Gareth Price
Language, Society, and the State

Language and Social Life

Editors
David Britain
Crispin Thurlow

Volume 9

Gareth Price

Language, Society, and the State

—

From Colonization to Globalization in Taiwan

ISBN 978-1-5015-2651-0
e-ISBN (PDF) 978-1-61451-464-0
e-ISBN (EPUB) 978-1-5015-0044-2
ISSN 2192-2128

Library of Congress Control Number: 2018961667

Bibliographic information published by the Deutsche Nationalbibliothek
The Deutsche Nationalbibliothek lists this publication in the Deutsche Nationalbibliografie;
detailed bibliographic data are available on the Internet at http://dnb.dnb.de.

© 2021 Walter de Gruyter Inc., Boston/Berlin
This volume is text- and page-identical with the hardback published in 2019.
Typesetting: Integra Software Services Pvt. Ltd.
Printing and binding: CPI books GmbH, Leck

www.degruyter.com

Acknowledgments

I have benefited greatly from the intellectual sustenance and warmth of friends, colleagues, and teachers, including Enam Al-Wer, Edna Andrews, Christina Bratt-Paulston, David Britain, Erin Callahan, Rebecca Clift, Giles Dudley, Luciana Fellin, Gustavo Procopio Furtado, Robin Hewat, Jane Hindley, Hae-Young Kim, Shiuan Liu, Michael Newcity, Liliana Paredes, Peter Patrick, Ian Rowen, Dave Sayers, Alison Sealey, Yasemin Soysal, Julie Tetel Andresen, Jennifer Wei, Jason Whittaker, and Billy Zaidi. My sincere apologies to anyone I have inadvertently left off this list. I am grateful for the probing questions and spirited debate among students in my annual Language and Politics seminar at Duke University; I have learned more from them than I have taught them. The magnanimity and pragmatism of the people of Taiwan are qualities celebrated in this book.

Special thanks go to A-chin Hsiau, who inspired me to begin this research for my PhD dissertation, and, along with Hsin-huang Michael Hsiao, kindly sponsored me as a visiting scholar at the Institute of Sociology at Academia Sinica, Taipei, in 2015. Rosa Wu and Chung Ting-yu were indispensable research assistants on this project. Dick Watts read the original proposal; the series editors, Dave Britain and Crispin Thurlow, provided helpful comments on the final drafts; while Lara Wysong at De Gruyter shepherded this book through the production process. Cat Thomas did a formidable job of copy-editing and fact-checking, and Michael Turton graciously read the draft manuscript in its entirety. All blunders remain resolutely mine.

Research for this book was generously funded by the UK Economic and Social Research Council; the Centre for Chinese Studies at the National Central Library, Taipei; and the Chiang Ching-kuo Foundation for International Scholarly Exchange. It would not have been possible to write it without their support. Part of chapter six was previously published in 2014 as "English for all? Neoliberalism, globalization, and language policy in Taiwan" in *Language in Society* (Vol. 43, No. 5). I thank Cambridge University Press for permission to reproduce parts of that article here.

Last, but by no means least, my parents Mary, Vic, and Michael, and my brother Robbie, have always encouraged me in my pursuits of verbal sparring, language games, and crosswords. My decision to return to graduate school was sparked by Dominika Baran lending me a book on sociolinguistics; she has always been my intellectual partner, and she eventually agreed to be my wife. Our daughter, Salomé, who can usually be found busily writing her own stories, gives me hope for the world. This book is dedicated to them all.

Contents

Acknowledgments —— V

Preface —— XI

List of Acronyms —— XXIII

1 Language, society, and the state: Defining the terrain —— 1
1.1 Introduction —— 1
1.2 Language —— 2
1.2.1 Language, communication, and evolution —— 2
1.2.2 Naming and un-naming languages —— 4
1.2.3 Measuring linguistic diversity —— 5
1.2.4 Language, thought, and culture —— 7
1.3 The state and society: The analytical terrain of political sociology —— 9
1.3.1 On the relative autonomy of the state —— 10
1.4 The state —— 12
1.4.1 Institutions, means, and ends —— 13
1.4.2 Characteristics of the state —— 15
1.5 Society —— 22
1.5.1 Civil society —— 24
1.5.2 The civil society argument —— 26
1.5.3 The public sphere —— 29
1.6 Conclusion —— 31

2 Towards a political sociology of language —— 33
2.1 Introduction —— 33
2.2 Language and the state —— 34
2.2.1 Language planning and policy: An overview —— 35
2.2.2 The administrative bureaucracy and the business of rule —— 39
2.2.3 Literacy —— 40
2.3 Language and colonization —— 42
2.3.1 Colonization and LPP —— 42
2.3.2 Administrative monolingualism —— 43
2.3.3 Administrative bilingualism —— 44
2.3.4 Elite bilingualism —— 45

2.3.5	Decolonization —— 46	
2.4	Language and nationalism —— 48	
2.4.1	Monolingualism and national identity —— 48	
2.4.2	Minority languages and multilingual nationalism —— 51	
2.5	Language and globalization —— 52	
2.5.1	The spread of English —— 53	
2.5.2	Superdiversity —— 56	
2.6	Language, rights, and transitional justice —— 57	
2.6.1	Language-based rights —— 58	
2.6.2	Language policy and transitional justice —— 62	
2.7	Language, society, and democracy —— 66	
2.7.1	Minority languages and the public sphere —— 67	
2.7.2	Multilingualism, pluralism, and civil society —— 71	
2.7.3	Language movements and language revitalization —— 72	
2.8	Conclusion —— 73	
3	**The coming of the state: Taiwan encounters China and Europe —— 75**	
3.1	Introduction —— 75	
3.2	Early Chinese encounters with indigenous Taiwan —— 76	
3.3	Dutch encounters with indigenous Taiwan (1624–1662) —— 80	
3.3.1	Multilingualism and political organization —— 82	
3.3.2	The missionary-colonial complex —— 84	
3.3.3	Vernacular literacy —— 89	
3.3.4	Dutch-spread policy —— 91	
3.4	Chinese influences on Taiwan (1624–1895) —— 93	
3.4.1	Chinese settlement and co-colonization —— 93	
3.4.2	The Zheng era (1662–1683) —— 96	
3.5	The liminal state: Qing rule (1683–1895) —— 97	
3.5.1	Interpreters and middlemen —— 98	
3.5.2	Chinese immigration and indigenous assimilation —— 101	
3.6	Conclusion —— 107	
4	**State against society: The Japanese and KMT regimes —— 109**	
4.1	Introduction —— 109	
4.2	Japanese rule (1895–1945) —— 110	
4.3	Language and political reform in Meiji-era Japan —— 110	
4.3.1	*Genbun'itchi*: Unifying speech and writing —— 111	
4.4	Japanese rule of Taiwan: The contemporary modern state —— 113	
4.4.1	The early years (1895–1919) —— 114	

4.4.2	The doka period (1918–1937) —— **120**	
4.4.3	The kominka period (1937–1945) —— **125**	
4.5	KMT Rule and Martial Law (1945–1987) —— **128**	
4.5.1	The rise and fall of Nationalist China (1911–1949) —— **130**	
4.5.2	The sociolinguistic context of Mandarin —— **131**	
4.5.3	KMT rule on Taiwan (1945–1949) —— **134**	
4.5.4	Language policy under Governor Chen Yi —— **135**	
4.5.5	The 22–8 Incident and its aftermath —— **139**	
4.6	Martial law and the ROC in exile (1949–1987) —— **141**	
4.6.1	Language, the state, and nationalism —— **141**	
4.6.2	Language and the public sphere —— **145**	
4.7	Conclusion —— **147**	

5 Democratization, pluralism, and multilingualism —— 150
5.1 Introduction —— **150**
5.2 The context of democratic reform (1979–1987) —— **151**
5.3 Language and democratization (1987–2000) —— **152**
5.4 On the campaign trail —— **156**
5.5 DPP language policies (2000–2008) —— **158**
5.5.1 The cultural politics of *bentuhua*: Equality without independence —— **158**
5.5.2 Status planning and transitional justice —— **161**
5.5.3 Language-in-education policies —— **173**
5.6 KMT policies (2008–2016) —— **183**
5.6.1 De-Taiwanization and re-Sinicization —— **184**
5.6.2 The social consensus —— **185**
5.6.3 The Hakka Basic Law —— **187**
5.6.4 Language-in-education policies: The twelve-year national curriculum —— **188**
5.7 Conclusion —— **189**

6 Globalization, neoliberalism, and immigration —— 191
6.1 Introduction —— **191**
6.2 English for all? Globalization, neoliberalism, and education —— **192**
6.2.1 Between localism and globalism: The context of DPP English language policy —— **192**
6.2.2 English as capital —— **196**
6.2.3 The-earlier-the-better argument —— **204**

6.2.4	The future of English —— **211**	
6.3	Foreign spouses, new immigrants, and "othered" languages —— **212**	
6.3.1	Metrolingual Taipei: Visible and invisible languages —— **213**	
6.3.2	Foreign workers and linguistic capital —— **215**	
6.3.3	Foreign spouses, language "problems", and language policy —— **219**	
6.4	Conclusion —— **227**	

Epilogue —— 228

Appendix: Languages in Taiwan —— 237

Bibliography —— 239

Index —— 262

Preface

On February 28th, 1947, soldiers from the Chinese mainland beat a Taiwanese cigarette seller in a park in Taipei City, sparking mass rioting and a near uprising against the brutality of the occupying Kuomintang (KMT) state. Local mobs marauded through the streets, attacking newly-arrived mainland Chinese immigrants. With little distinction in racial characteristics, the mainlanders were identified by the languages they spoke. In the tumult, Dai Guo-hui, a Taiwanese writer, found himself confronted by one such gang. As a Hakka speaker, he was unable to speak the dominant Taiwanese language, Hoklo. Thinking on his feet, Dai burst into a rendition of the Japanese national anthem, in Japanese. It saved his skin: he proved that he was not a mainlander by singing in the language of Taiwan's former colonizers. This vignette, as related by Hughes (1997: 28), aptly captures the welter of language, politics, and identities in Taiwan, the subject of this book. Though a fleeting moment in the middle of the twentieth century, the underlying themes resonate much further: back into the past to Dutch rule of the island in the seventeenth century, and forward in time to the current situation of democratization in the twenty-first. They are themes of complex linguistic and political loyalties, and of often violent antagonisms between the state and society. They are continuities which structure a historical narrative, but blur the distinctions between colonization and decolonization, and nationalism and globalization.

This book uses Taiwan as a case study to develop a theoretical framework of a political sociology of language. As such, it traces the contours of the relations between language, society, and the state in Taiwan across different historical-structural paradigms. The research questions articulated here are interrelated: What are the constants in the relationships between language, society, and the state as their precise dynamics are transformed? How does language operate as a fulcrum between society and the state in terms of both state-making and political resistance? What socio-political structures and historical processes have influenced Taiwan's contemporary linguistic situation? How are linguistic nationalisms produced in and by local contexts? How are these articulated in the post-national and denationalized context of globalization?

This brief preface sketches Taiwan's contemporary geopolitical situation as well as its sociolinguistic context. It then outlines the structure of the book as overall, and the narrative trajectory that it takes. Notes are also included on the difficulty of ethnic categorization, and the terminology used for different groups, as well as the Romanization conventions used.

1 Contemporary Taiwan in geopolitical context

A rugged volcanic island lying across the Tropic of Cancer approximately 160 km off the south-eastern coast of China, and 650 km south-west of the Japanese island of Okinawa, Taiwan is variously described as shaped like a yam, or sweet potato, or a rolled tobacco leaf. Around 400 km long and 145 km across at its widest point, the island is home to some 23.5 million people mainly crowded into lowland areas around the coast; half the island is covered by rough jungle terrain, making parts of Taiwan some of the most densely populated areas on the planet. Its small size belies its considerable influence in south-east Asian and global political affairs. Taiwan is a contentious piece of strategic territory, ever in the diplomatic or military cross-hairs of China, its larger neighbour across the Taiwan Strait, or the US, its chief ally across the Pacific. Beijing has long viewed Taiwan as a renegade Chinese province to be "reunited" with China, by force if necessary; it aims some 1,600 missiles at the island to underscore its point, though it has not seriously rattled its sabres since the first free elections in 1996. But Taiwan has never been part of the political unit of the People's Republic of China (PRC) since the latter's inception in 1949, and so Beijing's goal of "reunification" may be more accurately described as "annexation". The PRC has a "three noes" policy: no independence, no "two Chinas" or "one China, one Taiwan", and no Taiwanese membership in international organizations where statehood is required. Part of the difficulty for the PRC is the fear that if it allows Taiwan to declare itself as a free nation-state, then others in the Sinosphere – most notably, Tibet and the Uighur homeland of Xinjiang Province – will follow suit.

The US, under the Taiwan Relations Act, is legally obliged to offer certain defensive assistance to the island, but this is contingent on Taiwan not declaring itself as an independent country, even though to all intents and purposes it functions as one. It has its own democratically-elected government, an independent judiciary, and a standing army, navy, and air force. Its free-market, export-oriented economy – developed through the "Taiwan Miracle" of industrialization in the 1960s and 1970s – means Taiwan is often referred to as one of the four "Asian Tigers", along with Hong Kong, Singapore, and South Korea. It maintains its own immigration and border controls, has its own flag, national anthem, and currency, and over 90% of the population identify themselves as in some way Taiwanese according to survey data (ESC 2017a). Largely unrecognized by the international community, however, Taiwan exists in a diplomatic no-man's-land as a nation without statehood.

These tensions fundamentally structure Taiwan's internal politics; since 2000, elements of the pan-green coalition, led by the Democratic Progressive Party (DPP), favour independence while elements of the pan-blue coalition, led by the

Kuomintang (KMT), favour if not unification per se then increased rapprochement towards the PRC. In reality, centrists in both the DPP and KMT occupy an ideological middle-ground; in line with the wishes of most of the population, who have no desire to be embroiled in a costly and potentially unwinnable war, both parties have been content to maintain an uneasy status quo. For Ma Ying-jeou, former KMT president, this meant a different sort of "three noes" policy than Beijing's: no unification, no independence, and no use of force. Maintaining the status quo is seen by many as a pragmatic way to retain the economic and political freedoms that have allowed Taiwan to become a prosperous liberal democracy. Absent an opportunity to assert full independence and sovereignty, energies have been channelled into a form of cultural nationalism, in which both the pan-blues and pan-greens have deployed a multi-ethnic, multicultural, and multilingual Taiwanese identity for political purposes.

2 The sociolinguistic context

The complexities of Taiwan's sociolinguistic context are the subject of this book, and so it is only possible to give a brief summary here. Contemporary Taiwan is richly multilingual, with sixteen living Austronesian languages spoken by indigenous groups out of an original twenty or so, and over forty known dialects (see Appendix). Additionally, three mutually unintelligible Sinitic languages – Mandarin, Hoklo, and Hakka – are spoken widely in society. The Sinitic languages were brought by immigrants from China who arrived in various waves between the seventeenth and mid-twentieth centuries. Since the mid-1990s, cross-border marriage migration, mainly from south-east Asia, has brought languages such as Vietnamese, Tagalog, and Cambodian into Taiwan's sociolinguistic situation. Of course, there is also the presence of the global language of English, learned seemingly by everybody but spoken by relatively few. Table 1 summarizes the languages, origins, and demographic distribution of these groups, while Table 2 summarizes the percentages of languages used at home by age group, according to the 2010 census.

Mandarin is the dominant national language, used for official purposes, the medium of instruction in education, and in the media. Since 2017, Taiwan's indigenous Austronesian languages have been elevated to co-national status, though this is largely symbolic since almost half are classified as endangered. With this said, according to census data 1.4% of the Taiwanese population use indigenous languages at home (DGBAS 2016), with slightly over 2% identifying as indigenous, though this is shifting among younger speakers with less than 60% of speakers aged six to twenty-four using their language at home, compared to some

Table 1: Language distribution in Taiwan. Populations are approximate given the difficulty of establishing ethnic identities, and do not total 100% due to rounding.

Ethnolinguistic group and historical language(s)	Origin and date of migration to Taiwan	Approximate % of population by ethnic group
Hoklo		
Hoklo also known as Hokkien; Southern Min/M*innanhua*; *Tai-gi*; *Tai-yu*; Taiwanese	Southern Fujian Province, China	70%
Sinitic branch of Sino-Tibetan	17th century onwards, during Dutch colonial rule	
Mutually unintelligible with Mandarin or Hakka		
Mainlanders		
Taiwan Mandarin or *guoyu* (possibly a creoloid derived from Mandarin/ Wu/ Cantonese/Gan etc. language contact)	Various provinces, China 1945–1949, following end of Japanese colonial rule (1895–1945) and KMT defeat in Chinese civil war (1949)	10%
Sinitic branch of Sino-Tibetan		
Mutually unintelligible with Hoklo or Hakka		
Hakka		
Hakka	Guangdong Province, China	15%
Sinitic branch of Sino-Tibetan	17th century onwards, during Dutch colonial rule	
Mutually unintelligible with Mandarin or Hoklo		
Formosans/indigenous peoples		
20+ languages/40+ dialects (see Appendix)	Asian mainland	>2%
Formosan branch of Austronesian	4500–4000 BCE	
No phylogenetic relationship with Sinitic languages		

Table 1 (continued)

Ethnolinguistic group and historical language(s)	Origin and date of migration to Taiwan	Approximate % of population by ethnic group
New immigrant spouses		
Mandarin; various south-east Asian languages	China; Vietnam; Indonesia; Thailand; Philippines; Cambodia 1990s–2000s through cross-border marriages	~2%

Sources: Huang (1995); Ethnologue (2017).

Table 2: Percentage use of languages at home by age according to relative frequency in census data from 2010. Respondents may use more than one language at home. For Hoklo, reported language use exceeds the number of nominally "ethnic" Hoklo, indicating its function as a society-wide lingua franca. The relatively high percentage of "other" languages among those aged 65 or over is likely due to the lingering effects of Japanese-spread.

	Mandarin	Hoklo	Hakka	Indigenous	Other
Total	83.5	81.9	6.6	1.4	2.0
6–14 years	96	69.7	3.8	1	0.8
15–24 years	94.9	78.6	4.8	1.3	1
25–44 years	91.2	83.7	6	1.4	2.1
45–65 years	77.9	86.4	8.2	1.5	2.6
65+ years	45.3	81.7	10.1	1.3	3.1

Source: DGBAS 2016.

three-quarters of those aged over sixty-five. Hakka, like indigenous languages, has undergone shift to Mandarin, particularly among younger speakers; according to the same census data (DGBAS 2016), perhaps 6.6% of the total Taiwanese population speak Hakka at home (compared to as many as 10.1% of over-65s), though some 15% of the population identify as ethnically Hakka. Hoklo remains resilient, spoken at home by upwards of 95% of the population in some areas, and around 81.9% of the population overall (DGBAS 2016), with the number of speakers exceeding the number of nominally "ethnically" Hoklo indicating its status as a lingua franca and the prevalence of Mandarin/Hoklo bilingualism or Mandarin/Hakka/Hoklo trilingualism. Hoklo language shift is occurring among younger speakers, however; 81.7% of over-65s use it at home, compared to 69.7% of speakers aged between six and fourteen. However, apparent age-graded shift in Hoklo does not take into account the fact that speakers may return to the language after university and when entering the workforce (particularly when returning to family businesses).[1] Foreign spouses speaking south-east Asian languages often learn Mandarin or Hoklo to integrate or assimilate into Taiwanese society, though they are often traditionally discouraged (or prevented) from transmitting their languages to their children.

The historical-structural reasons for language shift are explored in chapters three and four. However, state- and civil society-driven strategies have been mobilized for the purposes of language maintenance and language revitalization as the result of increasing socio-political liberalization since 1987. Multilingualism is strongly associated with democratization and a pluralistic national identity. This has been focused on indigenous and autochthonous languages, but new immigrant languages are increasingly included in revitalization and maintenance programs, both ideologically and practically. The political context of language revitalization is explored in chapters five and six.

3 The problem of ethnic categories

Ethnicity is a problematic category when writing about Taiwan, and this complicates the definition of ethnolinguistic groups (see Table 1). The indigenous peoples – sometimes called Aboriginals or Formosans – share a common linguistic ancestor in proto-Austronesian, and have collectively suffered the blunt end of colonial interventions since the seventeenth century. I refer to "indigenous peoples" as a collective group, but it must be remembered that they are culturally and linguistically disparate and distinct. The Hakka- and Hoklo-speaking ethnolinguistic populations – that is, the historical ethnolinguistic groups that can be defined by assuming a one-to-one correspondence with ethnicity and language – migrated from China from the seventeenth century. I call these groups collectively "Han", in order to distinguish them

---

[1] Chen (2010) paints a more pessimistic picture of age-graded language shift, taking into account both reported fluency and reported language use at home. She uses a considerably smaller and less statistically robust sample than the DGBAS (2016) data from the 2010 census. In addition, her data is from 2003, only shortly after language revitalization strategies in schools and wider society had been put in place.

from both the indigenous groups and the "mainlanders" who themselves constitute a nominally ethnic group, according to Brown (2004: 10), and who migrated from China between 1945 and 1949, as well as from the Japanese and Dutch colonizers. The problem here is that the mainlanders are – in terms of cultural practices such as religion, festivals, and ancestor worship – also ethnically Han. Furthermore, intermarriage between male Han settlers and indigenous women has, historically, diluted any claims to "pure" Han ethnicity. The designation of Han for the Hakka and Hoklo groups is thus a convenient sociological and political fiction that gets around the thorny problems of describing both older and newer migrants from China as collectively "Chinese", as well as collectively describing indigenous and Han groups as "Taiwanese" (which would suggest that they historically saw themselves as such, or at least collaborated as sociopolitical actors, which was rarely the case).

4 A note on Romanization

In and of itself, the decision about which system of Romanization to use to phonetically represent Mandarin words can be politically and ideologically contentious. Since January 1st, 2009, the official Romanization system in Taiwan is Hanyu pinyin. I have chosen to use the Hanyu pinyin system for pragmatic reasons: it is, to my mind, a simpler and more coherent transliteration. For place names, I have used the transliteration likely to be most familiar to Taiwan specialists and non-specialists alike. Somewhat confusingly, these can be a mixture of either Hanyu pinyin, the previously-used Tongyong system, or the older Wade-Giles system, and may or may not be the version used on official documents before 2009. Thus, for example, the common rendering of "Miaoli" is the same in Tongyong and Hanyu pinyin; the older Wade-Giles "Kaohsiung" is the most common transliteration, though its Hanyu pinyin equivalent is in fact "Gaoxiong", a term rarely, if ever, seen; and so on. For proper names, I also use the most common transliteration: Sun Yat-sen, for example, retains the common transliteration of his Cantonese name, as opposed to the uncommon Mandarin rendering Sun Yi-xian. For contemporary politicians, I use the most common transliteration from media reports and other documents; different politicians adopt different (and sometimes idiosyncratic) Romanization conventions. Names referring to the authors of academic texts follow their published forms verbatim. All Chinese and Japanese surnames in this book come before the first name (e.g. Chen Shui-bian), except in a few cases where an English first name and Chinese surname are used commonly by authors, public figures, or politicians (e.g. Annette Lu).

5 Structure of this book

This book is comprised of three roughly equal parts of two chapters each, examining theoretical, historical, and contemporary aspects respectively. The structure reflects the central premise of the book, namely that perspectives on Taiwan's contemporary language politics can only be understood in their historical contexts, and that these in toto can be best understood through building a theoretical framework that synthesizes both sociolinguistic and political sociological approaches. As such, the first section, which develops the theoretical foundations of a political sociology of language, complements the other two, which are both empirical in nature. The second section is organized as a broadly linear historical narrative, while the third section addresses the contemporary situation – i.e. post-martial law after 1987 – somewhat more thematically. A standalone seventh chapter provides a conclusion to the book.

Part I: Theoretical foundations

In the first part, chapter one defines the analytical terrain of the book by outlining working definitions of language, society, and the state. These single terms index vast fields that deploy a multitude of concepts and positions, and so defining – or at least delimiting – is a Sisyphean task that is a necessary but never sufficient means to orient readers of different disciplinary stripes as to the ways in which they are used in this book. The following chapter attempts to synthesize these more coherently, so the objective of chapter one is to keep these definitions relatively isolated from each other, and they are presented consecutively and somewhat parsimoniously. Nevertheless, their amorphous nature means that definitions are only ever partial and cannot be entirely prevented from existing in dialogue with each other. Language, therefore, is treated as a political, sociological, and cultural phenomenon, as opposed to investigating its structural or psychological dimensions. Keeping society and the state – the analytical terrain of political sociology – separate is an even more arduous task; as Poulantzas (1980: 600) notes, "according to whether we choose the state or society as the focal point of our research, our approach to the other term will necessarily be different". Defining, or attempting to delimit, these key terms provides the foundations on which to build a theoretical framework of a political sociology of language.

Chapter two develops this framework, with an emphasis on a *political sociology* of language, and not a *political* sociology of language, which is to say that the concerns of political sociology – the relationships between society and the state – are used as a framework to understand language, and that it is not, for various reasons, an attempt to advance an explicitly politicized version of a conventional sociology of language, or, that is, a *political* sociology of language. Put another way, the aim of this chapter is to view relations between society and the state as a sociolinguistic concern, and language as a concern for political sociology; the critical, ethical, and normative perspectives of the "social bases of politics" (Lipset 1959) and the political bases of society have, it is argued, sociolinguistic dimensions. Specifically, this chapter deals with language and the (modern) state in terms of the bureaucratic imperatives of language planning and policy (LPP); the relationships between language and colonization, nationalism, and globalization; the notion of language rights and transitional justice; and the ramifications for multilingualism when considering the democratizing potential of pluralist public spheres and civil society. In all of these areas, it is argued that LPP decisions are always contextualized by the given historical-structural paradigm in which a state is located, and that they are always complex calculations between administrative practicality and political ideology.

Part II: Historical contexts

The second part locates Taiwan's language politics in their historical context. Chapter three begins by tracing the earliest recorded encounters, in the mid fourteenth century, between the Austronesian-speaking indigenous populations, who migrated from the Asian mainland to the island some six thousand years ago, and the Chinese. These contacts were to structure Taiwan's "imagined geography" (Teng 2006) as a peripheral territorial that lay, for all practical purposes, beyond the frontiers of the Chinese empire. With the arrival of Dutch colonists in 1624, indigenous Taiwan becomes enmeshed in state (or state-like) structures and processes imposed from without. The political economy of merchant capitalism facilitated labour migration from China for the agricultural colony, thus transforming the island into a majority Sinitic-speaking (rather than Austronesian-speaking) territory, with language politics, and politics and society more broadly, being managed by what I refer to as the "missionary-colonial complex". In this way, the linguistic resources and moral codes of the missionaries are leveraged for the colonial Dutch state's political and economic rationales. The final part of this chapter examines Qing rule of the island between 1683 and 1895, drawing a distinction between earlier practices of socio-spatial and sociolinguistic differentiation imposed until around 1750, which served in part to shelter indigenous language and cultures from shift and death, and assimilation processes afterwards, which accelerated the loss of linguistic diversity.

Chapter four deals with two periods of modern history, namely Japanese colonialism between 1895 and 1945, and the subsequent martial law period imposed by the KMT between 1949 and 1987. While Dutch colonization introduced the embryonic modern state, it came in more sophisticated form with the arrival of the Japanese, and the KMT finessed the technologies of statecraft even further. This chapter examines the continuities and discontinuities in colonial and authoritarian policies aimed at inculcating language shift among Taiwan's inhabitants. It begins by contextualizing Japan's internal socio-political and sociolinguistic reorganization during the Meiji Restoration from 1868, which dismantled a feudalist system with high internal dialect diversity and replaced it with a modern state that had a common language and script. This left Japan poised to experiment with becoming a colonial power, with Taiwan as its laboratory. Three main periods of colonial rule are identified, specifically the early years, and the subsequent *doka* and *kominka* programs, which differed in their approaches to sociolinguistic and cultural assimilation of different Taiwanese ethnolinguistic groups and social classes, depending on the exigencies of colonial and regional politics. KMT rule from 1945, at the conclusion of the second Sino-Japanese war, is then addressed, beginning with LPP on the Chinese mainland. From there, KMT language policies under the initial period of rule under Governor Chen Yi are examined, and then those after 1949 that successfully, if ruthlessly, spread Mandarin Chinese.

Part III: Contemporary perspectives

The third and final part focuses on the contemporary dynamics of language politics in Taiwan, particularly the period after the end of martial law in 1987 to the present day. Chapter five examines the politics of local languages, and the role of multilingual policies as a cornerstone of the transition to liberal democracy from martial law. Specifically, it begins by contextualizing democratic reform and political liberalization from the late 1970s, before assessing the role of language in democratization between 1987 and 2000, focusing in part on the use of local non-Mandarin languages in political campaigning. From there, DPP policies during their initial two-term tenure between 2000 and 2008 are analyzed, making the argument that the promotion of multilingualism was an adjunct to a form of cultural nationalism, or *bentuhua*, that has been an outlet for independence-oriented sentiment in the absence of an opportunity to assert full sovereignty. This section then turns to transitional justice dimensions of the ultimately unsuccessful National Language Equality Law (NLEL) and National Language Development Law (NLDL), before using ethnographic and interview data from 2007 to investigate how political factors, including local and regional autonomy, socio-economic differentiation, and party-political organization, structured differentiated access to mother-tongue language education (MLTE) in schools. The final section of the chapter investigates what, if any, changes occurred under the return of the much reformed KMT, who ruled for two terms between 2008 and 2016, following Dupré (2017) in concluding that path dependencies laid down by DPP policies forced the KMT to continue to promote multilingualism alongside democratization, albeit less vigorously.

Chapter six examines the influence of the nexus of globalization, neoliberalism, and immigration on Taiwan's sociolinguistic and socio-political situation. Two main themes are elaborated. The first is the phenomenon of English, the global language that comes laden with neo-imperialist and neoliberal baggage, thus threatening the egalitarian orientation towards democracy that the nationalist project of *bentuhua* rests on. The second theme considers the languages of the island's newest immigrants – so-called foreign spouses and migrant workers, which must be included from the perspective of democratic multilingualism, but which do not fall neatly into the categories defined by the often-parochial impulses of *bentuhua*. The first half of the chapter examines stratified access to English, arguing that, in practice, socio-economic and geographical factors mean that despite the "English for all" mantra that has framed LPP, English remains a valuable capital available only to a few. In particular, it assesses the existence of a shadow private education sector that competes, in neoliberal fashion, with the official state-funded education system. The second half addresses foreign spouses and migrant workers, and the otherization of their languages in state discourse, the public sphere, and civil society more broadly. In particular, the "language problems" of foreign spouses are discussed in terms of how their resolution – often through the expectation of linguistic and cultural assimilation – is fundamental to how they are constructed as "good citizens" in the eyes of the state and as "good Taiwanese" in the eyes of civil society.

The book concludes with an epilogue that assesses the prognosis for multilingualism in Taiwan and the contributions that a political sociology of language may make to the study of language politics more broadly.

List of Acronyms

CCP	Chinese Communist Party
CIP	Council of Indigenous Peoples
CKS	Chiang Kai-shek
DPP	Democratic Progressive Party
EGIDS	Expanded Graded Intergenerational Disruption Scale
ELE	English language education
ESC	Election Study Centre, National Cheng Chi University
GEPT	General English Proficiency Test
GIDS	Graded Intergenerational Disruption Scale
GSAT	General Scholastic Aptitude Test
HAC	Hakka Affairs Council
HBL	Hakka Basic Law
HLDL	Hakka Language Development Law
ICCPR	International Covenant on Civil and Political Rights
ICESCR	International Covenant on Economic, Social, and Cultural Rights
ILDA	Indigenous Languages Development Act
IPLDL	Indigenous People's Languages Development Law
JCCE	Joint Central College Examinations
KMT	Kuomintang/Chinese Nationalist Party
LPP	Language planning and policy
LSE	London School of Economics
MOE	Ministry of Education
MOI	Ministry of the Interior
MTLE	Mother-tongue language education
NCPPNL	National Committee for the Promotion and Propagation of the National Language
NIA	National Immigration Agency
NLC	National Languages Committee
NLDL	National Language Development Law
NLEL	National Language Equality Law
NTUE	National Taichung University of Education
PRC	People's Republic of China
ROC	Republic of China
TSU	Taiwan Solidarity Union
UDHR	Universal Declaration of Human Rights
UNDRIP	United Nations Declaration on the Rights of Indigenous Peoples
UNDRM	United Nations Declaration on the Rights of Persons Belonging to National or Ethnic, Religious and Linguistics Minorities

1 Language, society, and the state: Defining the terrain

1.1 Introduction

This chapter outlines some working definitions of language, society, and the state. The aim is to orient readers from different disciplinary paradigms – specifically, sociolinguistics and political sociology – and provide the basis for building a theoretical framework of a political sociology of language in chapter two. Since chapter two is thus a synthesis of these concepts, the definitions in the present chapter are kept relatively separate, and are presented consecutively. However, their precise articulations are inescapably influenced by each other. Language, therefore, is presented in terms of its social and political dimensions, and not in terms of its abstract structures. The concern of political sociology is the relationships between society and the state, and thus these are described in terms of their mutual dependencies.

The structure of the chapter is as follows. It begins with language, briefly considering its communicative functions and evolutionary basis. From there, the conceptual difficulties of seeing specific languages as discrete entities are discussed; the postmodern call to abandon the notion of singular languages is sketched but ultimately rejected, since languages are indeed perceived as real and distinct for social and political purposes. The current state of language diversity is considered in the next section; following that, the argument is made that linguistic diversity represents human cultural diversity, and that this is worth conserving.

The analytical scope of political sociology is then examined as a prelude to defining society and the state. As Poulantzas (1980: 600) notes, "according to whether we choose the state or society as the focal point of our research, our approach to the other term will necessarily be different". For the purposes of this book, the focal point is the state, and so society is defined subsequently in those terms. The state is addressed from a neo-Weberian perspective, examining its nature as an institution of institutions and a political organization with specific means available to it – chief among them the monopoly of legitimate force – and having identifiable and relatively durable characteristics of operation. The characteristics of coercion and legitimacy, organization and bureaucracy, territoriality and sovereignty, and nationalism and citizenship are emphasized. The concluding section considers the concept of society, beginning by outlining the problems of methodological nationalism, and partly resolving them by viewing society as a set of overlapping systems. The notion of civil society is then defined, before turning to the pluralist "civil society argument" and some criticisms of this approach. The public sphere is then briefly described, in terms of its relation to civil society and its potential as a forum for democratic deliberation, but also the problems of stratified access based on class, gender, race, and language.

1.2 Language

Definitions of "language" vary depending on the unit and level of analysis, and on the disciplinary approach in question. For syntacticians, for example, human language is a set of underlying if abstract structures operating primarily at the level of the sentence (Chomsky 1965), while discourse analysts see sentences as one element of "texts" that also have broader social and political dimensions (Gee 2011; Halliday and Webster 2014). Variationist sociolinguists seek to understand the social correlations of language use – such as class, age, and gender – from a linguistic perspective (Labov 1972; Trudgill 2000), while more critically-inclined applied linguists have inveighed against variationists' traditional under-theorization of society and politics, and the reliance on static social categories (Cameron 1995; Pennycook 2001). At a much more micro-level, phoneticians and phonologists ignore these concerns; they study language as a set of sounds and "wonder what all the noise is about" (Lippi-Green 1997: 7), apparently both literally and metaphorically. At the heart of these perennially roiling debates lie the questions of whether language should be analyzed on its own terms as an abstract system or set of systems, or in the social and political contexts in which it is embedded; and, if the latter, which social and political contexts matter and to what extent. From the title of this book, it should be clear that I take the critical sociolinguistic position that language is best understood in terms of its relationships with other aspects of our sociological, political, and economic realities. Specifically, I take a (political) sociology of language approach (Fishman 1972) that is less concerned with language itself, and instead with how language and languages affect social and political structures. In other words, here language is used as a prism to understand society and politics, and not the other way around.

1.2.1 Language, communication, and evolution

Language is the most fundamental means of communication among humans, and thus the basis for any form of human society (Noble 2000). As Bickerton puts it, language is also a "system of representation, a means for manipulating the plethora of information that deluges us throughout our waking life" (1990: 5). Many animals – from birds, to bees, to baboons – can communicate, and base complex societies upon this communication. But, to the best of our knowledge, animals cannot use language to represent abstract concepts or concrete phenomena that are not temporally or spatially present, among other features which make human language uniquely human (Adornetti 2015). It is far from settled whether human language is a branching-off from animal systems of communication or, as Chomsky (2000) holds, it is so different that it must have emerged in humans spontaneously and discontinuously (Knight et al. 2000), but it clearly has some evolutionary basis. Despite obvious evolutionary disadvantages to individuals in terms of expending time signalling or freely exchanging information, clearly language and thus cooperation has evolutionary benefits for social animals (Smit 2014: 159). One proposal is that human language emerged around the same time as tool-making; language makes it easier to assign social roles and tasks to members of a group (Stout 2010; Steele and Uomini 2009).

A more complex assessment of why, evolutionarily, humans became languaging beings can be found in Tetel Andresen (2014), but it is a demonstrable fact that children acquire language for the most part effortlessly, given normal cognitive development and opportunities for linguistic input from other humans. In Chomsky's (1965) early theorization, this was due to the innateness of language, which presumed that human brains were hardwired with some sort of language acquisition "device" that would adapt to the specific parameters of the target languages around them. Even at the time, scholars in the then-emergent field of sociolinguistics balked at this emphasis on language as a biological function. As Dell Hymes wrote, along with acquiring competence from innate rules of a universal grammar underlying all language(s), children must also acquire communicative competence in the social context of language use, since "a child from whom any and all the grammatical sentences of a language might come with equal likelihood would be of course a social monster. Within the social matrix in which it acquires a system of grammar, a child acquires also a system of its use" (Hymes 1974: 75; emphasis added). Social contexts of language use are determined by the child's immediate home environment and by his or her wider society. Traditionally, these were defined as the "speech community", though this notion is by now highly contested even in sociolinguistics (Rampton 2000; Patrick 2004). Chomsky was explicitly concerned with a stable speech community, writing that the object of linguistic study should assume an "ideal speaker-listener, in a completely homogeneous speech community" (1965: 3). Whatever a speech community is, however, its homogeneity is sociologically impossible; Chomsky has thus been reasonably criticized as developing "a theory of language without human beings" (Coulmas 2003: 576). A crucial dimension is that children will not only acquire languages in their speech communities, but they will acquire knowledge of the value of those languages within the social, economic, and political systems of their communities.

1.2.2 Naming and un-naming languages

For the purposes of this book, the unit of analysis is not "language" as an abstract system (or set of systems) in the singular, but named and distinct languages such as Dutch, Japanese, Mandarin Chinese, Hoklo, Hakka, Basay, or English. However, the very idea of named and distinct languages has come under attack in recent years from postmodernist scholars such as Makoni and Pennycook (2007). Languages might need to be "disinvented" insofar as they "were, in the most literal sense, invented, particularly as part of the Christian/colonial and nationalistic projects in different parts of the globe" (Makoni and Pennycook 2007: 1). As Errington (2008) shows, the European colonial project deliberately invented linguistic and ethnic distinctions where they did not exist, and erased them where they did. Nationalist impulses towards constructing and mythicizing traditions, cultures, and identities (Hobsbawm and Ranger 1983) have long been recognized as codifying, homogenizing, and standardizing languages at the expense of a vast diversity of accents, dialects, and repertoires (Anderson [1983] 1991; Wright 2016). Borders between national languages have been historically drawn by modernist "grand narratives" for political purposes, resulting in diminishing hybridity and diversity at the liminal edges of speech communities, and the socio-political marginalization of these mixed forms. Re-thinking language in contemporary sociolinguistics, for Garcia and Wei, is to conceive of it as an "open-ended, complex, [and] adaptive system" (2014: 31), and the project at hand is "to make visible the complexity of language exchanges ... that [have] been buried within fixed language identities constrained by nation-states" (2014: 21).

These perspectives, and others, give very good reasons to think that linguistic difference and individual named languages are to a large degree socially constructed. But, be that as it may, people understand themselves in national, sub-national, and ethnic terms on the basis of the distinct languages they speak, and not all the sociolinguistic borders that groups have drawn between "them" and "others" can be traced historically to the emergence of European colonialism or nationalisms. This is evident in the fact that many non-state societies have long distinguished themselves linguistically, even if they have not named their own languages; though, of course, linguistic distinctions were not always as abruptly delineated as they are now by national borders. Furthermore, distinct languages are specific manifestations of the underlying human capacity for language. They have their own discrete structures and systems, and can be empirically demonstrated quite easily. A monolingual Malay speaker and a monolingual Swahili speaker, marooned on a desert island together, will find ways to communicate with sufficient inclination, but only with great difficulty; they obviously do not speak the "same" language.

Such diversity seems to be an odd outcome in evolutionary terms: humans are endowed with the same universal material for language acquisition, and humans appear to be essentially the same in neurobiological and cognitive respects. As such, one might wonder why humans have ended up with multiple languages rather than a common one, which, according to the dominant monogenesis paradigm, we presumably started with (Atkinson 2011). Wright (2016: 6, after Laycock 2001), suggests that groups of people may "simply prefer [linguistic diversity] that way . . . a distinct and singular language contributes to their sense of self". In other words, having a common language may be part of a baser "human instinct to establish and maintain social identity . . . and a profound need for people to show they belong somewhere" (Chambers 1995: 250). The corollary of this is that there is potentially a desire to actively construct differences and barriers to understanding, since a common language can mark both inclusion within and exclusion from a particular social group: linguistic difference is used to exclude, marginalize, and dehumanize certain individuals and groups within societies.

1.2.3 Measuring linguistic diversity

Most sources put the total languages in the world at around 7,000. Even with this rough estimate, it seems that societal multilingualism is the norm among the 193 UN-recognized nation-states and the handful of territories with some (viable) aspiration to nation-statehood; this reality stands in stark contrast to the persistent myth of the monolingual nation-state. At the time of writing, Ethnologue (2017) tallies 7,099 extant languages. This is higher than the 6,909 than the earlier Ethnologue (2009) survey, but it does not mean that the world has grown nearly two hundred languages in the intervening period, since new languages emerge slowly. Languages are sometimes discovered in remote and unexplored places, but this is rare in contemporary times with most of the world politically (or cartographically) parts of established nation-states (Middleton 2015). Instead, the discrepancy between the two numbers is better explained by the political and linguistic difficulties of, and changing criteria for, counting languages and dialects (Baker and Jones 1998: 346–353), as well as whether one counts a barely viable language as alive or extinct.

Reclassifying barely viable languages as living accounts for most of the rise in the number of languages in Ethnologue between 2009 and 2017, but it masks the fact that languages are dying. Whole (speech) communities and their languages may disappear as they and their identities are absorbed into dominant ones. Younger generations may shift from their minority languages to ones that are politically or economically more muscular, and that are perceived to – or do – offer better access to social, political, economic, and geographical mobility. Migration to urban centres for economic purposes often leaves only older members behind to maintain community languages and cultural practices. Furthermore, language shift can be deliberately or accidentally influenced directly by state language policies, or more indirectly through social, economic, and political policies. Lewis and Simons' (2010) Expanded Graded Intergenerational Disruption Scale (EGIDS), based on Fishman's (1991) Graded Intergenerational Disruption Scale (GIDS), measures the vitality or endangerment of a language according to whether it is transmitted from one generation to another. According to the EGIDS, a language is "vigorous" if it is used "used for face-to-face communication by all generations and the situation is sustainable". "Developing" languages are "in vigorous use, with literature in a standardized form being used by some, though this is not yet widespread or sustainable." At the other end of the scale, a language becomes "dormant" when the last native speaker dies and while "the language serves as a reminder of heritage identity for an ethnic community ... no one has more than symbolic proficiency". Dormant languages can be kept alive – or even reinvigorated – with appropriate language, cultural, and socio-economic policies, and the will of the state and the community. But languages finally do go "extinct" when the last native speaker dies and "no one retains a sense of ethnic identity associated with the language".

The rate of language extinction is difficult to accurately measure, though two rough calculations are usually cited: that 50% of languages will disappear by the end of the twenty-first century at the current rate of attrition (Krauss 1992: 6), and that one language dies every two weeks (Crystal 2000: 28). These are suspiciously apocalyptic, but the outlook for global linguistic diversity is bleak even with more modest (and more scientific) estimates. Ethnologue (2017) counts 360 languages as having become extinct since 1950, at a rate of 5.4 per year; Campbell et al. (2013) estimate this rate at 3.5 per year. In the Ethnologue. some 35% of languages are classed as endangered according to the EGIDS; Campbell et al. give a figure of 43%. This means that between one-third and one-half of the world's languages are under threat of extinction, and some 200 of these will likely go extinct in the next half century. Although Ethnologue data suggests that the number of speakers of a language does not always correlate precisely with its endangerment, there is a dim prognosis for the 140 languages with under ten speakers, and it is not much better for the 338 languages with ten to ninety-nine speakers. By comparison, the largest 101 languages are spoken by around 60% of the world's population, with just six languages accounting for almost 29% of speakers (Ethnologue 2017). However, there are perhaps some grounds for cautious optimism. In the 2017 edition of Ethnologue, four languages were classified as having gone extinct over the previous year, which is broadly in line with Campbell et al.'s (2013) estimate, but two languages were reclassified as living. The sociological and political complexities behind language revitalization are one theme of this book, and the increased emphasis on pluralism and multilingualism as liberal democratic norms has played a significant role.

1.2.4 Language, thought, and culture

Whatever the rate of the decline in linguistic diversity actually is, it remains to be seen what can be done about it. Normatively, sociolinguists take it as axiomatic that something ought to be done about it, but let us play devil's advocate for a moment: there are arguments that the homogenization of languages and identities is natural, or at least beneficial. A shift towards fewer languages, and perhaps eventually a single dominant language, would presumably facilitate communication and thus cooperation between the world's peoples. In other words, reducing linguistic diversity may well lead to a reduction in human conflict. No longer would we have to abide the "zones of silence" and "razor edges of division" that are created by our "destructive prodigality" and the "implausible variety" of multilingualism (Steiner 1998: 56–8, cited in Wright 2016: 6). However, this is to risk imposing a highly Darwinian view of both linguistic and sociological evolution. While language attrition is the expected outcome of conflict, contact, and migration, this does not necessarily make it natural. Indeed, the contemporary rate of attrition, even at the most conservative estimates, appears unprecedented. It coincides with the distinctly *unnatural* emergence of the state (Mann 1986: 49–70) and concomitant social and political phenomena, such as colonization, nationalism, industrialization, and globalization.

Furthermore, this argument also overlooks the question of what is lost when a language disappears. Ken Hale, who was influential in putting language endangerment on the sociolinguistic research agenda in the early 1990s, once told a reporter that when a language is lost, "you lose a culture, intellectual wealth, a work of art. It's like dropping a bomb on a museum" (*The Economist*, 2001). Intuitively, Hale's point has a good deal of validity: the customs, beliefs, and ways of life of a community or society are connected at some fundamental level with language. In this view, language is a bearer of particular kinds of knowledge about the world, and when a language is lost, so too are valuable and particular cultural understandings. This is an intuitively appealing line of argument, but some dubious claims have been made on its behalf, and it requires tempering. The most obvious and familiar claim is the essentialist theory of linguistic determinism – the belief that a language fundamentally constrains the thought of its speakers – that held sway for much of the twentieth century.

Linguistic determinism has its roots at least as far back as Humboldt's claims in the mid-nineteenth century that each language gives rise to different conceptions of the "Cosmos". Later, Wittgenstein wrote that "the limits of my language are the limits of my world" (1922: 74). In more recent times, linguistic determinism is most widely associated with the Sapir-Whorf hypothesis which, in what is often described as its "strong" form, holds that language constrains thought to the extent that speakers of one language fundamentally perceive the world differently from speakers of another. For Sapir (1929: 207), "human beings do not live in the objective world alone ... but are very much at the mercy of the language which has become the medium of expression for their society". Sapir's student Whorf ([1940] 2012a: 272) further argued that the grammatical structure of a given language is "not merely the reproducing instrument for voicing ideas but rather is itself the shaper of ideas ... we dissect nature along lines laid down by our native languages". Whorf's argument is based on his work with the Native American language Hopi. For Whorf, the lack of a morphologically marked verb tense system meant that Hopi speakers could not perceive time in the same way as speakers of English or European languages. Specifically, the lack of past tense marking meant that Hopi speakers had "no general notion or intuition of time as a smooth flowing continuum in which everything in the universe proceeds at equal rate, out of a future, through the present, into a past" ([1936] 2012b: 73). It is by now well-documented that Whorf's work was conceptually and methodologically flawed; it is not clear that he understood the Hopi language very well (McWhorter 2008: 142) and, as Edwards (1997: 208) points out, he seems to have "presumed, rather than examined" the English tense system. Specifically, even if there are different words and conceptualizations of time in Hopi, these differences have nothing to do with verb tense marking and, in any case, they do not mean that Hopi speakers are unable to conceptualize in the same way as speakers of other languages. Furthermore, if language encoded reality to the extent proposed by the strong form of the Sapir-Whorf hypothesis, some concepts would be literally untranslatable, an observation refuted perhaps earliest by Black (1959). Fundamentally, linguistic determinism, the strong form of the Sapir-Whorf hypothesis, emphasizes deficit, not diversity.

However, a weaker – or less extreme – form of the Sapir-Whorf hypothesis exists, and is subscribed to by perhaps most contemporary sociolinguists. Known as linguistic relativity, this is a more plausible account of the relationship between language, thought, and culture, and allows for the fact that particular languages and cultures do indeed construct the world in different ways, that this has some effect on how speakers perceive the world, and that cultural concepts can sometimes be only clumsily translated. But it rejects the deterministic view by positing that these relationships are relative rather than fixed. In this version, as Gumperz and Levinson put it, "culture, *through* language, affects the way we think, especially perhaps our classification of the experienced world" (1996: 1, original emphasis). In other words, language may influence thought, and, in turn, language may be influenced by the non-linguistic basis of culture. Various empirical work has shown how at least some colour terms (Berlin and Kay [1969] 1991) and counting systems (Dahaene, Izard, Spelke and Pica 2008) are culturally constructed but, while they may be reflected in language use, it is not the case that language is constraining thought or determining culture. Rather, language is adaptive to what is culturally or socially relevant. Pinker (2007), after Pullum (1991), satirizes the old myth that Inuit speakers have more words for "snow" than, say, Southern American English speakers; even if they did (they don't) it is absurd to reason that their language gave Inuit speakers a better grasp of different types of snow; instead, culture, and its interaction with the natural environment, is much more likely to be the correct order of cause and effect. Put more simply, if Inuit speakers did in fact have more words for snow, it might be because they have more snow. Though the long-held notion that all languages are equally complex, in linguistic terms, has come under some recent scrutiny (Joseph & Newmeyer 2012: 357–61), the fact that a language has more or fewer terms for a concept than another language is likely the result of practical necessity of organizing and rationalizing the social and political relations of that community.

1.3 The state and society: The analytical terrain of political sociology

Before defining the state and society in more detail, it is worth briefly sketching the analytical terrain of political sociology.[2] At its broadest level, political sociology is concerned with the relationships between the state and society. As Lipset (1959) puts it, the main field of analysis for political sociology is "the social bases of politics" and, conversely, the political bases of society. Fundamentally,

---

[2] More substantial treatment of this broad field can be found in e.g. Faulks (2000); Orum and Dale (2009); Nash (2010); Amenta, Nash, and Scott (2016).

political sociology takes it as axiomatic that "political actors ... operate within a wider social context. [They] therefore inevitably shape, and in turn are shaped by, social structures ... Such structures ensure that political influence within society is unequal" (Faulks 2000: 1).

Political sociology traces its roots to Hegel, Marx, Durkheim, and Weber, though it only appeared as a distinct field of sociology and/or political science after WWII. A *political* sociology is distinct from a more general sociology, which is concerned with society, social relations, and social structures and processes that are not explicitly political (Cohen and Arato 1992: 429). In particular, political sociology takes as its focus civil society, a specifically politicized instantiation of society constituted by social processes and structures that are not part of the state but have some bearing on the way that the state operates. However, in important ways, political sociology is also distinct from political science, though these distinctions are harder to pin down (ASA 2008). One way to imagine the contrast between political sociology and political science is to consider political sociology as avoiding the analysis of the mechanisms of operation of specific state institutions, such as the judiciary, elections, or parliamentary process, or what Sanders acerbically calls the "tendency towards mindless empiricism" in political science (1995: 66, cited in Faulks 2000: 14). Instead, it asks the "big questions" about the state and society: who rules, and who is ruled? What modes of rule are accepted or resisted? What are rights, and how can they be distributed, claimed, and defended? These questions are essentially structured by notions of power.

A driving force in distinguishing political sociology from political science came from the new institutionalist movement in the mid-1970s and early 1980s (e.g. Evans, Rueschemeyer, and Skocpol 1985). This sought to recover the traditional macro-level and sociological emphasis on state institutions – that is, the concerns of Marx, Durkheim, and Weber – and was a reaction against the dominance of the mid-twentieth century "behaviourist" emphasis on quantifying individual political action (e.g. Easton 1953). In other words, it sought to realign understandings of the state and society in macro-structural perspective, rather than in terms of micro-political behaviour. This movement was particularly concerned with theoretically re-centring the state as an autonomous political actor compared to civil society.

1.3.1 On the relative autonomy of the state

The relationship between the state and civil society is interdependent. As noted in the introduction to this chapter, from a definitional perspective, "according to whether we choose the state or society as the focal point of our research, our approach to the other term will necessarily be different" (Poulantzas 1980: 600). From a theoretical perspective, this question turns on the relative autonomy of the state from civil society, and specifically whether we view the relationship between society and the state as society-centred or state-centred. In other words, our approach depends on whether we view society as shaped by the state or vice versa.

A detailed examination of the various positions taken on these questions is beyond the scope of this book, but they can be briefly summarized as follows. In the Hegelian tradition, the two separate spheres of civil society and the state could co-exist and their relationship could be "successfully mediated by public-spirited civil servants" (Faulks 2000: 3). Conventional Marxist approaches were more pessimistic; the state was one aspect of civil society and, specifically, a servant of dominant class interests; only the destruction of the state along with the class conflicts that required the state in the first place could finally liberate society in general from capitalism (Faulks 2000: 3, 33–34). As such, in Marxist approaches the state is perceived to have limited relative autonomy from civil society. Pluralists take similar views on the society-centredness of the state-society relationship, though with the important distinction that they see the democratic potential of civil society (albeit often conveniently ignoring its conditioning by capitalism) as a counterweight to the potential excesses of the state, rather than class conflict in civil society as the state's underlying principle and organizing logic. For Weber, in contrast, the state has such autonomy that society itself is in danger of being overpowered by the state's bureaucratic rationality: "once fully established, bureaucracy is among those social structures which are the hardest to destroy" (Weber, 1946a: 232). Neo-Weberians – another term for the new institutionalists – take a more nuanced view than simply fearing the state's autonomy; as Skocpol puts it, "states ... may formulate and pursue goals that are not simply reflective of the demands of the interests of social groups, classes or societies" (1985: 9); in other words, through its relatively autonomy, at least in some contexts the state can act neutrally or even positively to foster the democratic potential of civil society.

Assessing the relative merits of these perspectives is complex, but this book takes the neo-Weberian position that the state has a relatively high degree of autonomy from civil society. Historically, authoritarian and colonial contexts demonstrate that states can act in ways that benefit certain elites but, contra Marxist explanations, are not solely reducible to economically-defined class relations. Pluralist accounts – as we will see when we discuss the "civil society argument" (Walzer 1991; cf. Foley and Edwards 1996) below – tend to nostalgize the inherently democratic nature of civil society and its potential to act as a counterweight against the excesses of the state, but the state frequently has to act as the arbiter of conflict caused by illiberal tendencies in civil society.

Globalization, meanwhile, is giving rise to notions of a "global civil society" (Keane 2003; Nash 2010) and more interlinked and interdependent national economies. These are certainly reconfiguring the relative autonomy of the state, but not entirely eroding it: the state remains sovereign in the management and implementation of globalization structures and processes (Sassen 2007), although the relative autonomy of the state in this regard is arguably stronger in the global north than in the south. As such, state autonomy is relative to the social, political, economic, and historical circumstances in which each state is specifically located.

1.4 The state

Humans have not always lived under the state. Anatomically modern humans have been around for some 200,000 years, while spoken language developed between 60,000 to 100,000 years ago, and the capacity to use symbolic representation systems, such as cave paintings, dates back perhaps 30,000 years. However, the first recognizable proto-states emerged in Mesopotamia only around 3000 BCE (Hall & Ikenberry 1989: 16), coinciding with the development of writing systems. The modern state, which is the concern of this book, is even younger. Developing initially in Europe, embryonic forms of the modern state correlate with the decline of feudalism from the thirteenth century or so onwards. This is not to suggest that the state emerged teleologically; as Faulks (2000: 20) argues, to do so "may appear to endorse evolutionary theories of political community, which understand human society as advancing gradually from 'primitive' non-stateness towards the present 'civilized' stage of the liberal state". The modern state is not the result of the inexorable march of progress, but a highly particular and contingent mode of organizing societies in response to the historical context of medieval Europe. Its emergence drove, as much as it was driven by, processes of modernity, and in particular the transition from rural, agrarian, and feudalist societies to urban, industrialized, and capitalist ones (Pierson 2011). Similarly, the fact that the modern state model emerged first in Europe and was adopted elsewhere is not the result of the natural evolution of societies; instead, the modern state was sometimes directly imposed by Europeans through war-making and colonization, and sometimes adopted as a political model precisely to resist European colonization. Many societies did just fine without the modern European state, and often considerably worse with it.

The modern state is not a monolithic entity, and variation in the structural composition of any given state is the product of prevailing and countervailing social, political, and economic forces in a given historical context. As such, there are questions as to whether it is possible or worthwhile to define the state at all.

Foucault suggests that the state may be "no more than a composite reality and a mythicized abstraction" (1991: 103). In less extreme fashion, Jessop (1990, inter alia) makes the convincing argument that the state might be better conceived as a set of social and political processes that give rise to "state effects", rather than a concrete entity with distinct characteristics that is able to exercise power. Nevertheless, as Pierson (2011: 6) puts it, empirically there are real "political structures, institutions and practices which it makes sense to try and explain under the rubric of the state". The definitions advanced here rely on this perspective, and particularly Weber's formulations of institutional nature of the state and certain characteristics that appear to hold relatively constant in most manifestations of modern states around the world.

1.4.1 Institutions, means, and ends

"The state" is often used synonymously with "the government" in everyday discourse and, at least in the Anglo-American contexts, this is usually pejorative. Intuitively, they are related at some level, but the state and the government are not the same entity. Any number of institutions, and their associated structures and processes, are unambiguously part of the state, but they are less clearly part of the government as such. The highways agencies, for example, are certainly part of the state, but only the most ardent libertarian believes that getting a speeding ticket is the nefarious government at work. More accurately, the government is only one of many institutions that constitute the state more broadly. To be sure, it is a privileged institution in terms of being the supreme and sovereign organ of legislation and policymaking; however, it is up to other state institutions to implement policy (Orum and Dale 2009: 42). The institutional character of the state is at the core of most contemporary understandings and definitions (Mann 1984: 112). The state is an institution in itself, but more importantly it is an "institution of institutions" or an "organization of organizations". What gives a state its precise character in a specific historical context is the configuration of the relationships between these institutions. An institution, for March and Olsen (2006: 3) is

> a relatively enduring collection of rules and organized practices, embedded in structures of meaning and resources that are relatively invariant in the face of turnover of individuals and relatively resilient to the idiosyncratic preferences and expectations of individuals and changing external circumstances

One way to define the state, therefore, would be to list its institutions but, as Jessop (2007: 3) points out, such lists tend only to consist of a "core set of institutions with increasingly vague outer boundaries"; in other words, general agreement could likely be found on what constitutes the state's core institutions – the government, the judiciary, the legislature, the police or army, etc. – but less towards its margins. Even this would depend on the state in question at a specific time, given its institutional arrangements, as well as on the political or epistemological stance of whoever was compiling the list. As such, lists "typically fail to specify what lends these institutions the quality of statehood" (Jessop 2007: 3). An alternative route is to specify the ends of the state: that is, what the state or its institutions actually do or do not do. However, this is similarly problematic. The state does a great many things and, as Weber (1946b: 77) argues, "sociologically, the state cannot be defined in terms of its ends. There is scarcely any task that some political association has not taken in hand". Elsewhere, Weber points out these tasks range from the seemingly essential ("provision for subsistence") to the peripheral ("the patronage of art") (1978: 55). Conversely, there is "no task that has always been exclusive and peculiar to those associations" (1946b: 77).

Weber's (1946b: 77–8; original emphasis) most famous definition of the state – its *"monopoly of the legitimate use of physical force* within a given territory" – explicitly rejects the notion of defining the state according to its many potential ends; he insists that "one can define the modern state only in terms of the specific *means* peculiar to it". In other words, what the state, in any given situation, does in terms of its ends is less important that how it ultimately achieves them. The qualifier "ultimately" is important, here; violence is not the only means available to the state, but it is the coercive technique of last resort where others fail. But this does not tell us very much about what the state is *for*. Certainly, the bloody history of the twentieth century bears out Weber's observation that the means of the monopolization of violence can be "under certain circumstances, elevated into an end in itself" (1978: 55) and, as Orwell wrote in 1984, "the object of torture is torture". Under normal circumstances, however, these tautologies are insufficient, since the state is presumably not monopolizing violence for the sheer sake of doing so. Unless we take literally Foucault's notion of the state being a "mythicized abstraction", the empirically observable institutions and means of the state must be directed towards achieving something. How, then, can we express the broad aims or purposes of the state without listing all its institutions or everything that it can (or could) do?

Poggi (1978: 1) offers an elegant answer to this question: the state is concerned with the "business of rule", and the state is thus "a complex set of institutional arrangements for this rule" over a "territorially-bounded society". As Migdal (2001: 111) describes, this approach is common to most contemporary definitions, which emphasize the state's central purpose – or the "business of rule" – as being the making of rules and ensuring they are followed. For Anter (2014), there are two senses of the term "order" at play: the state gives "orders" for the maintenance of social and political "order". The maintenance of this latter notion of order is essential for the maintenance of the state itself, since disordered politics and society threatens the state's existence. The giving of orders, and the extent to which they are followed, turns on "the degree to which the state's institutions can expect voluntary compliance with their rules (legitimacy) or need to resort to coercion" (Migdal 2001:111).

Despite his considerable influence on contemporary understandings, Weber did not develop a specific sociology or theory of the state; his writings on the subject are instead "scattered throughout his work ... [h]e always deals with the state in passing, with remarks that are seldom pursued beyond a few sentences" (Anter 2014: 1). Perhaps Weber's most coherent single definition can be found in the following passage, in which he expands his earlier definition of "the monopoly of the legitimate use of physical force" and gives it an institutional context. Note that Weber sees the state as a contingent form of a "compulsory political organization" (as distinct, in his example, from a nomadic encampment):

> A compulsory political organization with continuous operations will be called a 'state' insofar as its administrative staff successfully upholds the claims to the *monopoly* of the *legitimate* use of physical force in the enforcement of its order ...
>
> [The modern state] possesses an administrative and legal order subject to change by legislation, to which the organized activities of the administrative staff, which are also controlled by regulations, are oriented. This system of orders claims binding authority, not only over members of the state, the citizens, most of whom have obtained membership by birth, but also to a very large extent over all action taking place in the area of its jurisdiction. It is thus a compulsory organization with a territorial basis ... The claim of the modern state to monopolize the use of force is as essential to it as its character of compulsory jurisdiction and continuous operation. (1978: 54–6; original emphasis)

1.4.2 Characteristics of the state

Parsing the passages from Weber, above, and avoiding listing all the institutions of the state, or the means and ends to which they are or could be put, one approach is to sketch certain characteristics of the modern state in terms of how it conducts the "business of rule" (Poggi 1978: 1). These can be summarized thematically as follows:
- Coercion and compulsion
- Authority and legitimacy
- Impersonal power and charismatic leadership
- Organization and bureaucracy

- Territoriality and sovereignty
- Nations and nationalisms
- Citizenship, inclusion and exclusion

The outlines of these characteristics are sketched in the following section (for a more elaborated discussion, see instead Pierson 2011). Here, I adopt Weber's "ideal-type" approach (e.g. 1978: 19–22), which offers a minimal definition of the state without constant recourse to empirical examples. In theory, this should capture the state along a continuum between liberal democracy and authoritarianism; the modern state compared to earlier forms; and the modern state in the historical-structural political contexts of colonialism, nationalism, and globalization.

1.4.2.1 Coercion and compulsion

Coercion refers to the state's ultimate recourse to enforcing its will, namely the monopolization of the use of (legitimate) force.[3] This can be expressed through various actions such as arrest, detention, or corporal or capital punishment, by various agents of the state, including the police, the military, and sometimes private companies. However, as Weber stressed, except in highly authoritarian contexts, coercion is "neither the sole, nor even the most usual, method of administration of political organizations" (1978: 54). Instead, compulsion through the mere threat of force is usually sufficient; it is thus "*control over* the means of violence, rather than the direct and frequent recourse to their employment," that is characteristic of the state (Poggi 1990: 3; emphasis added).

"Control", in this case, can be taken in the more obvious sense of "domination", but also – for the modern state – the precision involved in meting out violence, that is, its controlled use in practice. This stands in contrast with the pre-modern state, which was rather more arbitrary and brutal; this relied on what Mann (1984: 113) calls "despotic" power, which is exercised "without routine, institutional negotiation with civil society groups". Mann argues that the modern state has comparatively more developed "infrastructural" power, which is "the capacity of the state to actually penetrate civil society, and to implement

---

[3] This is not particularly important for our purposes, though it warrants clarification. Other groups or individuals might use force, but the key here is that the state holds the monopoly over the *legitimate* use of force. Individuals may be permitted to defend themselves or their home, for example, and therefore this is legal and legitimate use of force; however, this permission derives solely from the state's authority to grant it, hence the state's *monopoly*. Illegal use of force is by definition illegitimate.

logistically political decisions throughout the realm". The range of the modern state is greater, through increased capacities in surveillance, policing, bureaucracy, and administration; there is thus less need to exercise coercion through the "costly ostentation" of "spectacular and discontinuous interventions" (Foucault 1984: 61). Perhaps the most coercive state of all is the modern authoritarian state, which has high levels of both infrastructural and despotic power; this type of state penetrates deeply into civil society and is also arbitrary and brutal in its effects.

1.4.2.2 Authority and legitimacy

Ensuring compliance through coercion and compulsion can be effective in the short term, but both ineffective and inefficient in the long term. Coercion imposes the state's authority whether people like it or not, and very often they do not, with ramifications for the overall maintenance of stability in the social and political order, and the very survival of the state itself. As Sharp (2008: 17) puts it, "repression, even brutalities, do not always produce a resumption of the necessary degree of submission and cooperation for the regime to function" and, in fact, may produce precisely the opposite sort of effect. Compliance is more effective and efficient when it is granted willingly, paradoxically leading to a stronger state. Poggi (1990: 7) frames this as a reciprocal relationship whereby the state is seen to have a moral entitlement to issue orders, and citizens have a moral obligation to comply. In this case, the state's rule is legitimate in that it is generally accepted, or at least not violently opposed in any organized manner, by most of the population for most of the time (Pierson 2011: 25). Legitimacy is fundamentally a belief system, in which the ruled (and to some extent the rulers) see rule as valid, and thus "rules are followed because they are seen as natural, rightful, expected, and legitimate" (March and Olsen 2006: 7). State violence often inversely corresponds to its legitimacy; the state that lacks legitimacy has more need to resort to violence (thus further undermining its legitimacy), while the state with more legitimacy has less need to resort to violence, recursively increasing its legitimacy.

Pre-modern rulers often appealed to "traditional authority" (Weber 1978: 215), or some version of the "divine right of kings". Since the Enlightenment and the rise of more secular political organizations, such claims have been less convincing. Instead, modern states generally derive legitimacy from "legal authority", specifically a belief not merely in the moral rectitude of rule, but "in the legality of enacted rules and the right of those elevated to authority under such rules to issue commands" (Weber 1978: 215). Legitimacy is particularly cemented when the state can convince its citizens that it "embodies and expresses the (sovereign) will of the people" (Pierson 2011: 23). Democracy has been an important ideology in this regard (Poggi 1990: 28), though it is not a necessary ingredient.

1.4.2.3 Impersonal power and charismatic leadership

The shift from traditional to legal authority parallels another general tendency in the genesis of the state, namely to the depersonalization of political power. The personal and hereditary sovereignty of the pre-modern monarch, and the barons and landlords who made up subsequent strata of political organization, have been replaced by politicians and bureaucrats, giving rise to "impersonal rule bound by rules" (Ray 2012: 241). Sovereignty thus rests with the impersonal state, rather than with a specific person or group of people, and the state as an institution is relatively durable in the face of personnel changes (March and Olsen 2006: 3). There are, however, some caveats to this general observation. Poggi (1990: 20) remarks that while the institution of hereditary monarchy

> Seems to personalize power utterly...[t]he very fact that the accident of birth can assign to any individual at all... the supreme political position, indicates that the position itself, not the individual holding it, is the pivot of the system (Poggi 1990: 20)

Conversely, Weber (1978: 215) points to the notion of "charismatic authority", which encourages "devotion to the exceptional sanctity, heroism, or exemplary character" of an individual leader". This can be seen in the modern state even with the rule of law or relatively impersonal bureaucracy. Striking examples come from authoritarian contexts in the twentieth century. As Greenfeld and Eastwood (2005: 254) observe:

> Adolph Hitler, the Fuhrer who ardently believed that he represented the will of the German people, was but a bureaucrat, as was Joseph Stalin... who did not believe in any such thing but made sure that everyone else did.

Charismatic leaders are also frequently seen in contemporary liberal democracies, particularly with the growth of the mass media and the meticulously managed public images of politicians. As Beetham (2012: 123) notes, however, it would be a stretch to suggest that "both liberal democracy and fascism are different varieties of charismatic authority, one more rule governed than the other".

1.4.2.4 Organization and bureaucracy

The state is an institution and as such it is often referred to as a unified entity: the state is a subject that does certain things, or has certain qualities. However, the state is in fact made up of any number of institutions, each undertaking its own activities, under different remits, and with different jurisdictions. For Poggi (1990: 30), the contradictions between these unitary and heterogeneous tendencies are partly resolved by the state administration or bureaucracy. The bureaucracy co-ordinates the state's moving parts; put another way, it organizes the state's organizations. It has its own specific qualities, and enjoys a certain degree of autonomy from the (non-bureaucratic) supreme organ of sovereignty, such as Parliament, the Congress, or the Crown. The concept of the bureaucracy is implicit in the ideals of impersonal power and legal authority. It was central to Weber's understanding of the modern state, and he identified several normative characteristics (1946a: 196–7).[4]

- The authority to issue commands is "distributed in a stable way and is strictly delimited by rules concerning the coercive means ... placed at the disposal of officials". This implies a hierarchical organization of the bureaucracy; orders come from above, and "there is a supervision of the lower offices by the higher ones". This means that coercive measures are controlled, in the senses discussed previously; agents of the state should not be able to exercise arbitrary and unsanctioned violence. Furthermore, the bureaucracy "segregates official activity as something distinct from the sphere of private life" – that is, it should operate impartially and not at the personal whim or preference of administrators.
- The bureaucracy is based on the existence of "written documents ('the files') ... preserved in their original or draught [sic] form". Records of individuals must be kept tallying what symbolic and material resources should be allocated to whom. Policies and laws must be written down to ensure that the bureaucracy applies rules impartially.[5]
- The impartial, impersonal, and hierarchical aspects of the bureaucracy require that "only persons who have the generally regulated qualifications to serve are employed". Typically, this takes the form of educational qualifications, but may also be assessed through performance on competitive civil service exams. This has the function of ensuring a degree of homogeneity, which gives institutions relative durability in the face of personnel turnover. Here, the distinction is made clear between the non-elected, bureaucratic, and qualified civil servants who must implement policy and the non-bureaucratic, elected, but unqualified governments who make it.

---

4 Unattributed quotes in the remainder of this sub-section are from these pages.
5 Writing and literacy are of particular importance to the development of any kind of state, hence their emergence concurrently in Mesopotamia and elsewhere; they enable stability insofar as they "enable messages to be transmitted through the state's territories by its agents" (Mann 1984: 117), as well as account for who possesses and who owes what. In the earliest manifestation of the state, writing was the preserve of the bureaucracy. This will be addressed in chapter two.

1.4.2.5 Territoriality and sovereignty

The state occupies a defined geographical territory within which it is sovereign; that is, it exercises authority within that territory, solely within that territory, and it is the sole (legitimate) authority within that territory. This arrangement was codified – though not produced – by the Treaty of Westphalia in 1648, and it remains the basis of contemporary international law (Brown 2002: 22–35; Taylor 1994: 153). In general, with the exception of island nations, state borders do not coincide with physical features, but are arbitrary political segmentations of territory; borders only exist insofar as states agree that they exist, and states will jealously guard them to the point of going to war over strategically useless pieces of land or sea (Pierson 2011: 12).[6] Through territoriality and sovereignty, the state is therefore always a geopolitical entity in relation to other states and not an isolated unit (Mann 1988: viii). Pre-modern states were less well-defined. Like non-state societies, they had forms of territoriality but their edges were frontiers rather than borders, whereby political control was weaker at the periphery compared to the centre (Giddens 1985: 4). This is not to claim, however, that these organizations did not exercise sovereignty. Relative autonomy in practice at the periphery – caused to a considerable degree by the challenges to effective and rapid communication – did not mean an "actual claim to autonomy; autonomy is a practical response to problems of distance" (Brown 2002: 5). It became briefly fashionable at the end of the Cold War to claim that increasingly globalized or transnational processes and structures were eroding the bordered sovereignty of (nation-)states. In practice, bordered sovereignty has been transformed rather than eroded; the nation-state is still the arbiter of the parameters of globalization processes (Sassen 2007).

1.4.2.6 Nations and nationalisms

Poggi (1990: 22) quotes an unnamed Italian jurist, who suggests that "the state does not have territory, it is territory." Poggi uses this to illustrate the "hard" and "soft" aspects of the state's complex relationship to territory. The former is the factual basis of the state, such as its physical borders. The latter is more abstract, but, to its members, no less important: it is the relationship evidenced in the commonplace associations with mythical notions of "land", in terms such as motherland, fatherland, promised land, or homeland. Such associations are most clearly expressed in nationalism.

---

[6] Even oceans may not be a physical barrier, since territory may be expanded through war or colonization, with the effect that territory may be sovereign but not geographically contiguous with the political centre.

In Gellner's formulation, nationalism is "primarily a political principle that holds that the political and national unit should be congruent" (1983: 1). The political unit is the state, while the national unit is the nation; this gives rise to the "nation-state" that is hyphenated in practice and fused in everyday symbolism (Smith 1986: 228).[7] The nation is a group having various criteria in common, including language, religion, culture, or ethnicity, or some combination thereof. Nations are ideally recognized as such by others, but more fundamental is whether members see themselves in this way; that is, as being "fundamentally homogenous" enough to transcend issues on which they are "only superficially divided", and as a "unique sovereign people" (Greenfeld 1992: 3, 8). For Anderson (1991), members of a nation belong to an "imagined community": no member can meet all, or even most, of their fellow members, but their commonalities allow them to entertain the "image of their communion" (Anderson 1991: 6).

Nationalism can be divided into established and emergent types. Established nationalism is where the national unit is already congruent with the state; this begets nationalist sentiment including civic pride, patriotism, and belonging, but also its darker manifestations such as racism, xenophobia, and jingoism. The fusion of the state with the nation, and the co-opting or active production of nationalist sentiments, can be a powerful adjunct to state legitimacy. Emergent nationalism, on the other hand, presents more of a problem, since it is "a form of politics, primarily opposition politics" against an existing state (Breuilly 1982: 11). In its mildest form, an aspirant nation is content to co-exist with other groups, perhaps in return for certain rights, recognition, or autonomy in some spheres. In its strongest form, aspirant nations seek de facto or de jure independence and self-determination as their own states; that is, they seek their national units to be congruent with their own political units. Existing states are almost uniformly opposed to such movements: they threaten territorial integrity, and secession is the failure writ large to maintain social and political order. States may opt to assimilate or marginalize aspirant national identities; the last resort against secession, of course, is violence.

1.4.2.7 Citizenship, inclusion, and exclusion

Citizenship defines the extent of the reciprocal rights and obligations between the state and its members. As such, it overlaps with legitimacy, since state-

---

[7] The hyphenation of the nation-state in everyday language is something more than a diacritic; as Butler and Spivak (2010: 2) ask, "what work does the hyphen do? Does it mark a certain soldering that has taken place historically? Does it suggest a fallibility at the heart of the relation?"

granted rights (as opposed to universal human rights) are often framed in moral terms and in exchange for compliance. Citizenship can also be related to nationalism, since it defines the boundaries of inclusion and exclusion; in this regard, it is concerned with the questions of who "belongs" and thus who has the right to participate, and to what extent, in the political community. As a fact of social and political life, citizenship goes back to the city-states of ancient Rome and Greece. Foreigners, women, peasants, and slaves had fewer rights than full citizens, who were men and (usually) propertied. At least until Magna Carta in 1215, feudal and absolutist states in Europe held their members to exacting obligations, yet conferred few rights. The modern conception of citizenship, recovering the Greco-Roman form, emerged with democratic nation-states, particularly the American and French revolutions of the late eighteenth century. As Turner puts it, there are "two parallel movements" in this historical period, whereby "a *state* is transformed into a *nation* at the same time that *subjects* are transformed into *citizens*" (1990: 208; original emphasis).

In post-war Europe, a "series of interlocking legal, institutional and ideological changes affected the concept and organization of citizenship" (Soysal 2012: 384), which to some degree have spread elsewhere. Specifically, nation-state defined citizenship rights became oriented towards the emerging, normative, transnational, and universal human rights paradigm, locating them within a "postnational" context (Soysal 1994). These contemporary transformations of citizenship call into question an issue raised earlier, namely the erosion of the bordered sovereignty, and thus the autonomy, of the state. Once again, however, the state defines the parameters of rights and obligations within its territorial jurisdiction. Ultimately, it is the state that decides the extent to which it accepts and implements normative transnational rights structures. The state recognizes no other sovereign entity within its borders; as such, state sovereignty as a political principle is left largely intact. Immigrants, in particular, remain excluded from citizenship by definition, though they may have certain social, civil, and political rights. Paths to citizenship for immigrants, where they exist at all, often require demonstrating knowledge of a national or official language, as well as an understanding of the host state's politics, laws, customs, and social norms.

1.5 Society

While fields such as sociology and political sociology have no shortage of concepts and theories to explain how "society" works, explicit definitions of the term are scarce and sparse. Even academic dictionaries can be remarkably coy in their elaboration. Bruce and Yearley's (2006) SAGE Dictionary of Sociology, for example, opens with the following:

> Society: It may seem a curious discipline that has trouble succinctly defining its core term but this word carries a wide variety of meanings. (Bruce and Yearley 2006: 286)

A curious discipline indeed: we are reminded of Bagehot's quip about the nation, that "we know what it is when you do not ask us" (1872: 15, cited in Hobsbawm 1990: 1). Bruce and Yearley (2006: 286) reject the notion that society is the "totality of human relations" as being "broadest and least useful"; indeed, as Adorno ([1968] 2000: 30–31) remarked, this risks being a sociological understanding that is "no more than the trivial observation that 'everything is connected to everything else'". Particularly problematic is that, in this definition, "society" could feasibly be taken to mean an entirely borderless system consisting of all human relations, when we know that distinct societies exist; at the same time, somewhat paradoxically, this definition could be understood as societies being impermeable and closed: the totality of relations within a given society, with no influence from outside. Despite these caveats, we should bear in mind the fact something called "society" does indeed empirically exist as the result of multiple and overlapping sets of human relations, from the fleeting and dyadic to the more durable and larger-scale. These relations are held together and governed by norms, taboos, and social institutions, as well as – of course – language.

Bruce and Yearley (2006: 286) instead favour the definition that society is "any self-reproducing human group that occupies a reasonably bounded territory and has a reasonably distinctive culture and set of social institutions". This has intuitive appeal, but even here we run into difficulties. The notion of a "reasonably bounded territory" tends to privilege the nation-state as the unit of analysis; this is in fact made explicit when Bruce and Yearley go on to state that "we commonly refer to nation-states as societies" and that "we may also use the term for a particular people within a state" (2006: 286). We risk, here, falling into what Ulrich Beck (2003) calls "the trap of methodological nationalism", which unreflexively naturalizes the nation-state as the locus for sociological analysis. Although Beck's intention, in part, was to devise a sociology that accounted for contemporary globalization processes, Mann (1986: 2) much earlier warned of this tendency. Mann thus opts for a middle ground: society is "a unit with boundaries, and it contains interaction that is relatively dense and stable; that is, it is internally patterned when compared to interaction that crosses its boundaries" (1986: 13, cited in Pierson 2011: 66; emphasis added). The operative word here is "relatively": while discrete societies can be identified, their boundaries are always porous, and defined patterns of interaction are most clearly demarcated only when compared to those of other societies. Within the nation-state, multiple and overlapping societies exist, and this is particularly clear when we consider that practically all nation-states are multilingual, and that different sectors of national societies contend, compete, and collaborate over the distribution of politics and power.

Mann's definition accounts for multiple societies within the nation-state and the reconfiguration of nation-states in globalization processes, but also for societies that are not based around nation-states. As Held (1992: 73) notes, the similarities between state-defined and non-state societies are perhaps more striking than their differences. Very few of the latter now exist, since most have been incorporated, usually coercively, into the states or state-centred societies around them. However, both are social systems founded on complex and overlapping social relations and arrangements, and that have broader "social institutions" that manage essential social processes including the policing of social norms regarding kinship, marriage, and other interpersonal behaviours; resolving conflict and facilitating cooperation; enabling the transmission of learning; and the organization of power. Both face the same "two fundamental and inevitable human dilemmas: the problem of social order, and the management and distribution of material and cultural resources" (Faulks 2000: 23). They differ mainly in their approaches to solving these dilemmas. State-centred societies, by definition, address these issues through the state and its associated structures, processes, and institutions. Non-state-defined societies merely have different – but no less structured or complex – methods of addressing these issues; their characteristics are defined by other social and political forces.

1.5.1 Civil society

In its broadest definition, civil society is the space between the state and either the individual (e.g. Cohen and Arato 1992) or the family (e.g. Kopstein and Chambers 2008).[8] Most versions of civil society rule out political parties and certain specifically politically-oriented organizations, since these are concerned

---

[8] The precise arguments for including or excluding the family from civil society are not considered here, but excluding the family is usually premised on a stricter understanding of civil society as the public and not private domain of social life. From a sociolinguistic perspective, the use of language(s) in the family is important for language revitalization and maintenance; as such, a looser definition – i.e. including the family – is adopted here.

with running (or seeking to run) the state itself, though trade unions are almost always included; civil society is always politicized, in that it is conventionally held to provide a counterbalance to the state, but it is not the state itself. Usually, the economy is also excluded, for reasons we will explore later in this section. Cohen and Arato (1992: ix), here ruling in the family to civil society, thus offer the following definition:

> We understand civil society as a sphere of social interaction between economy and state, composed above all of the intimate sphere (especially the family), the sphere of associations (especially voluntary associations), social movements, and forms of public communication. Modern civil society is created through forms of self-constitution and self-mobilization. It is institutionalized and generalized through laws, and especially subjective rights, that stabilize social differentiation.

Ray (2012: 241) identifies civil society as a concept and material reality that emerged alongside the modern state in Europe. The rule of law and private property rights enabled voluntary economic exchanges; civic freedoms facilitated the formation of civic associations; and representative government allowed citizens to make collective political demands. The designation "civil" was originally intended to distinguish a broad and inclusive concept from "society" on its own; in older usage, "society" referred narrowly to the aristocracy (Drake 2010: 119). The independence of civil society, empirically or normatively, has been a concern since Locke and Hobbes in the seventeenth century to Hegel and, later, Marx in the nineteenth century; it continues to vex contemporary political sociologists and others in allied disciplines. Ray (2012: 242–243) offers a concise account of these historical origins and intellectual trajectories, noting that the academic concept (though not its actual manifestation) "passed into disuse ... for much of the twentieth century" (Ray 2012: 243) before being revived in the 1970s to explain political changes in Europe and Latin America, and again in the early 1990s as the Soviet Union collapsed. Contemporary approaches wrestle with whether civil society is or should be separate from, pitted against, in support of, in dialogue with, or beyond the state; whether it is a "partner, zone, or source of government" (Dean and Villadsen 2016: 401); or, as seems more likely, some combination of the above (Kopstein and Chambers 2008; see also Mouffe 1992; Chambers and Kymlicka 2002).

Engagement with explicit theorization of civil society has waned somewhat since the late 2000s (though cf. e.g. Dean and Villadsen 2016). However, these issues continue to be explored through specific case studies, particularly with regards to the growth of social movements (de Bakker, Den Hond, King, and Weber 2013); a renewed interest in civil society activism, and a concomitant rise in disaffection with political parties (Aarts and Cavatorta 2013); the potential for social media to facilitate such activism (Enjolras, Steen-Johnsen, and Wollebaek 2013); and in the relatively recent concept of a global civil society (Keane 2003; Colas 2013; Kaldor 2013). The aim of the following section, therefore, is to outline a critical view of the contours of the theoretical debates as they emerged from the 1990s. In the following, what Walzer (1991) calls the "civil society argument" is briefly sketched; this is fundamentally in favour of civil society and aligns with classical liberal/pluralist theories that see liberal democracy as a normative goal, and civil society as a means to achieve this. Some critiques of this position are then advanced.

1.5.2 The civil society argument

The "civil society argument" (Walzer 1991) holds that civil society is a necessary democratic counterweight against the excesses of state power. This rests on several assumptions. First, it invokes the classic liberal view that human beings are normatively free and equal and that they are entitled to pursue their political and economic interests and opportunities, so long as they do not restrict the freedoms of others, without intervention from the state. Second, it relies on pluralist accounts that citizens should be able to articulate their diverse interests against the state and, while different interests will compete in a "marketplace of ideas", the inherently democratic nature of civil society will ensure that no single interest will dominate in all political domains. This leads to consensus, not in terms of agreement on the substantive issues of identity or opinion – on these, in fact, there are agreements to disagree – but on the basic "rules of the game" of how politics and political discourse should be conducted (Pierson 2011: 59; Ray 2012: 246).

In this view, civil society is thus an egalitarian arena and the source of genuinely popular decision-making about the political allocation of symbolic and material resources in society. It exists to yoke the responsibilities of the state closely to the rights of the individual, and it behoves the state to serve the people, and not the other way around. Foley and Edwards (1996) parse the civil society argument into two threads, namely civil society Type I, and civil society Type II. "Civil society I" is the socio-political force that enhances accountability and maintains a democratic balance in an already-existing liberal democracy. "Civil society II", meanwhile, is found as resistance to authoritarian states, where the goal is achieving liberal democracy. Civil society is therefore seen as "an essential ingredient in both democratization and the health of established democracies" (Foley and Edwards 1996: 38). At least in what Foley and Edwards (1996: 38) call the "rough pastiche that has become the commonly accepted version" of the civil society argument, the power of civil society (in either Type I or II) is grounded in "dense network[s] of civil associations". Civil society associations are strictly voluntary in nature, and highly diverse; they encompass religious movements, sports clubs, parent-teacher committees, self-help groups, historical societies, professional organizations, NGOs, charities, special interest and advocacy groups, and trade unions, among many others. Whether these associations, taken individually, are specifically oriented towards overtly political activities is less important than the ways they combine to form a civil society that is collectively political or politicized (Putnam 1995). Civil society is political insofar as it is based on (or seeks to achieve) freedom of association, which is held to enable the cultivation of solidarity, trust, and cooperation; fostering these sentiments among the polity – and the deeper and denser the networks that do this the better – is healthy for democracy itself.

Social movements are perhaps the strongest evidence in support of the core argument that social and political change can and does emerge from civil society. These may be oriented towards the state and elite political institutions, through effecting policy or legislative changes, or towards civil society itself, by changing public attitudes (Nash 2010: 88–91). In popular laypersons' usage, the term refers "loosely to all relevant popular collective action, or at least all relevant popular collective action of which they approve" (Tilly 2004: 6), though sociological definitions are more circumscribed. Tilly (2004: 3–4) defines as social movements only those that have a synthesis of three elements: a sustained campaign, employment of various political actions from a social movement repertoire, and public displays of worthiness, unity, numbers and commitment. Snow et al. (2004: 6), summarize various definitions in the literature as revolving around three or more of five axes: "collective or joint action; change-oriented goals or claims; some extra- or non-institutional collective action; some degree of organization; and some degree of temporal continuity" (see also Tarrow 1998; Della Porta & Diani 2006: 20–29).

In these definitions, social movements are made distinct not only from spontaneous social political action, such as riots, but also from the more passive dimension of interlocking voluntary associations in civil society that are only collectively political. Tilly (2004) dates their emergence in the forms outlined above from around 1750. As Nash (2010: 88–91) argues, "traditional" social movements, such as nineteenth century feminism, were often concerned with single-issue identity politics. These were replaced by what are now called the "old" social movements, such as organized labour, which were oriented towards achieving more universalistic economic and political goals. "Old" movements were succeeded by the "new" social movements of the 1990s and 2000s, but these "new" movements have much in common with the "traditional" movements: Nash draws parallels between their single-issue politics, as well as – in contrast to e.g. the labour movement – an emphasis on non-hierarchical organization and grass-roots direct action. A final point to note is that social movements may eventually be incorporated into political parties, or (particularly with "old" movements) become fully-fledged parties on their own; that is, they morph from being strictly civil society elements to becoming part of the state itself, rather than merely seeking to influence its composition or direction.

The classical liberal pluralist position underpinning the civil society argument is plausible enough, and has some validity. Certainly, it has noble goals in its normative assumptions of freedom and equality; these are at the heart of modern democracy, and Mouffe (1992: 1) argues that "it is not possible to find more radical principles for organizing society". However, the civil society argument has tended to become "a somewhat uncritical celebration of the concept" (Chandhoke 2004: 143). In particular, the theoretical basis for the argument does not seem to play out empirically, and "mechanisms by which such 'microsocial' effects translate into 'macropolitical' outcomes are weakly specified or contradictory or both" (Foley and Edwards 1996: 47); furthermore, proponents of the civil society argument tend to presume, rather than show, that freedom of association, or fostering sentiments of solidarity and trust, in themselves lead to democratic stability. At most, these are necessary, but not sufficient, conditions for the possibility of a viable liberal democracy and some restraint on the excesses of state power.

A further problem is with the notion that civil society is an egalitarian arena in which all interests may be advanced; for Chatterjee (2004: 4), civil society is "the closed association of modern elite groups, sequestered from the wider popular life of communities, walled up in enclaves of civic freedom and rational law". Marxist approaches have long held that the economic interests of the bourgeoisie are the ideas that dominate, that property rights are inherently unequitable, and that economic exchange – especially wage labour – is never free. Indeed, for these critics, civil society props up the capitalist state rather than acts as a counterweight against it. More recent Marxist-inspired critiques, particularly those aimed at neoliberalism, are similarly suspicious of ruling the market in to civil society, since it is only in principle open to all. For Nash (2010: 15), the market is potentially "as much of a danger to the peaceful solidarity of civil society as are repressive states", a concern articulated in similar terms by Cohen and Arato (1992: viii). Walzer – who is otherwise a proponent of the civil society argument – takes a similar view, writing that "autonomy in the marketplace provides no support for social solidarity" (1991: 95). Meanwhile, unfettered freedom of association (and freedom of speech) may not be always desirable. Far right nationalism, for example, is permitted by unchecked freedom of association but undermines the sorts of multiculturalism that should, in theory, be guaranteed by pluralism. For Rosenblum (2000: 494), therefore

> The effects of many voluntary associations are positively antidemocratic. Their internal organization is hierarchic; their leadership is authoritarian; they disregard due process and fairness; their agendas are antithetical to civic norms. Secret societies and hate groups are only the most obvious examples.

Civil society, therefore, may in practice be "defensive about social transformation, nostalgic in its vision of the social order, and hostile toward the redistributionist state" (Benhabib 1999: 293). The polarized conception of a virtuous civil society against the perennially evil state is thus questionable in light of these observations (Cohen and Arato 1992). While the state, particularly in authoritarian contexts, may be a threat to civil society it may be, in fact, a necessary counterweight precisely to the profoundly illiberal tendencies of civil society. The state may serve to curb certain antidemocratic elements that, left unchecked, civil society would be neither inclined nor compelled to address. These include regulating hate groups and hate speech, guaranteeing certain constitutional rights, or intervening in intra-societal conflict and violence based on, for example, race and religion (Sivan 1989; Kaldor 1993). State regulation of markets has also been necessary to ameliorate the deleterious effects of untrammelled capitalism, such as poverty and environmental damage; economic crises, or the funnelling of vast sums of wealth to elites, has tended to coincide with periods of weak regulation (Tonkiss 2000; Stiglitz 2002; Harvey 2007), and the same is true for environmental catastrophe.

1.5.3 The public sphere

There is a close relationship between the public sphere and civil society; as Habermas observes, the public sphere "cannot be abstracted from the unique developmental history of civil society" ([1962]1989: xvii). However, it is important not to conflate the two. Delanty (2001: 42) offers the following distinction: the public sphere emerges prior to civil society, and while civil society indicates "specific forms of mobilization and citizen participation", the public sphere is "a domain of civic communication and civic contestation". If civil society is the space between the individual or the family and the state, then the public sphere is the space between civil society and the state (Drake 2010: 124). This space can in principle be anywhere – newspapers, radio (especially pirate radio, see Urla 1997), the street, the internet – that "communication is public rather than in private but that is still not part of the state" (Drake 2010: 124;

emphasis added).⁹ The public sphere is the forum (or set of forums) for the contestation of affairs of state, conceptions of the common good, including what constitutes "the good life", and matters of concern to everyone, including ethical and moral dimensions of how society should operate.

The concept of the public sphere as an academic concern was first articulated in Habermas' *The Structural Transformation of the Public Sphere* ([1962]1989). Habermas undertook a historical sociology of the emergence of the (bourgeois) public sphere in early modern Europe as feudalism gave way to capitalism. Whereas under feudalism only the state or the sovereign had control over the tools of mass communication and spectacle, and thus "the ruler's power was merely represented before the people", the emergent bourgeoisie gave rise to "a sphere in which state authority was publicly monitored through informed and critical discourse by the people" (McCarthy 1989: xviii). The development of the public sphere thus transformed the relations between the rulers and the ruled: "[state] authority was consolidated into a palpable object confronting those who were merely subject to it and who at first were only negatively defined by it" (Habermas 1989: 18).

The public sphere clearly has a sociolinguistic dimension; for Fraser, the public sphere "designates a theatre ... in which political participation is enacted *through the medium of talk*" (1992: 110; emphasis added). In the early development of the public sphere, face-to-face interactions in coffee houses and salons were key sites for public discussion among private citizens; these were eventually supplemented – through what Anderson (1991) would later call "print capitalism" – by the development of newspapers and journals, thus contributing to a general rise in literacy, at least among the bourgeoisie. In its contemporary manifestations, traditional and social media provide the main sites for discussion in the public sphere. As we shall see in chapter two, public spheres have dominant languages; so-called "official" public spheres usually follow the dominant language of the nation-state in which they are located, while unofficial or "counterpublic" spheres may operate in marginalized (or proscribed) languages (Fraser 1992; Urla 1997).

At least in Habermas' conception, the notion of the public sphere as a space for democratic deliberation gives rise to several idealized assumptions, which Fraser (1992: 59) sums up:

---

9 Two caveats should be noted at this point. The first is that state-funded (though not controlled) media may be an important part of the public sphere, the British Broadcasting Corporation being an example (Curran 1991: 42). The second is that social media, such as Facebook, is blurring the distinction between public and private.

the public sphere connoted an ideal of unrestricted rational discussion of public matters. The discussion was to be open and accessible to all, merely private interests were to be inadmissible, inequalities of status were to be bracketed, and discussants were to deliberate as peers. The result of such discussion would be public opinion in the strong sense of a consensus about the common good.

In practice, however, these assumptions are romanticized and nostalgized. Habermas to some degree recognizes this, but sees the Utopian potential of the public sphere as going unrealized, because private (mainly economic) interests made compromises between themselves and with the state and "non-bourgeois strata gained access to the public sphere", ending acrimoniously in social polarization and class struggle, and the fragmentation of the public into a mass of competing interest groups (Fraser 1992: 113). For Fraser (1992), however, rather than the ideal of unrestricted access simply going unrealized, "the official public sphere rested on, indeed was importantly constituted by, several significant exclusions" (Fraser 1992: 113) on the (often interlinked) bases of class, gender, and race, which were quite deliberately constructed from the outset. In other words, it was not that the eventual erosion of exclusions simply did not reach its full potential, but rather that exclusions on the basis of social inequalities were integral to bourgeois civil society. We can see in the contemporary manifestations of the public sphere that access to full democratic deliberation is still similarly restricted on the basis of class, gender, race, and – importantly for our purposes – language.

1.6 Conclusion

This chapter has outlined definitions of language, society, and the state as a prelude to synthesizing them into a theoretical framework of a political sociology of language in chapter two. Let us now summarize these definitions, and consider some of their implications.

Sociolinguists generally subscribe to the idea that linguistic diversity is something to be protected. There are several rationales for this position. If language, as Bickerton (1990: 5) puts it, is the means by which we process the deluge of information we encounter on a daily basis, then it seems intuitive that it is a burden to ask people to process daily life in a language that is not "theirs", however problematic the notion of language ownership might be. Language is also essential to our sense of identity and community, regardless of whether we take literally Makoni and Pennycook's (2007) call to disinvent named languages. Furthermore, through its linking with cultural diversity, linguistic diversity offers something, however intangible, to the stock of human knowledge about the world. These understandings have filtered through into contemporary conceptions of rights-based liberal democratic norms, namely that multilingualism is an integral aspect of social, cultural, and political diversity that should be respected. Historically, however, colonial, authoritarian, and nationalist impulses have been to ignore linguistic diversity, or even actively stamp it out.

These shifting historical contexts have driven and been driven by changes in the complexion of the modern state. The modern state is an identifiable entity with specific characteristics that are relatively durable across different contexts; it is an institution of institutions, or organization of organizations, that are co-ordinated through the administrative bureaucracy. These characteristics define the state as a bundle of contradictions. The tensions between coercion, authority, and legitimacy are fine lines to tread, since some measure of coercion – or, more accurately, the threat of coercion – is necessary for the state to maintain social and political order, though this can easily tip over into excess. Similarly, nationalism is a powerful adjunct to the state's legitimacy, yet it can be used to demonize, marginalize, and oppress non-dominant groups within the state's jurisdiction, a phenomenon that the state may find difficult to control. Citizenship defines the state's obligations to its population, but citizenship regimes may distribute rights unequally, particularly in the case of migrants.

The shorthand term "society" may inadvertently cast social relations as monolithic and homogenous. This is true for incautious uses of the term even by sociologists, and especially the case when it is used by sociolinguists. We can see from the foregoing that societies, even within the same nation-state, are multiple and overlapping. Civil society is a specific instantiation of society, one that is inherently politicized as a space for civic participation, association, and mobilization, and potentially a counterweight to the excesses of the state. However, we have also seen that civil society, despite the "civil society argument", is not an inherently liberal democratic space; it often gives rise to distinctly illiberal tendencies, such as hate speech or far right associations. The state must sometimes step in to mitigate these effects, and guarantee certain fundamentals of liberal democracy. In this way, it exercises a good deal of autonomy from civil society. The concept of the public sphere is related to civil society; it is the space between civil society and the state. However, while it has a potential as an arena for democratic deliberation, in practice access may be highly stratified along socio-economic and other lines.

2 Towards a political sociology of language

2.1 Introduction

The central concerns of political sociology are the relations between society and the state. These include critical questions about ethical and normative parameters of liberal democracy; who rules and who is ruled; how rule is conducted and how it is accepted or resisted; how symbolic and material resources are allocated; and what constitutes rights and how they can be distributed, claimed, and defended. These questions have sociolinguistic dimensions: which languages of the state are used to conduct the business of rule; the vitality and status of languages in civil society; how language is used to access rights; how democratic participation is structured based on language; how linguistic capital is valued within overlapping markets; and so on. As such, the present chapter develops a theoretical framework of a political sociology of language. It should be stressed that this is a *political sociology* of language, and not a *political sociology of language*; that is, it is not simply an explicitly politicized version of a conventional sociology of language approach. Instead, it is to bring the concerns of political sociology to bear on language and, conversely, it is a sociolinguistic understanding of the relations between society and the state. The aim of this chapter, in other words, is to frame relations between society and the state as a sociolinguistic concern, and language as a concern for political sociology.

At a general level, a political sociology of language is concerned with some of the problems posed by the fact that "we will never share a single language, nor be in complete agreement on what we view as the good life and/or the good state of society" (Peled, Ives, and Ricento 2014: 296). Multilingual, multi-ethnic, and multicultural complexity characterizes social and political relations both between and within states, though this comes at the risk of "razor edges of division" and "zones of silence" (Steiner 1998: 56–8) if common ground, tolerance, and understanding cannot be achieved. An academic approach to these issues is to locate – historically, geopolitically, and contextually – the politics of language in a given society, and thus a political sociology of language addresses Pennycook's (1998: 126) concern that

> we cannot assume that the promotion of local languages instead of a dominant language, or the promotion of a dominant language at the expense of a local language, are in themselves good or bad. Too often we view these things through the lenses of liberalism, pluralism or anti-imperialism, without understanding the actual location of such policies.

Pennycook's point is that liberalism, pluralism, and anti-imperialism all have analytical purchase, but they cannot be used unreflexively. Instead, specific manifestations of the state – in the case of Taiwan, primarily under colonialism, authoritarianism, nationalism, and globalization – and their relations with society need to be considered in order to situate the politics of language in a given historical period. Furthermore, the historical trajectory of the state and language politics, comprised of critical junctures and path dependencies (Cardinal and Sonntag 2015), needs to be understood to analyze their contemporary manifestations.

This chapter is structured as follows. I begin with an overview of language and the state, outlining language planning and policy, and describing the role of language in the administrative bureaucracy and the "business of rule" (Poggi 1978: 1). From there, I turn to the relationships between language and colonization, nationalism, and globalization, which roughly follows the periodization of Taiwan's political history. Language and its relation to civil society and the public sphere is then described. Finally, the chapter addresses language rights, and develops a theoretical framework exploring the sociolinguistic dimensions of transitional justice. Given space constraints and the focus on Taiwan in subsequent chapters, this is only a limited elaboration of a theoretical framework of a political sociology of language; a more comprehensive attempt will have to be left for a later project.

2.2 Language and the state

The state has a vested interest in regulating language, since language is the medium through which the state *vertically* conducts its "business of rule", and through which citizens interact with each other *horizontally* in civil society. To the extent that it needs to, or at least that it can, the state involves itself in such matters. Language planning and policy is the most visible intervention in these areas by the state, even if the state is not the sole actor in such processes, and even if intervention in fact consists of doing very little and, through a laissez-faire approach, simply allowing social and political forces to shape sociolinguistic contexts (Schiffman 1996). Different states, different types of states, and states in different historical-structural paradigms approach this differently but, as we will see shortly, the emergence of the modern state coincides with more concerted and sophisticated efforts towards language planning. This section begins with an overview of language planning and policy, before looking at the relationship between language and the state bureaucracy.

2.2.1 Language planning and policy: An overview

Language regulation, of some description, has likely occurred since humans used language in the earliest social formations: anthropologists have demonstrated that seemingly all cultures have taboo forms, and specific terms for honorifics and kinship relationships, for example (Spolsky 2004: 39). Limitations on who says what to whom constitute language policy and planning (LPP) at micro-levels without the need for either codifying these norms or a broader state-based system of socio-political organization.[10] More explicit and centralized language regulation develops with early states or empires: language was standardized for written forms in China 3,000 years ago; Arabic was standardized as the liturgical Islam by the ninth century; and Latin was (and remains) the language of the Catholic Church until the Reformation in the middle of the sixteenth century split the church into sects with their own vernaculars. In the thirteenth century, Kublai Khan hired Phags-pa, a Tibetan monk, to invent a new orthography for Mongolian that was later to become the official language of court documents during the Yuan dynasty (Ferguson 1996: 318).

The modern state gives rise to more complex LPP processes, often codified as laws and policies. The English government of Edward III put in place the Statute of Pleadings act in 1362, requiring that trials be heard in "the English tongue" rather than in Law French (Ormrod 2003), and this was clearly related to the Magna Carta signed by King John in 1215, which enshrined the rule of law and due process as right. Later, in the mid-sixteenth century, the Acts of Union required that only English speakers could hold public office in Celtic Wales (Wright 2016: 34). In France, the Académie Française was established in 1635 and exists to this day, charged with ensuring the "purity" of the French language and, by analogy, the stability of French society itself (watched over by a committee whose members are known as *les immortales*, or "the immortals"). Modern nation-states have often privileged monolingualism as well as preferred "standard" varieties over others; the US, for example, has no de jure official language but English dominates in state-society relations. Some, however, have enshrined multilingualism into official language policy; India has Hindi and English as official languages at the national level, with some twenty-two languages officially recognized at the state (that is, provincial) level. In recent years, language policies in many liberal democratic contexts have been concerned with actively promoting bilingualism and

---

[10] We will leave to one side the potential distinction between "planning" and "policy", for convenience seeing them as nested and mutually implicative processes.

maintaining or reviving the languages of indigenous and minority communities; these are framed in *trans-national* indigenous and human rights paradigms.

Although LPP activities have a long genesis in practice, their theorization within the academic field of LPP research is far more recent. In general terms, LPP processes consist of the "deliberate efforts to influence the behaviour of others with respect to the acquisition, structure, or functional allocation of their language codes", in Cooper's widely-cited definition (1989: 45). Once again, it should be stressed that not all LPP processes are conducted by the state, but the reality and prevalence of multilingual polities – some 7,000 languages in the world are divided among just over two hundred existing or viably aspirant nation-states – mean practically all states must engage in LPP processes; it is possible for a state to be secular on the issue of an official state religion, but a taking a position on which language(s) are to be used is unavoidable (Wee 2011: 15). To elaborate Cooper's definition, these efforts are related to corpus planning, or interventions in the structure, script, or vocabulary of a language; status planning, or interventions in which languages are symbolically valued in which social, cultural, and political contexts; and acquisition planning, or interventions intended to ensure populations learn certain languages, sometimes at the expense of losing others. These approaches are, respectively, about language, about uses of language, and about users of language.

We can see from Hornberger's (1994; 2006) attempts to integrate these various perspectives into a single coherent framework (Table 2.1) that status planning is concerned with selecting official or national languages (or proscribing certain languages) when it is oriented towards "the what" or *policy planning* ("on form")

Table 2.1: After Hornberger (1994, 2006); based on Cooper (1989); Ferguson (1968); Haugen (1983); Kloss (1968); Nahir (1984); Neustupny (1974); Stewart (1968).

Approaches *Types*	Policy planning (on form/ selection) *Goals*	Cultivation planning (on function/ implementation) *Goals*
Status planning (about uses of language)	Standardization of status; Officialization; Nationalization; Proscription	Revival; Maintenance; Inter/intra-national communication; Spread
Acquisition planning (about users of language)	Group; Education/school; Literature; Religion; Mass media; Work	Reacquisition; Maintenance; Foreign/second language; Shift
Corpus planning (about language)	Standardization: Corpus; Auxiliary code; Graphization	Modernization: Lexical; Stylistic; Renovation: Purification; Reform; Stylistic simplification; Terminology unification

dimensions; and with implementing revival, maintenance, and spread etc. of a language in terms of "the how" or *cultivation planning* ("on function") dimensions. Acquisition planning is concerned with selecting the appropriate language(s) to be used in domains such as education or religion when oriented to the *policy planning* dimensions; and with implementing language maintenance or shift in terms of the *cultivation planning* dimensions. Corpus planning – though not the focus of this book – is concerned with various processes of standardization of whichever language(s) are being selected and implemented through status and acquisition planning approaches. The three basic types of interventions overlap; as Fishman (2006) and others have pointed out, there is an implicit status dimension to corpus planning, while acquisition planning usually requires language standardization through corpus planning, and so on. To give a toy example, suppose, in terms of status planning, the fictional country of Hoopland selects the fictional language of Bazoolish as its sole official language (the political reasons for this selection are not important here, but let us assume that it is to inculcate a monolingual nationalism); in terms of implementation, the task is then to encourage Bazoolish speakers to maintain their language, while spreading Bazoolish to non-Bazoolish speakers. This overlaps with acquisition planning dimensions; one way to achieve Bazoolish-spread is through selecting Bazoolish as the medium-of-instruction in schools, and this requires standardizing Bazoolish so that it can perform this function.

To generalize from this toy example, status planning is concerned with selecting one or more languages as dominant in either interactions with the state or the spheres of (civil) society that the state has some degree of control over. This can be achieved by promoting some languages or proscribing others; the state is also able to selectively implement status planning in areas such as the legal system or the mass media. Status planning is always about formalizing existing hierarchies or establishing new ones, with different languages being valued differently and allocated different political and social functions and domains. Crucially, this also involves legalizing, officializing, or otherwise legitimizing not just languages but attitudes towards or ideologies about language (Spolsky 2004). These attitudinal or ideological processes can have powerful social, political, and cultural effects beyond language itself, since language is indexically linked to speakers – either individuals or groups – and to their social, political, and cultural positions within society; status planning is therefore rarely solely about language. It should be noted here that status planning *in itself* is neutral; language-spread may lead to language shift, loss, or death, but it may equally lead to language maintenance of an endangered or marginalized language. Whether status planning is harmful or benign in *its effects* largely depends on the relation of the state to the languages and speakers in question, the sociolinguistic context, and political exigencies.

Status planning can also have unintended consequences: attempts to ban a language may in fact lead to its revival or maintenance among a community. Conversely, attempts to maintain a language may not succeed if the social, political, and cultural factors behind its decline are not addressed; in other words, language policy never operates in a vacuum.

Through status planning, choosing which language(s) should be the medium of interaction with the state often involves some form of officialization. De jure officialization codifies the status of various languages in law, usually either in legislation or constitutions; Stewart thus defines an official language as one that "functions as a legally appropriate language for all politically and culturally representative purposes on a nationwide basis" (1968: 540). Cooper (1989: 100), however, later pointed out that a language does not have to be de jure official in order to be de facto official; he distinguishes "statutory" de jure official languages from de facto "working" languages that are official in all but name. As such, languages may be designated "national", but still be "official" for all intents and purposes. Furthermore, Cooper devises a third category – "symbolic" official languages – which are official in principle but not used (or are not accessible for people to use) in practice. Framed another way, practically all states engage in some processes of officialization of certain languages at the expense of other languages used in society, whether or not they have a de jure official language. For Bourdieu,

> Official language is bound up with the state, both in its genesis and in its social uses. It is in the process of state formation that the conditions are created for the constitution of a unified linguistic market, dominated by the official language. (Bourdieu 1991: 45)

However, only the most drastic status planning measures can change the sociolinguistic composition of society in the short term; a language can be officialized at the stroke of a pen, but this does not mean anyone knows or uses it, or that a population will suddenly stop using their now politically dispreferred language. Instead, the state's goals of language spread, shift, loss, or maintenance are more effectively achieved through longer term acquisition planning. Although it is perfectly possible to undertake mass acquisition planning with adults on a voluntary basis, more susceptible are children within the mass compulsory education system. The language behaviours of children can be closely monitored and controlled in ways that adults' behaviours (particularly in private) cannot. Once again, acquisition planning in compulsory education does not happen in a vacuum; the education system can inculcate beliefs and ideologies about language which serve broader political functions, particularly those related to nationalism. It is here that children learn whether languages are associated with, for example, patriotism or treachery, or backwardness or upward mobility.

To borrow from Bourdieu, again, children in the state's educational system are the primary site for the cultural reproduction of a chosen dominant language.

2.2.2 The administrative bureaucracy and the business of rule

Communication has been a perennial concern since the establishment of the earliest state formations, whether between the centre of political power and its administrative peripheries, or between the state/empire and its citizens/subjects. Political formations that have better solved these issues have arguably been more successful at consolidating power and rule. Although the centre/periphery designation implies a lateral distinction, following Cooper (1989: 105), the socio-spatial metaphor invoked here is one of *verticality*; from a Weberian understanding, the state's communications with both its peripheries and citizens are both administratively conducted downwards through a bureaucratic hierarchy.

Effective communication between the centre and periphery – whether frontiers in earlier empire formations or the more defined borders of modern states (Giddens 1985: 49–50) – is necessary for administrative reach to maintain territorial control; increased territorial control leads to access to economic and natural resources, thus enriching and sustaining the administrative centre. Essential to this feedback loop is the ability to transmit stable and comprehensible messages. Writing has played an important role in this regard, since the written form is less prone to misinterpretation than oral messages committed to memory. However, equally important is a common language code – an "administrative vernacular" (Anderson 1991: 41) – along the chain of command through the bureaucratic hierarchy. In this way, commands can be "distributed in a stable way" and that, aptly for the metaphor of verticality, "there is a supervision of the lower offices by the higher ones" (Weber 1946a: 196–7). In other words, without the ability to internally communicate effectively, institutions would not function (Patten and Kymlicka 2003: 17). This does not entirely preclude bilingual or multilingual administrations, but it does suggest that the state is inclined towards "administrative monolingualism" for rational bureaucratic functioning.

Administrative monolingualism does not require societal monolingualism; it is not strictly necessary to impose a single language in society for the bureaucracy to function in a single language, and a relatively small number of bilingual bureaucrats will suffice. However, societal monolingualism – or at least sufficient numbers of citizens being bilingual in the state language – is preferable for the state for the business of rule: that is, a common language is helpful for the purposes of issuing orders – laws, regulations, edicts – to its citizens and, crucially, ensuring that they are understood. At least in more democratic contexts, this has a bidirectional aspect (Wright 2016: 35); along with persuading and reasoning (as opposed to merely issuing orders), the state tends to seek consensus by consulting on affairs of state with civil society. The point to be made here is that the preference for societal monolingualism is a practical function of the necessities of the business of rule as much as it is an ideological function of nationalism. Indeed, it is not just that monolingualism is ideologically useful for nationalism; nationalism *itself* is useful for implementing the monolingualism that state rationality prefers. In practice, of course, the preference for societal monolingualism must be balanced against the reality of multilingual polities, and the approach of a given state depends on equations in terms of economic costs (Grin, Sfreddo, and Vaillancourt 2010; Hogan-Brun 2017) or political costs, particularly in terms of legitimacy versus coercion.

2.2.3 Literacy

Chrisomalis (2009) notes that writing developed independently in at least four separate places – namely China, Egypt, Meso-America, and Mesopotamia – which are also places where proto-states were established. The proto-state did not *require* writing (though the development of writing seemingly required a proto-state), but proto-states that did have written systems had substantial advantages. Writing, of course, enabled stable messages to be sent throughout the territory (Mann 1984: 117); it also enabled the stable codification of laws, which provided some degree of internal socio-political coherence. Writing also allowed for accounting of who owned and owed what, and what surpluses were produced and, crucially, tally them at relatively large scales. These functions are essential for effective taxation systems that enable the growth and development of more complex states.[11] Lévi-Strauss (1961: 292) points to how the emergence of writing coincides with the increased coercive and repressive capacities of the state:

> At the moment when writing makes its debuts ... it seems to favour rather the exploitation than the enlightenment of mankind. This exploitation made it possible to assemble workpeople by the thousand and set them tasks that taxed them to the limits of their strength ... The one phenomenon which has invariably accompanied [writing] is the formation of cities and empires: the integration into a political system, that is to say, of a considerable number of individuals, and the distribution of those individuals into a hierarchy of castes and classes.

---

[11] Conversely, various scholars have pointed out that non-literate and non-state societies in general have fewer number terms, because there is little need for counting above a certain level (Pinker 2007; Gordon 2004; Everett 2005).

Writing is even more fundamental to the legal architecture of the *modern* state. For Weber, fixed laws and administrative regulations structure the bureaucracy and delimit the jurisdiction of each "office" or "bureau". Furthermore:

> The management of the modern office is based upon *written documents* ("the files"), which are preserved in their original or draught [sic] form. There is, therefore, a staff of subaltern officials and *scribes of all sorts*. The body of officials actively engaged in a "public" office, along with the respective apparatus of material implements and the files, make up a "bureau." In private enterprise, "the bureau" is often called "the office." (Weber 1946a: 197; emphasis added)

As mentioned in chapter one, "the files" contain both administrative regulations as well as the aggregate or individual information pertaining to the population of citizens. The files must be *written* so that a given institution – and the institution of the state more broadly – is able to function relatively durably in the face of turnover of personnel. The stability of the state itself, then, is grounded largely in the stability of language that writing affords. A key attribute of any bureaucrat is thus literacy; they are, in Weber's words, "scribes of all sorts" and thus conversant with multiple literacies of the state. It is one thing for a citizen to be able to read a form and fill it in; it takes a special type of literacy to write the form in the first place.

Widespread literacy and numeracy is a comparatively recent phenomenon. For most of the history of the state, what might be called *administrative literacy* would have been sufficient, confined to political, social, or religious elites and, more importantly, among the bureaucratic cadre that served the state. Mass literacy begins to emerge alongside the modern European state around the sixteenth century due to a series of interlocking social, political, and sociolinguistic changes, and I should stress here that "mass" is a relative term. A pivotal moment is the invention of the printing press by Johannes Gutenberg in Germany around 1440, a technology subsequently exported to other European countries within a few decades. As Cook (1995) argues, this could not have led to an immediate explosion in societal literacy since it was still an elite preserve, though doubtless the introduction and circulation of books had the effect of incrementally raising literacy rates and cultivating "reading publics" (Anderson 1991: 37 – 40). True mass literacy – over 70% – is established in several nation-states in Europe from about 1850 (Vincent 2000). This coincides with several socio-political and sociolinguistic phenomena: the languages of those nation-states having relatively standardized forms and stable scripts; the primacy placed on literacy in general in those societies; the expansion of democratic franchise; the exigencies and affordances of industrialization; and the development of compulsory mass education.

2.3 Language and colonization

The relationship between language and colonization is structured differently depending on the historical and contextual location of the colonizing states or state-like entities, their colonies, and the sociolinguistic situations in question. However, common organizing principles are the questions of which languages are the "languages of colonial command", and who commands these colonial languages and to what extent (Errington 2008: 2–3). The language of colonial command need not be the language of the colonizers; it may be a local lingua franca, the language of a dominant ethnic or socio-political group, or the language of most or all of the colonized. What matters is that it is the language through which the business of colonial rule is conducted; that is, that it is the language of the administrative bureaucracy and through which political control is maintained.

2.3.1 Colonization and LPP

Colonization is not a new phenomenon; expanding territory to exploit and control resources has been a defining feature of human history, particularly when proto-states and civilizations emerged as the dominant mode of political rule. However, improved technologies, communications, and the strengthening of the modern European state gave rise to the distinctively modern form of colonization from the sixteenth century onwards. The enduring legacy of European languages across vast swathes of the globe is testament to the success of the colonial language-spread policies of their respective metropolitan countries (Léglise and Migge 2007). In their wake, indigenous languages, though they may be numerically larger, have often been marginalized from public and political life or, where they are numerically smaller, sometimes lost altogether.

Two main modes of colonial rule can be identified, and these have different ramifications for the practical and ideological bases of language policies. Settler-type colonialism – the more strictly "colonial" modality in the sense of the Latin term *colonia* or "farm, settlement" from *colonus* or "farmer" – involves the transfer of a population from the metropolitan centre to a new territory. Economic exploitation-type colonialism is more closely related to the notion of imperialism, which comes from the Latin *imperium*, "to command"; this only requires sufficient military or political control to enable resource extraction to take place. Of course, this is not a rigid distinction; settler-type colonialism often has an underlying economic logic, and economic exploitation may require or permit some level of settlement.[12] These precise dynamics vary in practice, as do linkages with the metropolitan centre, according to political and economic exigencies. In some cases, the periphery is seen as a system separate from, but controlled by, the centre; the metropolitan state's political interest in these cases is pragmatic, concerned with the maintenance of order and the business of rule. In other cases, the colony is an extension of the territory of the metropolitan state and incorporated into the state's geopolitical orbit. Here, the state's interest becomes at least partly ideological; it is necessary to convince a colonized population that they are being incorporated into the metropolitan centre, sometimes with claims to be returning the colony to a putative motherland or fatherland.

In what follows, three different models of colonial LPP are identified: administrative monolingualism; administrative bilingualism; and elite bilingualism. As with colonial modalities in general, these distinctions are blurred and, in practice, more than one approach may be taken even within the same colony, depending on the objective in mind. All three models have ideological and practical dimensions, though they differ in their emphasis. Let us sketch these in turn.

2.3.2 Administrative monolingualism

Administrative monolingualism refers to the system whereby the colonized population's language practices align with those of the colonizing state. In these cases, the bureaucracy is (usually) already monolingual by default; what is necessary is achieving monolingualism for the business of rule. It should be stressed that, while societal monolingualism is the ultimate goal (and the legacy of European languages demonstrates it was in large part achieved in many contexts), it is possible for administrative monolingualism to function as long as a sufficiently high number of the colonized are bilingual. The maximum outcome of this approach is thus the full assimilation of colonized populations into the colonial language and culture. The minimum outcome is to reorganize the relative statuses of languages in the colonial context; more specifically, it introduces a new language into the sociolinguistic ecology. This often leads to forms of diglossia, with the colonial language occupying high status domains and functions, marginalizing local languages symbolically and practically.

---

12 As we will see in chapter three, the Dutch operated a perhaps unique hybrid model in Taiwan, using (non-slave) Chinese settler labour and, through the missionary-colonial complex, Dutch administrative political control.

Administrative monolingualism has a clear practical purpose: it enables the stable transmission of orders from the colonial state to the colonized, and requires that colonial populations interact with the colonial state in the state's preferred language. However, it also has a powerful ideological function, particularly for forms of colonial rule that are claiming territory and fashioning it into new configurations of empire. The effect is to create an overlapping, though not completely isomorphic, sociolinguistic and cultural identification between the colony and the metropole. This often ties metropolitan citizenship to language proficiency, and may have a racialized as well as cultural dimension: in Fanon's words (1967: 18), in the eyes of the French colonial state the Black colonial subject "will be proportionately whiter ... in direct ratio to his mastery of the French language".

There are several drawbacks to this approach for the colonial state. The first is that without extensive acquisition planning mechanisms, and/or relatively coercive forms of language-spread, widespread adoption of the colonial language is difficult to achieve. This almost invariably leads to elite bilingualism, discussed below, with its associated problems being exacerbated when it is implemented as a means and not an end. Second, enforced monolingualism may be passively or actively resisted in the colonized society, with language becoming a focal point for political resistance. Linguistic resistance is powerfully symbolic, and a less politically risky strategy than some other forms of civil disobedience, or outright armed struggle.

2.3.3 Administrative bilingualism

Administrative bilingualism refers to the system whereby colonial administrators learn the language(s) of the colonized sufficiently well so that the bureaucracy can operate and orders can be communicated and understood. Despite the preference of the state, in general, for administrative monolingualism, in all types of colonization administrative bilingualism is perhaps the most practically-minded solution; indeed, for the initial period of colonial contact, it may be the *only* practicable solution. It is certainly the least onerous on the colonized population. It requires fewer people – mainly colonial administrators or clergy serving the missionary-colonial complex – to learn a new language; administrators and clergy are already literate to begin with, and thus they are able to function in their bureaucratic roles relatively quickly. It does not require the infrastructure of mass acquisition planning, or the introduction of a new language into the sociolinguistic ecology. Indeed, if practicality is the only criteria, administrative bilingualism is the most rational solution to the linguistic dilemmas of the bureaucratic colonial state.

However, its pragmatic focus loses the ideological function of fashioning identification with the colonial metropole, and thus it potentially reduces legitimacy of the colonial state in the eyes of the colonized. In fact, that it was not used more often demonstrates that colonial language policies were rarely solely concerned with the practicalities of communication. Further difficulties come with choosing which language(s) to learn and to use in sociolinguistically and ethnoculturally heterogeneous situations. Choosing a single language risks disturbing often delicate ethnic balances of colonized societies, which creates administrative problems for maintaining order and political control. Of course, the likely finite capacities of (most) humans for second-language learning makes requiring administrators learn *all* languages infeasible.

2.3.4 Elite bilingualism

Although poorly-planned administrative monolingualism may lead unintentionally to elite bilingualism, elite bilingualism may be an end in itself. In this model, a cadre of local bilinguals mediate between the (monolingual) colonial state and the colonized society. Elites may be chosen from dominant ethnic groups who wish to maintain or assert their relative social and/or political positions in society, or from those educated in a colonial system, sometimes in the metropole, and thus ostensibly sympathetic to the colonial mindset. They offer a means of indirect political control over society that is embedded by their being established members of the community, with potential advantages for the colonial state's legitimacy. As with administrative bilingualism, it requires fewer people to learn the target language, and reduces the need for large-scale education systems.

Conversely, elite bilingualism may also serve as an intermediate stage between administrative bilingualism and administrative monolingualism. In other words, following the initial period of colonial contact, during which administrative bilingualism is the only practicable option, elite bilingualism may be a means to achieve administrative monolingualism. This model, as Calvet (1987: 72) describes, consists of two steps. The first "vertical" step refers to the spread of the colonial language into the upper social strata (or "class"), usually in the colonial capital, from which it is spread into the middle and lower strata. From there, the colonial language takes a "horizontal" step, spreading out geographically to smaller cities, then towns and villages. In some ways, this reduces the need for, first, coercive forms of language-spread and, second, complex bureaucratic and educational infrastructure, since access to elite status or privileges is an incentive for people to learn the colonial language, or encourage their children to do so.

The difficulty with this model for political administrations is that elite bilinguals can wield an enormous amount of social and political power and influence as a translator class. They can destabilize ethnic, social, or political balances within a society, and thus their compliance must be negotiated by the colonial state. A further issue is that that elite bilinguals, being the upper social strata, tend to be or become intellectual elites. Exposed to colonial languages, and thus to sometimes radical currents of political and cultural thought, they then become a political paradox: cultivated by the colonial state, but at risk of becoming opposed to it.

2.3.5 Decolonization

As mentioned above, the development of LPP research as an academic discipline is relatively recent compared to the long genesis of LPP practices, and it parallels the wave of decolonization in Africa and Asia in the 1960s (e.g. Ferguson 1968; Stewart 1968; Fishman, Ferguson, and das Gupta 1968). New nations were born out of liberation struggles, and states had to be constructed to fill the lacunae left by withdrawing colonial powers. Alongside questions of the allocation of political resources within only nominally democratic systems, and of the economic and infrastructural capabilities for self-rule, there came sociolinguistic questions of how to deal with complex multilingual societies. Although not all linguistic differences were "invented" by colonization and post-colonial nationalisms, it remains the case that many of these societies, and thus their ethnolinguistic constituencies, were artificially created. Colonial and post-colonial national borders were often arbitrarily inscribed around populations who did not necessarily see themselves as homogenous national groupings; for Greene (1978: 183), they were

> drawn by their former imperialist rulers, with complete disregard for ethnic and linguistic considerations, and in the great majority of these states the citizens are bound together by nothing more than a shared experience of foreign domination.

The "shared experience of foreign domination" created difficulties for language planning; colonial languages were tangible links to this shared experience, and maintaining them was antithetical to anticolonial nationalist struggles. Though somewhat Whorfian in its orientation, for Fanon

> to speak [the colonial language] means to be in a position to use a certain syntax, to grasp the morphology of this or that language, but it means above all to assume a culture, to support the weight of a civilization. (Fanon 1967: 17)

But nationalist impulses were in many cases outweighed by the need for a functioning bureaucratic state. Retaining the colonial language for official state purposes was considered as a way to provide this, as well as partially avoid the risks inherent in elevating one or more local languages over others. Local languages had their place, but usually – excepting cases where there was a relatively neutral local lingua franca – this was in a diglossic situation in which they were relegated to the home, market, and other low-status domains. On the surface, these were simply pragmatic solutions to the so-called "language problems of developing nations" (Fishman, Ferguson, and das Gupta 1968), but beneath them lay highly ideological rationales connected to the politics of development as seen by Western sociolinguistic experts who, in a noteworthy example of praxis, both researched sociolinguistic contexts and were called in to advise on language policymaking (Williams 1992). The dominant paradigm they worked from was modernization theory; this held that the economic and political underdevelopment of former colonies could be ameliorated if they could only "catch up" with the West. Official monolingualism in a "Western" former colonial language could grant access to political, technological, and economic innovations, the (equally Whorfian) implication being that local languages could not grasp such concepts without extensive corpus planning reform efforts. As Fishman (1968: 60, cited in Williams 1992: 126), for example, opined, a linguistically homogenous state tends to be "economically more developed, educationally more advanced, politically more modernized, and ideologically-politically more tranquil and stable". The realities of multilingualism were never denied by researchers, but they were perceived as impediments to the functioning of the state and to the adjunct to state legitimacy provided by national social cohesion. Postcolonial language policies were thus as important in cementing language spread as colonial policies.

It may seem unfair to castigate these uncritical perspectives fifty years later, and with the benefit of more enlightened hindsight. However, the modernization theory espoused by sociolinguist experts neglected engagement with alternative dependency theories emerging in sociology and political science at the same time (e.g. Sunkel 1969; dos Santos 1971; see Ferraro 2008). These theories proposed that the apparent problems with these new nation-states were precisely the result of colonial exploitation; it was not that new nation-states inherently lacked human or economic capital, but that those resources had been systematically extracted under colonialism. Applying this to sociolinguistic contexts, it was not that local languages were inherently incapable of being used for the state's political and economic purposes; instead, local languages had been constructed in specific and unequal diglossic relations with regards to the colonial language. Claiming that the colonial language was ethnically neutral ignored the fact that the inscription of colonial and postcolonial borders created the conditions for ethnic conflict in the first place.

However, the imposition of the former colonial languages by language planners did not mean that sociolinguistic resistance was impossible. Many writers and intellectuals made conscious efforts to graft metropolitan languages onto local contexts; postcolonial literatures have become a medium through which "the empire writes back" (Ashcroft, Griffiths, and Tiffin 2002). Ordinary speakers, meanwhile – whether consciously or through the natural processes of language variation, change, and mixing – adopted localized varieties of former colonial languages (Schneider 2007; Trudgill 2010). In many cases, these varieties became important sources of national identity in society; through their distinction from their metropolitan forms, they represented a break with the colonial past, not a legacy.

More critically-engaged approaches to LPP research began to emerge in the late 1980s. These were concerned with the kinds of historical-structural conditions and power relations that dependency theory had pointed to. Economic development for its own sake was critically reconsidered as a principle, as was the notion that the essentially monolingual European nation-state was the best (or only) model of analysis for how possible or successful language policies may be (Luke, McHoul, and Mey 1990). Multilingualism began to be regarded as less of a problem and more of a resource, while notions of rights and equality began to frame normative understandings of language policies.

2.4 Language and nationalism

Historically, nationalism has been associated with monolingualism, within the ideological framework that a single language should be contiguous with a single nation with its own state. In some, but by no means all, contemporary *official* nationalisms, multilingualism has been tolerated or promoted, in parallel with greater acceptance of multiculturalism, and particularly the rights of national or indigenous minorities. Of course, monolingualism is still the ideological default in many *public* imaginations of nationalisms, and is often a cloak for xenophobia, particularly when oriented towards migrant languages. This section discusses these historical and contemporary links between language and nationalism.

2.4.1 Monolingualism and national identity

As Wright (2016) relates, before the advent of nationalism in the nineteenth century, in Europe and elsewhere there existed long and relatively unbroken dialect continua among related languages. These were linguistic chains along which differences were almost imperceptible between adjacent points, and added up to constitute mutually unintelligible "languages" only at more distant ends. Where languages rubbed up against those of different phyla, imbricated patterns of bilingualism occurred. Societal multilingualism was politically tolerated to a large degree prior to the nation-state (Anderson 1991: 42). The Romans saw no purpose in imposing Latin in its territories, in fact considering its acquisition as "a privilege to be sought, like citizenship" (Lewis 1976: 180, cited in Edwards 2011: 163), and that social and political forces would naturally cause language shift. The Ottoman and Austro-Hungarian rulers, and the *ancien régime* in pre-revolutionary France, similarly practiced policies of benign neglect, generally unconcerned about who spoke which languages to whom as long as taxes were paid and political harmony was maintained (Edwards 2011: 163). In pre-nationalist Qing China, linguistic diversity was something to be overcome for the sake of practical political administration.

The drawing of the boundaries of the nation-state and the centrifugal processes of nation-state building served to sharpen these differences, leading to homogenized, distinct, and named languages emerging contiguously with these borders for political reasons (Makoni and Pennycook 2007; Wright 2016). The ideological relationship between a single language, single people, and single nation-state becomes cemented in the nineteenth and early twentieth centuries, but there is considerable disagreement among theorists of nationalism about how the link between language and nationalism operates. For primordialist theorists, nations are timeless entities that are awoken by nationalism. In this view, Herder and Fichte in late eighteenth and early nineteenth century Germany being perhaps its earliest proponents, a single ancestral language is a highly salient marker of a distinct nation since it represents a unique "world-view", akin to Humboldt's notion of each language giving rise to a singular perspective on the Cosmos. More specifically, nations have distinctive ways of thinking that can only be expressed through having their own (single) language, which in turn legitimizes their political constitution as nation-states. For modernist theorists, "nationalism is not the awakening of nations to self-consciousness: it *invents* nations where they do not exist" (Gellner 1964: 168). From this perspective, the relationship between language and nationalism is less clear cut. Kedourie believed that a single language was contingent to nationalism: useful but neither necessary nor sufficient (Kedourie 1960). In Kedourie's analysis, which was also espoused rather earlier by Renan, language only *invites* people to consider themselves as a nation. More important is the "daily plebiscite" (Renan [1882] 1992) that seeks consensual (re-)production of identities that coalesce around a complex bundle of political and cultural attributes. Kedourie's student Ernest Gellner, however, broke with his thinking (Joseph 2004: 114), recognizing the foundational character of language to nationalism. Benedict Anderson (1991: 6) disagrees with Gellner on the form and force of nationalism; he argues that the fact that nations are "invented" does not mean they are fictions or fabrications, as Gellner would have it. Anderson agrees, however, with the foundational relationship between language and nationalism, though he emphasizes the "lexicographic revolution" (Anderson 1991: 84) of print-capitalism and the increased literacy that "made it possible for rapidly growing numbers of people to think about themselves, and to relate themselves to others, in profoundly new ways" (Anderson 1991: 52).

Adopting the modernist paradigm, Wright (2016) points to the distinctions between "state-nations" and "nation-states" in terms of the role of language in nationalism as put into practice in Europe. State-nations, such as Britain, France, and Sweden, carved out their territorial borders first, then set about the task of fashioning relatively homogenous nations out of the groups that inhabited them. For these entities, religious unity was the primary concern; linguistic homogenization came rather later, particularly as monarchies gave way to democracies. Nation-states, such as Germany, approached the issue from the other way around: convincing people that they belonged together, usually through some appeal to mythical, timeless, and primordial unity, was the first step, before building the structures of the state around these new groups. In these cases, a shared language (or a belief in one) seemed to be the only commonality, and thus foundational to the nation-building enterprise from the beginning; as such, the coincidence of political with linguistic boundaries were not entirely arbitrary.

But despite the differences between the cause-and-effect relationship between language and nation-building, most European national states, and the national states elsewhere in the world that adopted the European nationalist model – China and Japan being just two examples – eventually cleaved towards the idea that official monolingualism was the best way to achieve unity: a single people possessing a single language, constituting a single nation deserving of a single state. Of course, this came with the danger that other groups who had different languages would want their own nation-states, too. Taylor (1997: 34) summarizes Gellner's argument in this regard thus:

> If a modern society has an "official" language, in the fullest sense of the term – that is, a state-sponsored, -inculcated and -defined language and culture, in which both economy and state function – then it is obviously an immense advantage to people if this language and culture are theirs. Speakers of other languages are at a distinct disadvantage. They must either go on functioning in what to them is a second language or get on an equal footing with speakers of the official language by assimilating. Or else, faced with this second distasteful prospect, they demand to redraw the boundaries of the state and set up shop in a new polity/economy where their own language will become official. The nationalist imperative is born.

2.4.2 Minority languages and multilingual nationalism

Almost all nation-states face obstacles to the idealized and practical goals of monolingualism and cultural homogenization in the form of indigenous or national minorities within their borders, speaking languages other than official or national language(s), with or without claims to political independence. Historically, the solutions have been to absorb, assimilate, or annihilate these groups, but contemporary states – at least since the post-WWII "rights revolution" (Ignatieff 2007) – are more constrained in their options. The basic philosophical tenets of liberal democracy emphasize equality, justice, tolerance, pluralism, and individual freedom. These norms guide both established and aspirant liberal democratic states, and are partly undergirded by formal integration into international or post-national rights frameworks. As we will see later in this chapter, certain provisions in the UN Declaration on the Rights of Persons Belonging to National or Ethnic, Religious and Linguistic Minorities (UNDRM, adopted in 1992), and the UN Declaration on the Rights of Indigenous Peoples (UNDRIP, adopted in 2007), make protection of national minority and indigenous languages explicit, and more protections can be inferred from other provisions oriented towards the more amorphous and overarching notion of "identity". In Europe, languages are protected and promoted by the European Charter for Regional and Minority Languages.

As such, the combination of liberal democratic norms and formal rights frameworks means that many (though not all) contemporary nationalisms in liberal democratic contexts have been discursively reconfigured to embrace multilingualism and multiculturalism. In some newly-emergent nationalisms – particularly those emerging from transitional contexts, such as post-civil war Sri Lanka and post-apartheid South Africa – multilingualism has been built in from the outset. Multilingualism and multiculturalism is embraced as a component of nationalism, rather than conceived as a threat to it. In these contexts, monolingual nationalism, with its impinging on the freedoms of individuals and groups to use their languages, often in tandem with suppressing civil and political rights, now seems rather anachronistic. Nonetheless, it is necessary to avoid a too-celebratory tone. Monolingual ideologies can be reactivated in subtle or not-so-subtle ways when right-wing governments take control of the state, liberal democratic norms notwithstanding. Furthermore, a distinction should be drawn between official and unofficial nationalisms. Even where official nationalisms ostensibly celebrate diversity, unofficial nationalisms constructed and propagated by illiberal elements in civil society can use language as a cipher for other forms of xenophobic discrimination. In these cases, the relationship between a single language, a single people, and a single state is stubbornly persistent.

Where they successfully exist, multilingual nationalisms recast, in important ways, the practical/ideological and vertical/horizontal functions of communication as they relate to the nation-state. First, assuming that multilingual nationalism translates into a multilingual state, the practical preference for *vertical* monolingualism in the bureaucracy and for the business of rule is overshadowed by the liberal-democratic ideological commitment to providing access to the state that is not restricted by language. This means that the state is making a political calculation with regards to legitimacy over purely bureaucratic rationality. Second, relatedly – though somewhat conversely – the ideological underpinnings of a common language for *horizontal* communication in civil society are reshaped in favour of a more pragmatic recognition of multilingual and multicultural heterogeneity. Once again, this becomes a question of legitimacy; in particular, it is the realization that the relationship between language, society, and the state has to be reconfigured for nationalism to continue to act as an adjunct to state power.[13]

The fact that nationalism can operate alongside multilingualism suggests that, at least in nationalism's modern form, monolingualism is useful for certain functions, but not strictly necessary. In other words, the ideological preference of the state for a single language of horizontal communication is not essential to the functioning of nationalism. However, it is important to emphasize that this does not appear to mean that language *in general* is contingent to nationalism; even multilingual nationalism still makes some appeals to language. As such, the state may choose what kind of relationship its nationalism has with language, but it is difficult to avoid the issue entirely.

2.5 Language and globalization

If we take the 1648 Treaty of Westphalia as our starting point, and draw a line from that through colonization and nationalism, then globalization – like colonization – is hardly a new phenomenon. Historically, in every epoch states have sought to re-position themselves in relation to other states, with each state carving out its sovereign territory while stitching together zones of co-operation. What is new about contemporary globalization is the deepening and intensification of these processes. As such the nation-state has not withered away, despite

---

[13] It is notable, however, that immigrant languages are rarely included in these new multilingual nationalisms. This is in many ways related to how migrants are discursively constructed as the key threat to national unity, and far more dangerous than indigenous or national minorities.

some predictions; instead the state remains the final arbiter of policies on how globalization should be implemented (Sassen 2007), even if there is good reason to think that, on issues such as climate change and human rights, the nation-state is not the best solution to our global problems. Indeed, the impositions engendered by globalization have been most acutely felt not at the level of the state, but at the level of civil society. On one hand, we have seen the emergence of a "global civil society" (Keane 2003) that can organize and energize on economic, environmental, or social issues at both the community and trans-national level. On the other, nationally-defined civil societies bear the economic and social burdens of neoliberalism, with corporate power diminishing democracy, entrenching inequality, and trumping civil and human rights. These dichotomies are mirrored in language. New sociolinguistic configurations have been produced by contemporary globalization. But, as Blommaert (2010: 1) drily notes:

> Sociolinguistically, the world has not become a village. That well-matured metaphor of globalization does not work, and that is a pity for sociolinguistics – a science traditionally more at ease when studying a village than when studying the world.

Instead, the world has become a "tremendously complex web of villages, towns, neighbourhoods, settlements connected by material and symbolic ties in often unpredictable ways" (Blommaert 2010: 1). The result is more complex patterns of linguistic interaction, with ramifications for theoretical notions of language rights and the practical design and implementation of language policies. Two main phenomena can be identified, at least as they pertain to this book. The first is the spread of English, the foundations of which were laid by colonialism, but continued by US hegemony post-WWII, and the processes and structures of neoliberal globalization since the mid-1990s. The second is the destabilization of categories such as "migrant" and "ethnic minority", and more complex language practices; these are held by some to be captured by paradigms such as translanguaging and metrolingualism (Garcia and Wei 2014; Otsuji and Pennycook 2010; Pennycook and Otsuji 2015).

2.5.1 The spread of English

In the early 1600s, the number of English speakers in the world was perhaps five to seven million out of a global population of some 560 million; by around 1950, this had increased almost fifty-fold, with some 250 million first-language speakers and 100 million or so having learned it as a foreign language, out of a population of 2.5 billion (Crystal 2002: 1 – 2). Crystal (2012: 6) suggests that, in the contemporary era, over 1.5 billion people speak English to some extent out of a population of some seven billion, with foreign language speakers outnumbering first-language speakers. In terms of first-language speakers, English ranks behind only Spanish and Mandarin, according to most estimates.

John Adams, the second President of the United States, foresaw the spread of English as early as 1780; "English," he wrote in a letter to Congress, "is destined to be in the next and succeeding centuries more generally the language of the world than Latin was in the last or French is in the present age". Just under a century later, in 1868, W. Brackebusch wrote a doctoral dissertation (in English) at Göttingen University, Germany, titled "Is English Destined to be the Universal Language of the World?". Brackebusch's central thesis is unambiguous by page five (Brackebusch, 1868: 5): English had *already* become the dominant global language, since it "reëchoes from the West Indian sugar and the East Indian opium plantation", to "the ruins of every city that was renowned in Italy or Greece or Palestine", and "over every sea that carries keels of wood". Warming to his theme perhaps a little zealously, Brackebusch declared that the English tongue rang out in no less than "every seaport-town in the Universe". For all the hyperbole, Brackebusch is correct about the interlinked structural reasons for English spread – British naval power, trade, and colonization – by the middle of the nineteenth century.

From the middle of the twentieth century, a different set of processes and structures cemented the dominance of English. As mentioned, decolonization left many former colonies with English as a postcolonial official language, albeit often in creolized or localized forms and not embraced by everyone. Post-WWII US cultural and political hegemony indexically linked English with technological and political modernization paradigms, and directly spread the language through "linguistic imperialism" (Phillipson 1992) in the guise of government- and private foundation-funded programs (Troike 1977: 2, cited in Phillipson 1992: 7). Recent work has suggested that an effective critique of the spread of English in the context of contemporary globalization needs to examine the specific and novel characteristics of the political economy of globalization itself (Block et al. 2012; Duchêne & Heller 2012; Park & Wee 2012; Price 2014). In this regard, Piller & Cho (2013: 24) urge us to "look outside language and link language explicitly to the socio-economic order". That order is neoliberalism, the currently dominant political and economic logic of globalization (Chomsky 1999; Harvey 2007), and it has profoundly influenced both states in the global context and their social, economic, and political dynamics at national and local levels.

Neoliberalism venerates unfettered capitalism and, at least for certain functions, such as welfare provision or environmental regulation, a diminished role for the state. In theory, this allows for the operation of supposedly more efficient market forces. It perceives market forces and "competition", rather than the state, as offering the benefits of "choice" for rational, autonomous individuals within free markets of both private and public goods and services, including language and education. In practice, however, neoliberalism is paradoxical, and rather more nefarious. The supposed virtues of competition are dubious when they encourage deleterious rivalry between states, regions, schools, and individuals (Harvey 2007: 65). As Harvey puts it, somewhat bluntly:

> Neoliberalism wears a benevolent mask of wonderful-sounding words like freedom, liberty, choice and rights that hides the grim realities of the ... reconstitution of naked class power, locally as well as transnationally. (Harvey 2007: 119)

For Block et al (2012: 6) the neoliberalization of education has entailed a "shift from pedagogical to market values [and] the abandonment of the social and cooperative ethic in favour of individualist and competitive business models". Not only is competition premised on pre-existing inequalities, but it results in the exacerbation of these inequalities and, arguably, the creation of new ones. Furthermore, choices are disproportionately available to those who possess sufficient economic, cultural, and social capitals (Bourdieu 1986: 46–53). Those lacking such capitals are blamed for failing to avail themselves of market forces. Their status is thus entrenched, and they suffer "the stigma and material consequences whether in education, personal development [or] work" (Nash 2010: 28).

The neoliberal mantra of choice and competition is evident in the spread of English in a number of ways (see Phillipson 2008). There is no explicit coercion forcing states to emphasize English. However, given the interlinked and competitive nature of the global political and economic system, it is questionable whether, as the proponents of neoliberalism would have it, adopting English is exactly a "choice". Furthermore, state policies that emphasize English in compulsory education systems lead to the "commodification of language" (Heller 2010) as a valued cultural capital. Individual citizens have little choice, by definition, of studying English in a compulsory system. In addition, since the cultural capital of English competence acts as a gatekeeper to higher education and employment markets, students have little choice but to learn English well. An emphasis on English thus introduces another layer of competition into already-competitive compulsory examinations and higher education and employment prospects. This is particularly the case when shadow language education systems in the private sector offer advantages to those who can afford it.

2.5.2 Superdiversity

Superdiversity (Vertovec 2007) might be captured in a brief personal example: having lived in Taiwan, my wife and I – both white, English-speaking immigrants to the US – are Mandarin second-language speakers. At a local Asian supermarket and buffet near a university in North Carolina, we are usually greeted with "Hello! *Ni hao!*". This is an invitation from the staff, recent immigrants from China, to converse in either English or Mandarin, and my partner and I use Mandarin; it happens that our Taiwanese-accented Mandarin is quite close to the Fujianese-accented Mandarin of many of the staff, both varieties being considerably divergent compared to the Beijing Standard. At least some of the staff are from Cantonese backgrounds, and we hear them using Cantonese with overseas university students and other immigrants from similar language backgrounds. However, my Beijing Standard Mandarin-speaking graduate student from China tells me that if she doesn't reply to the staff's Mandarin greeting, then they will default into using English with her. While what is happening here can be captured by the traditional notions of bilingualism or socially-motivated code-switching (Gumperz 1982; Auer 1998), proponents of the more recent superdiversity (Vertovec 2007), translanguaging (Garcia and Wei 2014), and metrolingualism (Pennycook and Otsuji 2015) paradigms hold that these have better explanatory potential. Superdiversity provides a theoretical account of the political sociology of new migration flows; translanguaging and metrolingualism are ways to understand the language practices that result.

The main ideas of superdiversity can be summarized thus (Blommaert and Rampton 2011: 1): since the early 1990s, globalization processes and more diffuse patterns of migration have transformed the social, cultural, and linguistic diversity of societies across the globe. No longer is it possible to take for granted the stable categories (and sociolinguistic and socio-cultural features) such as "ethnic minority", "migrant", and "national identity". In particular, migration no longer happens in sustained, monolithic, and predictable waves; instead, superdiversity

> is characterized by a tremendous increase in the categories of migrants, not only in terms of nationality, ethnicity, language, and religion, but also in terms of motives, patterns and itineraries of migration, processes of insertion into the labour and housing markets of the host societies, and so on. (Blommaert and Rampton 2011: 1)

One sociolinguistic consequence of the superdiversity paradigm has been to cast language practices as multilingual repertoires and the creative use of linguistic resources, as opposed to being located in fixed language "systems". For Otsuji and Pennycook (2010: 244), metrolingualism "describes the ways in which people of different and mixed backgrounds use, play with and negotiate identities through language". Since then, their use of the term has shifted away from "playful or wilful creativity towards an understanding of everyday language use in the city ... a way of thinking about multilingualism centred around the everyday use of mobile linguistic resources in relation to urban space" (Pennycook and Otsuji 2015: 3–4). Similarly, translanguaging, for Garcia and Wei (2014: 18),

> offers a way of capturing the expanded complex practices of speakers who could not avoid having had languages inscribed in their body, and yet live between different societal and semiotic contexts as they interact with a complex array of speakers.

Despite its increasing ubiquity in the titles of publications and conferences, not everyone is quite so enamoured by the superdiversity paradigm. Pavlenko (2017), while not denying the usefulness of the concept for migration studies, calls it "academic branding", in which the term is overused and has become an empty slogan designed to grab attention, secure research funding, and publish. Others have criticized it on more theoretical grounds. Ndhlovu (2016: 35; after Turner and Khondker 2010: 176) suggests that "what is currently being described as superdiversity does not necessarily typify a new phenomenon ... these developments have always been there even in pre-modern times", pointing to the fact that some of the oldest mosques were built in China by and for Arab traders. Similarly, a common refrain is that the US, for example, and to some degree Australia, have *always* been superdiverse contexts, with unstable categories of migrants and complex sociolinguistic interfaces. Makoni (2012: 192–193), otherwise an advocate of the postmodern disinventing of languages, problematizes the celebratory anything-goes underpinnings of the concept: "superdiversity contains a powerful sense of social romanticism, creating an illusion of equality in a highly asymmetrical world". Kubota (2014: 2) makes the point that the "multi/plural turn" – in which she includes concepts such as superdiversity, metrolingualism, and translanguaging – risks being complicit in a "neoliberal multiculturalism that celebrates individual cosmopolitanism and plurilingualism for socioeconomic mobility". Not all languages are valued the same in metrolingual, translingual, or superdiverse concepts, and congratulatory postmodern approaches should be treated with caution.

2.6 Language, rights, and transitional justice

This section addresses two related issues: the concept of language-based rights, and the potential role of language policies in transitional justice contexts that are addressing previous systematic abuses of human rights more broadly. This discussion is framed within a *liberal democratic* conception of minority (language) rights (see e.g. Kymlicka 1995; Kymlicka and Patten 2003), whereby individual and group rights emanate from the state in the form of a social contract closely connected with the seeking of legitimacy. This contrasts, subtly or otherwise, with the final section of this chapter, which frames tolerance of multilingualism in civil society as potentially emanating, at least in part, from *participatory* democracy, whereby genuinely popular democracy is constituted by citizens' deliberations (Schmidt 2014).

2.6.1 Language-based rights

Language-based rights have been addressed since the 1990s in several disciplines – including political theory (e.g. Kymlicka and Patten 2003), legal studies and political philosophy (e.g. de Varennes 1995; van Parijs 2011; Poggeschi 2013), and sociolinguistics (e.g. Skutnabb-Kangas, Phillipson, and Rannut 1994; Kontra, Phillipson, Skutnabb-Kangas, and Varady 1999; Wee 2011; May 2012) – not least because of the realization that many social, civil, and political rights have linguistic implications. Virtually all serious scholarly accounts are clear that languages *themselves* do not have rights; instead, it is *speakers* – or in some cases communities (cf. Blake 2003) – who have specific rights, and these rights may have essential linguistic dimensions. The term "language-based rights" refers here to the types of rights that turn on two questions. First, and more obviously, to what extent should language-based rights guarantee the right to speak one's language in public or private domains (Wright 2007)? Second, to what extent should language-based rights guarantee that access to other universal and inalienable human rights is not impeded on the basis of language? In contrast to some uses (e.g. Skutnabb-Kangas 2006), I refer to these respectively as *language rights* and *linguistic human rights*. This is closer to Rubio Marin's (2003: 56) formulation, in which what I refer to as *language rights* are framed as "expressive" rights, which "aim at ensuring a person's capacity to enjoy a secure linguistic environment in her/his mother-tongues and a linguistic group's fair chance of cultural self-reproduction". Conversely, Rubio Marin frames "instrumentalist" claims – which are referred to in the present book as *linguistic human rights* – as those which:

> aim at ensuring that language is not an obstacle to the effective enjoyment of rights with a linguistic dimension, to the meaningful participation in public institutions and democratic process, and to the enjoyment of social and economic opportunities that require linguistic skills. (Rubio Marin 2003:56)

Thus, we have on the one hand "expressive" language rights, which are what most sociolinguists mean when they refer to the ability of citizens and communities to use, maintain, and revitalize languages in public and private life. On the other hand, and more the concern of political sociologists, we have "instrumentalist" linguistic human rights, which are guarantees that speaking or not speaking a particular language does not prevent access to other human rights – such as the right to a fair trial or education – that have linguistic dimensions. Let us now frame these in terms of universal human rights and indigenous/minority rights paradigms.

2.6.1.1 Normative frameworks
Universal human rights theoretically pertain to all humans simply by virtue of them being human; they are inalienable, applicable at all times, and in all places and contexts. They can be broadly summarized as the right to life itself and the right to dignity in living that life, and are enshrined in the 1948 Universal Declaration of Human Rights (UDHR). Two legal instruments put the UDHR into effect, namely the International Covenant on Civil and Political Rights (ICCPR), and the International Covenant on Economic, Social, and Cultural Rights (ICESCR), both adopted in 1966. Most countries are party to both treaties, though enforcement is problematic; states are legally bound to safeguard human rights, but there are few mechanisms for holding them to account if they fail to do so. The ICCPR is concerned with aspects such as freedom of speech, religion, and assembly, as well as voting rights and rights to a fair trial and due process; these are generally framed as *negative rights,* which prevent the state from interfering in the enjoyment of these rights, particularly through discrimination. In contrast, the ICESCR is framed as a set of *positive rights,* which require the state to actively provide certain rights as an affirmative obligation; in the case of ICESCR, these include the rights to family life, an adequate standard of living, social security, health, and education.

There are few language-based rights guaranteed by either the ICCPR or – perhaps more surprisingly, given the intuitive link between language and culture – the ICESCR. In fact, the ICESCR only provides, in Article 2, that rights will be "exercised without discrimination of any kind as to race, colour, sex, language, religion, political or other opinion, national or social origin, property, birth or other status". The ICCPR has effectively the same non-discrimination clause as the ICESCR in Article 2. Even here, however, the non-discrimination clause in both covenants specifies that individuals cannot be discriminated against on the basis of speaking language *X*, but not on the basis that an individual *does not* speak language *Z*. The non-discrimination clauses, therefore, only partially guarantee a weakly-specified linguistic human right. The ICCPR contains a more explicit linguistic human right, namely the right to a fair trial and due process in a language an individual can understand or, otherwise, with the aid of a translator (Article 14). Logically, however, it follows that other rights, such as voting, healthcare, and education, are similarly only accessible in one's own language, or at least a language one understands, but these are not specified. Between the two covenants, a single language right is specified in Article 27 of the ICCPR:

> In those States in which ethnic, religious or linguistic minorities exist, persons belonging to such minorities shall not be denied the right, in community with the other members of their group, to enjoy their own culture, to profess and practise their own religion, or to use their own language.

At the international level, language-based rights are protected rather more in two non-binding declarations adopted by the UN General Assembly. The first is the UN Declaration on the Rights of Persons Belonging to National or Ethnic, Religious and Linguistic Minorities (UNDRM), adopted in 1992 and inspired by but going beyond the minimal provisions in Article 27 of the ICCPR (Henrard 2000: 186). The second is the UN Declaration on the Rights of Indigenous Peoples (UNDRIP), adopted in 2007. These apply, in theory, to all (and only) member states, but pertain as rights only to members of defined minority groups. As such, the language-based rights of migrants, refugees, and unrecognized national minorities are, in general, not protected.

Article 2 of the UNDRM specifies that minorities should be able "to use their own language, *in private and in public, freely and without interference or any form of discrimination*." (emphasis added). Article 2 is a negative right, preventing interference by the state in language use. Article 4, meanwhile, establishes positive rights to ensure the development and survival of minority languages and cultures, including requiring the state to take "appropriate measures so that, wherever possible, persons belonging to minorities may have adequate opportunities to learn their mother-tongues or to have instruction in their mother tongue" (Art. 4 §3). Furthermore, states should integrate minority communities by fostering understanding of their cultural background among majority populations in education (Art. 4 §4), which may be read as offering (or requiring) language instruction in the minority language for majority language speakers. Conversely, §4 seeks to prevent linguistic or cultural enclaving of minority speakers by giving them "adequate opportunities to gain knowledge of" the majority language and culture, though this may have the unintended effect of causing language shift to the majority language (c.f. Wee 2011: 152).

Indigenous peoples, who constitute a specific type of minority group, are granted both language rights *and* linguistic human rights under the UNDRIP. Article 13(§1) provides language rights in terms of the "right to revitalize, use, develop and transmit to future generations their histories, languages, oral traditions, philosophies, writing systems and literatures", while (§2) requires states to provide linguistic human rights by "ensur[ing] that indigenous peoples can understand and be understood in political, legal and administrative proceedings, where necessary through the provision of interpretation or by other appropriate means". Article 13(§2) thus goes beyond the minimal provisions for due process and a fair trial in Article 14 of the ICCPR, since "political, legal and administrative" potentially covers a broad range of contexts, including voting and access to state services. A similar combination of language right and linguistic human right is protected in Article 14, which provides for the right of indigenous peoples to be educated in or to establish and be supported in establishing their own education systems; Article 16 makes further provision for indigenous language content and indigenous cultural representation in mass media. Notably, each article of the UNDRIP contains a positive and negative right, thus cognizant of contemporary theorizations of rights.

2.6.1.2 Implementation

The ICCPR and ICESCR (both promulgated 1966), the UNDRM (1992), and the UNDRIP (2007) are best seen as an evolving set of minimum standards regarding language-based rights. From a single linguistic human right regarding equality before the law (itself dating back to fourteenth century England), and vague provisions for language rights, emerge more comprehensive and robust protections, culminating in the UNDRIP document in which interlocking negative and positive rights do not merely restrain the state from interference, but require that it take affirmative action. The problem is that, while they are useful for codifying international norms on rights and committing states to moving in certain directions, neither the UNDRM nor the UNDRIP are binding legal instruments, and the two covenants that *are* binding have little scope for enforcement except for the most egregious human rights violations. As such, it falls to nation-states, or sometimes supra-national organizations such as the European Union, to implement language-based rights enshrined in these documents.

A crucial difficulty with relying on nation-states to implement language-based rights is that the very definition of the word "minority" is contested in international law (Jackson-Preece 2014). Nation-states are therefore given substantial latitude to define minorities or indigenous groups within their own borders. For indigenous groups, this creates something of a paradox, because (Western) liberal democracies are more likely to recognize them since language-based rights – and human rights in general – are located in (Western) liberal democratic norms (Kymlicka and Patten 2003: 6 – 7). Although indigenous rights were first brought into focus by New Zealand Maori, Canadian First Nation and Aboriginal peoples, Native Americans, and Australian Aborigines, as Brown (2002: 191) points out, "the majority of indigenous peoples actually reside in South American and Asian countries far less sympathetic to their cause than the aforementioned liberal democracies". National minorities are in a similar bind; although almost all states have at least one linguistic minority within their borders, there is a disincentive to recognize them as such in non-liberal democratic contexts where recognition is most needed and rights in most need of protection. The disincentive lies in the fact that recognizing minority or indigenous groups with rights to their own languages presupposes that they also have a right to their own culture and identity, different to and separate from that of the majority. In stable liberal democracies, this is not an insurmountable political problem; indeed, it may even have benefits in that it bolsters the legitimacy of the state, particularly in emergent or transitional contexts. But in non-liberal democratic contexts, it may be seen as undermining national identity or an outright threat to the unity of the state: granting separate language rights may be viewed as the prelude to claiming further rights and, ultimately, secession or some form of intra-societal conflict.

2.6.2 Language policy and transitional justice

In situations of civil or ethnic conflict, or authoritarianism or other political repression, human rights can be abused on systematic and massive scales; a *transitional justice* context is one in which a society or polity is moving away from war or repression towards a stable liberal democracy. Roht-Arriaza (2006: 2) offers the following definition:

> transitional justice includes that set of practices, mechanisms and concerns that arise following a period of conflict, civil strife or repression, and that are aimed directly at confronting and dealing with past violations of human rights and humanitarian law.

Abuses of language-based rights clearly pale in comparison to crimes against humanity, such as genocide or torture. But language can be an index of broader political repression, in the sense that language is a marker of ethnicity, social position, political ideology, or other attributes on which discrimination can be based; or may be itself one of the roots of the conflict (Kymlicka and Patten 2003: 4; Brown and Ganguly 2003). It follows that sociolinguistic reform can be used to achieve justice in post-conflict or post-authoritarian settings making the transition to stable liberal democracies, particularly through compensatory multilingual policies that better reflect sociolinguistic (and often ethnolinguistic) realities and provide for more equitable treatment. This is the focus of the following section, in which I attempt a theoretical account of the role of language policy in transitional justice contexts.

Roht-Arriaza (2006: 1; emphasis added) claims that transitional justice definitions have tended to "privileg[e] the legal aspects of coming to terms with the past ... overvalu[ing] the role of law and legislation, [which] may give *short shrift to the roles of education and culture and of distributional justice*". Law and legislation at the level of the state is insufficient for reconciliation, one of the main goals of transitional justice; it takes education and cultural change for people to learn how to live together again in post-conflict societies. Theoretical definitions have similarly given short shrift to language, possibly because language is bound up with education and culture in important ways; that is, if education and culture are not properly recognized as transitional justice sites, it follows that language would not be either. However, the role of language is given some emphasis in empirical accounts (e.g. the chapters in Arthur 2011 from a political sociological perspective; for a more linguistic approach to the language of truth and reconciliation commissions, see Anthonissen and Blommaert 2007). Furthermore, language is seen as an essential site for transitional justice in practical, on-the-ground contexts. To give some examples: the "rainbow nation" of post-Apartheid South Africa has put great emphasis on linguistic equality in its constitution (Lollini 2011: 25); post-civil war Sri Lanka has a single Ministry of National Co-existence, Dialogue, and Official Languages (UNPBF 2016); Croatia made bilingualism a priority following the Yugoslavian conflict in the 1990s (Ljubojevic 2016); and guidelines from a conference on Liberia's transitional justice stress the importance of language policy reform in dealing with two civil wars (TJWG 2008). It is clear from these examples that transitional justice in practice may have sociolinguistic dimensions, even if these have not been adequately theorized in the academic literature. Before going further, for the link between language (policy) and transitional justice to have any analytical purchase we should bear in mind that not all transitional justice contexts have a sociolinguistic dimension, though the examples above suggest that many do; conversely, not all (or even most) sociolinguistically unequal contexts necessarily have a transitional justice element. In other words, the transitional justice dimensions of compensatory multilingual policies do not obtain simply where two languages are of unequal status; instead, to be considered as having a transitional justice dimension, linguistic repression must be part of (or one source of) broader political conflict or repression. A further category can possibly be deduced, namely where a sociolinguistic context with transitional justice dimensions exists in a wider societal context which is not obviously transitional. Table 2.2 gives some examples of these different scenarios. South Africa has a

Table 2.2: Sociolinguistic contexts with/without transitional justice dimensions.

	Transitional justice context	Sociolinguistic context with transitional justice dimension
South Africa	Yes	Yes
Taiwan	Yes	Yes
Rwanda	Yes	Yes
South Korea	Yes	No
France	No	No
Wales	No	No
US/Canada	No?	Yes (e.g. indigenous boarding schools)

sociolinguistic dimension to its transitional justice context, whereas South Korea does not; conversely, Wales has an unequal sociolinguistic context between Welsh and English but, by most criteria, this does not have transitional justice dimensions. In the fourth category, indigenous boarding schools in the US and Canada are institutional sites for sociolinguistic inequalities that have transitional justice dimensions (Jung 2011), but not everybody agrees that the US and Canada are transitional societies *per se*. This final category is made more amorphous by the difficulty in designating as "transitional" those contexts that are not *proximately* transitioning from war, authoritarianism, or other form of repression; or, framed another way, the difficulty of distinguishing "transitional" from "ordinary" justice measures in established liberal democracies (cf. Winter 2013).

As a set of core practical measures, transitional justice is concerned with (a) *truth-seeking* to discover and acknowledge the realities of abuse; (b) *criminal prosecutions* and the punishment of perpetrators; (c) monetary, rights-based, and symbolic *reparations* for victims; and (d) *institutional reform* to ensure that ongoing or future rights violations are prevented (ICTJ 2009). For de Greiff (2012), these are all dependent and contingent on one another: monetary reparations may be viewed simply as "blood money" without criminal prosecutions for wrongdoing or truth-seeking, and so on. Fundamental to many contexts is the establishment or reestablishment of the rule of law. Crucially, transitional justice is not vengeance or "victor's justice", since that only perpetuates the problem of rights violations, with the former perpetrators now on the receiving end.

Clearly, there is likely little potential for compensatory multilingual policies to play a part in criminal prosecutions or establishing the rule of law. However, they may contribute to other measures in as yet undertheorized ways: truth-seeking can uncover the realities of linguistic repression and provide insight to other forms of political repression, not least because it allows the recovery of previously-repressed voices in civil society; compensatory language policies can provide rights-based and symbolic reparations for previous linguistic injustices to speakers or their descendants; institutional reform allows previously-repressed languages to be used to access state services and civil, social, and political rights. To avoid a victor's justice scenario, a compensatory multilingual policy should also be equitable; that is, it should not simply replace one form of sociolinguistic domination with another and, as such, it should take into account the former language of oppression or of the oppressors.

In de Greiff's (2012) theorization, these four core practical *measures* – and the "victor's justice test" – are (or ought to be) all oriented towards achieving two sets of *goals*, namely providing "recognition" and building "civic trust" as immediate goals and achieving "reconciliation" and "democratization" as final goals. In what follows, I briefly address the potential role of language policy in attaining these goals.

2.6.2.1 Recognition and civic trust

A key dimension of transitional justice is the notion of recognition: recognition that harm has been done, and recognition of those who have been harmed (de Greiff 2012: 42). A compensatory multilingual policy is potentially oriented towards recognition in several ways. First, it can recognize that harm has been done, and that harm has been done in part on the basis of language repression, either to speakers via the denial of language rights or to citizens via the denial of linguistic human rights, the distinction between which has already been made above. This aspect of recognition goes beyond establishing the simple *facts* of harm; instead, it acknowledges that language discrimination was sufficiently grievous to warrant intervention and recompense. Second, it recognizes the victims of such harm; there are linguistic communities and/or individual speakers in society who have suffered from unjust treatment through their *misrecognition* – a symbolic lack of respect of concern – as bearers of language-based rights. In combination, these forms of recognition constitute the foundation for a compensatory multilingual policy to make symbolic reparations for past injustices.

Rebuilding civic trust is necessary to refashion a functioning society (de Greiff 2012: 44–46). All transitional justice measures contribute in different ways to rebuilding civic trust, but a fundamental dynamic is the ability to trust (reformed) state institutions. Educational institutions are perhaps the most direct site for the transitional justice dimensions of compensatory multilingual policies: those that have marginalized languages, or punished children for speaking proscribed languages, are clearly not trustworthy in the eyes of those language speakers. Similarly, reforming the institutions of the police and courts has transitional justice-language policy dimensions. If citizens cannot understand, in their own language, the charges put to them then – even with the rule of law nominally operating – mistrust of the judicial system is not unreasonable.

2.6.2.2 Reconciliation and democratization

Reconciliation can be defined as peaceful co-existence based on mutual trust, respect, tolerance and understanding. Communities riven with animosity along ethnic, racial, religious or linguistic lines can only co-exist in the future if the past is addressed; this means more than simply "wiping the slate clean", since that leaves justice undone and resentments to fester (de Greiff 2012: 51). Instead, reconciliation requires the *normalization of social relations*, such that the potential for future injustices is limited. Normalizing and equalizing sociolinguistic relations may encourage previously conflicting groups to think about other aspects of identity – ethnicity, race, or culture – along similar lines. This is, in part, because of the unavoidability of language (Kymlicka 1995: 111; Wee 2011: 15–17) compared to other attributes. As such, compensatory and equitable multilingual policies are thus a highly visible and wide-reaching demonstration of the commitment to broader reconciliation, both symbolically and materially.

Democratization is a more mercurial category than the foregoing. One conception is of the establishment of the rule of law, but there is an obvious problem in the fact that unconscionable things can be done legally (Arendt [1964] 2006). As such, it is necessary to think of "a rule of law that ultimately involves a commitment to a more substantive conception of justice, one that calls for political participation" (de Greiff 2012: 55). Without full political participation rights are not rights at all, but simply privileges granted at the whim of the powerful. The relationship between compensatory and equitable multilingual policies is somewhat oblique, but it hinges on the notions discussed earlier: that citizens should be able to understand the political process and be free to deliberate democratically in their own languages if we are to achieve, in Fraser's (1992: 118) words, "participatory parity". It is to this issue that we now turn.

2.7 Language, society, and democracy

Since the state never operates in isolation, the discussions of language and the state so far necessarily invoke society, whether explicitly or implicitly. I turn now to the specifically politicized instantiation of society, namely civil society, and its related domain of the public sphere. Following Schmidt (2014), the emphasis here shifts away from *liberal* to *participatory* democratic theory. The former is concerned with conceptions of "rights" granted by the state in a form of social contract (e.g. Kymlicka 1995), while the latter is concerned with the potential for society as the source of genuinely popular sovereignty and democracy through deliberation and decision making (e.g. Walzer 1984; Dryzek 1990; Wolin 2010). As Schmidt (2014: 399) points out, there is at least a small but energetic group of scholars addressing the inevitable linguistic diversity of the societies organized by nation-states – a premise which he calls *ontological multilingualism* – from the point of view of liberal democratic political theory, but practically no literature on the issue from the vantage of participatory democratic theory.

In what follows, I address the role of minority languages in the public sphere, relying on a reading of Fraser's (1992) reading of Habermas ([1962] 1989). I then address the relationship between multilingualism, pluralism, and civil society, including non-state language movements to promote revitalization and maintenance. At the heart of this endeavour lie two questions whose answers can only be partially sketched in the present book. What are the sociolinguistic conditions for democratic pluralism? Or, for that matter, the democratic conditions for sociolinguistic pluralism?

2.7.1 Minority languages and the public sphere

Let us recall from chapter one that the "public sphere", for Delanty (2001: 42), is "a domain of civic communication and civic contestation" and deliberation about affairs of state and the common good. Drake (2010: 124) puts it thus: "civil society refers to a *public* domain that is not part of the state, and the public sphere can be most readily understood as the space between civil society and the state." The public sphere as a field of academic enquiry was first proposed in Habermas' (1989) historical sociology of the concept, and it remains central to political sociological enquiry. However, despite Habermas' influence more generally, little attention has been paid to the public sphere in sociolinguistics and yet, as Wee (2011: 165) argues, "deliberative processes and the modes of reasoning that they embody cannot be divorced from language practices". Similarly, as Schmidt (2014) argues, little attention has been paid to language by political sociologists working on the public sphere. The political philosopher Nancy Fraser is a notable exception, and it is to her work which I now turn. In particular, I consider Fraser's (1992) critical reading of Habermas (1989), using Fraser's notion of heterogeneous "counterpublics" in an attempt to situate a political sociology of language within the parameters of *participatory* democracy.

Fraser discerns four underlying assumptions in Habermas' historical reading as they pertain to understanding the potential of *contemporary* public spheres to create the conditions for "participatory parity" (Fraser 1992: 118) in deliberative political democracy, and we use two of them as our points of departure.[14] These are, to quote them in full:

> 1) The assumption that it is possible for interlocutors in a public sphere to bracket status differentials and to deliberate as if they were social equals; the assumption, therefore, that societal equality is not a necessary condition for political democracy
> 2) The assumption that the proliferation of a multiplicity of competing publics is necessarily a step away from, rather than toward, greater democracy, and that a single, comprehensive public sphere is always preferable to a nexus of multiple publics (Fraser 1992: 117)

Fraser's broader challenge to the first assumption is made clear from the outset: participatory parity in political democracy is incompatible with social inequality, and yet social inequality is an endemic function of stratified societies in already-existing liberal democratic states. The specific flaw in Habermas' premise, for Fraser, is that interlocutors can merely "bracket" inequalities and deliberate *as if* they are equals. Even if social inequalities are not the basis for "formal exclusion" from the public sphere, they can be "informal impediments to participatory parity" (Fraser 1992: 119). These are questions for political sociology, but Fraser frames them in terms of language, designating public sphere participants as "interlocutors" and defining the public sphere as being constructed through "the medium of talk" (1992: 110). A stubborn index of social inequality can be found in language and speech styles, and Fraser points to the example of unequal turn-taking and interruptions between men and women in faculty meetings. She cites Mansbridge (1990: 127; cited in Fraser 1992: 119) to further make her point: "even the language people use as they reason together usually favours one way of seeing things and discourages others".

Of course, sociolinguists have long recognized that, while practically all humans are endowed with the capacity for language, not all speech is socially valued in the same way; furthermore, speech styles are well understood as indexical of unequal social categories. But much sociolinguistic work has tended to see this in terms of its conventionally sociological dimensions – that is, its interpersonal or institutional functions – rather than its *political* sociological dimensions. Put more simply, sociolinguistic variation is not just interesting from a linguistic perspective, nor is it merely something to be correlated with (unequal) social

---

[14] The two assumptions not focused on here relate to: (a) undesirability of "private interests" in the public sphere (which Fraser points to as often working for the ends of masculinist ideology); and (b) the necessity of strictly separating the state and society in the public sphere (which Fraser challenges with a notion of weak/strong publics that, in a representative democracy with parliamentary sovereignty, may better link deliberation to decision-making).

categories; instead, it has implications for democracy itself in terms of participatory parity in the deliberative public sphere. Significantly for a political sociology of language, we thus start with a model that potentially links not just citizens but *speakers* to the possibility of macro-level political democracy, with the intervening variable – more familiar to sociolinguists – being categories of social inequality.

Both Fraser and Mansbridge then extrapolate from this micro-level speech behaviour at the level of citizen-speaker deliberation up to the macro-level of the speech community, though they do not use that term explicitly. Not only are individuals constrained by the socially iniquitous valuation of speech in the public sphere, but so too are groups. Mansbridge (1990: 127), again:

> Subordinate groups sometimes cannot find the right voice or words to express their thoughts, and when they do, they discover they are not heard. [They] are silenced, encouraged to keep their wants inchoate, and heard to say "yes" when what they have said is "no".

It is thus possible, without much difficulty, to cast this line of argument in terms of minority languages. As Urla (1997: 280) frames it, "mandatory silencing" in the public sphere is "especially clear in the case of those citizens who do not or will not speak the language of civil society". Of course, the conventional response is to urge speakers to bracket their status differentials by linguistically assimilating. But, if Fraser is correct about the impossibility of simply bracketing difference, this is at worst coercive and, at best, a hegemonic process where consent to sociolinguistic domination is a prerequisite for access to deliberative democracy. In either case, as Schmidt (2014: 408) observes

> Requiring significant blocs of a political community to adopt the language and other cultural practices of the dominant group is an inherently anti-egalitarian move ... and violates the most basic criterion for a participatory democracy.

Turning now to Habermas' second assumption, Fraser challenges the idea that a "single, comprehensive public sphere is always preferable to a nexus of multiple publics" (Fraser 1992: 117; see also Benhabib 1996; Asen 2000). For Fraser, "where social inequalities persist, deliberative processes in public spheres will tend to operate to the advantage of dominant groups" (1992: 122). The dominant public sphere is conducted in the dominant language, thus informally excluding minority language speakers; as such, "insofar as [dominant] public spheres are monolingual", it is difficult to see how they can "constitute an inclusive communications community of all those affected" (Fraser 2014: 25). The solution, for Fraser, is that *multiple* public spheres, constituted by what Fraser calls "subaltern counterpublics" likely offer better opportunities "partially to offset, although not wholly to eradicate, the unjust participatory privileges enjoyed by members of dominant social groups in stratified societies" (Fraser 1992: 124). This implies multiple multilingual spheres, rejecting the apparent consensus – or at least the implicit assumption – among democracy theorists and laypersons alike that a common language is necessary for meaningful deliberation to take place; the assumption, in other words, that "having multiple speakers of multiple languages engaging in public discourse in the public square would seemingly inhibit, if not distort and stifle, active discussion and debate" (Schmidt 2014: 406).

Two main points can be made here. The first is that bilingualism or translators are needed to avoid *implicit enclaving* in which minority speakers are free to deliberate among themselves yet have no stake in the dominant public sphere. Some level of individual multilingualism, therefore, is healthy and perhaps essential for participatory parity and genuinely popular democracy, particularly as it contributes to "nested" (Taylor 1995) public spheres. The second is that, as Fraser makes explicit, it is engaging in interpublic contestation and competition that constitutes participatory parity in democratic processes. Framed another way, it is contestation over affairs of state and the common good, and not merely reaching consensus, that is the authentic basis of democratic deliberation. This stands in contrast to Habermas' emphasis on the public sphere as mainly concerned with finding agreement on what we have "in common", which is effectively a form of status bracketing through assimilation. As Schmidt (2014: 405) puts it, "becoming accustomed to interacting with those speaking different languages can help us realize that we can all learn from each other's perspectives and values in relation to fundamental questions of human existence"

In sum, then, in the broadest sense:

> however difficult it may be, communication across lines of cultural difference is not in principle impossible, although it will certainly become impossible if one imagines that it requires bracketing of differences. Granted, such communication requires multicultural literacy, but that, I believe, can be acquired through practice ... Briefly, we need a critical political sociology of a form of public life in which multiple but unequal publics participate. (Fraser 1992: 128)

To finesse this final point, we might add that we need a critical political sociology of *language,* in order to understand the participation of minority language speakers in public life. In other words, our endeavour here is to understand the sociolinguistic conditions that make democratic pluralism possible, and the democratic conditions that make sociolinguistic pluralism possible. The following section elaborates these in the context of civil society itself.

2.7.2 Multilingualism, pluralism, and civil society

We have already seen in chapter one that, in the "rough pastiche that has become the commonly accepted version" of the civil society argument, the power of civil society is grounded in "dense network[s] of civil associations" (Foley and Edwards 1996: 38). Civil society associations are strictly voluntary in nature, and highly diverse; they encompass religious movements, sports clubs, parent-teacher committees, self-help groups, historical societies, professional organizations, NGOs, charities, special interest and advocacy groups, and trade unions, among many others. In an ideal multilingual civil society, individual bilingualism or multilingualism would be such that members could move relatively seamlessly in and out of civil society associations and networks, drawing on linguistic resources to code-switch and translanguage as necessary. In practice, sociolinguistically and socially stratified societies and limited bilingualism mean that this is not always possible, giving rise to relatively isolated monolingual strands – in both dominant and minority languages – in these dense networks of civil society. This comes with the danger of implicit enclaving raised above, in which networks and associations conducted in minority languages are marginalized from the dominant networks and languages of civil society.

Although it comes with its own political caveats, it might be suggested that some sort of bilingualism is necessary for full participatory parity (Wee 2011: 256). This brings us to normative questions about the state's role in fostering participatory parity in civil society, since – the emphasis on participatory democracy notwithstanding – it is not yet possible to talk of civil society as entirely separate from the state, nor get rid of the state entirely. More specifically, one question relates to the state's role in the provision of opportunities for language education, in order to create the conditions for both sociolinguistic and democratic pluralism. In this regard, the state's options can be typologized as follows. It can do nothing, and allow the sociolinguistic context to find equilibrium according to the prevailing and countervailing social and political forces in civil society. However, while democratic in theory, this may militate against pluralism, since it almost inevitably entails language shift and assimilation of minorities into dominant groups. Alternatively, it can provide education opportunities in the dominant language for minorities. While this provides for a certain amount of participatory parity in civil society, it serves to symbolically and practically marginalize minority languages from public and political life, as Fraser (1992) and Schmidt (2014) have been seen to argue in the previous section. The most democratic option is to provide multilingual education that offers access to the dominant language and thus to participation in broader civil society, but also provisions to protect minority languages from shift and assimilation, backed up where possible with status planning changes. In an ideal situation, and where practicable, minority language education will also be provided to majority language speakers who desire it, thus fostering a truly bilingual or multilingual civil society (Schmidt 2000: 226 – 234; 2014: 408).

A further issue for the state is how to deal with illiberal and antidemocratic tendencies in liberal democratic civil society. Not everyone thinks that multilingualism is necessary or desirable, particularly when nationalism is a powerful force within civil society and monolingual ideologies are a cloak for far-right xenophobic impulses. Here, the issue becomes whether the state has a responsibility, right, or even capacity to *enforce* some sort of sociolinguistic pluralism in civil society (Laitin and Reich 2003: 81), which is related to the question of the extent to which it should (or can) mandate democratic pluralism more generally. While the state can hardly ban illiberal viewpoints, as with dimensions of race or sexuality an onus may be on the state – at least in theory – to prevent civil society discrimination on the basis of language as a component of civil rights. These are difficult and as yet unanswered questions for theorists and lay proponents of liberal democracy alike. Conceptions of liberal democratic minority language rights, as we have seen earlier, tend to frame them in terms of non-intervention by *the state* in the freedom of their enjoyment.

2.7.3 Language movements and language revitalization

Language maintenance and revitalization programmes may be undertaken by the state through a variety of acquisition and status planning activities. However, the note of caution about illiberal and assimilationist tendencies notwithstanding, civil society offers multiple non-state sites for minority language use and thus language revitalization. Some of these are directly oriented to language, such as language learning clubs, language and culture celebrations and festivals, or book clubs and other literacy-spreading associations (Kosonen 2008). Others are less directly linked to language revitalization, but offer structures and opportunities for social interaction among minority language communities, and are especially useful when they can facilitate inter-generational transmission. This is especially the case where broad-based civil society associations – religious, cultural production, and sports, for example – overlap both in terms of their sociolinguistic and social remits, and with each other (Wright 2016: 291).

Civil society groups *directly* concerned with language revitalization and maintenance may constitute wider language movements, which are a specific type of social movement. Language movements are usually oriented towards changing repressive or non-egalitarian state language policies and language use in public life. However, they may also focus on the ostensibly *private* domains of language use, such as promoting a minority language in household use. Such movements may also be Trojan horses for other political demands – particularly nationalist and separatist projects – framing them in ways that do not constitute outright opposition to the state. However, while language movements may therefore be ways to institutionalize political resistance in civil society without taking up arms, the risk is that languages themselves can be flashpoints for conflict. As Spolsky (2004: 2) notes, civil war over language is rare, but Horowitz (2001) finds language to be a contributing factor in a number of what he calls "deadly ethnic riots". As Patten and Kymlicka (2003: 2 – 3) put it, the world has seen "a growing range of political conflicts and challenges ... that are centred on linguistic diversity ... affecting the stability and sustainability of a wide range of political communities".

Language revitalization and maintenance has implications beyond merely ensuring the survival of languages, and by extension their cultures, for their own sake; it may mitigate social problems that weaken community ties and thus civil society networks. An emergent body of research in the US, Canada, and Australia, has focused on the correlation between language shift and loss and poor mental health outcomes in indigenous communities (Strickland, Walsh, and Cooper 2006; Hallett et al. 2007). Language revitalization and maintenance improves academic success for indigenous schoolchildren (Cherubini and Hodson 2008). Some studies report better *physical* health among communities maintaining or reviving languages (Hodge and Nandy 2011: 797). Not without some justification, then, King, Smith, and Gracey (2009: 78) state that "language revitalisation can be seen, therefore, as a health promotion strategy". This research demonstrates that communities are not just important sites for language revitalization (though they indeed are), but also that language revitalization strengthens communities and thus the dense networks of civil society associations. It makes intuitive sense that communities with better health and social outcomes, better developed and utilized human capital (that of indigenous knowledge and experience), and lower rates of social exclusion, are better able to resist assimilation. This potentially strengthens the democratic basis of pluralist civil society and its public spheres.

2.8 Conclusion

As mentioned, given space constraints, this chapter is a limited elaboration of a theoretical framework of a political sociology of language, and it will need refinement and expansion to become more generalizable and unified. Nevertheless, it provides a framework for analyzing Taiwan's contemporary and historical language politics and, recursively, its application to a single case study in subsequent chapters will offer opportunities for such refinement and elaboration.

A political sociology of language takes as its starting point the relations between society and the state, and how these relations bear on sociolinguistic contexts. Once again, to paraphrase Poulantzas, which aspect we take as our frame of reference will determine our approach to the other. Here, it should be clear that the emphasis is on the state, with society invoked at various levels of implicitness and explicitness throughout. Fundamentally, the state's most visible influence on sociolinguistic contexts is through language planning and policy, and this varies depending on the prevailing and countervailing social and political forces – that is, the historical-structural paradigm in which a given state is located. It is also influenced by complex calculations between practicality and ideology, and the constitution of rights regimes and liberal democratic norms; furthermore, the state is not the sole actor in language policy: the state is the conduit for supra-national and internal civil society dynamics. In sociolinguistic issues as much as in any area in which it holds sway, the state exercises a good deal of autonomy, but never acts in isolation.

A brief roadmap may serve to sketch how aspects of this framework are applied in subsequent chapters. Chapter three is concerned with the colonization of Taiwan by the Dutch and later the Qing, and thus the indigenous societies' first encounter with state-like structures and the political economy of merchant capitalism and imperial tribute, and the transformation of their sociolinguistic ecologies as a result. Chapter four examines the enhanced colonial program of the Japanese from 1895, as well as that of the KMT from 1945, and the deepening and intensification of the processes and structures of the modern state on the island's population, characterized by more deliberate policy attempts to influence language practices as a means of socio-political control. In chapter five, we turn to the era of liberalization and democratization; here, multilingual nationalism, framed by conceptions of pluralism, rights, and transitional justice, is the organizing logic, underpinned by a commitment to protecting and promoting linguistic diversity that enhances the liberal democratic credentials needed for acceptance as an independent state by the international community. Finally, in chapter six, the perils of globalization are addressed, namely the difficulties the state has in formulating policies to deal with the spread of English and the multilingual realities of superdiverse forms of immigration; here, the tension between nationalism and globalization – between, in Chen's (2006) words, indigenization and internationalization – becomes apparent.

3 The coming of the state: Taiwan encounters China and Europe

3.1 Introduction

According to archaeological, linguistic and genetic data (Blust 1996, 2014; Bellwood and Sanchez-Mazas 2005; Bellwood and Dizon 2008; Ross 2008; Greenhill, Drummond, and Gray 2010), the ancestors of Taiwan's contemporary indigenous populations are likely groups who began to cross from modern-day south-eastern China around 4500–4000 BCE. No linguistic traces of these groups are found in China; they were likely absorbed into other populations over time. However, the indigenous languages of Taiwan are related to those spoken in a vast swathe of territory from Hawai'i in the north to New Zealand in the south, and from Madagascar in the west to Easter Island in the east, thought to be the result of waves of further migration out of Taiwan from about 2500 BCE. Taiwan is thus potentially the cradle of Austronesian, a family of some 1,250 languages, or approximately one-sixth of the world's total, spoken by 270 million people (Bellwood, Fox, and Tryon 2006: 1). If this is the case, then it has significant implications for protecting what is left of the island's rich linguistic and cultural diversity, which has been under threat since the arrival of the colonizing Dutch in 1624. Politically, this era heralds the coming of the state to Taiwan – or at least state-like structures and the political economy of merchant capitalism – and the first substantial encounter by indigenous groups with systems of socio-political governance other than their own.[15]

This chapter is structured as follows. I begin by outlining early Chinese encounters with Taiwan, which were minimal and only sparsely recorded in the diaries of seafaring adventurers. The focus of the remainder of the first half of the chapter is on Dutch colonization, including the political organization of indigenous multilingualism into a coherent (European) framework that the Dutch could use as the foundation for the business of rule. I then outline what I call the "missionary-colonial complex", in which the moral codes and linguistic resources of missionaries were put to political use. From there, the spread of local vernacular literacy is addressed, as well as limited programs to propagate the Dutch language. The second half of the chapter focuses on

---

[15] I use the term "indigenous" rather than the alternate "aboriginal" or "aborigines", which are sometimes used by other authors. This avoids the pejorative connotations of the latter two terms, and is in line with the official English translation of the Council of Indigenous Peoples (*Yanzhu Minzu Weiyuanhui*), which was previously known in English as the Council of Aboriginal Affairs.

Chinese influences on Taiwan. Before the Zheng (1662–1683) and Qing (1683–1895) regimes, it was in fact Dutch policies of "co-colonization" (Andrade 2008: 115) that transformed Taiwan from an Austronesian- to Sinitic-speaking island through the importation of agricultural labour from China. The Zheng era is a brief historical footnote, but some socio-political and language education structures were inherited from the Dutch and bequeathed to the Qing, marking a certain continuity. Qing rule is then addressed, with a distinction drawn between practices of socio-spatial and sociolinguistic differentiation imposed until around 1750, which largely sheltered local languages and cultures from shift and death, and assimilation processes afterwards, which accelerated the loss of diversity.

3.2 Early Chinese encounters with indigenous Taiwan

Although Taiwan is mentioned as early as the third century in Chinese seafaring accounts (Cauquelin 2004: 3), the earliest known first-hand Chinese account of the island, according to Thompson (1964), is Wang Ta-yuan's *Daoyi Zhilue* or *Brief Accounts of the Island Barbarians*, in 1349, towards the end of the Yuan dynasty (1279–1368); the next, Chen Di's *Dong Fan Ji*, or *Account of the Eastern Barbarians*, comes some 250 years later in 1603, towards the end of the Ming dynasty (1368–1644).[16] This long gap indicates how, despite lying just one hundred miles from the Fujian coast, indigenous Taiwan largely remained *terra incognita* to China until the seventeenth century. Its remoteness was largely structured in terms of political economy: the island of Taiwan proper was thought to have few natural resources that could be profitably traded, and there was therefore little need to exercise jurisdiction (Shepherd 1993: 6–7; Ts'ao 1997; Knapp 1999: 4–5). But Taiwan's isolation was never absolute (Teng 1999). Song dynasty seafarers (960–1279 CE) would have had little trouble navigating even the deep currents of the Taiwan Strait, save for the occasional typhoons which blew in from the east (Wills 1999: 84), and by 1349 fishermen, farmers, and traders from Fujian province had settled on the island of Penghu in the Pescadores, some twenty-five miles from the coast of Taiwan proper. Many of them, according to Wang Ta-yuan's account, were "long-lived", meaning old, suggesting that populations were not simply sojourning mariners. As Wang describes, the territory was administratively attached, at least nominally, to

---

16 Thompson (1964) translates both accounts. Wang Ta-yuan and the title *Daoyi Zhilue* are rendered in the older Wade-Giles Romanized form, as used by Thompson.

Chin-chiang County in the prefecture of Chuan-chou in Fujian province, from where the Chinese settlers hailed. He relates that, under the early Yuan dynasty between 1280 and 1294, "a sub-county magistrate was assigned there to be in charge of the annual tax fixed on salt" (Thompson 1964: 168), and Wills suggests that officers were occasionally stationed on the islands from 1170 (Wills 1999: 86). The Chinese settlements on Penghu, Wang opined, were a demonstration of "how great and far-reaching is the awe-inspiring virtue of China" (Thompson 1964: 167). China did not, however, exercise more than nominal control over Penghu, and exercised none over Taiwan itself.[17]

On Taiwan itself, Wang makes no mention of the presence of settled Chinese. He did, however, encounter its indigenous peoples, and discusses them in brief, impressionistic terms. He notes that "the customs [of the inhabitants] are unlike those of Penghu", but the islanders have kinship relations, and he notes, not unsympathetically, that they had some functioning system of socio-political government, since "they know to respect their barbarian lords and chiefs" (Thompson 1964: 168). However, he does highlight, in rather lurid detail, the practice of head-hunting, especially when "a person from another country offend[s] them" (Thompson 1964: 168–169), suggesting that some contact between the indigenous peoples and (presumably) Chinese did occur, perhaps in limited ways. Unfortunately for our analysis, he has nothing to say about the language situation in either place, and so his observations are chiefly relevant for the early roots of the discursive binary construction of the "civilized" Chinese and the "savage" indigenous peoples, which would continue in official narratives throughout the twentieth century (Teng 1999).

Isolationist Ming policies doubtless contributed to the lack of official narratives between Wang Ta-yuan's account in 1349 and Chen Di's in 1603. As Wills (1999: 86) points out, settlers would have been evacuated from Penghu under the early Ming maritime restrictions in the early fifteenth century, designed to thwart pirates; any settlers that remained would be "completely outside the law and no record of them has been found". Maritime restrictions, however, gave rise to the precise opposite of their stated intention, and allowed Japanese pirates or *wako* to flourish, using Taiwan as a base from which to make raids on the Fujian coast. In 1603, Chen Di – a retired garrison commander on the Great Wall – joined a successful mission to rout the *wako*; apparently, he did not participate in the battle, but went along because he had a "taste to see the sea" (Teng 1999: 449).

---

17 This is an important observation, given that some contemporary official PRC pronouncements argue that, in a form of "metonymic reasoning" (Munsterhjelm 2014: 13), nominal Chinese historical jurisdiction over Penghu justifies the PRC's political control of Taiwan as a whole today.

Subsequently, he ventured to see the island, particularly the villages around the area of present-day Tainan, the observations from which are recorded in *Dong Fan Ji*. It was the first significant account of the indigenous peoples on Taiwan proper, though the first English translation and publication was not until Thompson's in 1964.

Chen Di's pastimes during his retirement merit a brief mention, since they presumably shaped the anthropological lens through which he viewed Taiwan. He was, by all accounts, an interesting character and something of a polymath; as well as an explorer, he was an early modern travel writer, philologist, and social anthropologist. He was a noted early variationist phonologist; in one of his most important works, *Maoshi Guyin Jiao* (translated by Thompson as *Phonological Studies on the Mao Version of the Canon of Poetry*), Chen Di's central proposition was that the relationship between sounds and symbols, specifically the pronunciation of ancient Chinese characters, varies geographically and temporally, but this variation is structured according to a unified and consistent system (Norman 1988: 343). His interest in language can be seen in several places in *Dong Fan Ji*; indeed, the first reference to language comes in his second paragraph describing the indigenous Formosans:

> They do not have the etiquette of kneeling or bowing. They have no calendar and no writing. They count to the full moon as one month, and take ten months as one year. After a time they forget these [calculations], and therefore they cannot reckon their ages. If one asks an old man about it, he doesn't know. In business transactions they use the *quipu* to keep a record. (Thompson 1964: 172)

Chen Di's observation is essentially Whorfian: it is the Formosans' lack of writing which prevents them from remembering their ages and passing the marking of time; it likely would not have occurred to Chen Di that the converse may be more accurate, and that they did not have writing in part because they had no need to do such things. More specifically, it is *Chinese* writing that they lack. The *quipu* refers to a system of counting using knotted strings, a practice found in many early cultures around the world.[18] As Harrell (2011: 15) relates, the use of knotted strings for counting has long been significant in Chinese historiography; it has been viewed as a form of proto-writing, apparently appearing in Chinese anthropological accounts of indigenous minorities up to the 1950s. This stands in contrast to the system of Chinese characters, which in mythology were invented by the "wise sages" Fu Xi and Huang Di and bequeathed to the Chinese people

---

[18] Somewhat confusingly, *quipu* is a Quechua word borrowed by Thompson into English via Spanish, to translate Chinese describing an indigenous Taiwanese practice.

"in order that they might be civilized" (Teng 1999: 451). He returns to this theme, though for Teng (1999), his romanticizing of their "innocence" is merely a cipher for their construction as "barbaric":

> To the present day they are completely without the calendar and writing – how strange indeed! The Southern and Northern Barbarians all have writing like the ancient ... "bird-tracks" [script of China]; one presumes that at the beginning there were wise men who invented it. Why should this [place] alone have been lacking [such wise men]? But [these Eastern Barbarians] when they have eaten to the full and are enjoying themselves, contented and happy, what need have they for wise men? (Thompson 1964: 177)

Chen Di's observations are too fleeting, and his anthropological lens perhaps too untrustworthy, to give us much information about actual language practices among the indigenous groups he meets, but we do get tantalizing glimpses in several places. In one passage, Chen Di relates that

> During the time when they are tilling they do not talk or kill, and the men and women working together in the mountain wilds are very quiet. [Meeting] on the road they will [only communicate] by glances; the younger will stand with his back turned while the older passes by, without any exchange of words. If a Chinese insults them [at this season] they will not get angry. When the crop has ripened they resume their original behaviour[19].
> (Thompson1964: 174)

In the mention of insults, there is a key reference to the presence of Chinese engaging in some level of interactional co-existence with the indigenous groups. There were certainly Chinese settlements on Taiwan at the time of Chen Di's visit, though whether they existed out of sight during the maritime restrictions, or flourished after their lifting, is not clear. Interaction is sometimes framed merely as Formosan groups making raids on Chinese settlements and the Chinese placating the Formosans with fish and salt (Wills 1999: 86), but Chen Di's note about different responses to Chinese "insults" suggests perhaps more than this. This is further adduced by Chen Di's later observation that Chinese settlers "frequently [are able to] translate their language[s]", and trade with them". On this account, we cannot know the sociolinguistic situation that obtained here. There could have been bilingualism, code-mixing, or a pidgin variety (or varieties), but Chen Di's description is indirect evidence that language contact was taking place.

---

[19] It is not clear what Chen Di refers to as "mountain wilds". He supposedly visited the villages around modern-day Tainan, and thus would have encountered the Sirayans, who were plains-dwelling. It is highly unlikely that he ventured into the central mountains.

By 1600, as Spence (1990: 7–9) argues, in many respects China looked very much like Weber's description of a bureaucratic modern state; indeed, more so than many European states did. In particular, it laid claim to territory to an extent unparalleled in the world at that time, large parts of which it could claim sovereignty over with considerable legitimacy. It also was able to enter into relations with other states in which, as the dominant military, economic, political, and cultural power, it usually had the upper hand. The bureaucratic system and specialized institutions were complex and had a much longer history than comparable institutions in the west (see e.g. Feng 2013); the bureaucrats who held office were drawn from those who had passed the competitive civil service examinations, a tradition that dates back to at least the Sui dynasty (581–618 CE) (Zeng 1999: 8). Culture, writing, and the state system were also linked through the Ming dynasty's ethnic Han culture, explaining Chen Di's fascination with the lack of writing among the indigenous populations. As Melissa Brown (2004: 23) puts it:

> The association of Han culture with Chinese national identity derives from a historic narrative of unfolding which links China as a political entity (*zhongguo*) and Han (or Hua or Xia, as it was sometimes called) *wenhua* (culture, civilization, education). In simplified form, this narrative says that the essential elements of *wenhua* – writing, a state system, a code of ritualized hierarchical relations (*li*) including patrilineal ancestor worship – developed in the historic Shang and legendary Xia dynasties three to four thousand years ago in the Yellow River valley, while peoples in the rest of what is today China were illiterate and tribal "barbarians". (Brown 2004: 23)

At the time Chen Di was writing, late Ming China could have exercised political control over Taiwan had it wished to, but it was chiefly interested in suppressing Japanese piracy and, presumably, propping up its ailing regime which would fall to the Qing just four decades later. As such, although patterns of Chinese settlement meant it was by no means "pristine" indigenous territory, the Dutch could lay claim to colonial control of Taiwan without much geopolitical pushback. The "imagined geography" of Taiwan (Teng 2006) structured it as a peripheral territory that lay, for all practical purposes, just beyond the frontiers of the empire.

3.3 Dutch encounters with indigenous Taiwan (1624–1662)

The arrival of the Dutch on Taiwan in 1624 is a critical juncture in the development of Taiwan's socio-political institutions and its contemporary sociolinguistic profile. It heralds the advent of its modern – and textual (Stainton 1999: 28) – history and the end of its relative isolation from China and the rest of the world (Shepherd 1993: 49). In particular, it represents the coming of the embryonic modern state as a corporate political actor, and thus indigenous peoples' first encounter with systems of socio-political governance different from their own, and the ending of the age of "Aboriginal Taiwan" (Chiu 2008: 6). Of course, the state did not simply fall out of the sky, fully formed, with the Dutch; instead, the production of the state – the "making of colonial state space" (Goswami 2004: 32) that did not characterize previous Chinese interactions with the island – was a limited set of indigenous encounters with a limited set of state-like institutions, processes, and structures. Crucially, the Dutch colonial program was not directly instigated by the Dutch state itself, but rather in a complex way through its quasi-autonomous proxies, chiefly the Dutch East India Company or *Vereenigde Oost-Indische Compagnie* (hereafter VOC) and the Dutch Reformed Church. The VOC was a private company granted a monopoly on Asian trade routes, and certain political and legal jurisdiction over its colonial possessions, including the ability to make and sign treaties, by the mercantilist Dutch government (Andrade 2008: 185). The Protestant Reformed Church, while not the official state religion, had strong links with the Dutch Republic, in part because of the Dutch state's emergence out of territorial and religious conflict with Catholic Spain, as it broke away from King Phillip III's Habsburg Empire.

As Chiu (2008: 4) relates, Taiwan was acquired by the Dutch state rather accidentally. Having been repelled from Macao by the Portuguese – the Dutch were primarily interested in the lucrative port and its links to East Asian trading routes – the Dutch settled initially on Penghu in 1622. The governor of Fujian, who would not tolerate foreign troops stationed at China's front door, "suggested" the Dutch retreat to Taiwan proper, which was outside of China's sphere of sovereignty. The governor's "suggestion" was eventually backed up by several warships and a few thousand troops. The Dutch were joined in Taiwan by Spanish missionaries and traders who arrived in 1626 and, in part, this was a factor in developing Taiwan as a productive colony rather than merely a strategic entrepôt (Shepherd 1993: 49). The Spanish and the Dutch continued their religious, territorial, and trade rivalries on Taiwan as they waged a low-level war for influence; the Dutch sought to expand control of the south from their base in the Bay of Tayouan near Tainan, while the Spaniards held control of the north from their base, Fort San Domingo, in Danshui.[20]

The Dutch expelled the Spanish by 1642, and there appears to be little evidence of Spanish linguistic influence on Taiwan. Spanish is not a legacy language, and there is no surviving contact variety. It appears that there were

---

20 Sometimes rendered as the Hoklo name Tamsui, such as on the Taipei Metro at the time of writing.

cultural contacts with indigenous populations, and Nakamura (1956: 27; cited in Shepherd 1993: 57) reports that the missionary Esquivel had founded a small school for indigenous children and the children of the small number of Japanese and Chinese residents. Missionaries seemingly made some attempts to learn and document indigenous languages. Borao (2001: 12) and Klöter (2008: 208) note that Spanish missionary records refer to a grammar and a dictionary of an unspecified Formosan language(s); this was likely the now-extinct Basay dialect of Ketagalan, spoken around Fort San Domingo. Neither work is extant; Borao (2001: 122) suggests they may not have ever been formally published, and so little can be known about the policies and practices of the Spanish missionaries on Taiwan. Borao Mateo (2009: 113) intriguingly suggests that contact between male Spanish soldiers (and ostensibly chaste clergymen) and indigenous women may explain why Basay *puta*, a pejorative term for a prostitute, is the same word in Spanish. However, while this is both sociologically and sociolinguistically plausible, Borao Mateo unfortunately offers no linguistic evidence for an attested borrowing, and it may be a chance correspondence.

In contrast, the Dutch had a more significant influence on the sociolinguistic situation in Taiwan. In particular, language was a central concern of the twin socio-political projects, namely the "civilizing process" (Chiu 2008), conducted largely by the Church, and "co-colonization" (Andrade 2008: 115) that brought Chinese labour to operate Taiwan as an agricultural colony under the auspices of the VOC (Shepherd 1993: 50). This I will refer to this as the aforementioned "missionary-colonial complex". In the following sections, I examine the "problem" of multilingualism for Dutch political organization, the use of missionaries as translators, the legacy of literacy, and policies for Dutch-language spread. I then address the catalyzing effects of Chinese immigrants, encouraged by the Dutch, on the transformation of the Austronesian-dominated sociolinguistic landscape into one dominated by Sinitic languages.

3.3.1 Multilingualism and political organization

It is difficult to provide accurate indigenous population figures prior to colonization, especially since the indigenous peoples lacked written systems, and – without the exigencies of the state – perhaps even the terminology in their languages to even count at such large scales. Dutch censuses in 1647, 1650, and 1655 put the population of the western plains and northwest tip, where Dutch and Chinese settler activity was focused, at 60–70,000; estimates of mountain-dwelling groups take the population to 100,000 (Shepherd 1993: 7, 40–41, 451 fn.20). The focus of Dutch and Chinese activity was a pragmatic response. The central mountain groups lived in dense, remote jungle and were prone to bellicosity against invaders, and headhunting raids against other tribes and colonial encampments. They were thus not amenable to either pacification or proselytization. The eastern coastal areas were too remote to be explored; the overland route through the central mountains would have been treacherous given the terrain and hostility of the local indigenous groups, and the east coast consists largely of sheer cliffs and gorges that make it difficult to access by sea.

The western plains-dwelling groups spoke at least ten languages, many with high dialectal diversity (Ferrell 1969). The Dutch clearly perceived the high diversity of indigenous multilingualism as a problem in and of itself, aside from the problems of translation. Framed in terms of the colonial Self/Other dichotomy, indigenous peoples looked and sounded different enough from the Europeans to constitute a single homogenous people, but they certainly did not behave like one; inter-village warfare was the normal course of affairs. From missionary accounts, the Dutch saw multilingualism as connected to the socio-political conflict that they observed between and within indigenous groups. The early missionary Candidius, cited in Campbell's (1903) translation of contemporaneous missionary records, remarked that "they do not speak one, but several languages, and they have neither King, governor nor chief. They do not live at peace with each other; one village being continually at war with another village" (Campbell 1903: 9). The later missionary Gravius (cited in Klöter 2008: 209) wrote that:

> [What] has greatly hindered the advancement of the work is the manifold variety of languages in the island, so that scarcely four or five villages have the same language; this apparently arising from the endless quarrelling of the people and their consequent want of mutual intercourse.

Gravius seemingly sees multilingualism as arising from conflict, or the "quarrelling of the people", rather than the other way around. The situation was further complicated for the Dutch by the fact that even groups who *did* share a common language did not appear to act in unity. Alliances and enmities between villages were not solely determined by whether they spoke the same language, or even shared a common cultural grouping. Shepherd (1993: 32) sums this up: "ethnolinguistic groups were never corporate actors in indigenous Taiwan". Nevertheless, somewhat successful attempts were made to organize and integrate the two main villages and what the Dutch dimly grasped as broader cultural sub-groupings. Having pacified or subjugated key villages through either missionary or colonial work (or violence), the Dutch required that the benefits gained by acquiescing to Dutch rule were premised on recognizing the VOC as a state-like sovereign entity.

The Dutch organized meetings – or *Landdag* – on an annual basis between the colonizers and indigenous groups to reaffirm allegiances, settle disputes, and appoint elders for the villages. These were forums for European-style political debate, though conducted under the auspices of the Dutch state and not public spheres as such. In fact, they were quite literally political spectacles, as Andrade (1997) relates: grand affairs presided over by the sovereign body of the King, or more accurately his proxy, the Governor, and conducted with the pomp and circumstance of European state traditions. These included processions, speeches, and the occasional public execution, usually of a Chinese petty criminal. This latter display underscored the Dutch state's monopolization of legitimate violence to the indigenous peoples; it was a visible reminder of their ultimate fate for non-compliance with colonial or missionary will, which sometimes required reinforcing through massacres or the burning of whole villages.[21] The *Landdag*, however, partially replaced the need for coercive practices, by ensuring obedience through legitimacy and authority.

The organization of the indigenous groups in the *Landdag* was according to geographical area, though this was clearly a somewhat arbitrary system in terms of actually-existing socio-political, cultural, and ethno-linguistic affiliations. The resulting multilingualism of these meetings themselves obviously presented a language policy dimension: edicts and agreements needed to be translated so that the groups could understand them. The Dutch adopted official indigenous lingua franca for the meetings and translated their various aspects through interpreters (Chiu 2008: 199). Choices of lingua franca must have been pragmatic solutions to the challenges posed by the multilingual context and the lack of competent personnel to translate into all languages. However, they must also have been both reflective and constitutive of the socio-political power relations between the Dutch and the various groups.

3.3.2 The missionary-colonial complex

In general, the contemporary modern secular state is circumspect about claiming divine legitimation for its rule. In the seventeenth century, however, reli-

---

[21] Unfortunately, given the arguments being made and the focus on the political sociology of *language*, I have had to gloss over the intermittent brutality shown by the Dutch towards the indigenous peoples. Such actions today would likely constitute crimes against humanity.

gion and political-economic power were less clearly demarcated. It is no coincidence, therefore, that the extension of the European state through colonization proceeded in tandem with the work of missionaries for the next two centuries. For missionaries, there is the conviction that souls must be saved through conversion to the outsiders' religion, backed up with the force of the state where necessary. For the colonial state, displacing the moral and cultural codes of a society, and aligning them more with closely with those of the colonizers, produces more pliant and "civilized" subjects. From a sociolinguistic perspective, neither project can make much headway if their intended beneficiaries cannot understand what is being said; "missionary linguistics", therefore, overlaps with "colonial linguistics" (Stolz & Warnke 2015). For both, translation, language teaching, or the outright destruction of indigenous languages have been the modus operandi for achieving religious conversion or the maintenance of political order (Errington 2008).

Dutch rule on Taiwan was an exemplar of the missionary-colonial complex. Blussé (1995: 176) argues that organizational and institutional features led to an inter-dependent relationship between the VOC, the Dutch state, and the Dutch Reformed Church. Due to the integration of political and religious work in the missionary-colonial complex, missionaries therefore saw that "extension of Dutch rule was necessary to spread the Gospel (and that spreading the Gospel was necessary for the preservation of Dutch rule)" (Shepherd 1993: 50). In a wry symbolism, the firing of muskets was the sign for local people to come to the missionary church, at least as reported in one village in 1638 (Campbell 1903: 163). In 1628, the early missionary and first ordained minister on the island, George Candidius, unsuccessfully requested permission from the colonial authorities to appoint "a 'legal representative' to punish those who did not listen to him" (Heylen 2001: 207). From the perspective of legitimacy, it would be difficult to mete out punishment judiciously to distinguish those who could not understand him from those who simply refused to obey. Colonial officials were happy to use missionaries to spread the state's moral code, sometimes usurping religious instruction by, as one missionary report claimed with dismay, "handing [ecclesiastical control of the indigenous villages] over to political functionaries with the one object of civilising the people for political purposes" (Campbell 1903: 302). But Candidius' request was likely denied because the missionaries' role was not to invoke state *force*; that could be done by soldiers. Instead, the missionaries were to act as civilian mediators between the colonial state and the local people. In this regard, a key function of the missionaries was to translate and interpret between Dutch and local languages, including promulgating peace treaties, such as the *Pax Hollandica*, and other colonial edicts pertaining to political and economic control (Chiu 2008: 113–119). Missionaries played a key role in translating in the *Landdag*, though a limited number of colonial officials were apparently competent enough to assist (Chang 2014: 142).

The missionary-colonial complex focused initially on pacifying and converting the village of Sinkan (sometimes rendered Hsinkang) and surrounding villages that lay closest to the Dutch fort Castle Zeelandia at Tayouan, near present-day Tainan. The inhabitants of Sinkan spoke a dialect of Siraya, known as "Siraya proper"; other villages used at least two related dialects, Taivoan and Makatao. There was perhaps a total Siraya-speaking population of around 20,000 at its height (Chiu 2008: 6); it is possible that Siraya was a lingua franca for other speakers in the western plains, and it certainly became so as the result of colonial administration and missionary work (Adelaar 2013: 212). Missionary-colonial records show that Siraya remained the focus of linguistic work, but as the Dutch extended their locus of political control northwards, missionaries would turn their attention to the Favorlang-Babuza language by 1650 (Klöter 2008: 210).

The first ordained missionaries, George Candidius and Robert Junius, pioneered learning the local languages in order to teach the catechisms and other religious practices. This was a characteristic, in general, of Protestant missionary work; Protestantism was founded precisely on the rejection of the Catholic insistence on using sacred Latin, rather than vernaculars, as the liturgical language (Spolsky 2004: 49). Of Junius, one Rev. Sibellius wrote approvingly in 1650 that Junius "with great paines and speedie diligence, in a short time, even now in his adult age ... happily learned the barbarous Language and rude *Idiome* of those *Heathen*, who were of differing Speech and Manners" (Campbell 1915: 33). This quote indexes language ideologies of both the difficulty of "broken" foreign languages, and the younger-the-better argument for foreign language learning. Both Candidius and Junius produced written materials for other missionaries to use; these materials are no longer extant and so, as Klöter (2008: 210) points out, we cannot judge their success as "fieldworkers" in purely linguistic terms. Eventually, efforts were made to learn an unspecified language or languages of the regions south of the Dutch fort; this is possibly Paiwan, since the Paiwan and Siraya lived roughly either side of modern-day Kaohsiung. However, these efforts appear to be haphazard and sporadic, the product of conflict between missionary and colonial policies and objectives (Campbell 1903: 302–4; Heylen 2001: 234).

Utilizing missionaries as intermediaries and translators was quite obviously a language policy solution to a socio-political problem, and likely the most expeditious one in the circumstances. Teaching Dutch to the local people was impractical if not impossible; investing in the human capital required for all colonial officials to speak or understand one or more indigenous languages was similarly prohibitive in terms of effort and costs. Relying on Chinese settlers as translators clearly presented its own difficulties, as a third party in the transaction with an advantage in linguistic resources, the Chinese would have their own interests to advance in the negotiations. Instead, given that missionaries were already learning local languages, the colonial state could co-opt for its socio-political purposes the linguistic resources being acquired by the missionaries in their religious work. As Campbell puts it:

> Of course, those reverend gentlemen had to make a deliberate study of the language for prosecuting their spiritual work, but having once acquired a good working knowledge of it, their value to the ill-equipped local government became apparent. (Campbell 1903: 552)

Within a short space of time, it became policy that – rather than the colonial authorities making do with the subsidiary outcomes of missionary linguistics – candidates for promotion in the missionary system were required to have knowledge of the local languages, or the talent and motivation to acquire it (Campbell 1903: 80–81). Linked to this policy was the belief that indigenous languages were "difficult" and required long periods of familiarization. This may well have been true, but it usefully underpinned the Church's argument that missionaries were necessary in the villages, thus ensuring the continuance of the process of spiritual conversion of and ecclesiastical jurisdiction over the inhabitants. Candidius, for example, wrote that:

> In three or four years [a replacement for or assistant to Candidius] would not be able to master the language, but in ten or twelve he might obtain a complete mastery of it. It would be no doubt possible to speak a little and to teach the people something at the end of three or four years. This, however, is not speaking the language, but only having a kind of smattering of it which is most disagreeable to listen to. And so ... in ten or twelve years' time, those who come out will be able to express their thoughts in the language, and to pronounce it well ... Hence also the necessity of having several always working at the language, so that they may be ready to take the places of those who die or have to leave the country. (Campbell 1903: 92)

However, this had unintended consequences, and the missionaries' language competence made them a victim of their own success. Missionaries who found the burden of political service onerous, and its earthly nature conflicting with the spiritual dimensions of missionary work, could end up with their linguistic resources effectively trapping them in their posts. In 1636, the missionary Junius, in a letter to the Consistory at Batavia, called political service "a burden that still rests heavily on our shoulders", though he was optimistic that the authorities had seemingly approved that "Lieutenant Johann Jurieansen should soon come here to learn the language, and thus qualify himself to relieve us" (Campbell 1903: 150). Yet Junius was still pleading his case in early 1643. The Governor-General in

Batavia – present-day Jakarta, Indonesia, where the VOC was headquartered – wrote a letter stating:

> Mr Junius persists in his desire to leave for Batavia ... Mr Bavius, however, we do not consider able, *on account of his imperfect acquaintance with the language*, to undertake the political duties which Junius performed in addition to those of his spiritual office. Moreover, Junius and Candidius have repeatedly requested to be discharged from this political service; on the ground that it was contrary to their spiritual vocation, and brought them into contempt. (Campbell 1903: 191; emphasis added)

One catechist, Joost van Bergen, was "married to a native woman" and seemingly had fewer scruples about conflating religious and political roles, unlike the "persons belonging to the Church [who] often render us their services as interpreters with excessive reluctance and in an ineffectual way" (Campbell 1903: 197). It was thus "resolved [in 1643] to appoint [van Bergen as a] special interpreter upon whom the title of 'deputy' may be bestowed ... so that he may be able to assist us in all political and judicial matters". A report in the Day-Journal relates a meeting of the *Landdag* in 1647, during which:

> Joost van Bergen, a free citizen and sheriff, was employed as an interpreter to the Formosans. He was well acquainted with the Sinkan [Siraya] language ... The schoolmaster of Favorlang was appointed interpreter to the people of that place. Interpreters who knew the Camachatsian dialects and that spoken in the mountains, were also engaged. (Campbell 1903: 222)

Here, in the employment of schoolteachers and colonial interpreters, we can see the problem of the scarcity of missionaries compared to the desire for colonial expansion. A potential solution was proposed by Candidius and Junius in 1634, namely sending a handful of Sinkan youth to be educated in Holland; "the aim was clear: let the locals spread Christianity using their own languages" (Chiu 2008: 197). The project stalled, apparently because the colonial authorities in Batavia had attempted – without success – something similar with children from the Dutch colony in Indonesia (Chiu 2008: 291 fn.91). Instead, from 1636 the missionaries established schools staffed by Dutch schoolteachers. In theory, this greatly increased the reach of the missionary-colonial complex; schoolteachers could learn local languages and give religious or secular instruction, but be supervised more efficiently by an ordained minister who could act peripatetically rather than being stationed in one village. However, this came with its own problems in practice. Schoolteachers were mostly "soldiers taken from the ranks to learn the language and instruct the people" but, unlike the presumable chaste clergymen, they were notorious for "drunkenness, fornication and adultery; in fact, most led scandalous lives", as one official put it (Campbell 1903:

211). Indeed, the official noted with chagrin that "three Dutch schoolmasters who were more proficient in the language than many of the others fell into this grievous and shameful conduct"; accrued linguistic capital was squandered if they had to leave the village suddenly or, as in at least two cases, they met an untimely demise at the hands of outraged villagers.

To supplement the diminishing contingent of trustworthy Dutch personnel, from 1639 Junius began to train indigenous people as schoolteachers; by 1643, fifty indigenous schoolteachers were paid a monthly salary by the VOC, and stationed in Sinkan and the surrounding villages (Chiu 2008: 198). Indigenous schoolteachers were drawn from those who had already studied in the village schools and who displayed particular aptitude for "penmanship" (Campbell 1903: 179), in a manner somewhat resembling an idealized, meritocratic bureaucracy. The indigenous schoolteachers were thus trained, presumably from a relatively young age, in the missionary-colonial institution and subsequently put to work perpetuating its values.

3.3.3 Vernacular literacy

The primary function of the schools was to inculcate the religious, moral, and political habits of the Dutch, even if the various stakeholders in the missionary-colonial complex differed on the emphasis that should be given to each. Their subsidiary function, however, was to propagate literacy in the indigenous languages, which was particularly important for the missionary program with its emphasis on holy written texts. As Heylen (2001: 206) argues, Candidius was fascinated by the pre-literacy of the indigenous populations as well as their apparently non-hierarchical and decentralized socio-political systems, reasoning that these made them ripe for conversion to Christianity. Early on, he took the view that it was difficult to supplant the belief systems of, for example, the Chinese they had encountered elsewhere in Asia, who had "systems and ceremonies embodied in written laws, with priests who thoroughly study these writings and are well versed in their creeds" (Campbell 1903: 90). The indigenous peoples had neither writing systems nor priests, and thus the missionaries could teach the Formosans both "to read and write, and impart to them concisely the contents of our religion; so that being instructed in one system, they would be taught to call upon God with one heart and mind" (Campbell 1903: 91).

According to the missionary records in Campbell (1903: 182), by 1639 religious instruction was given twice a week in the Sinkan school, while literacy was taught on the other days. Elsewhere, literacy instruction was underway in several villages by 1638, and by 1643, one report suggested that some of the six hundred schoolchildren in six villages "can write tolerably well in Latin characters" (Campbell 1903: 192). Another report of 1643 gave more specific figures: of "eighty scholars and twenty-four others attending a writing-school ... eight to ten of them [are] already able to write a tolerable hand" (Campbell 1903: 195). It seems to have been important to report hard numbers to the colonial authorities who, after all, were operating within the framework of a political economy concerned with trade, tax, and profit from its agricultural colony, and thus keen on counting things. Indeed, the authorities periodically wondered whether the numbers of saved souls being claimed by the missionaries were being inflated to justify their expense. As part of the colonial bureaucracy, missionary activity was thus under constant scrutiny and oversight. In September 1643, the colonial authorities evidently wanted to ascertain the veracity of the missionaries' successes in literacy, likely with a view to understanding how it could be put to use for maintaining social and political order, but also to ensure the missionaries were implementing policy correctly. They did this through a rudimentary language testing regime, examining "two persons who had learned to write, to see whether they could put down their thoughts in writing, and spell correctly different words mentioned to them" (Campbell 1903: 196). Apparently, the colonial authorities were satisfied enough to continue the missionaries' school system; as late as 1657, reports from the Tayouan Consistory discuss the use of indigenous languages for religious instruction in the village schools (Campbell 1903: 303), and schoolmasters were still resident in the villages in 1661, as the Dutch were being routed by forces of the Chinese warlord Koxinga (Campbell 1903: 324).

Candidius' original materials are no longer extant, but Junius produced several texts in the Romanized Siraya language. These include his short *Formulary* of the catechisms, republished in Campbell (1903: 345–379); a version of the Lord's Prayer (reprinted in part in de Lacouperie 1887: 470); and a speller. The latter two were published in Delft after Junius had left the island in 1643. The literacy program in the schools presumably continued after Junius' departure, since Gravius went to the trouble of translating and publishing a Sirayan form of the Gospel of St. Matthew and St. John (1661) and a Formulary of Christianity (1662); these were printed in Amsterdam but apparently never made it to the Formosans in the confusion and bloodshed of the Dutch defeat. An anonymous and undated, though probably seventeenth century, dictionary of Siraya, the *Vocabularium Formosanum* – known more commonly as the Utrecht Manuscript – was later found in the University of Utrecht archives and published by van der Vlis in 1842 (Klöter 2008: 212).

Perhaps more noteworthy for a political sociology of language is the discovery by Robert Swinhoe, a British Consul who arrived in Taiwan in July 1861, of the Sinkan Manuscripts (Steere [1874] 2008; Murakami 1933; Chiung 2001; Chiu

2008: 225), a series of mainly land contracts – mortgages, sales agreements, and leases – drawn up between the inhabitants of Sinkan and surrounding Siraya-speaking villages, and Chinese settlers. Of 101 manuscripts collected by Murakami (1933) and 170 collected by Paul Jen-kuei Li and colleagues (Li 2010), the most recent is from 1818, while the earliest is from 1663 or, more reliably, 1683 (Li 2010: xiii). A Chinese traveller in 1685 observed that:

> There are some who can write the characters of the Redheads [i.e. Dutch]. These are called chiao-ts'ei. *All accounting of the incoming and outgoing [goods] passes through their hands.* [They use] a sharpened goose quill dipped in ink, and [in contrast to the Chinese] write horizontally, from left to right, not in vertical lines. (Thompson 1964: 183; emphasis added)

This suggests that the Romanized written system for Siraya had taken root and was passed down inter-generationally. Literacy was likely not widespread in Sinkan or any of the surrounding villages, but rather the preserve of a small elite. However, as a political unit, Sinkan's monopoly of a written system put it at an advantage over other indigenous groups, and potentially on an equal footing with the Chinese settlers. This is significant: the legacy of literacy seems to have profoundly altered the balance of political and economic power for some 150 years after the end of Dutch rule in 1662. For Heylen (2001), this is key to the development of indigenous nationalism, and Chiu (2008: 226) argues that

> the Sirayan schoolmasters and pupils showed adequate proof of their acquired knowledge of spelling and writing in their own language inculcated by Dutch education and transformed it into a cultural weapon to fight for indigenous rights and privileges [against the Chinese].

3.3.4 Dutch-spread policy

It seems likely that the Chinese traveller from 1685 encountered Romanized Siraya, the written form looking much like Dutch "characters". However, there is the outside possibility that it refers to Dutch itself, since some efforts were made to introduce the language in the late 1640s (Heylen 2001: 223–225). Two French Jesuit priests, Father de Mallia, visiting in 1714, and Father du Halde, visiting in 1720, claimed to find indigenous groups using Dutch. Their accounts (published respectively in Campbell 1903: 510 and Davidson 1903: 66) are highly similar, thus appearing to corroborate each other. As de Mallia wrote:

> We have met several who are able to speak the Dutch language, who read Dutch books, and who, in writing, use their characters. We have even found in their hands fragments of our five books (? the Pentateuch) in Dutch. (Campbell 1903: 510; parentheses in original)

It would appear that the order to introduce Dutch came from Batavia in 1643, and was initially pursued by then-Governor Le Maire. Le Maire's reasoning seems to have been that, unlike Formosa, other Dutch colonies in Asia had extant lingua franca such as Malay or Portuguese, greatly simplifying the task of learning multiple languages for governance purposes (Campbell 1903: 197); conversely, the lack of an extant lingua franca in Formosa made the introduction of Dutch easier (Heylen 2001: 223, 225). Le Maire's successor, Governor Caron, was less enthusiastic about introducing Dutch, proposing instead to use two or three local languages as island-wide lingua franca (Heylen 2001: 224), likely co-opting the language policies already being put into practice for the *Landdag*. According to Heylen, Governor Overtwater finally introduced Dutch officially in 1648, with Dutch being taught in the village schools (Heylen 2001: 224).

Several thousand prayer books, catechisms and other religious texts were printed, and the missionaries and colonial officials periodically wrote to Batavia extolling the enthusiasm of the indigenous people towards learning Dutch. In relative terms, Heylen claims that this policy was "more successful than in the other colonies" (2001: 223), but, beyond this, it is difficult to ascertain how widespread knowledge of Dutch actually was. Initially, Heylen (2001: 225) argues, the missionaries "welcomed the Dutch language because it partly solved the shortage of capable schoolmasters and clerical labour", but within a few years "in as much as education was subordinate to religion so too was the Dutch language policy". It would seem, then, that at least some of the missionaries themselves quietly sabotaged the plan and, at most, Dutch was taught as a supplementary language. A report in 1656 mentions disagreement between the clergymen as to the best language to use (Campbell 1903: 300), and Chiu (2008: 200) suggests that even eight years after its introduction, Dutch did not entirely replace Siraya as the language used by the clergymen with the indigenous inhabitants. In 1657, records note that a bilingual program was in place in some village schools, with religious instruction taking place in indigenous languages in the morning, and Dutch being taught – presumably for administrative purposes – in the afternoon (Campbell 1903: 308). This would suggest that Siraya was considered a more effective vehicle for missionary work than Dutch, but that Dutch was still seen as a language of colonial command. By November of 1657, the Governor and Council of Formosa proposed a different bilingual policy, teaching Dutch to children while maintaining religious instruction in local languages for the elders (Campbell 1903: 311–312).

It is not clear, therefore, that the Dutch language ever penetrated to any significant depth or breadth among the Siraya. Data from the time of names for foreign objects (introduced by the Dutch, but also by contact with earlier Chinese traders) in Siraya indicates that word-for-word translation through calquing, rather than borrowing, was the norm (Chiu 2008: 177). Davidson (1903: 48) reports there were no attested Dutch borrowings in indigenous languages by the end of the nineteenth century, at least in then-extant dictionaries, though the absence of evidence is not necessarily evidence of absence. If the French Jesuit de Mailla's account is to be believed, and the Dutch language did survive as late as 1714, it was likely confined to limited domains and among a small elite. Compared to Romanized Siraya, maintaining Dutch – if it was not a lingua franca and no longer useful to communicate with the colonizers – would have conferred fewer direct social, political, and economic benefits. Widespread bilingualism or language shift therefore did not occur, and probably could not have occurred, as a direct result of Dutch language policy.

3.4 Chinese influences on Taiwan (1624–1895)

The remainder of this chapter outlines three distinct phases of Chinese influence on Taiwan, namely the co-colonization that occurred as Chinese settlers came to Taiwan to operate the island as a Dutch agricultural colony, the brief Zheng era, which replaced the Dutch and drove them from the island, and the much longer Qing era, which extended and deepened Chinese settler colonization, though with only minimal direct political control.

3.4.1 Chinese settlement and co-colonization

So far, the analysis has focused on more-or-less direct interventions by the Dutch state – through colonial or missionary linguistics – in the sociolinguistic landscape of Formosa. This section now turns to indirect interventions in the form of colonial political, social, and economic policies geared towards operating Taiwan as a productive agricultural colony. The crucial aspect here is Dutch policies that encouraged and facilitated the migration of ethnically Han Chinese labourers from across the Taiwan Strait, who hailed mainly from Fujian and Guangdong provinces and spoke the Sinitic languages Hoklo and Hakka. To borrow the title of Andrade's (2008) book, this sociolinguistic and ethnic change is at the heart of the explanation of "how Taiwan became Chinese", and the intention here is to link language with Andrade's historical analysis of the political economy and political sociology of colonization. Specifically, Andrade's central thesis is that the Dutch colonial project progressed in tandem with Chinese immigration to Formosa, a process that he describes as "co-colonization":

> A Dutch military and administrative structure co-evolved with a much larger Chinese agricultural and commercial colony in a process of co-colonization. Without the Dutch East India Company, Chinese colonisation would not have occurred when and how it did; without Chinese labour, entrepreneurship, and social organisation, the Dutch would not have been able to create a prosperous land colony. (Andrade 2008: 118)

As mentioned previously, some Chinese settlers were already on Formosa when the Dutch arrived in 1624. Shepherd (1993: 40–41) estimates the pre-Dutch Chinese population at between 1,500 and 2,000, as compared with an indigenous population of some 100,000. The magnitude and permanence of Chinese settlement increased dramatically under the tenure of the Dutch, particularly from the 1640s. A 1650 Dutch census put the number of Chinese at 15,000 (Chiu 2008: 4). By 1661 at the tail end of Dutch rule, Shepherd (1993: 86) estimates that they may have numbered between 35,000 to 50,000, some one-fifth to one-third of the population.

Chinese settlers initially acted as translators between the Dutch and the indigenous peoples, the Dutch and Chinese using Portuguese which was "the lingua franca of Far Eastern commerce at the time" (Shepherd 1993: 83 fn. 196; see also Boxer 1941: 415). The Dutch could have therefore made use of the trilingual resources of the Chinese as a matter of policy, and doubtless did use them ad hoc in certain situations. However, as mentioned, relying heavily on a third linguistic party presents challenges to the social and political dynamics between the colonizers and the indigenous population. Some form of pidginization between Hoklo (or perhaps Hakka) and indigenous languages may have occurred. Andrade (2008: 32) cites a Dutch visitor to the village of Soulang in 1624, the first year of the Dutch era, who complained that "there is scarcely a house in this village ... that does not have one or two or three, or even five or six Chinese living there" and, through contact with Chinese, that the indigenous people spoke "a mixed and broken language". The Dutch visitor, however, was not a linguist, nor conversant in the local language. Language contact was certainly taking place, but despite the visitor's ire the early Chinese settlers were too few in number to effect language shift, and were likely adopting Siraya.

The Dutch had needed labour to turn the island into a productive and profitable agricultural colony. Their fellow Dutch were presumably not inclined to move from relatively comfortable and prosperous Holland to a south-east Asian island with a reputation for privation, disease, and hardship. The VOC was marginally involved in the Atlantic slave trade – a few African slaves were in the service of missionaries and colonial officials, including Junius, on Taiwan (Campbell 1903: 241, 326, cited in Brown 2004: 37) – but a mass import of slave labour would have been impractical. Meanwhile, the indigenous populations were unwilling to be co-opted into agricultural production above subsistence levels, which offered the Dutch no profit (Brown 2004: 38). Instead, the Dutch opened Formosa to enterprising colonists willing to farm the land. In principle, the colony was open to anyone. However, Chinese, mainly from Fujian province on the opposite coast, were particularly attracted: Formosa offered the promise of economic (and to some extent political) freedom, but it was not a distant frontier. The VOC leased tracts of land to *pachter* or Chinese tax-farmers, who in turn leased it out to peasant farmers or employed migrant labour. As the colony grew prosperous, it attracted even more willing pioneers. As Andrade puts it, "the company catalyzed the Sinification of Taiwan ... by making colonization safe and calculable" (2008: 118).

The migration and settlement of Taiwan through co-colonization transformed Taiwan from a majority Austronesian-speaking to majority Sinitic-speaking island. The majority of migrants were native Fujianese from Zhangzhou and Quanzhou counties, and spoke two mutually intelligible dialects of Southern Min or *Minnanhua* (Feifel 1994); these dialects merged to form the basis of modern Taiwanese Hoklo (Young 1988), and this group will be referred to with the demonym Hoklo throughout the remainder of this book. A smaller number of settlers were Hakka, mainly from Guangdong province, who sought both economic opportunities and freedom from persecution: the demonym Hakka (*kejiaren*) euphemistically means "guest people" but, historically, they were made distinctly unwelcome throughout China. Hakka is a Sinitic language, like Southern Min, but the two are mutually unintelligible. Ethnically, the Hoklo and Hakka were (and are) Han Chinese, as opposed to Taiwan's indigenous peoples. However, the "sub-ethnic rivalries" (Lamley 1981) between the Hoklo and Hakka meant they did not automatically constitute a unified ethnic group, even in the frontiers of Taiwan (Brown 2004: 6–7). Competition over resources meant that the numerically stronger Hoklo succeeded in isolating the Hakka, often in mountainous regions; notably, this isolation seems to have preserved or produced five distinct contemporary dialects.

Within the Dutch-administered political system, Andrade (2008: 123) makes the observation that the Chinese were viewed as burghers or citizens. Theoretically, they were under the rule of law, which conferred certain rights and responsibilities in a reciprocal relationship with the VOC and, ultimately, the Dutch state. For example, the Chinese were subject to taxation, but were protected from arbitrary seizure of land and other assets. A court system based on Dutch law adjudicated grievances between the VOC and the Chinese, and between Chinese and the small number of Dutch residents, and was apparently independent enough that judgments were sometimes issued in favour of Chinese. In contrast, the indigenous peoples were viewed as vassals in a feudal system, whereby pledging loyalty to the sovereignty of the VOC entered the Dutch and the indigenous peoples into a compact of mutual defence (Andrade 2008: 123). The Dutch attempted to prevent the Chinese from harassing the indigenous inhabitants and, in general, leased land to the Chinese outside of indigenous areas. In return, the indigenous peoples undertook to assist the Dutch militarily when it came to maintaining order (Brown 2004: 37). These policies of socio-spatial separation arguably prevented the wholesale domination, assimilation, or elimination of indigenous languages and cultures in the short term.

3.4.2 The Zheng era (1662–1683)

Across the strait, China was embroiled in civil war as Manchu forces sought to depose the Ming dynasty and install the Qing in its place. The Ming were routed from the north by 1644, but maintained some control over the south, including Fujian province, until the last bastion of resistance fell in 1662. The Ming loyalist warlord Zheng Zheng-gong, also known as Koxinga, saw Taiwan as potential base from which to continue to battle the Qing. The Dutch initially negotiated with Koxinga, but were betrayed by their Chinese interpreter, Pinqua, who revealed their military plans (Campbell 1903: 390; Spence 1990: 55; Chang 2014: 145). Koxinga's armies swept through the Dutch controlled areas with brutality. Resentful of the economic and military burdens imposed by the Dutch, Chinese settlers on the island – whose numbers were swelled by refugees from the war on the mainland – supported Zheng's forces, as did indigenous groups who had previously sided with the Dutch to quell Chinese peasant rebellions. The Dutch were defeated, and forced to flee the island. Apparently, the missionaries had gravely misjudged indigenous enthusiasm for Western learning and salvation: "being free of the obligation to attend school, the [Formosans] were jubilant as they destroyed their textbooks replete with Christian edification and went out headhunting Dutch residents" (Chiu 2008: 222; see also Campbell 1903: 318).

Koxinga did not have time to savour his victory, dying of malaria in June of the same year; his son and putative heir, Zheng Jing, ascended to power to continue the Zheng regime at least in name. The Qing initially had devices on Taiwan, but quickly lost interest in directly conquering and controlling the island. The Zheng regime attempted to negotiate with the Qing, with a view to operating Taiwan as a Chinese tributary in the same vein as Korea and Japan. These overtures were rebuffed on partly linguistic and cultural grounds. The Qing reasoned that there had been "no precedent since the Five Dynasties for permitting tributary autonomy of a regime of Han Chinese language and culture" (Wills 1999: 97). Taiwan, in the eyes of the Qing, had linguistically and culturally become an ineffable part of China, even if they were not particularly interested in asserting direct political control. The Zheng regime had a linguistic advantage in terms of administration; the Chinese majority spoke Southern Min, as would have Zheng and his troops, who hailed from Fujian province. They seemingly understood that subjugation through socio-cultural means could be more efficient than rule through sheer force or, in other words, that legitimacy had more political versatility than simple coercion. Notwithstanding the indigenous groups' lack of enthusiasm for schooling, the education system established by the Dutch could be put to use to these ends. As Wills (1999: 99) describes:

> [The Zheng regime] made some efforts to replace Dutch projects of 'civilization', establishing schools where children were to be taught the Chinese language and the basics of proper behaviour. The prestige and magic of text and writing, the focus on male cultural and political leadership, the breaking of the web of magic and custom in favour of productivity, universalized religious and cultural values, and propriety – were all striking continuities from the Dutch civilizing project to that of the Chinese.

3.5 The liminal state: Qing rule (1683–1895)

Zheng Jing died in 1681, and with his death came instability brought about by Zheng family intrigue over choosing an appropriate successor to the dynasty. This was compounded by resource shortages: in 1682, troops were moved to insurrection over unpaid wages, while a severe grain shortage in 1683 is "said to have caused rumblings of rebellion among several aboriginal tribes" (Shepherd 1993: 104). Capitalizing on these crises, the massive naval fleet of Qing Admiral Shi Lang secured Taiwan's surrender in 1683. Spence (1990: 56–57) relates that there was heated debate within the Qing court as to what to do next with Taiwan. The emperor was inclined to abandon Taiwan and its inhabitants altogether; he dismissively called the island "a ball of mud", among other epithets. The counsel of his courtiers was equally scathing, since there was little in the way of potential revenue from the island. Shepherd (1993: 137) points out that "in 1683, the Qing court was impressed more by the burdens of the incorporation of Taiwan into the empire than its benefits". As Teng (2006: 34–5) describes, these views were in line with the prevailing "imagined geography" of Taiwan as a "place beyond the seas" – that is, both metaphorically and physically outside of China – inhabited by "savages".

Shi Lang, in contrast, reasoned that Taiwan's proximity to China offered a potential offshore bulwark against the inevitable incursions of maritime trade and warfare around Asia, and that it would be dangerous to allow it to become a base for a rival colonial power (Shepherd 1993: 106). The emperor was persuaded over his own misgivings, and in 1684, Taiwan was subsequently annexed as a prefecture of Fujian province. For administrative purposes, it was divided into three counties, each with a civilian magistrate, with the capital at present-day Tainan. Taiwan thus came under formal control of the Chinese state for the first time. However, this control was at best nominal. Ambivalent and often conflicting Qing policies "ensured Taiwan's development as an unruly dependency, a kind of rough-and-tumble frontier society, only peripherally bound to the administrative structures of the Chinese state" (Spence 1990: 58).

This background is required to understand the ambivalent centre-periphery relations between Taiwan and the imperial capital that would define its politics, society, and sociolinguistic situation for the next two centuries. The Qing era can be divided into two parts, the early period from 1683 to 1750, and the late period afterward, until 1895. A detailed chronological account is impossible given space constraints, so the remainder of this section treats these periods according to two themes. The first is the political role of Chinese settler interpreters in the early Qing period, who translated between the indigenous societies and the state. The second is the broader effects of Chinese migration to Taiwan on Austronesian languages, particularly in the context of the Qing's lax approach to socio-spatial separation after around 1750.

3.5.1 Interpreters and middlemen

At least initially, Qing officials and troops were sent from Fujian province (Shepherd 1993: 108), which was politically and administratively a level higher than the prefecture of Taiwan, as well as being geographically proximate. In Southern Min, the Hoklo-speaking settlers thus had a common language with the immediate representatives of the regime. Communication between Qing officials and the indigenous peoples was done through Chinese settlers who were bilingual in Hoklo and one or more indigenous languages. Often, they were stationed in indigenous villages, sometimes alongside Chinese village "headmen", though frequently as the sole interface with the regime (Shepherd 1993: 116–117). The role of the interpreter was a powerful and often lucrative one, since their linguistic capital allowed them to frame interactions between the state and the local people in ways which suited their own interests. As Shepherd (1993: 116) puts it, the indigenous peoples' "inability to deal with or appeal directly to government officials left them subject to the exactions of predatory middlemen". Of course, this inability was not entirely due to the language barrier, but also because of indigenous societies' unfamiliarity with the social and political structures of the

Qing state. By way of illustration of the above points, in the following, I highlight a few examples of this situation from various contemporaneous sources.

In 1697, the Chinese explorer and entrepreneur Yu Yong-ho visited the island, compiling a tract titled "Observations on the Aborigines in Taiwan" as a part of a wider collection titled *Small Sea Travel Journal*. Yu marvelled at the foreign phonology of the indigenous language(s) he encounters: "Their language is full of sounds like 'du-lu gu-lu': to drink liquor is called 'da-la-su'; to smoke is called 'du-mu-gu'; and in general it is like this" (Thompson 1964: 189). He is initially ambivalent about the "barbarians"; he sees them as becoming more "uncouth" when he encounters them further from the Chinese-settled towns and villages, which is presumably code for being less assimilated into the cultures of the Chinese. Later, however, he muses that it is "because they are of a different race [that] we hold prejudice against them" (Thompson 1964: 198) and ends up overall rather sympathetic towards the indigenous groups, references to "barbarians" notwithstanding. This accords with the general attitude of Qing literati "who objected to the exploitation of the indigenes on humanitarian grounds, as well as out of a Mencian concern for the well-being of imperial subjects", though it is at odds with some of the more chauvinistic travel writing of the time (Teng 2006: 77). Yu is fiercely critical of the Chinese interpreters stationed in the more remote villages; he calls these "village bullies" and "criminals" fleeing from justice on the mainland. It is worth quoting his observations in this regard at some length, since they constitute a rare eye-witness account of, and insight into, the nexus of power relationships between language, society, and the state under the Qing:

> They hide themselves in distant, out-of-the-way places uninhabited [by Chinese], where they scheme to act as [village headmen] and interpreters. With the passage of time they acquire an intimate knowledge of the language. When the father dies the son succeeds him, thus perpetuating the evil endlessly ...
>
> The village [headmen] are changed every year or so, but these fellows [the interpreters] would not leave till they die.
>
> [They] take advantage of the simplicity of the barbarians, and also want very much for them to be poor. If they are simple then they are completely ignorant, and easy prey; if they are poor than they are easily oppressed, and do not have the strength to resist. (Thompson 1964: 197–198)

The interpreters, then, were bureaucratic officials, but their positions were obtained through nepotism rather than meritocracy or civil service examinations. This stood in contrast to the system in China; while corruption and malfeasance doubtless existed, it was not a blatant premise for governance, and a great emphasis was placed – at least outwardly – on meritocracy in the bureaucracy. Although the indigenous people were imperial subjects, the intermediary function of the interpreters prevented them from claiming fair treatment from the Emperor. Indeed, they were subject to the interpreters' self-interested, arbitrary, and sometimes malicious rendering of state policy. Yu Yong-ho, again:

> [The interpreters] continually get [the Formosans] into trouble. Then, even if there are some who appeal to justice, the judge cannot get at the facts of the case because of the language barrier, and he still has to ask the interpreter to explain. The interpreter turns right into wrong and wrong into right, and it is the barbarian who gets a scolding. The interpreter furthermore tells him, "The district magistrate is very angry with you because you have disobeyed the interpreter and the [headman]." Therefore the barbarian dreads the [interpreter] even more, and serves him like God Himself. They are without redress, and those in charge of them have no way of knowing about it. In the whole world there are none more deserving of pity than these barbarians. (Thompson 1964: 198)

Almost two decades later, in 1714, the Jesuit priest Father de Mallia, whose remarks on literate Sirayan speakers' use of Dutch characters were cited earlier, is similarly scathing about the interpreters, calling them "unworthy harpies" and "petty tyrants". He also contextualizes their role in terms of the scalar political organization of Qing Taiwan and that of the indigenous villages, both mediated by the interpreters to their advantage. He notes that the mischief that the interpreters could make by virtue of their linguistic capital did not endear them to Chinese officials any more than it did to the indigenous peoples; in other words, they constituted a powerful class theoretically answerable to the Qing state but able to circumvent its strictures.

> Although these islanders are entirely subject to the Chinese [i.e. the Qing state], they have still some remains of their ancient government. Each townlet elects three or four of the elders who enjoy the greatest reputation for probity ... Their tributes to the Chinese [i.e. revenue to the Qing state] are paid in grain. As regards to these tributes, there is in each townlet a Chinese conversant with the language, who serves as interpreter to the mandarins [i.e. officials]. These interpreters, who ought to assist these poor people, are themselves unworthy harpies who prey upon them pitilessly: indeed they are such petty tyrants that they drive even the patience of the mandarins to the verge of extremity as well as that of the islanders; who, however, are abstained from interfering with them for fear of courting still greater complications. (Widely cited; e.g. Colquhoun and Stewart-Lockhart ([1885] 2008: 547); Campbell 1903: 509–10; a slightly different translation appears in Davidson 1903: 68)

In 1716, efforts were made to curtail the role of interpreters by frontier officials concerned that the interpreters could provoke rebellion. The interpreters were also obstacles to the officials' economic function of extracting revenue (Teng 2006: 77; Shepherd 1993: 120–122). A 1717 article in a local gazetteer (cited in Shepherd 1993: 120) put it thus:

> The aborigine revenue tax is the responsibility of the interpreter just as among Chinese subjects the land tax is the responsibility of the village [headman]. However, Chinese

subjects can pay their taxes by the method of "self-seal and deposit," but the aborigines are uneducated and can neither write nor figure, so it is not possible to institute [this method] among them. Thus, among the Chinese subjects the village [headman] can be eliminated, but among the aborigines the interpreter cannot be eliminated.

Putting together these different descriptions, the interpreters were clearly a paradox for the Qing state. When the interpreters were behaving themselves, they played a key role in the political functioning of the state, most obviously in the collection of revenue and tribute, but also for policing and surveillance. It was thus difficult to remove them without losing an effective means of political control. However, when they were cheating the indigenous villagers, which seems to be more often than not, this caused ill-will towards Chinese officials and the state, thus undermining the state's legitimacy. The interpreters therefore embodied the difficulties of operating an ethnically and sociolinguistically complex frontier territory. A further paradox is the indirect protection of sociolinguistic diversity. While marginalizing (at best) indigenous people, the roles of the interpreters as middlemen meant that less powerful indigenous languages were to some degree protected from shift and decline, because bilingualism in Sinitic languages was deliberately restricted. Interpreters had their own self-interested reasons (and presumably means) to prevent rival Chinese settlers from encroaching on their territory. The combined effects of socio-spatial and sociolinguistic separation under the Dutch, Zheng, and early Qing regimes contributed to the fact that language shift and death does not appear to happen in significant ways until the late eighteenth century. This is the focus of the final section.

3.5.2 Chinese immigration and indigenous assimilation

During the early Qing era, immigration was limited; indeed, upon taking control of the island, the Qing sought to reverse immigration that had occurred previously. Settlers without property or wives were repatriated, some 40,000 out of a maximum population of 120,000 at the end of the Zheng regime (Shepherd 1993: 106). As has already been demonstrated, efforts were also made to keep indigenous peoples and the remaining Chinese settlers separated. Policies were not always successful, not least because they were not always strictly enforced. Migration could only be controlled to a certain degree, and socio-spatial separation must be understood in the context that "the government's priority was to preserve control … not to defend aborigine societies" (Shepherd 1993: 107). However, taken together, Qing policies broadly served to "shelter from change many aspects of the accommodation of [indigenous] societies to [Chinese] traders and Qing rule" (Shepherd 1993: 137). It seems reasonable to assume that languages were similarly protected, and the sociolinguistic evidence suggests that this is the case. Interpreters were key political interfaces in this earlier period, and even now-extinct languages survived up to (at least) the end of the nineteenth century. The Qing formally reversed the anti-migration policy from around 1725, apparently for two reasons (Shepherd 1993: 137–139). At the risk of oversimplifying the complexities of frontier economics, first, additional land needed cultivating, which was crucial for increasing tax revenues. Second, in a complete change of thinking, the Qing appear to have decided that migration might perhaps *prevent* unrest; an influx of new settlers would dilute rebellious elements on the island that had flourished in spite of earlier policies, and allowing women and families to migrate would temper the male-dominated frontier culture of gambling, drinking, and general rowdiness.

To be sure, immigration policy was much more haphazard than can be done justice to here (see Shepherd 1993: Ch.6, esp. 160–162), and it is important to note that periodic, though usually unsuccessful, attempts were made to reverse immigration. However, what is crucial here is that the Chinese population continued to grow over the next 170 years or so, dwarfing the indigenous populations and often assimilating them in its wake. By 1905, the year of the first Japanese census, the Chinese population numbered around 2,890,000, compared to around 82,700 plains-dwelling indigenous peoples, and an unknown number of mountain-dwelling indigenous peoples, later estimated to be 150,000 in a 1935 survey (Shepherd 1993: 161, table 6.4). In addition to raw migration, the "Chinese" population numbers were almost certainly increased, as Brown (2004) argues, through intermarriage and plains-dwelling indigenous assimilation to Han Chinese identities. This was due to earlier policies of socio-spatial separation giving way to more lax approaches to cultural and sociolinguistic mixing as the result of Han territorial expansion. Taking these together, we would expect to see an increase in bilingualism, and eventual language shift and decline. Most vulnerable to language shift would be the languages nearer the focal points of Chinese settlements in the east and north. Piecing together eyewitness accounts from visitors to the island, this appears to be precisely what happened.

An explosion of European and American interest in Taiwan occurred in the mid-nineteenth century, facilitated by the development of colonial and trade networks in south-east Asia. Naturalists, physicians, traders, explorers, diplomats, and missionaries became bewitched by the "beautiful island", as the Portuguese had named it. Many of these visitors viewed Formosa through anthropological lenses of various levels of sophistication, and some of these make reference to language. Of course, these cannot be treated as entirely representative data, and nor do they meet the standards of modern sociolinguistic fieldwork. Some of them are deeply tinged by the hyperbolic racial discourses of colonialist anthropology characteristic of the period, seeing essentialized racial dimensions where nuanced cultural differences should be; they are, of course, framed by an Anglo-European imaginative geography of the so-called Orient (Said 1977), and structured by a dichotomy between "barbarians" and "civilization" just as marked as in earlier Chinese travel writing. However, we should perhaps not discount all folk linguistic interpretations as sociolinguistic fictions. In what follows, I offer a few vignettes that appear to support the idea that language shift, via bilingualism, coincided with historical changes in policy and varied according to geographical factors.

A British doctor, Sir Patrick Manson, writing in 1873 (Manson [1873] 2008: 435), had been stationed in Taiwan for five years previously. As he puts it:

> In this part of the country the villages of [Hoklo], Hakkas and Pepo-whan [a Chinese term for plains-dwelling indigenous peoples] are mixed up together, their territories not strictly defined. There is, however, a general arrangement by which the Pepo-whan is thrust back on the rough, unclaimed lands at the foot of the hills: the Hakka preys upon him as soon as he has got anything to steal, and the [Hoklo] upon both. So the different waves of civilization have advanced across the land, the last one leaving the [Hoklo] in possession of nearly everything worth having ... And so we feel, that not many years hence, the Pepo-whan will be numbered among the extinct race.

There are immediate problems with this account of the sort just mentioned. First, and perhaps most obviously, casting all Hoklo as ruthless exploiters, and all Hakka as thieves, is highly generalizing. Second, the notion that that indigenous peoples were simply pushed off the plains into the mountains is an old folk narrative that is far too blunt a description of actual processes of migration and assimilation (Brown 2004: 35). Furthermore, it robs indigenous peoples of any agency, rendering them as hapless victims; indigenous groups were highly adept warriors who knew their land, and how to survive on and from it, far better than the Chinese or Europeans did. However, it is a fact of history that the Hoklo ended up in a position of dominance – social, political, economic, cultural, and linguistic – vis-à-vis both the Hakka and indigenous groups, largely through assimilation, oppression, and exploitation. Furthermore, geographical dispersals of indigenous peoples are attested, away from or within the western plains (that is, towards the foothills) as the result of colonization processes. Manson's account thus provides an overview of the socio-political processes occurring at the time that, at a very broad level, is not entirely inaccurate.

The British consular officer T.L Bullock ([1874] 2008: 440–452) and the American naturalist J.B. Steere ([1874] 2008: 453–459), undertook quite extensive linguistic fieldwork, generating comparative word lists from five extant languages, which do not have recognizable names but seem, based on geographical and demonym details, to be Siraya, Paiwan, Thao, Seediq/Taroko, and an undetermined language that could be Pazeh, Atayal, or a dialect of Favorlang distinct from Babuza. In Bullock (2008), these five languages are compared against each other, as well as to Favorlang-Babuza, the latter based on the dictionary collected by the Dutch missionary Happart in 1650, and subsequently translated and published by Medhurst (Happart 1840). Bullock presumes that Favorlang-Babuza is extinct, being unable to find indigenous settlements where Medhurst's maps indicate they should be: "the unfortunate speakers ... either were ground to nothing between the wild savages and the Chinese, or were absorbed by the latter" (Bullock 2008: 442). Once again, the notion of "wild savages" is a problematic colonialist category; what he means is groups who are less pacified and thus less "civilized". Thao, Seediq/Taroko, and the undetermined language appear to be still viable at the time Bullock writes, for the obvious reason that Bullock is able to derive word lists from fieldwork with living speakers, though there are some gaps in the wordlists for Seediq/Taroko. These languages are located in the central mountain region, and thus outside of the most intense regions of Chinese settlement. He briefly describes the phonology, morphology, and syntax of these three languages, suggesting that they languages were still spoken widely. Shift to Hoklo in the Paiwan and Siraya villages they visited is evidenced by the extensive gaps in Bullock's word lists; there were no longer indigenous terms for these words. Steere (2008: 451), who was on the same expedition as Bullock, describes the encounter in the Sirayan village in more detail, and we can see the classic signs of significant language shift whereby the language is only known by elderly informants:

> They no longer speak their aboriginal language, using Chinese [Hoklo] instead. I procured the list of words from a very old woman at Kongana, who said that this language was little used even in the time of her parents, Chinese having already become general. There can be no great dependence put upon the list of words, as the woman was old and toothless, and found it difficult to pronounce the words she could remember. (Steere 2008: 451)

Returning to Manson's account from 1873, he seems broadly sympathetic to the processes and problems of language shift and decline. He also encountered an elderly speaker of Siraya, though it has a rather fascinating twist. Some context is required. The term *-hwan* or *-whan* was used by the Hoklo to refer to both (Dutch) Europeans and indigenous peoples, both of whom were "barbarians" in their eyes. As such, the Hoklos' use of the term *-hwan* had apparently convinced the Siraya that they were ethnolinguistically the same as the Europeans, and, thanks to Dutch colonization, had been mythologized as some sort of distant relatives[22]:

> Their language is dead already; only once have we met anyone who could speak it. Many of them believe our language to be identical with their own forgotten one. The Chinese call us 'whan' or foreign, just as they call the [Siraya] 'whan', and so the latter come to consider our races the same. One afternoon we visited in a village where Europeans had never been before. A visit from a fair-skinned foreigner had evidently been long looked for by the villagers, as an opportunity of testing this theory of identity. No sooner had we sat down than an old woman, blind, grey and venerable, was escorted to where we sat, and began to address us in a language we could not understand. She was a relic of the past, and spoke in the language of her childhood, the old [Siraya] tongue. She was evidently much disappointed, as were the bystanders. "No," she said, addressing them in Chinese, "No, we are not the same." (Manson 2008: 436)

Siraya was thus not a language in common usage among the middle-aged or young; it is doubtful whether it was even a lingua franca among the elderly. We might estimate Siraya, at least in this village, as nearly extinct or dormant. If the testimony of Steere's native informant is to be believed, and her language was last spoken in her grandparents' time, assuming a generation age of twenty-five years, we might conservatively put Siraya as still viable somewhere around 1750.[23]

An anonymous account in *The Chinese Recorder* (*The Chinese Recorder* [1885] 2008: 293) refers to the language planning efforts of Rev. William Campbell, the nineteenth century Scottish Presbyterian missionary whose translation of seventeenth century missionary records in Formosa under the Dutch (Campbell 1903) is referred to liberally above.

> An interesting experiment is proposed for adoption in South Formosa, where most of the converts to Christianity are of aboriginal blood. It is found very difficult to teach them the Chinese language with its cumbersome characters; and the use of books with Roman letters has its drawbacks. The Rev Wm. Campbell is therefore devising a scheme for writing the language of the aborigines with characters made of Chinese elements.

This refers to developing literacy for a spoken form that must have survived to the extent that it was a viable language. It is unclear, however, which language this was. The reference to south Formosa is vague, but this would suggest the language of the Siraya or Paiwan groups, who shared a border of sorts immediately due north of present day Kaohsiung. The latter is a possibility, though the

---

[22] Janet B. Montgomery McGovern (1922: 69–83) relates a similar tale of being welcomed as a god of the white Dutch rulers by the Atayal. Tu, Tsai, and Chang (2011: 55–64) make the rather striking (and highly speculative) claim that the Shau indigenous group, who lived or live near present-day Sun Moon Lake, may be descendants of the Dutch.
[23] The difficulty of determining generation lengths is compounded by the Sirayan practice of preventing women under thirty-seven from bearing children. By all accounts (e.g. Shepherd 1995), the Dutch largely eradicated the practice.

Paiwan were hostile to outsiders, beheading a group of Japanese settlers in the Mudan Incident of 1871, which sparked the brief and ill-fated Japanese invasion of 1874. If it was Siraya, then this would suggest that not all villages had shifted to Hoklo, and that assimilation was a more socio-spatially differentiated process than Hoklo settlers simply wiping out indigenous populations from the western plains. The emphasis on indigenous literacy for missionary work reflects its continued importance in the nineteenth century, a continuation of Dutch efforts two hundred or so years previously.

Finally, we have the account, from 1869, of an American customs officer, Edward C. Taintor, who undertook an expedition to an unspecified indigenous village in northern Formosa. He refers to the people as Pepo-hwan, the broader term for plains-dwelling and assimilated groups, but specifies that they go by the endonym Kabarab (likely a version of the modern demonym Kavalan). In this case, bilingualism was pertaining apparently without language decline:

> The whole people, men, women and children, speak the local Chinese in addition to their native language. Some few of the men can read and write a little Chinese, having been at Chinese schools. (Taintor 1875: 61)

Kabarab or Kavalan appears to be still viable, at least in this village, though bilingualism is occurring. This is likely explained by the geographical location. Siraya declined because the areas in which Siraya speakers dwelt was one of the focal points of Chinese settlement. Meanwhile, the mountain-dwelling groups, as a result of their remoteness, experienced far less language shift. Kabarab speakers lie somewhere in between.[24]

Aggregating these nineteenth century European accounts, and generalizing somewhat, it appears that Siraya was threatened, perhaps severely, with other Formosan languages rather more viable. This does not necessarily negate the possibilities that Siraya was more viable in some locations than others and, similarly, that other languages were being pressured to different degrees in areas not visited by the Europeans. But the broader observations of language shift and decline seem to be corroborated by all sources. Historically, bilingualism and language decline occurs following the lifting of migration restrictions in the mid-eighteenth century. This does not mean that languages were not in decline before then, since Chinese settlers and indigenous groups were in contact and conflict since the Dutch. However, an increase in the sheer numbers of Chinese settlers, as well as a lack of commitment to earlier Qing policies

---

[24] Taintor 1875 also produced a comparative vocabulary of the Kabaran and Yukan languages of North-Eastern Taiwan; Yukan is a dialect of Atayal.

of socio-spatial separation, would have accelerated these processes. What is clear is that it is not Qing language policies which are causing language shift and decline, but rather that these are occurring indirectly as the result of laissez-faire policies and the Qing's general disinterest in governing the island, compared to the earlier, if brief, period of Dutch rule.

3.6 Conclusion

This chapter has a broad historical scope which begins with the arrival of the indigenous groups some six millennia ago and ends in the latter years of the nineteenth century, shortly before – as we will see in the following chapter – Taiwan becomes a Japanese colony. Limited space and sparse literature means that the chronological narrative is necessarily abbreviated, but the central organizing theme is the coming of the state – or at least state-like structures and processes, and the political economy of merchant capitalism, agricultural colonialism, and imperial tribute – with the arrival of the Dutch. Before this, Taiwan's indigenous inhabitants had little contact with the outside world and practically no experience of systems of socio-political governance different from their own. Dutch policies – conducted through the auspices of the missionary-colonial complex – reconfigured the island's socio-political, socio-spatial, and sociolinguistic arrangements. In what is by now a classic hallmark of colonialism, socio-political and ethnic differences were uncritically mapped onto linguistic differences, producing specific and identifiable groups upon whom techniques of political and social control could be inscribed. Language policies towards the indigenous group sought not to destroy these differences through linguistic homogenization, but instead use local languages to spread the colonizers' political and moral codes among the indigenous groups. The most drastic change to the island's sociolinguistic situation was not directly through language planning and policy interventions. Instead, it came from the socio-political policy of co-colonizing Taiwan via the importation of Chinese labour to turn the island into a productive agricultural colony. As such, the sociolinguistic profile shifted from being overwhelmingly Austronesian-speaking to increasingly Sinitic-speaking. Even here, however, strategies of socio-spatial and sociolinguistic separation meant that many indigenous languages were protected from shift and death.

Qing statecraft had various similarities and differences compared to that of the Dutch. Clearly, if colonization is determined by the intent towards territorial control and economic expropriation, then the Qing were as much a colonial power as the Dutch. However, although eventually reasoning that the sociolinguistic and cultural Sinicizing of Taiwan meant that the island was an ineffable part of China, their initial approach to rule was ambivalent and perfunctory at most. Until around 1725, they were concerned with *removing* their own subjects from the island and preventing further migration, and using interpreters and village headmen as the main socio-political interface between indigenous societies and the state. In this way, they maintained and even enhanced the strategies of socio-spatial and sociolinguistic separation they inherited from the Dutch. After 1725 we see significant policy shifts such as relaxed controls on colonial migration and little oversight of settler expansion, though even here it is the absence of policy rather than its presence – indicating a continued laissez-faire attitude to rule – that is key. If nineteenth century travellers' accounts are to be believed, these policy changes coincide with language shift and death among indigenous languages. Once again, the most drastic change to the sociolinguistic context comes indirectly from macro-level social, economic, and political policies, and not through direct interventions in language itself.

The theoretical implications for a political sociology of language can be summarized thus. The early modern state – in either the Dutch or Qing variants – is not concerned with the ideological functions of language policy, even if we rule in religious conversion by the Dutch as ideological in nature. Instead, it is concerned with the problems of language within the vertical dimensions of the administrative bureaucracy and the business of rule; insofar as religion is ideological, it is in fact the vehicle only for the imposition of the moral code of the colonizers as a means for political control by the colonizing state. Similarly, there is no sense that nationalism, monolingual or multilingual, plays a role in either the Dutch or Qing attempts at rule; loyalty – the indigenous peoples as *subjects* – is to the state or its proxies, not a nation, and nor does there appear to be an oppositional nationalism resisting colonial rule on the part of the Formosans, or any sense of separateness in national terms on the part of Chinese settlers. Furthermore, the notion of "rights" – civil, social, political, or linguistic – is very distant during the Dutch and Qing periods. The early modern state – and the colonial state more generally – has only an embryonic social contract between ruler and ruled. With this said, the moral rights of the indigenous inhabitants are partly recognized through the religious teachings of the Dutch missionaries and the Mencian notions of governance of the Qing.

In conclusion, this chapter leaves us at a point where far more well-developed structures and processes of the modern state come into play. In chapter four, the Japanese and KMT assume political and economic control over Taiwan, with far more direct political interventions in the language practices of Taiwan's societies.

4 State against society: The Japanese and KMT regimes

4.1 Introduction

If Dutch colonialism marked the coming of the embryonic modern state, it arrived even more fully-fledged in 1895, as Japan took control of Taiwan. The *Kuomintang* (KMT), whose rule replaced that of the Japanese in 1945, finessed the technologies of statecraft even further, achieving one-party control of state institutions, and substantial – though not total – suppression of dissent in civil society, largely thanks to the imposition of martial law from 1949. The Japanese period is bookended by geopolitical conflict: a regime newly-emboldened by the internal socio-political and sociolinguistic reforms of the Meiji Restoration flexed its muscles as an Asian regional power at the conclusion of the first Sino-Japanese war; the second Sino-Japanese war ended with Japan's surrender, via the atomic bombs dropped on Hiroshima and Nagasaki, within the broader context of the end of WWII. The KMT regime similarly begins in earnest with conflict, namely the Chinese civil war between the Nationalists and Communists, and ends with the transition from martial law to democratization. For very different reasons and in very different ways, both regimes sought to spread their respective official languages alongside their political ideologies.

This chapter is divided into roughly equal parts focusing on the Japanese and KMT periods respectively. The first section begins by addressing Japan's internal socio-political and sociolinguistic modernization during the Meiji Restoration from 1868. From there, I address language and social policies in Taiwan during the Japanese colonial period, emphasizing the distinction between the early years and the subsequent *doka* and *kominka* programs, with their different approaches to assimilation. The second section begins by describing the rise and fall of the KMT in China as the Nationalists lost the civil war to Mao's forces, before examining the socio-political and sociolinguistic underpinnings of Mandarin Chinese. I then turn to the arrival of the KMT Governor Chen Yi in Taiwan and his determination to enforce vertical and horizontal monolingualism, the 22–8 Incident and its aftermath, and language policy, civil society, and the public sphere under martial law.[25]

---

[25] I refer here to the 2–28 "Incident", which is not an unproblematic term. In English usage, it runs the risk of glossing over the violence of the event(s), and is in danger of rendering it as a mere disagreement between the state and civil society groups. However, it is one translation of the commonly used Mandarin term 事件 (*shijian*) which, according to Corcuff (p.c.), "can be

4.2 Japanese rule (1895–1945)

The first Sino-Japanese war broke out in 1894, as both parties contested influence over the Korean peninsula. An internally weakened Qing dynasty was forced to sue for peace and, as part of the terms of the Treaty of Shimonoseki, Taiwan was ceded to Japanese control in 1895. Even though it was a restive, peripheral, and largely neglected province, losing Taiwan still involved losing face for the Qing. We begin our narrative, however, somewhat earlier, namely in the Meiji Restoration era of mid- to late-nineteenth century Japan. Socio-political modernization had led to the military strengthening of Japan, causing the shift in the balance of Asian power that led to their victory against China, and would lead them to be the first non-Western colonizing power. Part of this modernization had a sociolinguistic dimension: the fashioning of a standard national language that would the basis of a unified national identity that, in turn, would be an adjunct to state legitimacy. From here, we turn our focus to the colonization of Taiwan. As is conventional in the literature (e.g. Long 1991: 26–27; Ching 2001), the following sections divide Japanese rule of Taiwan into three eras: the early years (1895–1918), the *doka* or "assimilation" period (1918–1937), and the *kominka* or "imperialization" period (1937–1945). In abbreviated form, these timeframes correspond, respectively, to consolidation of rule in the face of armed resistance; pacification and more liberal processes of assimilation; and, from the start of the second Sino-Japanese war in 1937, a more urgent repression of Taiwanese identity.

4.3 Language and political reform in Meiji-era Japan

The feudal Tokugawa regime, which ruled Japan during the Edo period from 1603, pursued isolationist foreign policies or *sakoku*, and imposed strict controls on domestic social and cultural life. By the mid-nineteenth century, however, the regime was experiencing internal decline; externally, the British, Americans, and French, through diplomatic and naval brinksmanship, pressured Japan to open its ports to foreign trade, culminating in the unequal US-Japan Treaty of Kanagawa in 1854. The Japanese astutely realized that the foreign powers

---

used for serious events and does not necessarily neutralize the horror". The alternative term in use (at least in English) is "massacre", which is no doubt factually correct but a highly emotive term in English. "Uprising" is also in use, but it suggests that the islanders somehow instigated the chain of violent events. In conversations with Taiwanese, the period is often referred to simply as "2–28" (*er-erba*).

prowling Asia would devour them unless they could significantly modernize. This included a drastic reorganization of feudalism, and the abandoning of *sakoku* in favour of learning how colonial mindsets operated. Under what became known as the Meiji Restoration, from 1868 the emperor's role was rehabilitated from being a mere figurehead – the lords and samurais under the Tokugawa had been the real power brokers – into the supreme source of political authority. The same year, the emperor declared that "knowledge should be sought throughout the world and thus the foundation of the Imperial polity will be strengthened" (Röhl 2005: 23).

The result was the rationalizing and modernization of the state infrastructure – including banking, finance, and taxation systems; transport and communications networks; and the legal code – according to various European models (Westney 1982; Röhl 2005). A comprehensive civil service examination system was developed in the mid-1880s, giving a bureaucratic basis to the modern state (Spaulding 1967; Tsai 2009: 52). Industrialization provided the economic backbone to these political reforms. These changes required and produced widespread social upheavals, which were traumatic in a society that valued tradition, stasis, and rigid vertical and horizontal stratification (Wert 2013). Fundamental to these shifts was the need to fashion a Japanese national identity as a means to underpin the legitimacy of the new state, and this required substantial intervention in language and literacy practices (Twine 1991; Gottlieb 2005; Heylen 2005). Language became a key political battleground for moderate reformists, ultra-nationalist reformists, and traditionalists/conservatives.

4.3.1 *Genbun'itchi:* Unifying speech and writing

As Coulmas (2002: 204) argues, the development of the modern Japanese nation-state rested on improving vertical communication between the state and its citizens and within the bureaucracy. It also required facilitating horizontal communication between citizens themselves, to facilitate a common national identity. Fundamental in this regard was the program of *genbun'itchi*, or the "unification of speech and writing", led by language reformer Maejima Hisoka.[26] In theory, two sociolinguistic contexts worked to reformists' advantage. First, due to over two centuries of isolationism, Japan was and remains relatively monolingual. Second, an emphasis on cultivating a civilized and

---

26 See a useful biography of Maejima Hisoka in Hunter (1988).

cultured population under the Tokugawa Regime meant that literacy rates in the late Edo period reached perhaps 40%, higher than the comparable rate in Europe (Deal 2007: 228; Gottlieb 2005: 40). As such, reform worked from the foundation of a single language and relatively widespread literacy. Despite this, language modernization was no easy task, and in practice it became "one of the most significant and bitterly contested reforms of the Meiji period" (Twine 1978: 333).

The first difficulty was that although it was nominally monolingual, Japanese had high internal dialectal diversity. Under the feudal system of political rule and social organization under the Tokugawa shogunate, over two hundred autonomous domains were each ruled by a feudal lord or *daimyo*; to protect the central military government's authority, the power of the *daimyo* was limited to their respective regions, and this was partially achieved by restricting most citizen-subjects from travelling outside of their own region. As Gottlieb (2005: 7) observes, "the linguistic consequence of [the feudal arrangements] was that local dialects flourished, unaffected by more than occasional contact with passers-by from other places who spoke a different dialect". Fashioning a national language, therefore, required choosing a standard dialect and it was decided that the standard should be based on the capital city, which, having previously been Kyoto, was now Tokyo (Gottlieb 2005: 8).

The second difficulty was that although literacy was relatively high, there were four orthographic systems in use, namely *kanbun, sorobun*, wabun, and wakankonkobun. These differed in whether they used Chinese characters (*kanji*), Japanese phonetic symbols (*kana*), or a mixture of both (Gottlieb 2005: 40–42). To add further complexity, each of these systems was based, stylistically and syntactically, on classical Chinese or Japanese literary conventions, and each had their own sub-conventions (Heinrich 2012: 43–44), meaning that they were in practice only accessible to those with specific training. Framed another way, quantifying literacy rates depends on what kind of literacy, and in what system, is being described. For reformists, "the extant system of languages and styles was a reflection of the obsolete social order: hierarchic, inflexible, and highly stratified" (Coulmas 2002: 204). For traditionalists and conservatives, of course, such distinctions suited their own interests in maintaining social and political power. The practically complex and politically contentious nature of language reform ensured that debates continued into at least the early 1930s. All four written systems were retained to varying degrees, indicating how both corpus and status planning were dictated by the contours of political compromises.

The role of Chinese characters in the new written system warrants a brief discussion for the political dilemma it posed for nationalism. For practical reasons, some reformists wanted to reduce them or, for Maejima Hisoka and others, abolish them entirely, since their non-phonetic nature made them difficult to read without learning them individually. Traditionalists took umbrage, but so did ultra-nationalist reformists, who might have been otherwise expected to support a distinctively "Japanese" system. Chinese characters were perceived as being quintessentially Japanese instead of a polluting foreign influence; they had been borrowed – along with Buddhism and other cultural influences – in the sixth century (Gottlieb 2005: 41). *Kanji*, then, were mythologized as timeless parts of Japanese heritage and thus central to its national identity; attempts to abolish them were an "attack on national values", since "they had become not just a form of writing, which could be altered as circumstances demand, but a value-laden cultural institution" (Gottlieb 2005: 45). Related to this debate was the attitude towards adopting Romanization and abandoning *kana* and *kanji* altogether, which even for reformists was a modernizing (and Westernizing) step too far; Kitta (1989: 53, cited in Gottlieb 2005: 47) notes that a student-led movement to introduce Romanization was repressed by the secret police.

Mass education was the vehicle for sociolinguistic acquisition planning as well as social and political reform and the inculcation of a national identity; Japan's new leaders and bureaucrats "fully recognized that education was the cornerstone upon which the whole process of national transformation would come to rest" (Horio 1988: 26, cited in Coulmas 2002: 204). Plans called for one elementary school for every six hundred people (Storry 1990: 113). While this was probably not uniformly achieved, it was a policy as progressive as it was ambitious; Japan introduced compulsory education in 1872, rather earlier than many European countries that it supposedly emulated (see Soysal and Strang 1989).

4.4 Japanese rule of Taiwan: The contemporary modern state

The contemporary modern state arrives with the Japanese; their rule was austere, and sometimes brutal, and rampant discrimination against the Taiwanese stifled upward mobility. However, it is undeniable that they brought some benefits of the modern state to Taiwan, investing massively in infrastructure, such as sanitation, transportation, and communications, and developing the island's economy through sugar and rice production and, subsequently, industrialization. Most importantly for our purposes, they created systems of relatively mass education and raised literacy levels, in addition to spreading the Japanese language. To view these outcomes – a sort of "progressive despotism" (Phillips 2003: 17) – as part of a coherent program, however, is to miss the haphazard trajectory of colonial policy under the early years, and the subsequent *doka* and *kominka* eras.

4.4.1 The early years (1895–1919)

The Qing bequeathed to the Japanese a complex sociolinguistic situation on the handover of Taiwan in 1895. Hoklo speakers were the dominant group on the island. Competition for resources was pushing the Hakka off the fertile plains to mountainous regions where they preserved, or developed, five distinct dialects. Since interactions (and often clashes) with Hoklo still occurred, their geographical isolation was not total, and it seems likely that at least some Hakka were bilingual enough in Hoklo for limited trade and commercial purposes. Hoklo had a rudimentary written system, Peh-oe-ji, left by British missionaries (Klöter 2005), but literacy in this would be limited, in terms of both population and domains. Hakka had no such system indigenous to Taiwan, though it is possible that the Phak-fa-su system, developed by Presbyterian missionaries in China, had spread in limited ways. Meanwhile, Classical Chinese was taught in Qing-era holdover private schools that catered to wealthy elites from both Hoklo and Hakka groups. Overall, literacy was about 5% (Tsurumi 1984: 283). Both groups, the Hoklo in particular, had dominated indigenous language speakers in assimilated areas, leading to language shift (by and large towards Hoklo) and language death, particularly from 1750. The Han population – that is, the Hoklo and the Hakka – numbered around 2,890,000, according to the Japanese census in 1905.[27] The same survey identified around 82,700 plains-dwelling indigenous peoples, with an unknown number of mountain-dwelling indigenous people estimated later, in a 1935 survey, at 150,000 (Shepherd 1993: 161, table 6.4). The indigenous groups spoke various languages; as we have seen in the previous chapter, assimilation, shift, and some language death occurred particularly after the mid-eighteenth century.

The political context was no less complex. The first three years of Japanese rule were "characterized by aimless drifting and chaos" (Chang and Myers 1963: 434), and punctuated by periodic revolt. Both indigenous and Chinese groups were opposed to the colonial takeover from the outset, presumably reasoning that Qing governance (or, more accurately, the lack of it) was preferable to the

---

[27] In this chapter, "Han" refers to the Hoklo and Hakka Taiwanese whose descendants had migrated to Taiwan since the time of Dutch rule. They are thus distinct as socio-political actors from the Japanese colonists and indigenous groups, but also from the "mainlander" Chinese who arrived with the KMT after 1945. Of course, the latter group are also ethnically Han, so the term is more of a socio-political designation that avoids the problems of conflating the Han and the mainlander Chinese as "Chinese". When talking about Han elites, however, it must be remembered that the Hoklo had the upper hand over the Hakka. The terms "islanders" and "Taiwanese" refer to both the indigenous and Han Taiwanese populations collectively.

unknown vicissitudes of the Japanese. In May 1895, a group of rebels proclaimed the Republic of Taiwan, but disorganization and the lack of a central government or state institutions stymied their plans, as did the refusal of the Qing to assist (Davidson 1903: 275–289; Lamley 1968). Davidson (1903: 365–366) suggests that some 8,000 Taiwanese died resisting the Japanese in 1895 alone. 6,000 were killed in a single event, the Yunlin Massacre, in 1896 (Lamley 1999: 207). Another 8,000 people were arrested annually for sedition (Kerr 1974: 155–156). Support for resistance was partly class-based; "many wealthy [Han] islanders preferred the stability of Japanese rule to the lawlessness of those resisting colonization" (Phillips 2003: 17). Indigenous populations were particularly prone to insurrection, taking 1,900 Japanese lives in 1,132 incidents by 1903 (Takekoshi 1907: 229, cited in Simon 2015: 82).

Quelling rebellion and taking control was thus the first priority for the Japanese; this was achieved for the most part by 1898, with a colonial police force replacing occupying military troops, though sporadic uprisings and outbreaks of violence – particularly by mistreated indigenous groups – would occur at least until 1930. By 1898, the Japanese realized that, at least with the Han, coercive military measures contributed nothing to, and likely outright undermined, the legitimacy of the Japanese colonial state. The next priorities, therefore, were maintaining order, ingratiating themselves with sympathetic elites, and spreading Japanese.

4.4.1.1 Language, education, and gradual assimilation

On the second day of occupation in 1895, an education reformist named Izawa Shuji was appointed head of the Taiwan Bureau of Education. His philosophy was to introduce universal mass education from elementary to tertiary levels, arguing that this could persuade the Taiwanese of their rightful allegiances to their new rulers, and eventually to assimilate them. He immediately announced that the Taiwanese education system's immediate goal was to teach Japanese to its new citizens (Tsurumi 1979: 618). The Japanese language was widely seen as intricately entwined with Japanese socio-political norms – as seen in the *genbun'itchi* debates – and, for Izawa, thus a key vehicle by which the Taiwanese could be brought under Japanese tutelage. He set up sixteen language institutes, but by 1897 had vacillated on assimilation mainly for pragmatic reasons, arguing instead for a "policy of fusion" with Japanese and Chinese linguistic and cultural elements (Takeshi and Mangan 1997: 314). In 1898, the first chief civilian administrator, Goto Shinpei, arrived, and replaced the language institutes with "common schools". These were essentially elementary schools with a six-year curriculum, and segregated from schools for Japanese residents. Goto was even more cautious about assimilation, arguing that the different political and cultural histories of the Taiwanese meant they could not be Japanized any time soon (Lamley 1970: 500). Language and literacy education (and education in general) were for the time being necessary only insofar as they served the needs of the Japanese state for the purposes of maintaining order in the colony and operating it productively. Thus, as Kerr (1974: 56) puts it, literacy education should be

> Enough to improve [a student's] economic productivity and no more. On completing primary school he should be able to read orders, patriotic slogans, and simple technical information – the directions on a bag of fertilizer, for example ... but he would not be encouraged to think for himself. (Kerr 1974: 56)

Also in 1898, the Japanese government appeared to contradict Goto's position on assimilation by promulgating an edict, the Government-General's Common School Regulation, which stipulated that: "the common school should teach Taiwanese children ethics and practical knowledge, thereby cultivating in them qualities of Japanese citizenship and also lead them to be well versed in the *kokugo* [Japanese language]" (cited in Coulmas 2002: 214). However, this still did not intend for substantive incorporation of the Taiwanese into the Japanese empire. The dynamics of how the Japanese saw the Taiwanese in relation to themselves and their state is indicated in the use of the term *kokugo* rather than *nihongo*. *Nihongo* refers to the language spoken by the ethnically Japanese, and thus those who are full citizens of the metropole; *kokugo*, meanwhile, refers to Japanese for foreigners or, in this case, colonial subjects. As *kokugo* speakers, therefore, cultivating the "qualities of Japanese citizenship" in the Taiwanese was not the same as bestowing de jure citizenship. Through this ethnicized and politicized differentiation of terms for the same language, the colonized are viewed not as rights-bearing citizens, but rather subjects who owed certain responsibilities to the Japanese state. This mirrored the logic of colonial rule.

Reticence on the issue of assimilation was certainly ideological but, as Tsurumi (1979: 618) points out, plans for education and thus language-spread had to contend with the dull practicalities of operating a bureaucratic state, not least of which were budgetary considerations in a colony that was not yet economically productive. Goto's superior, Kodama, decreed that, while universal comprehensive education was the longer-term goal, for the time being common schools were to be voluntary and established in limited numbers, mainly where wealthy Han were prepared to subsidize them (Tsurumi 1979: 618). This was also designed to curry further favour for the regime; wealthy elites, as mentioned, were already inclined towards accepting the relative stability of Japanese rule in preference to the lawlessness of the Qing, or at least not actively resisting it (Tsurumi 1977: 38–39). They were further placated with classes in classical

Chinese for four or five hours a week; the elites, of course, were likely educated in Qing schools and steeped in the Confucian tradition.²⁸

In terms of reach, common schools increased from seventy-four in 1898 to 181 by 1906 (Tsurumi 1979: 619). However, this still meant that only between 2% and 5% of the school-aged populations were enrolled, though this increased to some 15% by 1918 (Tsurumi 1979: 620). Furthermore, despite 70% of timetabled hours being devoted to Japanese language courses (Wu 1992: 310 cited in Hsiau 2000: 35), the proportion of the Taiwanese population able to comprehend and speak Japanese grew to a mere 2.6% by 1920 (Chou 1995: 119, cited in Hsiau 2000: 34), indicating sluggish progress for language-spread through acquisition planning. Part of the problem here, of course, was the huge gap between written and spoken forms of Japanese (Takeshi and Mangan 1997: 315); the *genbun'itchi* debates were still ongoing in Tokyo and, as such, there was no agreed-upon standard model of Japanese with which to teach. The common schools were also competing with private Han schools in what counted for Taiwanese civil society, which the Japanese tolerated likely as another means to placate elites. Kerr and others estimate that around 2,000 private Han schools existed upon the arrival of the Japanese in 1895, with some 30,000 attendees (Kerr 1974: 27; Tsurumi 1979: 619). They were often staffed by local teachers who refused to have anything to do with the Japanese education system, and would neither teach Chinese in the schools nor learn Japanese to the level required to teach other subjects (Tsurumi 1979: 620; Lamley 1999: 211).

In time, however "even gentry-scholar holdovers from [Qing] days who frowned upon the 'new learning' felt that their children needed Japanese language and modern subjects to win a comfortable and honoured life in the new society"; Han school enrolment thus declined to about 20,000 in 1907, though thousands continued to attend until 1918 (Tsurumi 1979: 621). In 1915, the first public middle school for Taiwanese boys was opened by the colonial administration, albeit reluctantly (Tsurumi 1979: 622). Takeshi and Mangan (1997: 319) point out a specifically political dimension to this: wealthy Taiwanese petitioned the governor on the basis that a middle school would be a reward for their assistance to the Japanese in campaigns against indigenous rebels, and the governor had little choice but to accept. Around this time, a select few Taiwanese were offered access to local higher education, though almost solely in medicine or teaching. Part of the rationale for the Japanese to develop local education opportunities was to stem the flow of the children of

---

28 Later, however, the Japanese would claim that classical Chinese instruction had been designed to foster a lingua franca among the different ethnolinguistic groups (Tsurumi 1984: 283).

wealthy elites, frustrated by a dearth of opportunities in Taiwan, studying in the colonial metropole, Tokyo.

The "common schools" were aimed at Han rather than indigenous groups. As mentioned, a crucial function of the schools, and thus language, cultural, and educational policies more generally, was to inculcate support for the Japanese colonial regime among established and emergent Chinese elites. The indigenous groups were neither elites nor power brokers within the nominally defined civil society/state relations; what power they did have usually came from actual violence against the colonial state, often in response to the state's own violence for the purposes of socio-economic marginalization and resource exploitation though this simplifies the complexities of aboriginal resistance (see e.g. Katz 2005). Some schools were built in mountainous aboriginal areas before the 1920s – the "Puyuma school" in Beinan, near Taitung City, was built in 1904 (Cauquelin 2004: 227) – but it seems that they were designed for rather blunter forms of colonial control, since non-assimilated mountain-dwelling indigenous groups were constructed as "savage", with their ability to ever be "civilized" in question (Ching 2001). The Japanese had come to this conclusion as a result of earlier, failed attempts by officials attached to the *Bukonsho* (or Office of Pacification and Reclamation) to ostensibly "learn indigenous languages and customs, protect them from outside exploitation, and gradually civilize the indigenous people through peaceful means" (Simon 2015: 81). Instead, forcible removal of the indigenous peoples from their lands, and linguistic and cultural assimilation, later became a fundamental part of Japanese policy.

Beyond limited assimilation and propitiating elites, the education system had another function, namely training interpreter-translators for the colonial bureaucracy. As Cheng (2014: 254) relates, in 1895 the Japanese had sent several hundred military interpreters to Taiwan, only to find that the interpreters spoke Beijing and Nanjing dialects of Mandarin, which were unintelligible to the Hoklo- and Hakka-speaking Taiwanese. While they could write down their messages, this meant they could only communicate with literate and elite Taiwanese, of whom there were few, and even this required orally relaying written orders to the rest of the residents, entrenching the status of the elite class by bestowing a specific form of linguistic capital. Furthermore, the territory and population of the new colony had to be surveyed and detailed for the purposes of bureaucratic governance, particularly since the Qing, with characteristic disdain, had done little in this regard. But, here again, the language barrier (quite aside from the rudimentary transport and communications infrastructure, which the Japanese would improve dramatically) was a formidable obstacle, particularly given the ethnic tensions and latent resistance. As Japanese colonial administrators moved out into the countryside, "simple private and personal misunderstandings such as haggling over the price of eggs or the hire of rickshaws could flash into a public quarrel erupting into a local riot" (Kerr 1974: 26). Interpreter-translators thus became essential to the basic operation of the colonial administration. Accordingly, very soon after occupation, a teacher-training college was established to train sixty Japanese in Hoklo and Hakka, and thirty Taiwanese in Japanese; and soon textbooks were produced to train hundreds of Taiwanese in schoolrooms and meeting halls, which was "a good beginning, but ... thousands were needed" (Kerr 1974: 27). By 1902, Kerr states that this had expanded to three teacher-training colleges, and four language institutes, alongside the instruction happening in the "common schools" (Kerr 1974: 84). Along with training interpreters, the next step was to teach conversational fluency to colonial administrators, police, and language instructors (Heylen 2005: 500; Cheng 2014). Notable here is that it seems that language instruction was first concentrated in civil society, rather than among agents of the state.

Translating in indigenous contexts was a more difficult proposition. Although the Japanese were initially optimistic about learning indigenous languages (Barclay 2005: 338), this proved to be more difficult than first thought. Individuals from remote indigenous groups could not be persuaded or coerced into becoming language teachers, nor was there much thought given, at least initially, to teaching them Japanese. The Japanese instead decided to use the older Qing system of Han interpreters who lived among, and were familiar with, indigenous groups and their languages. They therefore adopted an already existing socio-political, economic, and sociolinguistic nexus seemingly, at least from Nakajima's description (1896: 247–248, cited in Barclay 2005: 338), with few differences in the eyes of the indigenous groups. There were, however, additional levels of complexity in this arrangement. The Qing and the Han interpreters shared a common language (or enough of one), while the Japanese and the Han did not. This required embedding additional levels of translation into the process, made even more complex by the political organization of the Japanese state. As such, as Barclay (2005: 338) relates,

> A minimum of two interpreters, but usually three, brokered Japanese-Aborigine communication in the early years of colonial rule. Japanese men known as official translators interpreted for government officials to the Chinese interpreters. These Chinese interpreters stood between the official translators and the intermediaries known simply as "local men" (*sheding*) or "Aborigine women" (*banpu*). Despite their low official status, these *sheding* and *banpu* were indispensable for sojourns in the Aborigine territories.

In summary, then, Japanese language policies until 1919 were mostly pragmatic decisions oriented to spreading Japanese in limited ways through the common schools, gaining support for colonial rule among elites, and the practicalities of translation for the state's two main objectives: the giving of orders to maintain order in the colony, and operating it so that it was economically productive. A highly limited and gradual cultural and political assimilation program was oriented towards the Chinese. Around 1919 a shift in emphasis takes place, whereby *doka* – assimilation or integration – becomes a priority.

4.4.2 The doka period (1918–1937)

Although most armed resistance had been quelled by 1898, sporadic uprisings occurred. The largest of these was the 1915 Tapani Incident, which involved both Han and indigenous groups. Two main consequences of the Tapani Incident can be discerned (Takeshi and Mangan 1997: 318; see Katz 2005 for a more in-depth analysis). First, while it was not the last uprising, in general armed resistance was replaced by non-violent anti-colonial ideology among the Han, with the "young generation who had received an education playing a pivotal role" (Hsiau 2000: 29) and debating in what became a somewhat vibrant public sphere. Second, while the Japanese still ruled Taiwan with a rod of iron, they began to place greater emphasis on political, cultural, and sociolinguistic assimilation than previously. Assimilation had previously been assumed to risk *causing* revolt; now it was adopted as a means to prevent it, by aligning the Taiwanese with the Japanese world-view, fostering obedience to colonial authority, and thereby enhancing the legitimacy of Japanese rule. For Ching (2001: 6), the logic of the *doka* period was the urging – though not yet insisting – that the colonized become "Japanese".

4.4.2.1 Language, assimilation, and anticolonialism
From 1919 or so, the common school system was consistently expanded. This reflected shifts in colonial policy, which began to edge towards assimilation. However, subsequent governors vacillated over the issue, and the debate over the necessity or desirability of assimilation was still yet to be settled. As Roy (2003: 41) puts it:

> The pro-assimilationist view was that Taiwanese were increasingly alienated from China and would therefore become Japanized [...] The opposing view was that Taiwanese could never develop the mindset or patriotic spirit of the ethnic Japanese. Thus their destiny was to remain under a military government indefinitely.

General Akashi Motojiro, governor between 1918 and 1919, cautiously accelerated Goto's gradual approach, viewing partial assimilation of limited numbers of

Taiwanese as a means to maintain the internal status quo between colonizers and colonized, so that "Taiwanese with suitable training could be integrated into Taiwan's growing economy and be made more susceptible to Japanese national interests" (Lamley 1999: 20). As already mentioned, some higher education openings were already available to a select few Taiwanese, though restricted for the most part to medicine and teaching. Akashi expanded access to post-elementary education systems, opening institutions in agriculture, forestry, and engineering, recognizing not only the Taiwanese clamour for educational opportunities but the labour requirements of the colony (Tsurumi 1979: 622). Programs for Japanese residents were still closed to Taiwanese, but it was nevertheless a widening of educational possibilities.

In 1922, Taiwan's first civilian governor-general, Den Kenjiro, ostensibly advanced assimilation further, radicalizing the educational system by inaugurating an integrated school system, whereby entrance to top-ranking formerly segregated Japanese elementary schools was, in theory, to be based on proficiency in the Japanese language, and not on ethnic or racial determination (Tsurumi 1977: 92–93). In practice, however, the language barrier proved to be a difficult obstacle, one which ultimately ensured ethnic discrimination in favour of the Japanese (Tsurumi, 1979: 624), with the effect that segregation continued to limit full assimilation. At first blush, it might be reasoned that Taiwanese were simply not being exposed to Japanese language training to the degree that they were acquiring the necessary competence. But a more critical analysis suggests otherwise: competence was a socio-political construction rather than a linguistic measure, because by all accounts the Japanese-spread program was succeeding. 25% of children were enrolled in common schools in 1920 and 29% by 1922, meaning that the children of the upper class and most (male) children of the expanding middle class had received at least an elementary education; meanwhile, enrolment in the Chinese schools declined over the same period from below 8,000 in 1920, to around 3,500 in 1922 (Tsurumi 1979: 621–625). Furthermore, despite the objections of Han parents, classical Chinese was phased out in many schools under Governor-General Den (Ren 1923: 81, cited in Tsurumi 1979: 624 fn.23), effectively rendering these schools wholly monolingual and immersive in Japanese. Indigenous children, needless to say, were not permitted to attend desegregated schools at all. In some senses, then, Den spoke assimilation – and prescribed indoctrination (Lamley 1999: 227) – but paradoxically restricted educational opportunity; Akashi did the reverse.

By 1932, 90% of Han children were in free common schools. Perhaps more remarkable is that between 70% and 75% of indigenous children also were (Mendel 1970: 21; To 1972: 184). However, following the indigenous Mushe (or Wushe) Uprising of 1930 (Ching 2000), and particularly for the majority who lived in the remote mountains and not the "pacified" hills and lowlands, indigenous schools were likely more blunt forms of colonial control and discipline; indeed, colonial police doubled as teachers (Lamley 1999: 228), and the schools were called "instructional centres for barbarian youth" (To 1972: 184). Japanese language provision was through a four-year program. It is difficult to know how comprehensive this was. Colonial policy in the lowlands was linguistic and cultural assimilation; in the mountainous areas, it seems likely that instruction was only sufficient to ensure obedience to Japanese colonial authority. Drop-out rates were high, and a survey in 1944 suggested that just nineteen indigenous youth had any form of post-elementary education (To 1972: 184).

Following the education reforms in both 1919 and 1922, officials began to decree that the Japanese language should be promulgated to the wider (Han) society outside of the formal school system (Lamley 1999: 227). From 1929, a growing non-elite were acquiring Japanese in government-sponsored public programs, and 22.7% of the population comprehended Japanese by 1932 (Sugimoto 1971: 984). As Chou (1991: 64–65, cited in Friedman 2005: 108) describes:

> These programs were generally called "Japanese study programs" (*kokugo koshojo*). The Taiwanese aged between twelve and twenty-five who did not speak Japanese were eligible for enrolment. The programs did not charge any tuition; the minimum number of schooling days was one hundred days a year and two to three hours of study each day. One could finish the program in a period ranging from one year to four years. Yet, because of budget shortages and the need to accommodate the peasants' farm work schedules, the government offered a compromised version of this language study program, with a shorter study period (sixty days a year) for people over twenty-five. Schools of this sort were referred to as "basic Japanese study programs" *(kan'i kokugo koshojo)*. Their outreach programs expanded quickly. By April 1937, there were 2,812 "Japanese study programs," with 185,590 students, and 1,555 "basic Japanese study programs," with 77,782 students. (Chou, 1991: 64–65 cited in Friedman, 2005: 108)

This did not necessarily mean abandoning their Taiwanese languages, which managed to survive and, particularly for Hoklo, even flourish through borrowings. However, it did create a diglossic situation, whereby these languages became increasingly confined to the home and marketplace, and Japanese was dominant in the legal, government, and other official domains.

Limited assimilation through Japanese language-spread was proceeding somewhat quicker than in the early years. However, equality of treatment remained out of reach, not least because of the often-racialized ideology of Japanese superiority, and this remained a point of political contention among educated elites agitating for change. By 1922, across all levels, around 2,400 students were studying in the colonial metropole, Tokyo, in response to the limited education provision in Taiwan itself (Tsurumi 1979: 623). The colonial authorities were very much aware of the danger this created, namely that the Taiwanese would be exposed to more sophisticated currents of thought that would give them ideas above their station or, worse still, radicalize them (Tsurumi 1979: 621). University students would be exposed to international ideas, since Japan was in the process of modernization and looking outwards to the world for technological and political inspiration; of course, the years after WWI saw the emergence of the principle of national self-determination, which would be taken up in anticolonial struggles for the next half century.[29] The Japanese apparently weighed this as an acceptable risk compared to offering equal treatment or substantive assimilation for the majority of Taiwanese. The predictable effect was to create a core of bilingual Han elites both willing and able to lead social and political movements in opposition to the policies of the Japanese colonial state. For Hsiau (2000: 29), non-violent anticolonialism, contested in civil society and the public sphere, thus forms the basis of Taiwanese struggle from around 1920.

A variety of organizations were formed to advance the cause, beginning with the New People's Society (*shinminkai* in Japanese; *xinminhui* in Chinese), established in 1920 by a group of Taiwanese university students in Tokyo, backed by a number of wealthy donors (Hsiau 2000: 30). The last, the League for Attainment of Local Autonomy (*Taiwan chihojichi renmei*) collapsed in 1936 (Tsurumi 1979: 630). Since there was no local parliament, these constituted civil society organizations with political dimensions, rather than political parties as such; indeed, the lack of a Taiwanese parliament was a grievance petitioned almost annually to Japan's national Diet, without success. Agitating for local political representation and economic autonomy by the New People's Society "marked the turn toward a home rule movement, which became the motif for the reformist group for the next decade and a half" (Hsiau 2000: 30). Different factions had different goals (Hsiau 2000: 30–31; Mendel 1970: 23; though cf. Tsurumi 1979: 630), and disentangling competing visions is difficult. Below the home rule movement, at least for certain radical anticolonial elements of it, lay a simmering desire for full national independence. Conservatives aimed for the relatively straightforward reformist goal of assimilation and equal treatment between Japanese and Taiwanese residents, though they would claim a more radical position retrospectively. Perhaps more contentious were appeals to be returned to the "motherland" of China since, unlike the home rule/independence position, it was difficult to couch these in covert terms.

---

29 In addition, a sizeable number went to China for study; Lamley (1999: 220) also points to the anti-imperialist May 4th Movement in 1919 as helping to foster radicalism and nationalism.

In terms of the public sphere, the movement produced a number of pamphlets, newspapers, and journals to disseminate their ideas. Some of these would have had limited (and elite) readerships, but a few attained the status of relatively mass publications with high circulations (Liao 2006: 85). The main organ of the New People's Society was *Tai oan Chheng lian* (Heylen 2007: 242; Lan 2015: 154), the Romanized Hoklo translation of the Mandarin *Taiwan Qingnian* or *Taiwan Youth*, which was published between 1920 and 1922, before being renamed as *The Formosa (Taiwan)*, and closed in 1924.[30] The first two issues of *Tai oan Chheng lian* contained articles on language reform (Chang 1999: 265), and the front cover of the first issue is semiotically complex, with the English definite article "the" before the title in Romanized Hoklo and calligraphic Chinese, and publication information in printed Chinese and Japanese (using kanbun characters), indexing different spheres of local, colonial, and global cultural and political power. Despite the name, and the involvement of Cai Peihuo, who was deeply connected to the Hoklo Romanization movement (Heylen 2007), the journal was published bilingually in Japanese and Chinese, with the latter being either classical/literary Chinese, or (presumably *baihua*) Mandarin (Heylen 2007: 259 fn8). *Taiwan Minpo* (Taiwan People's News), was a newspaper from the same publisher of *Tai oan Chheng Lian* and *The Formosa*, first issued in 1923 and continuing until 1944. It was written mostly in Japanese with a column in *kanbun*, using Chinese characters that could be understood by literate Taiwanese, and "very openly published Taiwanese views and critical opinions"; furthermore, "when the newspaper was issued daily it published many popular and imaginative fictional works representing social realities" (Liao 2006: 91). The publication of fictional work was connected to the burgeoning Taiwanese New Literature movement of the 1920s and early 1930s (Chang 1999), which was the highly politicized cultural offshoot of the home rule movement. This had its own internal debates, with regard to writing *accessible* literature, about using modern vernacular Chinese instead of classical or literary Chinese.[31]

This did not mean that newspapers could print absolutely anything they wanted, of course; prepublication censorship was common (Liao 2006: 83). But it seems that the Japanese regime tolerated, at least at elite levels, some dissent

---

30 Not to be confused with *Formosa (Meilidao)* that was published in the later years of KMT Martial Law, though both have common intellectual traditions in Taiwanese independence and nationalism.

31 Intriguingly, Liao (2006: 83) further argues that criticism of the colonial government, corruption particularly, was prevalent through exposes, allusion, and satire even in the so-called official *Taiwan Nichinichi Shinpo* (Taiwan Daily News).

in civil society, and some degree of contestation and deliberation within the public sphere. The political rationale was presumably to provide a limited outlet for social and political dissatisfaction, in order to make visible and deflect any serious challenge to power. In this vein, as Mendel points out, the Japanese "imprisoned only the radical elements" of the movement, preferring instead to "suppress, subvert, or disrupt ... it encouraged the moderates and bought the loyalty of the more susceptible; [and] spread rumours designed to sow discord among the leadership" (1970: 24). Crucially, however, these organic intellectuals were Japanese-educated and conducted their dissent and deliberations mainly in the Japanese language, meaning that they were displaying at least some acquiescence to the assimilation program. The elite were increasingly "bilingual middlemen" (Heylen 2007: 239), mediating between the state and the more disadvantaged classes in a capitalist society (Chang 1999: 263), and controlling the elites meant, to some extent, giving them some political latitude, or at least the appearance of doing so. These elites would find themselves sociolinguistically and intellectually isolated when the KMT took control in 1945.

4.4.3 The kominka period (1937–1945)

With the outbreak of the second Sino-Japanese War in 1937, and with home rule civil society associations agitating for political reform, the Japanese made the decision that a more rapid and comprehensive assimilation was required under the auspices of *kominka*. As mentioned, for Ching (2001: 6, emphasis added) the *doka* and *kominka* eras are characterized by, respectively, the *"urging and then insisting* that the colonized become 'Japanese'". In contrast to *doka*, in which the Taiwanese were colonial subjects and were simply being assimilated, albeit in limited ways, under *kominka* they became thoroughly Japanese imperial subjects, whose allegiances were meant to be to the Japanese state and, ultimately, the emperor. But the reality was contrary to "the official discourse of a consistent and continuous colonial policy of equality and benevolence" (Ching 2001: 91). Increased assimilation was a function of the war effort, for which Han allegiances to and identification with China were dangerous, and was deemed necessary to neutralize any pro-home rule revolutionary or seditious tendencies (Roy 2003: 48; Meisner 1964). The emphasis on *insisting* on assimilation meant that the Taiwanese had little choice in the matter. Although it had a limited effect on stamping out "Chinese" identities among the Han population, *kominka* inculcated a powerful sense of Japanese-ness, and fundamentally – and finally – transformed its sociolinguistic situation.

4.4.3.1 Language, assimilation, and citizenship

As mentioned earlier, by 1932, 22.7% of the population apparently comprehended spoken Japanese (Sugimoto 1971: 984); furthermore, at the beginning of the *kominka* initiative in 1937, 25% of the (total) population had had an elementary school education, enabling them in theory to become literate in Japanese (Hsiau 2000: 51). Japanese-spread policies in the *doka* period, it seems, were becoming successful. But these paled in comparison to the rate that Japanese proficiency increased under *kominka*. Just three years in, by 1940, Japanese comprehension was reported to have doubled to just over half the population (Sugimoto 1971: 984), and reached 80% by 1944 (Hsiau 2000: 44). Of course, this must be taken with some caution; the Japanese would have had political motives for inflating the extent of assimilation to convince both themselves and their Taiwanese subjects of its success and, as we shall see, colonial authorities constructed political and socio-economic incentives for residents to claim Japanese proficiency. Nevertheless, qualitative data corroborates that a significant ramping up of Japanese-spread, as a function of more insistent assimilation under *kominka*, was occurring. Certainly, in 1945 the KMT inherited a polity in which Japanese was spoken widely, and this presented difficulties for its Mandarin-spread program.

Under the *kominka* program, local languages were banned from public life. Hoklo and Hakka-language radio programs, and the publication of Chinese-language sections in newspapers, were all prohibited, effectively closing down the public sphere for all but the Japanese-speaking elites. Meanwhile, a change in the system of socio-spatial organization of society led to further exposure to Japanese language and culture, in the hope that language shift would take place. The previous *hoko* system of household registration and surveillance that scaled up to villages and then to larger units was replaced by the *buraku* system in 1936. Administratively, this meant that household registration was a civilian rather than police matter. It likely did not look much different in the eyes of most Taiwanese, but for the state "the *hoko* system had long nurtured segregated localities where the Taiwanese speech and local Chinese customs were preserved" (Lamley 1999: 228). The logic here is clearly to prevent enclaving of the Sinitic-speaking communities, though the continuation of the surveillance function doubtless had the effect of policing the use of dispreferred (though still not totally proscribed) languages in public. A similar program, started somewhat earlier, relocated indigenous populations into designated villages on the plains, where Japanese-spread, and programs of colonial control and pacification, could be undertaken in earnest.

In addition to more coercive language proscription and socio-spatial engineering, the Japanese also utilized incentive schemes to promote the acquisition of the Japanese language and assimilation towards its culture. In one program, both Han and indigenous groups were encouraged (in the case of the indigenous peoples, more or less forced) to adopt Japanese surnames as a step towards achieving Japanese nationality and the rights associated with it (Roy 2003:41), though only 7% of the Han population took up the offer (Chou 1991:57, cited in Roy 2003:41). In addition, during the war, the Japanese authorities pursued a policy which:

> offered incentives to the Taiwanese to learn Japanese [...] Families that were certified as having learned a small amount of Japanese earned an emblem for display on the front gate of their house that brought small privileges from the local administration. (Roy 2003: 41)

Roy rather underestimates the "small privileges" that learning Japanese brought the Taiwanese in terms of their dealings with the state and its institutions. Acquiring Japanese effectively offered access to a whole different category of citizenship. As Chou (1991: 78, cited in Friedman 2005: 110) relates

> First, the children of such families would be allowed to enter an elementary school where the majority of students were ethnic Japanese ... Second, their children would enjoy favourable consideration when they were trying to enter a high school. Third, the members of such families would be given priority over others for employment in government offices ... and in public organizations. Fourth, the members of such families enjoyed better chances of getting certain business licenses ... Apart from these specific benefits, they were to "enjoy convenience and receive special favour whenever possible". (Chou 1991: 78, cited in Friedman 2005: 110)

However, this privileged citizenship came with caveats. Enhanced rights were not solely based on language proficiency alone, but were linked to other demonstrations of "good citizenship" and assimilation by the Taiwanese. These criteria included:

> (1) the extent to which family members communicate in Japanese, taking into consideration their motives, efforts, and duration, (2) the extent to which they had been Japanized in religion, clothing, and daily life, and (3) the extent to which they had become true citizens by paying taxes, interacting with the metropolitans, and involving [themselves] in community service (Fong 1993: 121, cited in Friedman 2005: 110)

Quite clearly, these caveats were designed to thwart the claiming of Japanese proficiency, or Japanese-ness in general, on spurious grounds. It must be stressed at this juncture that the linking of Japanese proficiency with certain categories of citizenship effectively framed civil society within the state's terms. "Good citizenship" was based on behaviours within civil society – religion, clothes, and daily life – as much as towards the state. Furthermore, Japanese-spread and thus the construction of civil society was focused mainly on the Hoklo and Hakka populations; though the Japanese would make use of indigenous fighters – the Takasago volunteers – during the Second Sino-Japanese war (Huang 2001), they were treated as second-class citizens for whom even language proficiency could not truly "civilize" them as members of state-defined civil society.

Japanese-spread, at least among the Hoklo, Hakka, and assimilated indigenous groups, was ultimately successful. It was widely spoken when the KMT took control and, as will be discussed below, they found it difficult to eradicate it from society. When I undertook fieldwork in Taiwan in 2007, it was not uncommon to meet elderly people who only spoke Hoklo and Japanese, having acquired the latter in the Japanese education system and missed the introduction of Mandarin by the KMT post-1945.[32]

A final footnote comes in the form of the only known Japanese-based creole – Yilan Creole Japanese – which is lexified by Japanese, has Atayal features, but based on a grammatical structure different from both languages (Qiu 2015). It is thought that the Atayal and Seediq, whose languages are part of the same Formosan subgroup, used Japanese as a lingua franca; the reasons for this are unknown, though Qiu (2015: 16) observes that its emergence in the 1930s and 1940s coincides with the establishment of educational facilities in indigenous areas. Of course, this also coincides with the beginning of *kominka*, when more attention was paid to Japanese-spread in indigenous areas. Another explanation, from Sanada and Chien (2010: 353) is that socio-spatial reorganization of indigenous groups – the movement of residents from the mountains to the plains for the purposes of assimilation and control – forced Seediq and Atayal populations "from different villages to live together and constitute new communities". With some 3000 speakers, according to Sanada and Chien (2010: 351), the language is not in imminent danger of death. However, it appears that transmission of the language has stopped, and those born after the 1980s do not speak the language (Sanada and Chien 2010: 352). At the time of writing, this puts the youngest speakers at approximately 40 years of age.

4.5 KMT Rule and Martial Law (1945–1987)

The Second Sino-Japanese war concluded in 1945 with Japan's defeat and, under the provisions of the San Francisco Peace Treaty, Japan agreed to cede control of

---

[32] Lin (2015) discusses how this group are discursively constructed as a language minority in Taiwanese modernity.

Taiwan. However, this is a complex area of international relations (Chen and Reisman 1972). It is not at all clear to which entity control was in fact ceded, since Article 2(b) of the Treaty only specifies that "Japan renounces all right, title and claim to Formosa and the Pescadores". The People's Republic of China (PRC) did not exist until 1949 and so could not have been the controlling power, thus undermining current claims by the PRC that Taiwan is a "renegade province". The KMT took de facto control on behalf of the then-ruling Republic of China (ROC), but de jure control is not specified in the ceding instruments, and thus the often-used term "retrocession" is technically inaccurate, because Taiwan was not legally "returned" to China. One legal theory holds that the United States, as the allied occupying power, took legal control, and thus the US can ultimately determine Taiwan's sovereignty; a more fringe version of this theory is that Taiwan is or should be the fifty-first state of the USA (Chen 2010: 162–172, 184–186, 198–99). US courts have declined to make a judgment on the issue, citing the political dimensions of the case that are more the preserve of the executive branch. Taiwan's status in international law remains muddled, and this has structured its internal and external politics up until the contemporary era.

Perhaps in part cognizant of their tenuous legal control of the island, and thus the implications for legitimacy, the KMT would operate Taiwan under martial law for almost four decades. The stated nationalistic logic – emphasized in inverse correlation to the soundness of its legal basis – was that Taiwan was being rightfully returned to the motherland of China. Initially, this was welcomed by at least some Taiwanese, though the enthusiasm rapidly dissipated in the face of the KMT's brutality and ineptitude. The broader cultural, social, and political project was the Sinification and de-Japanization of Taiwan, of which Mandarin language-spread was an integral part. In the remainder of this chapter, I discuss the political sociology of language under the KMT regime on Taiwan. I begin by contextualizing the political rise and fall of Nationalist China on the mainland after the dissolution of the Qing dynasty in 1911, and the KMT's flight to Taiwan after defeat in the civil war by Chairman Mao's Communist forces in 1949. I then give a sociolinguistic sketch of Mandarin and language policy in Nationalist China, before turning to language policy during the KMT period in Taiwan. Temporally, the narrative shifts around somewhat, so Table 4.1, below, lists some significant dates for guidance.

It is an unfortunate fact that the indigenous populations disappear somewhat from our narrative – though not from Taiwan – at this juncture. This is the effect of this study's concentration on the relations between the state and civil society. Although both the Japanese and KMT regimes focused on programs of pacification through assimilation, indigenous groups were never intended to be full citizens or members of civil society. This, in fact, would have been a useful adjunct to the discursive construction of Chinese-ness by the KMT: the ethnically

Table 4.1: Significant dates in the history of the KMT.

Date	Event
1912	*Foundation of the Republic of China (ROC) and the Kuomintang (KMT)*
1921	*Foundation of the Communist Party of China (CCP)*
1925	*Sun Yat-sen's death; Chiang Kai-shek (CKS) takes over the KMT*
1927	*Civil war begins between the KMT and CCP/People's Liberation Army (PLA)*
1937	*Beginning of the second Sino-Japanese War; civil war suspended*
1945	*End of the second Sino-Japanese War and WWII; civil war resumed; Japan cedes Taiwan*
1949	*CCP/PLA victory in the civil war; CKS and KMT exiled to Taiwan*

Han Chinese Hoklo and Hakka could be (re-)Sinicized and de-Japanized by returning them to the motherland of China; the indigenous groups were very distinctly othered in racial and ethnic terms. Nevertheless, indigenous languages will be treated as much as possible and where appropriate.

4.5.1 The rise and fall of Nationalist China (1911–1949)

As with the end of the Tokugawa regime in Japan, the demise of the Qing dynasty came about as the result of a combination of both internal and external political forces. In particular, China had been embroiled in conflicts with the European nation-states asserting their dominance in Asia and, later, with Japan. The aging, cumbersome Qing system could not modernize fast enough to be a match for these younger, feistier political units, who flexed their naval and economic power on China's doorstep. The loss of face to foreign powers, including the debacle of the two Opium Wars against the British, undermined the Qing's political legitimacy at the domestic level; weakened by warfare and unequal treaties imposed from without, revolutionary change came from within. In 1911, the Xinhai Revolution – a collection of revolts and uprisings culminating in the Wuchang Uprising on October 10th, and the abdication of Puyi, the six-year old "last Emperor" – ended the reign of the Qing and began China's republican era.

Dr Sun Yat-sen was a central political architect of the revolution (see the biography by Sharman 1934); military heft came from fellow revolutionary, the strongman General Yuan Shi-kai. Sun had developed a political philosophy of the "three principles of the people", based on nationalism, democracy, and economic wellbeing. He also saw the link between language and national identity, in the confluence of blood kinship, common language, and common customs. Sun declared himself faithful to the teachings of Confucius and Mencius, and thus effectively grafted Western political principles of nationalism onto pre-existing socio-political structures and currents of philosophy in Chinese society.

The Chinese Nationalist Party, or *Kuomintang* (KMT), was in fact a loose collection of groups that Sun consolidated as provisional President of the new political entity of the "Republic of China" (ROC). By 1921, the KMT were joined on the political stage by a nascent Communist Party of China (CCP) as Marxist ideology took hold. Following Sun Yat-sen's death in 1925, Generalissimo Chiang Kai-shek took over the KMT, and civil war between the CCP and KMT ensued, with a hiatus between 1937 and 1945 as the two parties joined forces against Japan in the Second Sino-Japanese War. As mentioned, Japan's defeat in 1945 saw Taiwan come under de facto control by the KMT-ruled ROC. In October of 1949, the CCP, under Chairman Mao Ze-dong, gained the upper hand in the civil war, taking control of most of the mainland and establishing the People's Republic of China (PRC). By December of that year, Chiang Kai-shek and the KMT fled to exile on Taiwan, along with up to two million Nationalist troops and refugees, and were thus left controlling the rump of the ROC's territory.

4.5.2 The sociolinguistic context of Mandarin

The abbreviated version of the remainder of this chapter is that the KMT state pursued a highly aggressive Mandarin-spread policy in Taiwanese society between 1945 and 1987. Before addressing KMT policies towards and discourses about Mandarin, however, it is worth giving some sociolinguistic context to the language itself. Mandarin is, in many respects, an invented language. Although it is now standardized in both China and Taiwan, and used for official and educational purposes, with the written and spoken forms unified, these are comparatively recent developments.

During the Qing period, the official language of the bureaucracy was the Tungusic language Manchu (or Jurgen-Manchu) of the ruling group, and the term *guoyu* (lit. "national language") thus referred to Manchu. But, as Norman notes, under the Qing (and other dynasties) "the vast bulk of government business was transacted in [Mandarin] Chinese and not in the languages of the ruling elite" (Norman 1988:133). In the Qing case, a situation of diglossia obtained within the state apparatus: the bureaucratic written system was a late form of literary Chinese, while verbal communication was conducted in a variety of the Beijing dialect of Northern Mandarin, "often strongly influenced by the local native [language] of the speaker" (Norman 1988: 133). The spoken form was known as *guanhua*, or the speech of the "officials" (or "mandarins", hence the English name for the language). But:

> neither of these forms of bureaucratic Chinese was codified in any fashion; they simply developed as a natural response to the need for a practical medium to carry on the day-to-day business of the empire. (Norman 1988:133)

In other words, vertical communication within the bureaucracy was conducted through a (diglossic) lingua franca. However, vertical communication for the purposes of giving orders was multilingual: laws, edicts, and the like would have to be translated from literary Chinese or spoken Mandarin into each of the many local languages throughout the empire. This was during a time when literacy was not widespread, most people knew only their own local languages, and the geographical mobility of both people and their languages was restricted. Before the nationalist era, there was thus no common language among the broader Chinese population; they were linked only politically through the administrative language of the bureaucracy.

In the early years of the twentieth century, reformists' perceptions of the need for China's modernization led to concerted efforts towards language reform (Kaske 2008). Doubtless looking towards the recent sociolinguistic and political modernization of the Japanese (Chen 1999: 14), for reformers the benefits – the necessities, even – of a "uniform and officially sanctioned language, both as a tool of education and administration and as a symbol of national unity" were clear (Norman 1988: 133). However, so too were the hurdles: the traditional literary language – *wenyan* – was an impractical vehicle for expanded literacy, even if updated and modernized; furthermore, there was a need for a new model of spoken Chinese to replace the uncodified lingua franca of *guanhua* (Norman 1988: 134), and it needed to be a genuinely popular language, not merely the preserve of the elite and the bureaucrats.

In 1909, the Ministry of Education under the ailing Qing regime developed language acquisition policies for promoting the teaching and study of a new national language based on Mandarin in schools (Norman 1988: 134). In 1911, shortly before the Qing dynasty collapsed, the *Tongyi guoyu fangfa* or "Act of approaches to the unification of the national languages" was passed, setting up a corpus planning committee to "decide on the standards of *guoyu* by selecting what is elegant, correct, and popular" and determine a standard pronunciation "mainly based upon the Beijing dialect ... the vocabulary and grammar should be mainly based upon *guanhua*." (Chen 1999: 15).[33] Furthermore, in terms of acquisition planning within the education system, it was recommended that "apart from

---

[33] The fact that acquisition planning proceeded *before* corpus planning, which seems illogical at first glance, is testament less to Nationalist disorganization than the intrinsic and overlapping relationship between corpus and acquisition planning processes.

being taught as a specific [school] subject, *guoyu* should gradually become the medium of instruction for all subjects" (Chen 1999: 16). Language planning efforts resumed immediately in 1912, after the fall of the Qing, with the Nationalists pursuing the agenda of the 1911 Languages Unification Act (Chen 1999: 17). In 1919, *baihua*, a vernacular-based written form, was chosen over classical literary *wenyan* (Norman 1988: 134; Chen 1999: 72). In 1920, the Ministry of Education decreed that Chinese subject instruction in years one and two of primary school should focus on *guoyu* and *baihua*, and in 1935 *Jiaoyubu guoyu tuixing weiyuanhui*, the "Committee for *guoyu* promotion of the Ministry of Education" was set up to coordinate national popularization of *guoyu* (Chen 1999: 22). However, the momentum of the national language movement was lost due to the outbreak of the second Sino-Japanese war in 1937; the intention was to resume Mandarin-spread in 1944, but little headway was made due to the resumption of the civil war between the Nationalists and Communists (Chen 1999: 23).

All this raises the question of the proportion of Mandarin speakers among the two million or so troops and refugees who fled to Taiwan in 1949. As the official and de facto administrative language even under the Qing, it was likely a lingua franca among Nationalist troops, the KMT's own bureaucrats, and teachers, who comprised a socio-politically and numerically significant contingent. However, even by 1949, it was largely uncodified and would have been relatively divergent in terms of accents and dialects. In terms of the civilians who arrived, theoretically some of them were from the north and native Mandarin speakers. However, it is attested (Klöter 2006: 209; Hsiau 2000: 129) that in general they were sociolinguistically heterogenous, many speaking a variety of southern languages and dialects such as those from the Wu, Gan, Min, Xiang, and Yue families.[34] If they had been exposed to Mandarin to any degree all, it would have been likely through schooling between 1920 and 1944, but we have already seen that amidst various political conflicts education policy had not been comprehensively or consistently applied, and virtually not at all between 1937 and 1944. At best, then, as Tsao (2008a: 274) puts it, "most of them could manage to communicate in Mandarin", but most were not first language speakers and many were not fluent second language speakers. As such, KMT Mandarin-spread policies may have been aimed at the mainlanders as much as the Taiwanese. What might be the case is that these groups – or, more likely, their children – were better positioned and better motivated to learn Mandarin relatively quickly compared to the Taiwanese (Hsiau 2000: 129). First, there was a need for a lingua franca in a sociolinguistically heterogenous yet politically homogenous community, and

---

[34] It would, of course, have been easier to flee to Taiwan from the south.

Mandarin was a residual linguistic resource given that at least some people already spoke the language to greater or lesser degrees. Second, they were likely politically motivated to learn Mandarin as the result of nationalist ideologies that equated learning Mandarin with Chinese patriotism; as a group, the common collective identity among the mainlanders was Chinese, in contrast to the Taiwanese, who were quickly coming to see themselves as a separate people.

Linguistically, then, Taiwan Mandarin is possibly a creoloid variety (Kubler 1985; LaPolla 2001). As Trudgill (1983: 106) describes, a creoloid is a variety which demonstrates creole-like features, such as an acrolectal-basilectal continuum, but was probably never a pidgin. Notwithstanding the standardization implied in KMT language planning efforts, creoloidization of Taiwanese Mandarin is thus perhaps "the result of imperfect learning by relatively large numbers of non-native adult speakers" (Trudgill 1996: 8). Some recent linguistic research bears out these ideas: Kuo (2005) suggests that modern day Taiwan Mandarin is the partly the product of language/dialect contact or koineization processes between speakers of different Sinitic languages; in other words, it is not solely the result of language contact between Hoklo speakers and a homogenous group of Mandarin speakers, though this has been an important influence. In this regard, several works detail the phonology and grammar of Taiwan Mandarin and its basis in but divergence from the exonormative standard of the Beijing variety (Cheng 1985; Kubler 1985; Baran 2007).

4.5.3 KMT rule on Taiwan (1945–1949)

Absorbing Taiwan into the Republic of China, the KMT took a disdainful and high-handed approach to rule from the outset. General Keh King-en echoed the "ball of mud" epithet bestowed on Taiwan by the seventeenth century Kangxi Emperor, calling the Taiwanese "a degraded people" and the island a "degraded territory" that was *guanwai*, "beyond the pale of true Chinese civilisation" (Kerr [1965] 2017: 54).[35] Although the Taiwanese perhaps recognized the similarity between the comments of the Qing and the new leaders, their "chilling implications were obscured in the general elation with which everyone welcomed the war's end and greeted the beginning of a new era" (Kerr 2017: 54). It would not be long, however, before some Taiwanese came to suspect that the Nationalist

---

35 Quotes from Kerr ([1965] 2017) refer to the most recent Camphor Press reprint of *Formosa Betrayed*. The book may be out of print at the time of the present book going to press; the publishers assure me a revised 2018 edition is planned.

government troops were simply another set of colonists, albeit a set inepter and with worse manners than the last, and a modern proverb emerged in Hoklo: "dogs go, pigs come". Taiwanese Han elites, many of whom had been educated in Japan, were broadly sympathetic, if not entirely loyal, to the Japanese worldview (Hsiau 2000: 52) leading many to privately see the mainlanders as "chaotic and backward" (Phillips 1999: 276), even as publicly many Japanese "collaborators" became "ardent and vocal Chinese patriots" (Phillips 2003: 42). The resulting tensions structured political, social, cultural, and sociolinguistic relations between Taiwanese civil society and the KMT state for decades to come. In this section, I focus on language policies of Governor-General Chen Yi from 1945; although his tenure was only four years long, it laid the groundwork for KMT policies that were fundamentally unchanged between 1949 and 1987. I then address the 2–28 Incident which, while having only tangential sociolinguistic dimensions, is the defining political moment of KMT rule of Taiwan.

4.5.4 Language policy under Governor Chen Yi

The first provincial governor of Taiwan, Chen Yi, had language politics firmly in his mind from the outset. On arrival, despite being fluent in the language, he "swore he would never speak a word of Japanese" (Hsiau 2000: 55), and was determined that nobody else would either. Apparently, he was also fluent in Hoklo, or at least mutually intelligible Southern Min), though neither did he deign to use that to communicate with the Taiwanese (Copper 1996: 35). Mandarin-spread was the goal from the beginning, and Chen Yi intended for it to happen quickly. However, Klöter (2006: 205) notes that, in practice, "Mandarin was by no means enforced abruptly" in Taiwan. Instead, more cautious and less coercive approaches were taken to begin with, the result of language planners' more realistic assessments of Taiwan's sociolinguistic situation compared to Chen Yi's dogmatism. Officially, initial policy was in fact to "to recover the Taiwanese dialect [Hoklo] so as to enable the public to learn the national language [Mandarin] by comparison between the dialect [Hoklo] and the national language" (Chang 1974: 51 in Hsiau 2000: 54; Tse 1986: 25–6). Furthermore, whether by accident or design, Mandarin-spread was greatly aided by the apparent fervour on the part of the Taiwanese for returning to the Chinese motherland. Government-sponsored Mandarin classes were eagerly joined by large numbers of Hoklo and Hakka; newly-found patriotism was doubtless one motivation, though Phillips (1999: 285) also points to the "release of curiosity stifled by the Japanese", while Hsiau (2000: 56) more cynically notes that at least "some were obviously opportunists who hoped to profit from the new political environment". However, enthusiasm was short-lived due to the increasingly noxious broader political climate of forced Sinification and de-Japanization. The latter was an attempt to stamp out loyalty towards China's wartime enemy. As such

> The zest for Mandarin ... was dampened dramatically within the first year ... Resentment at being stigmatized because of Japanese influence and being politically discriminated against proved ... part of the reason. (Hsiau 2000: 56)

With voluntary language acquisition waning, Chen Yi switched to more coercive measures. In April 1946, the KMT established a Taiwan provincial subcommittee of the National Committee for the Promotion and Propagation of the National Language (NCPPNL), with city and county level institutes opened across the island to implement policies developed by the committee, working closely with city governments and school systems (Tsao 2008a: 250). Formal schooling began in Mandarin in 1946. State industries and workplaces offered captive audiences for language instruction; in 1947, the UN officer Allan Shackleton, a New Zealand national stationed in Taiwan in 1947–48, recalls

> An interesting incident ... on coming by road to a railway station, I found what I thought was chanting in progress. On looking closer, I found all the Formosan employees assembled in one room being taught Mandarin. This, I found later, was a common occurrence anywhere where Formosans were employed. (Shackleton 1998: 77–78)

Japanese was banned from newspapers and periodicals in 1946 and thus excised from a crucial part of the public sphere. Authors who had written solely in Japanese found themselves expelled from literary circles, and the literary language was prohibited in the public domain more broadly (Hsiau 2000: 55).[36] Several authors observe that the native Taiwanese intellectual class, an organic elite that developed in the public sphere cautiously allowed by the Japanese, was officially rendered illiterate, almost overnight (Gates 1981: 264; Hsiau 2000: 55; Chen 2001: 98). Tolerance for Hoklo began to be strained and the initial project of "recovering" it for the purposes of teaching Mandarin foundered; Hakka may have been tolerated rather more, given that it was not a significant threat to Mandarin-spread, but by 1948 "local languages were declared inappropriate for academic and cultural communication" (Wu 2009: 105).

---

[36] The politics of literature is an important part of anticolonial resistance against both the KMT and Japanese. However, while closely related to the politics of language, it is beyond the scope of this book. For treatments see e.g. Hsiau (2000).

However, Mandarin-spread was proceeding slowly. This was a problem for state policy, but also acutely felt by the islanders when Mandarin fluency became mandatory for obtaining government jobs. This allowed Chen Yi's administration to frequently argue that lack of competence in Mandarin meant local Taiwanese were unable to effectively perform the required tasks (Hsu 1991: 166–7, cited in Hsiau 2000: 55; Lai, Myers, and Wei 1991: 65–7, 70). This led to more disenfranchisement of elites, as those Taiwanese officials who had demonstrated their loyalty and diligence to the Japanese were replaced with mainland administrators. Mayoral and district chief elections were postponed, also on the grounds of lack of competence in the language (Hsiau 2000: 55) There may have been a degree of truth to the administration's claims: certainly, the Mandarin-spread policy fundamentally misjudged the speeds at which spoken Mandarin could be learned to issue or follow orders compared to learning written Mandarin to understand or produce official documents (Phillips 1999: 285). But insisting on Mandarin proficiency was in reality a covert form of political discrimination. In particular, it hid the fact that Chen Yi was stuffing the bureaucracy with arriving mainlanders. For George Kerr, a US diplomat stationed in Taiwan between 1945 and 1947,

> In due course there were to be found on Formosa about 1600 generals, nearly 200 admirals and enough bureaucrats to govern the whole of mainland China. Room had to be made for all of them, and all had to be fed by the Formosan people. (Kerr 2017: 308)

As Hsiau (2000: 55) notes, the most pressing reason for preventing local Taiwanese from occupying political and bureaucratic office was, in Chen Yi's words, to avoid the island becoming "Taiwanese Taiwan". For Gates (1981: 263), then, Mandarin proficiency requirements

> Provided a rationale for excluding or demoting Taiwanese from responsibility. It placed the burden of effort, of awkwardness, and of linguistic ineptitude on a group that was already coming to be categorized as inferior because it was culturally different and politically impotent.

Chen Yi's initial language policy thus disenfranchised both those Taiwanese who had retained Hoklo and Hakka languages and thus a broader Han Chinese identity, often out of loyalty to the putative Chinese motherland and/or resistance to the Japanese, as well as those who had abandoned their local languages and embraced Japanese for social advancement.[37] The shared sense of

---

[37] The indigenous groups disappear from our narrative at this point, because they had no stake in administrative power, having been successfully assimilated by the Hoklo and Hakka, or marginalized by the Japanese.

disappointment surely fed into anti-mainlander sentiment, and served to foster an embryonic independent Taiwanese identity.

In an attempt at compromise, Chen Yi moved to nominally open up governmental positions through direct elections to the Taiwan Provincial Assembly, and to sub-committees at the county, city, and township levels. Spirited discussions ensued between elected Taiwanese and KMT commanders, but "served more to highlight hostility between the government and the Taiwanese community than to promote reconciliation" (Roy 2003: 66). Indeed, political communication in the Assembly and its sub-committees was difficult, since most Taiwanese did not understand Mandarin and most Mainlanders did not understand Hoklo, Hakka, or Japanese (Phillips 1999: 285). Negotiations were thus mediated through third-party translators. While translators in the Provincial Assembly and its committees had less direct economic interest in manipulating translations to their own ends than Chinese settlers who had translated for the Dutch or Qing, their political ambitions or affiliations, or sheer mischief, could presumably influence the nuances of interpretation.

As Kerr relates, the legal and judicial systems faced similar sociolinguistic challenges (Kerr 2017: 153); codes, laws, and other documentation were in Japanese, not to mention that they were framed within Japanese law; lawyers and judges had to be trilingual in Mandarin, Japanese, and a local language in order to function; and Japanese was banned but its use was often unavoidable. Chen Yi's penchant for cronyism, furthermore, meant that

> Although few mainland Chinese had both the linguistic and legal qualifications, they were given the highest appointments at Taipei. [However,] circumstances compelled Chen Yi to appoint qualified Formosans as district and local judges and procurators. The majority were bilingual, having studied literary Chinese while passing through the higher schools, and having taken law degrees at the Japanese universities.

Kerr (2017: 153) goes on to note that re-staffing the Japanese police force was similarly done according to non-meritocratic criteria. Police jobs were given to friends of mainlanders in the administration, who could rarely speak either Japanese or the local languages; combined with their inexperience and lack of training and discipline, this led to frequent (and sometimes violent) misunderstandings.

The Taiwanese began in important senses to view themselves as somewhat superior (Copper, 1996:35). As Roy (2003:59) notes, there were

> Abundant anecdotes illustrating the prevailing Taiwanese view that these troops were *t'u baotse* ('hicks'): crowds of soldiers staring in amazement at an elevator in a downtown Taipei department store, soldiers walking along the roads carrying stolen bicycles strapped to their backs.

As Kerr (2017: 81) puts it:

> For many years the mainland Chinese had had to endure the condescension implied in Western attempts to help 'backward heathens' develop modern techniques, but here they were being laughed at by their own people and an inferior people at that. That is, I think, one of the important keys to the situation on Formosa in all that followed.

4.5.5 The 22–8 Incident and its aftermath

In hindsight, sociolinguistic and socio-political tensions, and arbitrary and sometimes brutal state action, meant that the island was a powder keg. It would explode in the now notorious chain of events that began on February 27th, 1947, and forever remembered – though for decades taboo to mention – as the "2–28 Incident" for its aftermath the following day.

On February 27th, agents from the Monopoly Bureau found a woman peddler, Lin Jiang-mai, selling contraband cigarettes in a Taipei park. They seized her cash and tobacco and, in the ensuing fracas, beat her about the head with a pistol butt. An angry crowd surrounded the agents, one of whom fired a warning shot at the furious civilians; the shot killed an innocent bystander. The next day, some two thousand protesters marched on the Monopoly Bureau, demanding justice. They moved, fatefully, on to the Governor's office, where guards opened fire, killing four and seriously injuring two. A radio station briefly reported that a demonstration was underway, and soon crowds took to the streets across Taipei. The situation was quickly repeated in cities across the island. On the same day, Kerr poignantly notes, "martial law was declared at six o'clock as winter dusk settled over a tense, unhappy city" (2017: 212). Over the coming days, government troops would repeatedly turn their weapons on civilians, killing dozens and injuring hundreds. But this was just a taste of the violence to come.

Ethnic tensions in civil society came to a head, and for a brief period local Taiwanese mobs began to attack mainlanders. With little distinction in racial characteristics, the mainlanders were identified by the languages they spoke, turning the usual pattern of linguistic discrimination on its head. In the tumult, Dai Guo-hui, a Taiwanese writer, found himself confronted by one such gang. As a Hakka speaker, he was unable to speak the dominant Taiwanese language, Hoklo, when questioned. Thinking on his feet, Dai burst into a rendition of the Japanese national anthem, in Japanese (Dai and Ye 1992: 3, cited in Hughes 1997: 28). It saved his skin: he proved that he was not a mainlander by singing the language of Taiwan's former colonizers. Recalling the distinction between the Japanese as "dogs" and the Mainlanders as "pigs" mentioned above, and that

Taiwan is shaped like a yam or sweet potato, in his eyewitness account Kerr (2017: 211) writes that:

> Formosan schoolboys had an old joke in which they referred to the island as "Japan's sweet potato." Now mainlanders on the street were challenged "Are you sweet potato or are you pig?" and if the proper answer were not promptly forthcoming a hot chase took place, and sometimes a beating. (Kerr 2017: 211)

The events that transpired make for sobering reading. Chen Yi had stalled for time, adroitly manipulating Taiwanese civil society leaders for over a week, by sending out contradictory and confusing political messages. He had demurred on demands for the curbing of military power in society and more equal economic and political treatment for local Taiwanese, and vacillated on promises to lift Martial Law before imposing conditions that could not be reasonably met. Chiang Kai-shek, fearing an uprising on Taiwan when the civil war in China was beginning to tip in favour of the CCP, sent reinforcements. KMT troops, armed with American-made weapons, disembarked from ships that sailed silently into Keelung Harbour, north of Taipei. They marauded towards the capital, indiscriminately beating, raping, and murdering civilians and looting property as they went; within days they moved south to Kaohsiung and other major cities. If the first wave of KMT troops were seen as uncultured bumpkins and petty thieves, this was nothing compared to the wanton violence and sheer bloodlust now visited on Taiwan.

Community leaders and intellectuals were rounded up, tortured at length, and executed. Students and citizens who had assumed the role of guardians of law and order in the breakdown of KMT rule were identified and met the same fate; if they could not be found, another student or family member was taken hostage or executed in their place (Kerr 2017: 248–250). Schoolchildren and their teachers were liquidated, along with "anyone who in the preceding eighteen months had given offense to a mainland Chinese, causing him to 'lose face'" (Kerr 2017: 248–249). Finally, anyone who "spoke English reasonably well, or [...] had close foreign connections" was arraigned for interrogation (Kerr 2017: 249). The exact death toll from the massacre, which lasted for several weeks, is impossible to verify, and estimates range widely from 18,000 up to around 28,000, according to an Executive Yuan official report in 1992 (*Taipei Times* 2017). The massacre was the beginning of the White Terror period that would characterize the next few decades, during which perhaps tens of thousands more were disappeared, killed, or imprisoned for actual or suspected transgression including having Communist sympathies, opposing KMT dogma, or advocating for Taiwanese autonomy or independence. Ironically, Chen Yi would eventually meet his demise at the behest of Chiang

Kai-shek, who had him executed in 1950 ostensibly on charges of collaborating with the Communists while provincial chairman of KMT-held Zhejiang Province in China. It is hard to dismiss the possibility that Chiang's order was a punishment for Chen Yi's stunning mismanagement of the restive island to which the KMT would be exiled.

4.6 Martial law and the ROC in exile (1949–1987)

Although martial law was declared by Chen Yi after the 2–28 Incident in 1947, it was not made official in law until the "Temporary Provisions Effective During the Period of National Mobilization for Suppression of the Communist Rebellion" were put in place in Taiwan Province, effective May 20th, 1948, which formally suspended the Republic of China (ROC) constitution. In December 1949, effectively defeated by Mao's Communist forces on the mainland, Chiang Kai-shek and his Nationalist government retreated to Taiwan. Propped up with ideological, military, and economic support by the US as "free China", for decades they would officially cling on to the increasingly absurd delusion that they would eventually retake the mainland.[38]

4.6.1 Language, the state, and nationalism

After 1949, the Leninist (but not *Marxist*-Leninist) KMT party was isomorphic with the state; while two minor parties fled with the KMT, they had little influence and all new parties were banned (Hsiau 2000: 64). From the perspective of state theory, the KMT party-state was highly autonomous from civil society and inured from countervailing political and economic forces, both domestic and foreign (Gold 1994: 48). It well deserved the label "authoritarian"; state-society relations were structured in such a way that the state had enormous latitude in political, social, cultural, and economic affairs, and brooked no dissent under the White Terror program. Economic development offered opportunities for small businesses and entrepreneurs, and raised the general standard of living; as Gold (1994: 49) points out, this was a counterweight to government by sheer force, and

---

38 The ROC constitution was formally amended in 1991 to more accurately designate the territorial and jurisdictional distinction between the "Taiwan area" and the "Mainland area". Depending on the legal interpretation one takes, this may reflect the KMT's thwarted territorial ambitions. However, this question was not settled by the constitutional court when it came up in 1993 or subsequently. See Hwang (2012: 17–18).

"facilitated ... a perhaps grudgingly granted increase in the party-state's legitimacy". In most other respects, however, the KMT were heavy-handed and discriminatory, "alienating virtually all segments of the native population by inaugurating a military regime that treated Formosa as a conquered territory rather than a liberated area" (Meisner 1964: 147). Continuing Chen Yi's program, language policy was a key arena for the imposition of ideological and cultural power, with Mandarin-spread key to the twin nationalist projects of Sinification and de-Japanization. Quite clearly, the purpose of Mandarin-spread was to inculcate a "Chinese" national identity in the Taiwanese, since this was the only way in which the KMT could still lay claim to being the rightful government of all of China. The point was to align a single language with a single nation, since nationalism was a powerful – and perhaps the only – adjunct to the legitimacy of the single party-state.

Hiring for government positions favoured mainlanders, partly because many were associated with the KMT government in some form; partly because they were better educated than the local Taiwanese (and many educated Taiwanese had been killed in the 2–28 Incident); and partly, of course, because most of them knew at least some Mandarin (Tsao 2008a: 274). For more than two decades, then, the KMT effectively continued Chen Yi's initial combined policy of mainlander-favouring cronyism and the sociolinguistic Sinification of the administrative bureaucracy. Beginning in 1965, civil servants were required to use Mandarin during office hours (Hsiau 2000: 129). Orders from the state were promulgated in written Mandarin, though translation into Taiwanese languages took place, mainly through TV and radio broadcasts, for the benefit of the islanders; even authoritarian states must consider questions of practicality and political legitimacy in terms of enforcing orders that cannot be understood. But the burden of language learning was on the Taiwanese to learn Mandarin. As Hill Gates (1981: 263) puts it:

> Effective bilingual communication could have been established much more readily, had this been the only goal, by teaching the smaller group of generally literate mainlanders to speak [Hoklo] instead of obliging, as the KMT decided to do, millions of relatively unschooled Taiwanese to learn Mandarin. When we consider this fact, some of the political functions of making Mandarin the national language become more evident.

Gates is correct, at least at the macro-level of policymaking. However, some additional micro-level dimensions can be explored that suggest a more complex sociolinguistic situation. First, it is questionable whether the mainlanders, civilians in particular, would have been motivated to learn Hoklo beyond the absolute minimum: in addition to the effort needed to acquire Mandarin as a lingua franca if they did not already command it, ethnic tensions meant that they already held the Taiwanese, their culture, and their languages in low regard. Similarly, it seems doubtful whether many Hoklo speakers were willing to act as teachers to those who were perceived as invading colonizers; ethnic and political antagonisms obtained very early on. Second, in terms of interacting with Taiwanese, at least some bureaucrats, administrators, and police would have spoken mutually intelligible Southern Min; others likely picked up enough Hoklo in interactions to manage to communicate, or learned some of their own volition simply to do their jobs. A few may have done so because they quietly sympathized with the Taiwanese. Despite being officially monolingual, language practices in the bureaucracy must have been accommodating to some degree, since it could not have operated as such in practice, given the "relatively unschooled" islanders' inability (or, beyond the initial enthusiasm, unwillingness) to learn Mandarin quickly. As such, even the mighty KMT could not ensure the total dominance of Mandarin overnight in the operation of the state; there are, in other words, limits to status planning dictated peremptorily at the highest level.

To give a further example: a political wing was attached to the military to monitor pro-Communist tendencies and to drill soldiers of every rank into obedience to the KMT, and in the 1940s and 1950s, new recruits were encouraged to enrol in a Mandarin course first (Tsao 2008a: 254). However, as one former conscript wrote:

> In the Nationalist Army the use of the Japanese language was not permitted, but we Formosans used Japanese loudly on purpose. It was not by accident that we wrote letters in Japanese. We knew our letters were censored but we wrote them in the prohibited language intentionally. It was not from our love of Japan that we used Japanese, but the use of it certainly had a nuisance value as our tiny means of retaliation against the Nationalist regime. (Cited in Meisner 1964: 158)

The Japanese language was also a site for resistance in daily life. Despite officially banning it from the public sphere, as with the bureaucracy the KMT's reach was limited in terms of instant transformation of sociolinguistic reality. There were, however, generational differences in passive or active resistance. In 1964, Meisner wrote that

> Formosan "cultural nationalism" has taken the form of the continued use of the Japanese language and the maintenance of a variety of Japanese social habits and styles of life. For the older generation of Formosans, the use of the Japanese language and Japanese customs is largely a matter of habit. For younger Formosans it is usually a deliberate effort to assert their Formosan identity. (Meisner 1964: 158)

Notably, it was not yet a case of articulating a pro-independence, nationalist Taiwanese identity through the use of Hoklo or Hakka, perhaps ironically because these languages were not banned and thus perhaps were less effective in goading the mainlanders. But just before the end of Martial Law – somewhat surprisingly given the relative softening of Chiang Ching-kuo from the mid-1970s after his father's death – Hsiau (2000: 131) notes that banning local languages was seriously being considered:

> From 1983 to 1985, the Ministry of Education drafted the Language Law, one article of which stated that only the national language could be used in a public meeting, official business, and conversation in public domains. However, confronted with increasing public objection, the Ministry eventually abandoned the attempt to have the Language Law enacted.

4.6.1.1 Language in education

As Tsao (2008a: 249) relates, following Kubler (1985), the NCPPNL took an active role in discussions about the reconstruction of Taiwan as early as 1944, when Japanese defeat seemed probable. This left the committee poised to set up the infrastructure needed for Mandarin-spread after the KMT took control, with a contingent of educators and language planners, headed by a philologist and a grammarian, arriving in Taiwan in November 1945. With few qualified teachers to staff the Mandarin institutes, some thirty primary school teachers from Fujian Province, proficient in Mandarin and presumably Southern Min – mutually intelligible with Hoklo – and several dozen students from universities across the mainland, were drafted in to assist (Tsao 2008a: 249). Aside from the lack of qualifications to become teachers, it perhaps also points to the limited knowledge, in general, of Mandarin in the mainlander communities beyond a lingua franca, as we have already discussed. In 1959, the Taiwan provincial subcommittee of the NCPPNL was abolished (though it would be resurrected again in 1980), and replaced with a committee under the Department of Education. The reasons behind this are a matter for some intrigue. Ostensibly, the objectives of standardization and propagation were deemed to have been achieved, and promotion of the national language could be continued via efforts of the media, schools, and state-defined civil society as a whole, and these efforts could be co-ordinated by a lower-level committee (Tsao, 2008a: 251). The underlying rationale, however, seems to be that Mandarin spread among adult citizens was simply not as effective as had been hoped, at least after the initial enthusiasm for language classes had waned.

"Promotion of the national language" through compulsory education in state schools had several clear advantages. Mandarin immersion through medium of instruction could be blended with the Nationalist curriculum, thus ensuring that the habit of *speaking* Chinese could be cultivated alongside *thinking* as Chinese. Schoolchildren were also captive audiences, and much more susceptible to both language learning and uncritical acceptance of nationalist ideology. This was greatly assisted by the institutional structure of the education system – the KMT had brought their mainland innovations and grafted them onto the existing Japanese structures – which ensured a deep link between the state and the individual, effectively bypassing countervailing influences of civil society. The KMT apparently realized this sometime before abolishing the Taiwan provincial subcommittee of the NCPPNL. In 1956, non-Mandarin languages were banned in schools. Notoriously, children were punished – with apparently ever-increasing degrees of ingenious cruelty – for speaking these languages during school hours, policed by roaming groups of older, or more ideologically fervent, students.

Mainlanders were disproportionately represented as teachers in the education system (Gates 1981: 257). The effect of this, of course, was to render Mandarin as the sole medium of communication in the entire education system, particularly since austere language policing measures presumably remedied any defects in language pedagogy itself. As Tsao (2008a: 274) relates, directly or indirectly "students were taught that it was unethical and unpatriotic to speak their mother tongue if it was a language other than Mandarin". Evidently seeing results on the language and ideology front, though the economic exigencies of industrialization doubtless had some influence, in 1968 the six-year curriculum (that is, from the first year of primary school) was extended to nine-years. Two years later, the Department of Education prioritized "strengthening Mandarin in the schools", if this were at all possible. In terms of national policy, things would change little until the lifting of Martial Law in 1987, as we will see in chapter five. Some liberalization may have occurred outside of the purview of official state policy, especially in individual counties and schools, but in general there were few points of resistance for children within the educational system itself. For Hsiau (2000: 129), adopting Bourdieu's (1991) position:

> the educational system plays a decisive role in the construction, legitimization and imposition of an official language, which helps to fashion the similarities from which a community of consciousness derives, the cement of the nation ... In Taiwan, school plays this part rather successfully.

4.6.2 Language and the public sphere

Certainly, the KMT state was highly autonomous from society more broadly, and highly immune to countervailing social, political, and economic forces.

Furthermore, through its authoritarian system it controlled key parts of civil society and the public sphere throughout martial law. Mandarin-spread was highly successful, being inculcated in schools and acting as a gatekeeper to jobs in the party-state. But ideological and sociolinguistic control was never total, and there were numerous points of resistance. I briefly review some of these in what follows, examining the role of language in broadcasting and the media.

The KMT made adept use of the broadcast media and press to control a key part of the public sphere, to both impose ideological orthodoxy and suppress local language use in favour of Mandarin-spread. After the 2–28 Incident, the government-run *Hsin-Hseng* newspaper published an editorial describing as "criminals" those editors and reporters from non-government publications who were stirring up their readership – Mandarin-literate university students in particular – with anti-KMT rhetoric. As Rawnsley (2004: 210) relates, however, these outlets were not shuttered but brought into line, with varying degrees of coercion, in terms of transmitting the KMT's ideological world view: the superiority of Chinese identity over those of the islanders, the retaking-the-mainland narrative, and unquestioning deference to Chiang Kai-shek. A press ban in 1951 refused new newspaper licenses, restricting the number to thirty-one until 1987; the English-language *China Post* seems to have been exempted, beginning publication in 1952 and designed to spread the KMT's perspective to the world, and US audiences in particular.

Broadcast media was even more strictly controlled. Unlike newspapers, understanding radio and television broadcasts does not require literacy, making them even more effective as mass media. Radio stations were not all government owned – the KMT had to make some outward ideological pretence at capitalism to justify being called "free China" by the US – but commercial stations belonged to members of the elite (Lee 2000: 113). Aware of the combined power of sound and image, affectations to free enterprise were dropped when it came to the three television stations: one each were owned by the government, the KMT party, and the military, which amounted to the same thing (Lee 2000: 113). Restrictions were imposed on non-Mandarin language programming from the opening of the first television station in 1962, though these were not always adhered to: Hoklo programming, consisting of "soap operas, puppet shows, traditional Taiwanese operas, and commercials" reached a zenith around 1971; in 1972, radio and television programming in Hoklo was limited to one hour per day by the Bureau of Culture, and in 1976, the Radio and Television Law required a minimum of 55% and 70% Mandarin-language programming, respectively, and policy would become more restrictive over time (Hsiau 2000: 130).

But total ideological and sociolinguistic control of the public sphere was thwarted by several factors. These included left-wing reformist elements in the

KMT itself, as well as the commercial objectives of the press in a competitive marketplace, which sometimes outweighed political purism. More significantly, a burgeoning underground press and, later, pirate (or "free") radio constituted an alternative public sphere for subaltern counterpublics whose politics and languages were otherwise marginalized. Magazines – notable examples include *Formosa* and *Free China* – proliferated, since they were not covered by the 1951 press ban, which curiously only applied to newspapers. This alternative public sphere was not merely deliberative in the Habermasian sense, but a site for state-oppositional conflict and, as such, performed certain civil society functions. As Rawnsley (2004: 211) notes:

> Because the KMT prohibited the formation of political parties outside its control, underground publications provided a training ground for activists, eager to learn the arts of political participation, competition, and mobilisation. They performed many of the same functions as traditional political parties: they provided the movement with ideological direction, opportunities for patronage, the aggregation of interests, and the recruitment and training of leaders. (Rawnsley 2004: 211)

Pirate radio constituted important underground resistance in broadcast media. This is a highly subversive mass medium, which, again, does not require literacy, and is not confined to elites. Broadcasting in Hoklo and Hakka, pirate radio proliferated in Taiwan in the early 1990s and was well established by 1994, following the relaxation of the broadcasting laws and the climate of political liberalization more generally (Minns 2006: 216; Baker p.c.). However, Rigger (1999: 149) and Rampal (2011: 70) trace its emergence to earlier in the 1980s. Pirate radio became an outlet for radical political thought from the then-illegal *Tangwai* (or outside-the-party) movement, with its general secretary, Lin Chia-lung, operating perhaps the earliest station (Rampal 2011: 70–71). The *Tangwai* movement would eventually crystallize as the Democratic Progressive Party (DPP), which was formed in 1986. Later, pirate radio would be a democratic space for Taiwan's various social movements – such as labour and women's rights (see Hsiao 2011) – to jostle for the attention of the public (Rampal 2011).

4.7 Conclusion

From inauspicious beginnings characterized by violence and chaos, the Japanese went on to consolidate power in Taiwan, turning it into a productive agricultural colony with a relatively well-developed infrastructure and, for the most part, an ordered society with some limited opportunities for contesting the state in the public sphere. However, colonial rule was conducted with a rod of iron, and structured by racialized notions of Japanese superiority that, in important ways, shaped attitudes to the social organization and political representation of the Taiwanese inhabitants. Language was key to the assimilationist programs that began in limited ways in the early years of rule, were accelerated under the *doka* era, and became the organizing logic of colonial administration in the final few years of rule during the *kominka* era. Opportunities to develop proficiency in Japanese were initially withheld from the islanders for practical and ideological reasons; with the exigencies of the second Sino-Japanese war, the colonial state developed incentive schemes for learning Japanese that created a distinct and privileged category of citizenship for Japanese speakers.

The Japanese did not, however, succeed in eradicating Hoklo or Hakka, even if they managed to marginalize these languages in public and political life. Some indigenous languages fared slightly worse in terms of their survival, thanks to assimilation and pacification efforts, although the mountainous languages were still viable at the beginning of KMT rule in 1945 as a result of their isolation. Even so, both Kerr (1974: 167) and Lamley (1999: 228) remark on the effects of Japanese-spread on the possibilities of intra-group communication among indigenous groups through having a common language for the first time. This would become politically salient in subsequent generations; it marked a tentative collective indigenous identity. At the same time, somewhat paradoxically, it is important to note that Japanese rule created individual indigenous "nations", newly settled into villages with Japanese toponyms, where they did not exist before (Simon 2015), and constructed partly around sociolinguistic boundaries that, if not wholly "invented", in Makoni and Pennycook's (2007) term, were certainly sharpened through ethnic and political distinctions.

Under the KMT, Mandarin-spread was aggressively pursued and, on its face, highly successful. Within a generation or two, Mandarin was spoken or understood by the majority of the Taiwanese population, especially among younger and more educated people. As might be expected, there is evidence of language shift towards Mandarin monolingualism, with a degree of attrition in local languages. However, it did not cause *total* language shift, with bilingualism in Japanese, Hoklo, Hakka, or the indigenous languages still prevalent at the end of martial law. Politically, Taiwanese perceptions and articulations of KMT rule were in important senses structured by a lament, albeit one highly romanticized, for the relatively benign and stable Japanese occupation. As Phillips (2003: 40) notes:

> It is not clear what the Taiwanese "knew" had occurred during [Japanese] colonial rule or what they had experienced personally as opposed to the history they constructed in public though speeches, oral histories, and essays ... Nevertheless, that so many Taiwanese said

> or wrote similar things on the positive aspects of [Japanese] colonial rule, the defects of the Nationalist provincial administrators, their difference from Mainland China, and the resulting need for self-government indicates that these ideas rang true to their fellow islanders. (Phillips 2003: 40)

Independence and self-government were themes that would continue to develop throughout the KMT era, and in part these were structured by the desire for the freedom to speak local languages. Only relatively late – during the drafting of the Ministry of Education's Language Law between 1983 and 1985 (Hsiau 2000: 131) – did the KMT regime seriously contemplate explicitly banning local languages from public life. It came at a time when the political climate, following Chiang Kai-shek's death in 1975, was substantially liberalizing. One explanation, then, is that the final repression of languages in civil society and the public sphere was a last grasp at power of a regime that sensed seismic changes were coming.

5 Democratization, pluralism, and multilingualism

5.1 Introduction

From the beginning, the KMT had little legitimacy in the eyes of many Taiwanese. Not everyone, after all, was happy to see the backs of the Japanese, and while official discourses would portray the KMT as a liberating force returning Taiwan to the motherland, what goodwill the KMT may have had was squandered early on with the 2-28 Incident and Chiang Kai-shek's White Terror purges. Coercion became the standard modality for extracting social, cultural, and political compliance with KMT rule. However, by the 1970s, local, national, and international political forces began to converge and create the conditions for liberalization. At the international level, in 1971 the United Nations and several major countries switched diplomatic recognition from the KMT's Taiwan-based ROC to the PRC in Beijing; in 1979, the US – which had backed the KMT's "free China" against the communists on the mainland – belatedly followed suit, as Cold War geopolitical pragmatism began to win out over ideological purism. Weighing pragmatism over purism was not Chiang Kai-shek's forte, however; he turned down a seat at the UN under the name of Taiwan, resolutely claiming instead to be the legitimate government of China, a critical juncture that would strand the island in geopolitical exile for decades to come. On Chiang Kai-shek's death in 1975, his son Chiang Ching-kuo assumed power, first as KMT party leader and, three years later, as President of the ROC. Nationally and locally, a nascent movement for democratic reform and national self-determination began to take root in the 1970s and 1980s, though democracy was not won easily. The KMT's attempts at repressing local languages became a highly symbolic rallying point, and democratization would become inexorably linked with multilingualism (Wang, H. 2005).

This chapter begins by politically contextualizing democratic reform from the late 1970s onwards, before turning to the role of language in the democratization process after the lifting of martial law in 1987, including the use of local languages by politicians during election campaigns. DPP language policies between 2000 and 2008 are then addressed. The section begins by discussing the DPP's *bentuhua* program, with was a form of nationalist cultural politics that claimed a distinct, pan-ethnic, and multilingual Taiwanese identity but stopped short of a call for outright political independence. The chapter then turns to transitional justice dimensions of the ultimately unsuccessful National Language Equality Law (NLEL) and National Language Development Law (NLDL), particularly with regard to the potential for different scenarios of language officialization to meet transitional justice measures and goals. It then examines language-in-education policies during the DPP era, using ethnographic and interview data from 2007 to understand how local autonomy and differentiated socio-economic, sociolinguistic, and party-political factors influenced variegated access to mother-tongue language education (MTLE). The final section of the chapter investigates what – if anything – changed under the return of the KMT, who governed between 2008 and 2016.

5.2 The context of democratic reform (1979–1987)

Chiang Ching-kuo succeeded his father Chiang Kai-shek on the latter's death in 1975, first as KMT party leader then, three years later, as president. The younger Chiang shared his father's ideological commitment that Taiwan was an ineffable part of China, but – at least later in his tenure – differed in his more pragmatic attitude that rule through legitimacy was preferable to rule solely through coercion. While Chiang Ching-kuo was not averse to using the repressive apparatus of the state where necessary, he began slow and gradual approaches to political reform and liberalization, including an emphasis on increased equality between mainlander and native Taiwanese citizens, particularly through more balanced representation in politics and the bureaucracy (Jacobs 2016: 50–51). To some degree, Chiang Ching-kuo appears to have undertaken some genuine soul-searching in terms of his own politics and identity vis-à-vis Taiwan (Jacobs 2005: 33). To a greater extent, however, his position was shaped by an emergent democratization movement in civil society, that both influenced and was influenced by the weakening of the KMT state to the extent that it could no longer rule by dictatorial fiat alone.[39]

Political opposition to the KMT was galvanized in the aftermath of the Kaohsiung Incident of 1979, in which troops brutally quelled a pro-democracy and pro-human rights demonstration organized by the editorial board of *Formosa Magazine*, a group of *Tangwai* – or "outside the party" – political dissidents who were subsequently tried and imprisoned under sentences ranging from twelve years to life.[40] They escaped the mandatory sentence of execution for sedition, largely because the KMT were cognizant of the glare of the international

---

39 With that said, Jacobs (2016: 50–51) draws a distinction between liberalization and democratization, with the latter only instigated in any meaningful form by Lee Teng-hui, after Chiang Ching-kuo's death in 1988.
40 *Formosa Magazine* took its name from the Portuguese term for "beautiful island", which Taiwan was christened in 1544 by Portuguese sailors. Notably, Portugal did not attempt to colonize the island, and thus the magazine's name was an unabashed anti-imperialist stance.

community, which had already begun to diplomatically abandon the ROC in favour of the PRC, but also due to the work of two enterprising young lawyers, Chen Shui-bian and Frank Hsieh. As is now well known, Chen would go on to become the first DPP president between 2000 and 2008, while Hsieh would serve as premier. Fellow defendants Annette Lu, Chen Chu, Peng Ming-min, and Shih Ming-teh all became DPP heavyweights. Forged in the crucible of the *Tangwai* movement and the Kaohsiung Incident, the DPP was officially formed in September 1986, although opposition parties would not be technically legal for another half a decade. That year, the KMT announced that martial law was to be lifted, and this came to pass on July 14th, 1987. Until it was surpassed by Syria in 2011, Taiwan's martial law period was the longest in the world, at thirty-eight years and fifty-seven days.

5.3 Language and democratization (1987–2000)

As the gravitational centre of power shifted, the politics of multilingualism became fundamental to the contestation of state control and appeals to support from within civil society. For the DPP, the KMT's repression of local languages in favour of Mandarin was indexical of its repression of a distinctive Taiwanese political identity. For the KMT, conceding ground on sociolinguistic issues was presumably seen as a way to defuse more strident claims for outright democratization, which aligned with its gradual approaches to liberalization and political reform in general. In 1987, punishment for speaking non-Mandarin languages in schools was banned. Although far from a comprehensive reconsideration of language policies, it came symbolically in the same year that martial law was lifted. The edict proclaimed that:

> At every junior high school and elementary school in the province [of Taiwan] it is not permitted to continue the practice of using physical punishment, issuing fines, or using other such improper means to punish students for speaking dialects on school grounds. (Huang 1995: 57–8, cited in Sandel 2003: 530)

Doubtless this had immediate and concrete effects for schoolchildren at the sharpest end of policy implementation, but it had powerful symbolic dimensions in the broader political context: it was perhaps a recognition that coercive language policies were metaphors for state-society relations in general, and that these were in urgent in need of reform. The edict continued:

> The Bureau of Education points out that in recent years ... in implementing the national language policy, their methods have gone astray. Toward dialect speaking students the

means of punishment have been to hang the placard, hit heads, issue fines, and use other degrees of punishment. These measures have provoked people to falsely believe that the purpose of the government's national language policy is to eliminate dialects. (Huang 1995: 57–8, cited in Sandel 2003: 530)

It is difficult to understand what, if not to "eliminate dialects", the "purpose of the government's national language policy" actually was, especially given that between 1981 and 1983 the KMT had given serious consideration to banning non-Mandarin languages from public life entirely (Hsiau 2000: 131). But, assuming there was any truth in the government's assertion, it seems there was a recognition that the means of the language policy had long eclipsed whatever ends were in mind. The state's response, in part, was to blame the bureaucrats for overzealous interpretation of policy, which seems on its face to be a convenient scapegoating. However, as if to underscore their commitment to reform, the government eased restrictions on TV and radio broadcasting in non-Mandarin languages, which had become increasingly prohibitive since 1976 (Huang 2000: 144; Wei 2008: 21). In November 1987, three government TV stations began broadcasting news in Hoklo (Klöter 2006: 211).

Lifting martial law and some of its associated language restrictions was one of Chiang Ching-kuo's final acts before his death in 1988, and it appears to have coincided with a period of reflection and reassessment of his politics and identity. Less than two weeks after reinstating civilian rule of law, Chiang apparently told a dozen elderly people that "*wo yeshi Taiwanren*" or "I am also Taiwanese", which represented a turning away from China in spite of his commitment to unification (Jacobs 2005: 33; see 52 fn.63 for more context of the exchange). He also seemed to consider the role of a common language in vertical terms of the fundamental democratic requirement of a leader to communicate with the polity:

> Toward the end of his life, President [Chiang Ching-kuo] regretted that – unlike President Lee Kuan Yew of Singapore with whom he travelled around Taiwan – he could not speak [Hoklo] to talk to his own people. (Jacobs 2005: 33)

In 1984, Chiang Ching-kuo had nominated a native-born Taiwanese and accomplished state administrator, Lee Teng-hui, for vice-president, and he was duly officially elected by the national assembly. Lee succeeded to the presidency on Chiang's death in 1988. Lee was a peacemaker and a pragmatist, granting KMT rivals influential positions in his government. However, he was primarily a fearless reformist and a democrat, abolishing remnants of anti-dissent laws, and meeting with "Wild Lily" student demonstrators in 1990 to assure them that Taiwan was on the path to full democratic elections

(Tsai 2005: 179). He made good on his promise; the first democratic elections were held in 1996, with Lee comfortably winning the presidency (54% to 21.1%) against rival Peng Ming-min of the opposition DPP. The PRC sabre-rattled during the election, launching missiles into the Taiwan Strait and conducting military manoeuvres. This was a warning against formerly-exiled Peng Ming-min's outspoken nationalism and fiercely pro-independence standpoint. However, it was also directed at Lee's increasing advocacy of a "New Taiwanese" identity, which the PRC believed amounted to the same thing by different, softer means. In a speech in 1994, Lee had brought up the issue of language as it related to Taiwanese identity, which is worth quoting in its entirety here:

> I am more than seventy years old. Having lived under different regimes, from Japanese colonialism to Taiwan's recovery, I have greatly experienced the miseries of the Taiwanese people. In the period of Japanese colonialism, a Taiwanese would be punished by being forced to kneel out in the sun for speaking [Taiwanese languages]. The situation was the same when Taiwan was recovered: my son, Hsien-wen, and my daughter-in-law, Yüeh-yün, often wore a dunce board around their necks in the school as punishment for speaking [Taiwanese languages]. I am very aware of the situation because I often go to the countryside to talk to people. Their lives are influenced by history. I think the most miserable people are Taiwanese, who have always tried in vain to get their heads above the water. This was the Taiwanese situation during the period of Japanese colonialism; it was not any different after Taiwan's recovery. I have deep feeling about this. (Quoted in and translated by Hsiau 1997: 302)[41]

As Hsiau puts it, "this is an excellent summary of the past 100 years' history of the political suppression of Taiwan's local languages" (1997: 302). Language is indexical of the broader political struggle of the Taiwanese against two successive colonial regimes; as has already been argued, punishment for speaking local languages in schools is a metaphor for the coercive and arbitrary state more broadly, but it is also highly symbolic of the historical political humiliation of the Taiwanese people. What is crucial here is that Lee, as a sitting KMT president, is making this link explicit in the context of democratization. The admission of wrongdoing constitutes one form of language-based transitional justice, an issue to which we will return to in more detail later in this chapter. It came in the broader context of a re-evaluation of the role of Hoklo – and to a

---

[41] Lee used the term "tai-yu" ("Taiwan language"), which Hsiau renders verbatim in his translation in pinyin. Usually, and not without some controversy, this word refers to Hoklo, although Lee Teng-hui was ethnically Hakka. I have rendered this here as the literal gloss "Taiwanese languages" to give it the broadest meaning in the context.

lesser extent Hakka and indigenous languages – in public and political life.[42] As Wei (2008: 21, after Tse 2000: 161) puts it, some Taiwanese

> took a more drastic political stance ... feelings of resentment and inferiority ... found an outlet and even a platform ... [T]here was a trend toward the increased use of [Taiwanese languages] as a symbol of defiance against the establishment, as an expression of democratization, as a sign of localism, and as an assertion of ethnolinguistic identity. (Wei 2008: 21)

Indeed, as a report from *The Economist* in 1993 observed,

> Opposition politicians are discovering that the language can be a useful political tool. In parliament, they have recently taken to questioning government officials in [Hoklo], knowing the bureaucrats could not understand, simply to embarrass them. (*The Economist* 1993: n.p.)

Policymakers were astute enough to respond to the ways that language politics were shifting in state and civil society relations. By 1990, Yilan County was offering elective classes in non-Mandarin languages in its elementary and junior high schools (Klöter 2006: 211); by 1993, a number of county education bureaus – an article in *The Economist* (1993) reported seven, all in nativist anti-KMT heartlands – were encouraging the teaching of non-Mandarin languages in elementary school, leading to broader discussion of mother-tongue language education implementation (Wei 2008: 21). After Lee's election in 1996, the KMT sought to re-write language policies to actively promote and protect Hoklo and also Taiwan's other non-Mandarin languages (Klöter 2004; Cabestan 2005). In 1997, Article 10 was formally added to the ROC constitution, which stated that "the State affirms cultural pluralism and shall actively preserve and foster the development of aboriginal languages and cultures". This constitutional provision mirrored the provisions of the UNDRM and UNDRIP; the fact that Taiwan was not bound to these as an unrecognized state indicates its ambitions towards liberal democratic credentials and recognition from the international community. By 2000, progress on these issues was such that Tse (2000: 157) was optimistic enough to declare that "there is hope ... for the development of a multilingual and multicultural society where all languages and cultures will become truly equal in the not too distant future".

---

42 From 1995, indigenous names were allowed to be used on official identification cards, though only rendered "phonetically" in Mandarin characters. The Mandarin character requirement was dropped by 2006.

5.4 On the campaign trail

If the use of Hoklo was an act of oppositional political defiance, it had the effect of forcing mainlander KMT elites to use it as an act of deference, particularly on the campaign trail. In preparation for the 1996 elections, several top KMT leaders – including Chiang Hsiao-yen, grandson of Chiang Kai-shek, and then-justice minister (and later Taipei mayor and Taiwanese president) Ma Ying-jeou – had taken to learning Hoklo (Hsiau 2000: 126). Crucially, they ensured that their efforts were well publicized, extending to crooning popular karaoke songs in Hoklo on the stump. While "their proficiency and fluency could never match that of native speakers ... their efforts in [Hoklo] won them sympathy and support" and, of course, votes (Wei 2008: 40); "learning [Hoklo] represents the efforts of the [KMT] to 'localize' itself and win the support of the dominant ethnic group" (Hsiau 1997: 304). Indeed, Hughes (2011: 66) even suggests that, by the late 1990s, the increased use of Hoklo in the DPP primaries "effectively exclud[ed] Mandarin speakers from the democratic process". When, while canvassing for votes in 1998, Taipei mayoral candidate Ma Ying-jeou was asked by President Lee if he was a mainlander or a Taiwanese, "Ma replied in [Hoklo] that he was a 'new Taiwanese', drinking Taiwan water and eating Taiwan rice" (Teufel Dreyer 2003: 404–5). Even if this was clearly a bit of theatre, campaigning as a monolingual Mandarin mainlander was a political non-starter.

New presidential elections were held in 2000. Language proficiency again became indexical of political support during the campaigns. Lien Chan's failure – the KMT stalwart finished third far behind KMT-turned-independent candidate James Soong, with the DPP's Chen Shui-bian narrowly taking the presidency and ending fifty years of continuous Nationalist Party rule – is partly attributed to his general aloofness. However, he was not helped by his faltering Hoklo, his proficiency being perhaps as expected for a Hoklo raised on the mainland (Teufel Dreyer 2003: 406). Soong, on the other hand, had made serious attempts to learn Hoklo, or at least convinced many voters that that was the case.

Chen Shui-bian, meanwhile, used his existing multilingual resources to his political advantage. A southerner from Tainan, he rose from humble beginnings as a tenant farmer's son to graduate with a law degree from the prestigious National Taiwan University, formerly Taihoku University under Japanese rule. Being born in 1950, Chen was among the first generation to be educated in Mandarin. As an educated lawyer, Chen was conversant in the most formal, overtly prestigious, and standardized Taiwan Mandarin variety propagated officially by the KMT's Mandarin-spread policy. Chen used this acrolectal variety in most formal situations, though he spoke – or, for some, contrived to speak – the covertly prestigious basilectal form when communicating with his core political constituency.[43] In addition, he spoke Hoklo, and codeswitched between this and Mandarin varieties in political speeches. Wei (2008: 43–51) analyzes several of Chen's speeches between 1989 and 2001, demonstrating the highly strategic use of codeswitching with different audiences and to different effects, including the use of puns, rhetorical questions, and aphorisms known in Mandarin as *chengyu*. This has a symbolic, rather than practical dimension; it is designed to index a political identity and a political stance, rather than convey the intricacies of policy.

The use of Hoklo in political discourse is problematic, however, in that it only addresses the majority ethnic group, and not the 20% or so Hakka or the 2% indigenous peoples. Not without some justification, Hakka activist and former Hsinchu County Commissioner Fan Chen-tsung is said to have criticized "the great [Hoklo]-language chauvinism permeating the DPP" (Chang 1999: 8), and this was a problem with the DPP's conception of "Taiwan" and "Taiwanese-ness" more broadly. Politicians cannot afford to ignore the Hakka vote: they do not always vote as a unified bloc, nor consistently along party lines, and they are numerous enough to potentially play kingmakers (Martin 2005: 183). To mitigate the charge of ethnolinguistic chauvinism, Chen Shui-bian shrewdly took to campaigning in Hakka, being, as Teufel Dreyer (2003: 406) notes, the first non-Hakka to do so. This had practical as well as symbolic dimensions: many elderly speakers could speak only Hakka and Japanese, having missed out on Mandarin education and with little reason to acquire Hoklo given the relatively sociolinguistically homogenous rural areas in which Hakka traditionally live. Speaking in Hakka was one way to directly communicate the DPP's platform and policies.

As a political variable influencing voting behaviour, the significance of Hakka language use in political campaigns in the 2000 election is not entirely clear. Certainly, demonstrating solidarity through language use cannot have hurt Chen's performance, but Lien Chan and James Soong did not campaign in Hakka and still managed to win around 70% of the Hakka vote between them. The better explanatory variable is the deep integration of local Hakka politicians into KMT networks, particularly in the Hakka heartland counties of Taoyuan, Miaoli, and Hsinchu (and Hsinchu City) in the north. Furthermore, Soong and Lien Chan promised political positions for prominent Hakka. However, assuming that at least some Hakka are indeed swayed by issues of ethnolinguistic identity and do not merely vote out of rational calculation (c.f. Lee et al 2016), Chen's efforts at

---

43 See the discussion in chapter four of the possibility that Taiwan Mandarin is a creoloid variety that exhibits certain creole like features (such as the acrolectal-basilectal continuum) but is not a full creole.

speaking Hakka may have had some effect. While Chen came second to Soong in terms of raw vote tallies, he garnered 120,000 more Hakka votes than DPP strategists predicted he would need to win (Teufel Dreyer 2003: 406fn46).

In comparison, Chen did not campaign, at least to any notable extent, in indigenous languages, but politically there was perhaps not much point. Despite being officially separated into sixteen separate "tribes" based on linguistic (and cultural) distinctions that may in themselves have been invented under Japanese rule (Simon 2015), indigenous peoples are a more predictable and unified voting bloc than the Hakka and, at around 530,000 people or 2.3% of the population, could only be theoretical kingmakers in a very close election. In any case, at least until recently, indigenous groups consistently vote KMT over other parties, for a number of reasons: the indigenous groups have a historical animosity against the Hoklo due to centuries of ill-treatment, and the KMT had – as with the northern Hakka – successfully integrated its patronage system deeply into indigenous local politics (Simon 2012: 123; Rawnsley and Gong 2012: 100).

5.5 DPP language policies (2000–2008)

As has become clear in previous chapters, language has been a convenient way to differentiate Taiwan's different ethnic groups; whether imposed exogenously or derived endogenously, language is a means to create a shared "cultural interpretation of descent" (Keyes 1981: 4, in Constable 2005: 8). Language can be seen, for activists and citizens, as a relatively unbroken link to a shared cultural past, or at least a link that can be recovered through language maintenance and revitalization. As such, the dominant language ideology of *bentuhua* is peculiar compared to most historical and many contemporary nationalisms; it is multilingual rather than monolingual, and thus its language ideology corresponds more closely to sociolinguistic reality. Arguably, this correspondence is to a large degree part of its success. Embracing multilingualism has been a visible way to invoke ethnic equality, though it is far from uncontentious. It is to these issues we now turn, examining the transitional justice dimensions of DPP language policies between 2000 and 2008. Before doing so, it is necessary to contextualize the nationalist political project of *bentuhua*.

5.5.1 The cultural politics of *bentuhua:* Equality without independence

The concept of *bentuhua* is a synthesis of ethno-cultural equality, democratization, national identity, and self-determination but, as Jacobs (2005) and others have noted, it defies easy translation into English. A literal gloss is "original culture", though this loses the connotations in Mandarin and Hoklo of a process rather than a noun. A closer translation is thus "localization", though this contains a political implication that Taiwan is a local province of greater China (Jacobs 2005: 18), which is in fact the opposite political identity and orientation that *bentuhua* seeks to achieve. "Indigenization" (e.g. Schubert and Braig 2007: 7; Makeham 2005: 11) is another option, but it unavoidably refers to Taiwan's indigenous peoples at the exclusion of the rest of the island's population. Jacobs suggests that "Taiwanization" is the more appropriate term; Jacobs (2005: 17) quotes Lee Teng-hui as saying that "the goal of democratization, speaking simply, is the *Taiwanization of Taiwan*" (emphasis added). This has the added irony of being precisely what, in those very same terms, Governor Chen Yi tried to avoid by stuffing the immediate post-war bureaucracy with Mandarin-speaking mainlanders. Makeham (2005: 1) offers a similar definition; the *bentuhua* movement is a reaction against historical colonial oppression, and has "functioned as a type of nationalism that champions the legitimacy of a distinct Taiwanese identity, the character and content of which should be determined by the Taiwanese people".

In practice, *bentuhua* is the yoking together of several (often competing) subnational groups into a common and equitable pan-ethnic national identity. It has faced criticisms that it frames multiculturalism and politics in general as narrowly focused on ethnicity (Ngo and Wang 2011; Simon 2011). *Bentuhua*, in its implementation, has sometimes privileged Hoklo ethnicity over others, Han Chinese over indigenous groups, and only "Taiwanese" ethnicities over those of, for example, new immigrants. As Horowitz observes, "ethnicity is one of those forces that is community-building in moderation, community-destroying in excess" (1985: 13). Indeed, one of the functions of *bentuhua* is to sharpen the distinctions between these identities even as it seeks to unify them; in order to celebrate ethnic difference, it must have ethnic difference to work with. As Comaroff and Comaroff (1992: 54, cited in Constable 2005: 8) point out, "ethnicity has its origins in the asymmetric incorporation of structurally dissimilar groupings into a single political economy". Constable (2005: 8) adds to this that "the asymmetric or unequal relationships between ethnic groups is of central importance, as it is from awareness of inequality, not merely cultural difference, that ethnic consciousness develops".

As with many comparable nationalisms, *bentuhua* has both political/civic and ethnic/cultural dimensions. The political question is structured by the existential threat from Taiwan's larger and better-armed neighbour across the Strait, which believes Taiwan is a renegade province to be "reunited" by force if necessary, and aims some 1,600 missiles at the island to underscore its point.

Typically, the KMT have been in favour of greater rapprochement with China, though stopping short of voluntary unification (which would anger many Taiwanese); the DPP have been in favour of increased autonomy for Taiwan in the international sphere, while refraining from calling for outright independence (which would anger China). Although there are fringe elements and parties on both ends of the unification-independence continuum, both the major parties have been squeezed into an ideological middle ground, which both reflects and constructs popular opinion (Fell 2007). National Cheng Chi University Election Study Center survey data (ESC 2017b) shows that moving towards declaring independence (22.9%) was more popular in 2016 than moving towards unification with China (10.2%), a general trend since 1994. However, a plurality of 59.4% favour maintaining the status quo, likely for pragmatic reasons to avoid war; they are presumably content with Taiwan remaining as a de facto, but not de jure, independent state with limited international privileges as the price for peace. As such, without a juridical-political outlet in the international sphere, *bentuhua* finds expression in national cultural politics or, perhaps seen another way, as a highly-politicized type of national culture and identity.

In terms of ethnic and cultural dimensions, a further ESC survey (ESC 2017a) provides a bellwether of how national identity, and attitudes to identity, have shifted over time.[44] Between 1992 and 2016, the percentage of non-respondents has fallen, likely due to a decreased fear in expressing political opinions post-martial law (Jacobs 2005: 47). Solely Chinese identification has declined from 25.5% to 3.4%. Dual identification has also declined, though less so in relative terms, from 46.4% to 34.3%. However, solely Taiwanese identification – clearly a function of the "Taiwanization" project of *bentuhua* – has increased from 17.6% to 58.2%. Put another way, 92.5% identified as either solely Taiwanese or Taiwanese-Chinese in 2016, compared to 64% in 1992. The largest upticks in solely Taiwanese identity occur immediately after the first presidential elections in 1996 (+9.9%), after Chen Shui-bian's victory in 2000 (+4.7%), and immediately before and after (2007–2008) the return to power of the KMT under President Ma Ying-Jeou (+4.7%). Under Chen's DPP between 2000 and 2008, identification as solely Taiwanese climbed from 36.9% to 48.4%, (+11.5%); under Ma's KMT between 2008 and 2016, it continued to climb, from 48.4% to 58.2% (+9.8%).

---

44 Since 1992 for the identity question, and since 1994 for the unification/independence question, annual telephone polls have been undertaken with robust sampling methods weighted for gender, age, education, and geographical location. They are conducted by trained call-handlers who can switch from Mandarin into Hakka or Hoklo depending on the respondent's language preference. Indigenous languages are not used. (ESC, via email).

Several conclusions might be deduced from these shifts. First, spikes in Taiwanese identity may occur as the result of heightened nationalist feelings around highly contested elections, which is not all that surprising, though these do not appear to correlate with specific issues of nationalism and independence being the focus of election campaigns, at least when looking at data from Fell (2007; 2011) and Fell and Chen (2014). Second, and more intriguing, despite the KMT's stance towards greater rapprochement with China, their term in office between 2008 and 2016 did little to dampen the rising enthusiasm for claiming Taiwanese identity overall. One explanation is that this general trend continued due to the dual path dependencies laid down by Lee Teng-hui and the DPP; in other words, the KMT either did not or could not stop the broader cultural-political project of *bentuhua*, and that Taiwanization had taken root as a relationship between civil society and the state that was independent of the specific political party in power.

5.5.2 Status planning and transitional justice

Transitional justice has been a complex and protracted issue for Taiwan (Wu 2005; Shih and Chen 2010; Rowen and Rowen 2017; Stolojan 2017). On the one hand, Taiwan has emerged from an authoritarian regime and transitioned almost bloodlessly into a fully-fledged liberal democracy, despite a historically fractious ethnic composition. This is to the credit of its own people and politicians, even if anything else could have been used as a flimsy excuse for Beijing to step in and re-assert order. Gradual liberalization was a way to dissipate popular anger in a controlled way, while a genuine commitment to democratization led by then-president Lee Teng-hui created a path dependency that his successors had to follow. On the other hand, it presents dilemmas as to whether the transition itself constitutes justice being done. The KMT may have reformed itself and engaged in some level of truth-telling, but it has only conceded what it has had to, which is far from enough for certain elements in civil society. The DPP, meanwhile, have vacillated over formal and meaningful transitional justice approaches, partly due to holding the presidency but only a legislative minority between 2000 and 2008, and then being in opposition against a KMT legislative supermajority between 2008 and 2016.[45] As such, Taiwan is an example of how transitional justice

---

[45] President Tsai Ing-wen, however, committed to transitional justice in her inauguration speech in May 2016, and formally apologized to indigenous peoples for past mistreatment in August of the same year (Coolidge 2016).

processes can take years or decades *after* democracy has been achieved (Roht-Arriaza 2006) and how, in de Greiff's (2012) formulation, transitional justice may not just be precondition of democratic polity, but one consequence of such a polity, and one safeguard of its continued existence. In other words, it is Taiwan's democratization that is facilitating any concrete steps towards transitional justice, rather more than transitional justice is leading to democratization.

The following discussion uses Taiwan as a case study to develop a theme outlined in chapter two, namely the possibility for LPP status planning efforts to be sites for practical measures and theoretical dimensions of transitional justice. To reiterate from chapter two, the core transitional justice measures are *truth-telling, prosecutions, reparations*, and *institutional reform*; language policies rarely have potential for prosecution, and are more geared to the measures of truth-telling, institutional reform and (symbolic or rights-based) reparations. For de Greiff (2012), these measures should be or are collectively oriented towards achieving *recognition, civic trust, reconciliation*, and *democratization* in the sense of full "participatory parity" (Fraser 1992). Language policies more obviously have recognition, reconciliation, and democratization dimensions; more obliquely, they have a civic trust dimension related to institutional reform, since each recursively leads to the other. A (justice-focused) rule of law is usually a goal of transitional justice, though it is harder to see how this relates to language policy specifically. To be strenuously avoided is victors' justice, which is possible in cases where one regime of sociolinguistic marginalization simply replaces another, or one party inverts the previous dynamic of "logoclastic violence" (Gully 2011: 5) out of revenge. It is first necessary to situate this discussion within the policy framework of the National Language Equality Law (NLEL; *guojia yuyan pingdengfa*) which was drafted by the DPP between 2002 and 2003 (Dupré 2016). It ultimately failed to become legislation, but structured discourses in civil society and the public sphere, as well as non-legislative language policies pursued through bureaucratic channels (Dupré 2016: 417).

5.5.2.1 The National Language Equality Law

The NLEL was drafted between 2002 and 2003 under the auspices of the National Languages Committee (NLC), and approved by the NLC in February 2003. It was clearly influenced by the UNDRM of 1992, but also by the UNDRIP, which was not adopted until 2007 but had been in circulation in draft form since 1993, and framed language-based rights in terms of both "expressive" language rights and "instrumental" linguistic human rights (Rubio Marin 2003). As Dupré (2016: 419–420) relates, the NLEL consisted of twenty-five articles, relating to the languages of the eleven indigenous groups officially recognized as "tribes" at the time as well as

Hakka, Hoklo, and Mandarin. Mandarin was rendered as *huayu* or "ethnic Chinese language" instead of *guoyu* or (singular) "national language", to avoid using a term that would have the unintended effect of solely promoting Mandarin as the national language. Made explicit was the need to "tolerate and respect linguistic diversity as part of Taiwan's cultural heritage" (Article 4). Other articles provided for rights to use minority languages for personal names, in broadcast media, education, and legal proceedings; as well as obligations on the state (either at national or local governmental levels) towards language development (including orthographies) and protecting endangered languages. For our purposes, a notable inclusion was requiring public officials to be certified in minority language competence, as well as the latitude given to local governments to decide on an appropriate language for state functions "in accordance with the sociolinguistic situation of their jurisdiction", provided that this did not impinge upon the use of the other "national" languages.

A qualification to the term "national language" is important. "National" is the term used in Mandarin, and the complexity and contentiousness of the issue led to avoiding discussion of the "official" state language, while education Minister Huang Jong-tsun was forced in the Legislative Yuan to deny the "co-official" status of non-Mandarin languages (Dupré 2016: 421), and Council for Cultural Affairs Vice Chairman Wu Mi-cha said that "the term 'official language' will no longer exist" (Huang 2003: 1). However, from the perspective of language planning and policy research these would be very much state-sanctioned and thus de facto if not de jure "official" languages. With this qualification, we are able to talk about "officialization" and "de-officialization" of so-called "national" languages as aspects of transitional justice measures, without having to resort to the clumsier alternative of "nationalization".

For different reasons, various committee members, legislators, and civil society groups opposed either the NLEL itself or the details of its framing, particularly in terms of what was meant in intent and practice by the notion of "equality". KMT lawmakers were adamant that the NLEL constructed all languages as equal apart from Mandarin. Even the names of languages themselves were contentious: Hakka groups accused the Hoklo of ethnolinguistic chauvinism over the initial use of the term *taiyu* or "Taiwanese language" at the expense of other languages of Taiwan, and some Hoklo and Hakka disputed the term *huayu* or "ethnic Chinese language" for Mandarin, since their languages and identities too were ethnically (Han) Chinese, even if that ethnicity was different from the mainlanders. As Dupré (2016: 421) remarks, "while the Taiwanese were accustomed to societal multilingualism, the idea of official multilingualism was neither well-understood nor well-received". The DPP themselves seemed ill-informed about the proposal; DPP premier Yu Shyi-kun, for example, was forced to clarify that he supported the draft bill, with the qualification that he thought the legislation was not feasible due to the problems of translating all official documents in a dozen or so languages. Other opponents of the law warned that official multilingualism would lead to ethnic conflict, social unrest, and communication problems (Tiu 2007). Amidst such acrimonious debate, in 2003 the NLEL was re-drafted as the National Language Development Law (NLDL; *guojia yuyan fazhanfa*), with most of its provisions intact, though the idea of requiring public officials to certify their competence in minority languages was dropped. The change in title reflected the shift in emphasis from equality to development, and from status to corpus planning, which implied "the idea that local languages should be legislated upon not only to raise their symbolic status, but also to turn them into fully-fledged societal languages" (Dupré 2016: 422).

The emphasis of the NLDL was on multiculturalism and language rights, requiring the government grant negative rights of non-interference and positive rights of affirmative obligations. Dupré translates Article 1, for example, as reading:

> The languages used by domestic ethnic groups are national cultural assets; this law is specially drafted so as to respect and safeguard the linguistic rights of citizens, promote the growth of multiculturalism, so that all languages can be used and developed equally

The revised law was not much better received. To begin with, the notion of "development" implicitly excluded Mandarin, since Mandarin was the one language that did not require developing. Furthermore, political polarization and Chen Shui-bian's increasingly strident linking of declaring political independence with enhancing Taiwanese identity, of which *bentuhua* and language equality was a part, further disinclined the KMT to support the bill (Dupré 2016: 422–423). Shelved in 2003, the NLDL was revived in 2006, though by the time it was presented to the Legislative Yuan it had been significantly diluted to just eight articles, to the disappointment of both drafters and supporters, particularly those who argued that it did little to practically protect languages from shift and loss. It still was not sufficient for its opponents, doing little to assuage the fears that the law amounted to "de-Mandarinization" (*qu guoyuhua*) (Dupré 2016: 423–424), and tabled indefinitely with the KMT's return to power in 2008.

The NLEL and NLDL do not appear to be specifically framed with transitional justice in mind, though a resuscitated language law was briefly floated in 2007 as one of five concerted transitional justice measures. However, the foregoing gives some context to potential status planning scenarios in which transitional justice principles could operate. The following section outlines three such status planning scenarios: 1) the de-officializing of Mandarin, with or without officializing other languages, which was feared by the KMT and mainlander groups; 2) officializing Hoklo only, or making it co-official as a second language with Mandarin, which formed the basis of charges of ethnolinguistic chauvinism and was formally proposed by the ultra-nationalist Taiwan Solidarity Union (TSU) in 2002 but quickly rejected by the DPP, at least officially (*Taipei Times* 2002); or 3) officializing or achieving some other equal status for all of Taiwan's languages, including Mandarin, which was the intent and would have been the practical effect of the NLEL or NLDL, at least taken on its face. After assessing the dimensions of these policies in their more overt formations, for each scenario I address several covert and micro-level political processes: as Dupré (2016: 417) argues, the stalling of the laws in the legislative system led to

> a shift in focus from de jure language regime change to a single-handed reliance on bureaucratic channels in language policy-making, as these channels did not require approval from the legislature. (Dupré 2016: 417)

5.5.2.2 De-officializing Mandarin

It seems to have been tempting, at least for fundamentalist elements, to abolish Mandarin as the official language as a broader approach to de-Sinicization, and the KMT and mainlander groups had some justification to fear such an approach. Indeed, some of the wording of the NLEL – such as "the nation must tolerate and respect linguistic diversity as part of Taiwan's cultural heritage, especially Aboriginal languages, Hakka and Hoklo" – was interpreted as implying that Mandarin would not be protected to the same extent as other languages (Dupré 2016: 420). There are quite plausible transitional justice reasons for considering de-officializing Mandarin, with or without officializing other languages, in order to reflect Taiwan's multicultural identity and distance itself from assimilationist policies of the past. Mandarin was the language of colonial oppression and ineluctably linked to broader political authoritarianism; Mandarin-spread policies also rode roughshod over local languages and identities, marginalizing them from public and political life. As Hsiau (1997: 312) describes, for many Taiwanese

> The KMT state, the Chinese nation, the Chinese culture, and Mandarin are identified with one another. The enactment of the nation-state model as a solution to the problem of political unity culminated in the KMT's 'Chinaization' endeavour.

Furthermore, in independence-minded and more strident Taiwan nationalist quarters, Mandarin is associated not just with the KMT on Taiwan but also with the PRC. De-officializing Mandarin would be a means to ethnolinguistically differentiate Taiwan from China; most obviously, this would be a legitimating basis of a proposed Taiwanese nation-state, but from a transitional justice perspective, it would also be a symbolic severing of the connection with the Chinese civil war between the Nationalists and the Communists that caused the KMT's exile to Taiwan, and thus the authoritarian regime that it put in place.[46]

In practice, however, de-officializing Mandarin would meet very few transitional justice criteria. It does not seem have any significant *truth-telling* function; it merely constitutes a finding of wrongdoing rather than an admission. There is a case to be made that it offers certain potential for *institutional reform*, but the obvious rebuttal is that it is only the (symbolic or material) destruction of those institutions, not their reform per se. It follows from this that *civic trust* cannot be rebuilt in institutions that have been destroyed. The best candidate is perhaps *recognition*: to some degree, it would be a public acknowledgement that language repression and thus political oppression took place. However, it is difficult to see how the other requirement for recognition in de Greiff's (2012) formulation – the recognition of victims as subjects with agency, objects of unjust treatment, or as rights-bearers – is met. The simple abolition of Mandarin in fact creates victims out of not merely monolingual mainlanders, but out of those who have lost their home language through involuntary processes of language shift and loss. Reliable and cross-comparable statistics are hard to come by, but in 1991, Mandarin proficiency was estimated at nearly 90% (Huang 1995: 120); according to Chen (2010), 98.1% reported fluency in Mandarin in 2003; and census data from 2010 indicated that 83.5% of all residents over six years old used Mandarin at home, though this varied according to region and was age-graded, with older residents using Mandarin substantially less than young people (DGBAS 2010b). With victims being so problematically defined, it becomes unclear who *reparations* are being made to, or what they should entail.

In any case, de-officializing Mandarin fails one of the key tests of transitional justice, namely the requirement to avoid victors' justice, symbolically or otherwise. Abolishing Mandarin, officially or in education, would be a clear case of using "logoclastic violence" (Gully 2011: 5) to avenge the very same violence visited on local languages during the martial law era, and it would emphasize retribution over redistribution that called into question claims to liberal democracy, and would contribute little to *reconciliation* and *democratization*. Although, to my knowledge, it was never articulated explicitly, the transitional justice dimensions of de-officializing Mandarin made it an unrealistic policy goal.

---

[46] Martial law was imposed under the legal auspices of the "Temporary Provisions Effective During the Period of National Mobilization for Suppression of the Communist Rebellion", put into legal effect the year before martial law was declared.

More micro-level approaches to undermining Mandarin were taken via bureaucratic channels rather than legislative changes, however, and to some degree they succeeded. In 1996, when the DPP's Chen Shui-bian was mayor of Taipei, he renamed the road outside the presidential palace from *Jie Shou Lu* or "Long Live Chiang Kai-shek Road" to "Ketagalan Boulevard", honouring an indigenous tribe. The KMT's Ma Ying-jeou, who succeeded Chen as Taipei mayor (and as president in 2008), declined to change the name back. Not all changes to the linguistic landscape achieved such a level of consensus, however. The renaming, in 2007, of Chiang Kai-shek Memorial Hall to the Taiwanese Democracy Memorial Hall was far more controversial.[47] The KMT evidently viewed it as akin to a symbolic beheading, and thus far from a moderate transitional justice measure; then Taipei mayor Hau Long-bin (KMT) refused to alter maps, street signs and the metro station to reflect the change, and the KMT changed it back when in power in 2009.[48] This provoked furious protest, with some seeing a shrine to a dead tyrant as anachronous and offensive.[49] As a 2009 editorial in the *Taipei Times* thundered:

> With the Chinese Nationalist Party (KMT) so singularly unwilling to conduct even the slightest iota of reflection on its continued unwavering worship of dictator Chiang Kai-shek – a man considered by most of the rest of the world as a corrupt, megalomaniac butcher – it seems Taiwanese will never experience transitional justice of any form. (Taipei Times 2009: 8)

Klöter (2004: §16) points out a wry postscript to the issue of names and languages: while the Chinese name of the Mandarin Promotion Council (*guoyu tuixing weiyuanhui*) could not be easily changed without legislative wrangling, its English name could. In 2003, it thus became the National Languages Committee, translating *guoyu* alternatively, but perfectly correctly, as "national language" instead of "Mandarin", and pluralizing "languages" where pluralization is not obligatorily marked in Mandarin. The multilingual basis of national unity, and thus one element of transitional justice, was thus articulated in a foreign language.

---

[47] Several observers pointed out that "memorials" are usually to something long since dead, and thus the name was an odd choice for a monument to a nascent democracy.
[48] The KMT left the name of the plaza as Liberty Square (*ziyou guangchang*), with Vice-Minister of Education Lu Mu-lin saying that "the square plays an important role in Taiwan's democratic and cultural development" (Wang 2009).
[49] At least in 2015, the English name of the gift shop at CKS Memorial Hall was "Cheer for Chiang".

5.5.2.3 Officializing or co-officializing Hoklo

As the most widely-spoken language behind Mandarin (Chen 2010; DGBAS 2010b), but sidelined from civic and political life for a nearly a century under the Japanese and KMT regimes, Hoklo is conceivably a candidate to replace Mandarin altogether as the official language, if that had been a realistic policy goal. At the very least it is potentially a second co-official language.

On some transitional justice criteria, this approach fares somewhat better than de-officializing Mandarin. *Truth-telling* is admittedly an indirect function of co-officializing Hoklo, but it may be argued that recovering and re-legitimizing victims' voices, narratives, and languages in public and political life enables their experiences of wrongdoing through linguistic repression to be heard. For similar reasons, it makes symbolic *reparations* to those (or their forebears) who have experienced language and political repression, by re-centring Hoklo in public and political life. The dimension of *recognition* – of both public acknowledgement of wrongdoing and victims as subjects with agency, objects of mistreatment, and bearers of rights – is thus clear.

However, while having a practical aspect given the difficulties of achieving truly official multilingualism, it is unlikely to lead to *reconciliation*, since Hoklo just becomes another dominating language without other languages achieving equal status. Similarly, the participatory parity needed for *democratization* is not specified; it would give a former political minority parity with the formerly oppressing ruling elite ethnic group/class, but at the expense of speakers of smaller languages.[50] *Institutional reform* would likely be possible, though at the risk of simply relexifying the institutions with another hegemonic language without reforming them, and thus replacing one form of sociolinguistic domination with another, which has implications for rebuilding *civic trust*. This is particularly problematic given the claims of ethnic chauvinism, and constitutes a different type of victors' justice than de-officializing Mandarin: it would lead to oppression of the next most vulnerable minority languages – Hakka and indigenous tongues – unless they were also made official. It can be seen, therefore, that co-officializing Hoklo without achieving equality for other languages is overall problematic for a transitional justice-based compensatory multilingual policy.

Even micro-level and non-legislative changes to the language used within the state bureaucracy have caused problems of the sort outlined above. In 2003, the DPP changed the language of some questions on certain police and civil service examinations by using Chinese characters with pronunciations only Hoklo

---

50 For a discussion of ethnicity and class in elite KMT leadership, see Gates (1981)

speakers would understand. Despite abandoning the idea of co-officializing Hoklo, it was difficult to dispel the widespread suspicion that "the principle of equality was but a facade for the Hoklo to assert themselves as cultural majority" (Dupré 2016: 420). Perception of policy is as important as policy itself, especially in contentious or transitional contexts. The response from the KMT was predictably outraged. KMT chairman Lien Chan charged the DPP with "inciting ethnic conflict". As the *Taipei Times* reported in 2003:

> Speaking in Hakka, KMT Deputy Chairman Wu Po-hsiung and former deputy speaker of the legislature Yao Eng-chi echoed Lien and criticized the controversial questions on this year's national exams for civil servants.
>
> "It's discrimination against Hakka people," Wu said.
> [...]
> In a bid to put the language controversy to rest, Yao proposed drawing up an ethnic culture and religion equality law. (Ko 2003: 3)

Notable here is that rather than making it an issue of Mandarin being undermined, KMT legislators cast it as a problem for Hakka speakers. This was a shrewd move that framed, albeit implicitly, the issue in transitional justice terms: rather than threatening a dominant language, an act that at least some in civil society would be sympathetic towards, Hoklo is positioned as threatening the next most subordinated language. A thorny problem of institutional reform arose from the DPP's sensitivity to claims of ethnic chauvinism, in that it refused to create a bureau of Hoklo cultural affairs, as it had done for Hakka under the Executive Yuan to complement the equivalent Council of Indigenous Peoples. Instead, it allowed a Hoklo language sub-committee under the National Languages Committee (NLC) of the Ministry of Education, with limited autonomy in language issues being seen as sufficient enough to maintain the already dominant Hoklo culture. For this reason, some Hoklo activists in education and civil society refer to themselves as "the weakest majority". As one such activist told me during an interview in 2007:

> The Hakka and [indigenous groups] say, "We are weak, but you are strong ... you don't have to have a [bureau of cultural affairs]." That's why we call Hoklo people ... the Hoklo language group is ((laughs)) ... like, you have a lot of people who speak that language, so you are strong – but you are weak, actually, because you don't even have a [bureau] to promote your language and your culture. Now we can only promote the language first. We have no leaders involved in culture. If we can save the language ... then we can do that. We say, "our problem is we are the weakest majority"!

Despite limited institutional support, Hoklo remains vibrant in civil society. In 2015, a record number of 10,850 people nationwide voluntarily took the official

Hoklo proficiency test (Lin 2015), which had been retained in the face of bitter complaints over proposed cuts to the NLC's budget for the test.

5.5.2.4 Co-officializing all languages

Political hair-splitting on the distinction between national and official languages aside, it is clear that the intent of the two proposed language laws, the NLEL and the NLDL, was to elevate all of Taiwan's languages to official status, or at least that that would be the effect in practice. Hakka and indigenous languages are minority languages in the strictest sense of the term. They are the numerically smallest; 6.6% reported Hakka use at home according to the 2010 census (DGBAS 2010b) and 10.9% reported fluency in Chen's (2010) survey data from 2003; 1.4% reported indigenous languages use at home in the census (DGBAS 2010b) and 2% reported fluency in Chen's data (2010).

Once again, as with officializing or co-officializing Hoklo, certain *truth-telling* functions come indirectly from the rehabilitation of voices and narratives of speakers of previously repressed languages. *Reparations* for language and political repression can be clearly seen, simply through both the symbolic and actual re-configuration and rebalancing of the sociolinguistic regime. *Reform* is not merely the gutting of institutional structures, the re-peopling of institutions, or relexifying institutions with one language at the expense of others. As such, it is a recursive process of rebuilding *civic trust*. *Recognition* stems from the admission that the unequal statuses of the languages vis-à-vis Mandarin were unjust, and that speakers were victims and normatively should be bearers of (now restored) language rights. Co-officializing performs significantly better on other measures and dimensions compared to the two previously outlined status planning scenarios. Given their numbers and the arrangement of the sociolinguistic regime, none of these languages is ever going to replace Mandarin or Hoklo as the dominant language, and thus their co-officializing presents few dilemmas for hypothetical victors' justice scenarios. Quite clearly, as a result, an equitably multilingual polity has positive implications for *reconciliation*. For *democratization*, co-officialization offers the opportunity for full participatory parity in public and political life.

Institutional reform through bureaucratic channels is perhaps the one area where significant progress was made by the DPP in the absence of legislative solutions to achieve formal co-officialization. The Hakka Affairs Council (HAC) was established in 2001 by the DPP, partly in response to the *Huan Wo Muyu Yundong* or "Return our mother-tongue movement" in civil society; the Council of Indigenous Peoples (CIP) was established in 1996 by the KMT as the Council for Aboriginal Affairs, and renamed by the DPP in 2002. Both agencies fall under the purview of the Executive Yuan; among other remits, these have advisory and promotion roles for Hakka and indigenous languages and cultures.[51] Despite (or perhaps because of) being insulated from the legislature, the CIP was instrumental in getting the Education Act for Indigenous Peoples and the Indigenous Peoples' Basic Law passed in 1998 and 2005, respectively. The latter refrains from any discussion of official or national language status, and contains instead rather weak provisions for indigenous language broadcasting, academic linguistic research, and developing measures to give priority to indigenous peoples in civil service jobs and/or special civil service examinations based, in part, on language proficiency. This does little to stem the language and cultural shift caused by indigenous peoples' assimilation into Taiwan's increasingly complex urban society. An equivalent Hakka law was passed under the KMT in 2010, to which we will return. In addition, as we will see shortly, education curricula became a key battleground for quasi-officialization of Taiwan's languages.

5.5.2.5 Assessing transitional justice in Taiwanese language policies

Based on the foregoing discussion, the matrix in Table 5.1 summarizes how practical measures and goals of transitional justice may operate in three potential status planning contexts in Taiwan. The obvious conclusion to be drawn is that only co-officialization of, or granting some other equal status to, all languages meets all transitional justice criteria. De-officializing Mandarin, with or without officializing other languages, or officializing Hoklo, both fail the core test of avoiding victors' justice (and thus achieving *reconciliation*), hence making the other criteria somewhat moot. However, this aside, it seems relevant that both appear to fail (or succeed in only limited and qualified ways) on some common criteria. These are the practical measure of *institutional reform* and its related goal of *civic trust*, as well as the goal of *democratization*. We can see how these mechanisms might work by looking, perhaps counter-intuitively, at examples from *non*-transitional contexts. The literature in LPP research is clear that language policies which do not effectively address their institutional shortcomings seem to do poorly on achieving their goals of multilingual equality. Furthermore, institutional shortcomings seem to produce language policies that are not geared towards participatory parity in public and political life that stable liberal democracies require (Fraser 1992).

---

[51] Some Hoklo activists protested the formation of the HAC rather than, as my interviewee posed the problem, merely the lack of an equivalent Hoklo body.

Table 5.1: Assessing status planning and transitional justice criteria.

	Measures (e.g. Roht-Arriaza 2006)		
	De-officializing Mandarin, with or without officializing other languages	Officializing Hoklo only, or co-officializing with Mandarin	Officializing all languages
Truth-telling	Yes, with co-officializing; no otherwise	Yes	Yes
Reparations	No	Yes	Yes
Institutional reform	Yes, if drastically	Yes, but replaces one hegemonic language with another	Yes
Victors' justice test*	No	No	Yes

	Goals (de Greiff 2012)		
	De-officializing Mandarin, with or without officializing other languages	Officializing Hoklo only, or co-officializing with Mandarin	Officializing all languages
Recognition	Yes	Yes	Yes
Civic trust	No, because institutional reform insufficient to rebuild trust	No, because institutional reform insufficient to rebuild trust	Yes
Reconciliation justice test	No	No	Yes
Democratization	No	No	Yes
Victors' justice test*	No	No	Yes

* The "victors' justice test" is strictly speaking neither a transitional justice measure or a goal; instead it determines whether measures successfully attain their goals.

Other transitional justice contexts, such as Sri Lanka, Yugoslavia, and South Africa, have all made legislative efforts to co-officialize their various languages that were formerly sites of conflict. Taiwan, in fact, is a somewhat unusual example of a transitional context with a fundamental sociolinguistic component where legislative language reform has not occurred. However, a contrast should be drawn between Taiwan's lack of language legislation but effective bureaucratic channels for language reform in e.g. education, and cases such as South Africa, where lip service was paid to language equality in the constitution, but few steps taken to ensure it was realized in practice. In fact, this usefully returns us to the point made by Roht-Arriaza (2006: 2) noted earlier, namely that an emphasis on law and legislation in transitional justice contexts neglects the role of education and culture, the latter having the potential to be achieved outside of the formal legislative system.

5.5.3 Language-in-education policies

It has already been mentioned that, in the absence of the ability to pass a language law, DPP language policy entailed "a shift in focus from de jure language regime change to a single-handed reliance on bureaucratic channels in language policy-making, as these channels did not require approval from the legislature" (Dupré 2016: 417). In other words, language policy reform came not through legislation, but through the bureaucratic mechanisms of the state that the government controlled through the executive branch. This section discusses such channels in the context of the DPP's mother-tongue language education (MTLE) curriculum from 2001, which mandated one hour per week of local language instruction in elementary schools between grades one and three, and provided for local language electives in middle and high school. This required curriculum changes, but these fell under the bureaucratic purview of the relevant government ministries, the Ministry of Education (MOE) specifically. Furthermore, the devolved local autonomy implied in democratization and liberalization processes created spaces for resistance, either against DPP policies in non-DPP controlled locales or, conversely, for implementation that went beyond minimum requirements where local conditions warranted. The outcome was differentiated access to MTLE, based on a complex of ethnolinguistic, party-political, socioeconomic, geographic and rural/urban factors.

5.5.3.1 The political context of curriculum reform

The school functions as an extension of the national state (Bourdieu 1999) that regulates the production of citizen-subjects who have a shared conception of what the nation and the state are constituted by. History demonstrates its common past (and destiny); geography emphasizes its territorial control and integrity; social sciences frame "good citizenship" and the parameters of morally and socio-politically acceptable behaviour in civil society. Taken together, these elements serve to legitimize the abstract symbols – which are the basis of what Geertz (1973) calls culture – of the nation-state, such as flags, anthems, cuisine, and "values". It has long been recognized in this regard that education has a powerful hegemonic function.

Martial law-era education policies in Taiwan thus reflected the dominant ideologies of the KMT party and the ROC state. The traditional geography curriculum is sometimes lampooned as requiring the rote memorization of obscure railway stations in far-flung Chinese provinces. As with any satire, there is probably an element of truth to this; after all, the KMT maintained that they were the legitimate government of all of China, and simply temporary indisposed in their quest to retake the mainland, and rote memorization is the hallmark of an older and less enlightened pedagogy. Certainly, the "local" Taiwanese context was entirely subsumed under the "national" context of the ROC. History was similarly China-focused, with Taiwanese history considered peripheral at best. The Sinocentric paradigm largely ignored the influence of the Dutch and the Japanese, while the nationalist paradigm had little impetus to venerate the recently-deposed Qing (Wang, F. 2005: 63).

As Chang Lung-chih (2011) relates, beginning in 1989 the KMT gradually altered the broader curriculum to reflect the lifting of martial law and the wider context of liberalization and, belatedly, post-war cultural change. In the 1990s, Lee Teng-hui's nativist turn and the beginnings of the *bentuhua* movement forced a re-positioning of "Chinese-ness" within a "Taiwanization" discourse. Identity formation within the curriculum was conceived of as concentric circles scaling at local/national, regional, and global levels, whereby Taiwanese youth should "stand on Taiwan, have consideration for China, and open their eyes to the world" (Corcuff 2002: 87). In 1997, the re-writing of history textbooks flared into a hotly-contested dispute, with substantial media coverage and public protests over the speed at which the *bentuhua* paradigm was replacing that of Sino-centrism. For some, the new paradigm in history teaching was simply a replacement for the previous version of hegemonic ethnic chauvinism. The timing of the controversy is notable, as Wang Fu-chang (2005: 57) points out. It had not arisen when the KMT began curriculum reform in 1989; instead, it came in 1997 as the result of the politicization and sharpening of ethnic differences through democratization and *bentuhua* in the intervening period. For Chang Mau-kuei (2005: 252),

> [*bentuhua*] strives to achieve not only self-recognition but also other-recognition. The essentializing tendency in the construction of the opposing groups of 'peoples', however, can lead to nationalistic and ethnocentric pitfalls. (Chang 2005: 252)

Such arguments continued to dog the DPP's more strident approaches to nationalism in the curriculum. As late as 2002, Taiwanese children were still being taught that the capital of the ROC was Nanjing, China, instead of Taipei, prompting DPP legislators to point out the Faustian choice between teaching children nonsense to pass exams or teaching them facts that would cause them to fail. In 2003, the Ministry of Education proposed to teach Chinese history since 1500 as part of modern world history; this was met with much opprobrium, with KMT chairman Lien Chan calling it a replacement of unchangeable historical facts with ideology. A watered-down history curriculum was proposed in 2004, seemingly a compromise whereby pupils would learn "Taiwan's history" in the first year before being exposed to "China's history" (including the establishment of the ROC) in the second. Even this compromise was not enough for pan-blue legislators and their supporters, who again accused the DPP of promoting political independence by stealth through the education system. In early 2008, as their defeat in the presidential elections and loss of control over the bureaucratic machinery loomed, the DPP finally pushed through textbooks which emphasized Taiwanese history over that of China's.

5.5.3.2 Mother-tongue language education

As with history and geography curricula, educational language policies and ideologies are intrinsically related to the legitimization of the nation-state. Arguably, they are more so, given the unavoidability of language, the fact that language is often a key aspect of ethnic identity, and that ethnic identity is often a foundation of national identity. However, the adoption in 2001 of mandatory mother-tongue language education (MTLE) in elementary schools, and as electives in middle and high schools, proved rather *less* politically contentious in political and civil society discourses, attracting much less ire than reform of the island's self-perception of its historical trajectory and geopolitical location. This is likely for several reasons. To begin with, Mandarin was not de-officialized in education; in other words, it was not replaced as the medium of instruction, and this policy is aptly described by Scott and Tiun (2007) as being a shift from "Mandarin-only to Mandarin-plus". As such, its status in the education system – and by extension, as the language of the state – was not drastically changed. Furthermore, the KMT could hardly complain about language reforms since, first, it had instigated those reforms and, second, it bore responsibility for the indexing of linguistic repression with political repression during the martial law era. Even for hardliners, it was impossible to disrespect Lee Teng-hui's advocacy for democratization through, in part, sociolinguistic reform. Additionally, it seems that for all the fanfare over the NLEL/NLDL, the DPP toned down the nationalist rhetoric when it came to curriculum reform, meaning that reaching social and political consensus was easier to achieve. However, the DPP were nevertheless cautious in their approach A brief content analysis of the English-language MOE publication *Education in Taiwan* between 2001 and 2007 serves to underline this claim: it is not until 2007, towards the end of the DPP's tenure, that MTLE becomes emphasized.

The transition to democratization post-martial law allowed and indeed required increased autonomy for local county governments. According to the official government publication *Republic of China Yearbook* of 2002, Ilan County, on Taiwan's east coast, was the first to initiate Hoklo language courses in elementary and junior high schools in 1990, while Taipei County's Wulai district was the first to offer extra-curricular indigenous Atayal language instruction in schools the same year. In 1991, Pingtung County offered elective courses in Hoklo, Hakka, and the indigenous Paiwan and Rukai languages in selected schools. These counties extended MTLE outside of the formal education system into wider civil society by holding activities such as community speech and singing contests, which were later developed into an island-wide multilingual and multicultural music, arts, and dance program. Similarly, in 2001, the government launched a national proficiency certification program for indigenous languages, enabling citizens to receive official (if symbolic) credit for learning or maintaining them.

In an interview in 2007, Mr. Deng, an elementary school principal in Miaoli County, explained the historical context of Hakka language education in his school, initially outside of the formal instruction context. Here, we can see that at least some schools and counties emphasized the role of culture in MTLE, but that MTLE was also a way to buttress cultural preservation:

> The educational policy in our school, from the beginning to nowadays, is kind of like this. Our school started to incorporate local educational activity with the local language teaching around 1989. We have used unofficial [extra-curricular] courses like students' clubs, the dawn-twilight time [before classes start], after-school courses, or the summer vacations to do some activities related to local language teaching. But we did not merely teach the local language [Hakka], we also introduced the Hakka customs and culture to teach the language. [Mr Deng, school principal, Miaoli County]

The interview with Mr. Deng was one among several I conducted with elementary school principals and local education bureau directors during fieldwork in Taiwan in 2007. These took place in rural Miaoli County and Taitung County, which have Hakka and the indigenous language Amis respectively as their dominant local languages, and in Mandarin/Hoklo-speaking Taipei City. They were conducted in Mandarin with an interpreter, and designed to investigate the implementation of MTLE policies on-the-ground in local contexts. As well as being broadly ethnolinguistically representative, Miaoli County, Taitung

County, and Taipei City are broadly representative of Taiwan on various sociopolitical criteria. The metropolitan and urban centre of Taipei in the north contrasts with the peripheral and rural regions of central (Miaoli County) and southern (Taitung County) Taiwan. They also provide a cross-section of wealthier to poorer regions, and of political positions, from hard-line KMT (Taipei City), more moderate nativist KMT (Miaoli County), and fairly hard-line DPP (Taitung County). Cities and counties listed here are real, while localities, schools and people are anonymized. What emerged from these interviews was participants' perception of the need to tailor implementation by counties and individual schools according to the sociolinguistic contexts of their jurisdictions, in tension with the practical obstacles familiar to educationalists everywhere: district and school budgets, the availability of qualified teachers, and parental support and involvement. A related function of democratization and autonomy (and neoliberalism, which is a separate discussion) is the notion of "choice", which is appealing in theory but in practice ends up favouring dominant languages and their speakers. These issues structure the discussion in the following sections.

Where numbers warrant: Choosing local languages in schools

In theory, autonomy in MTLE implementation was meant to prevent the problem of every school on the island having to offer classes in every local language. In practice, it meant MTLE was not an individual right, but distributed according to the ethnolinguistic composition of the dominant minority (or minorities) in a given area. Children who were in a non-dominant ethnolinguistic minority in a particular locality or institution were not guaranteed their own language classes or teachers. Some schools remedied this by requiring that they studied their own language individually but, while well intentioned, this had the unintended effect of stigmatizing these children from their linguistic majority classmates. Other schools offered MTLE in an alternative language, thereby tacitly devaluing their actual mother-tongues as languages not worth teaching. Mr. Tang, a school principal from Taitung County with predominantly indigenous Amis children, explained the difficulties of teaching "minorities within minorities" during our interview:

> Gareth: Which language or mother-tongue should teachers teach in schools?
>
> Mr. Tang: It is pretty difficult to decide which local language to teach in schools ... [in our school] the indigenous students get together and an indigenous language teacher teaches the students. The Hoklo students get together and another Hoklo language teacher teaches the students. There are two main language groups in our school. There are very few Hakka students in our school so we do not have another Hakka group for them.

> Gareth: Which language do the Hakka students learn?
>
> Mr. Tang: They can choose the language they want to learn. They can choose the Amis language or the Hoklo language. [But] only the Amis kids learn the Amis language.

Choice, of course, is the watchword of neoliberalism, and Taiwan has embraced certain neoliberal discourses alongside the internationalization and globalization of its political economy. However, increased choice is also an outcome of democratization: it stands in contrast to the distinct lack of choice of language in education, and public and political life, under martial law. It is not clear who – Hakka pupils or their parents – is in reality making the choice in Mr. Tang's school, but the choice to learn Hoklo is oriented towards the dominant language in wider national society, not in the community or the school; Amis is the majority language and Hoklo is a minority language in the local context, with only 28% of the children at this school coming from Hoklo backgrounds. If Hakka parents are making these choices, it seems to be an instrumentalist decision of which language is most socially, politically, or economically valuable in society more broadly; Amis is not considered to be useful or desirable compared to Hoklo. If it is students themselves, then it would appear that instrumentalist valuation of languages occurs at a very young age, or children are valuing languages in different ways. I interviewed Ms. Long, principal of an elementary school in a relatively wealthy area of Taipei, who told me that her students *did* choose their MTLE options:

> Ms. Long: Three kinds of local languages are taught at our school. In 2007, we opened classes in *Minnanhua* [Hoklo], Hakka, and an indigenous language, Amis.
>
> Gareth: Why Amis? Why not other indigenous languages?
>
> Ms. Long: It is because we have the students choose by themselves. We count the three most popular languages chosen by the students ... we do not choose the languages by ourselves.

Rather taken aback, I failed to find out why students chose Amis. However, Amis is the widest spoken indigenous language in Taiwan and, perhaps more importantly for children, it has a relatively large presence in popular culture, especially through the new wave of indigenous pop music that emerged in the early 2000s. Knowing the area in which this school is located, it is highly unlikely that children were choosing the Amis language because they identified as Amis. Notably, Amis is valued by the schoolchildren in Taipei City, but not for the Hakka students in Mr. Tang's school in Taitung. There are further distinctions between the schools I visited in Taitung and Taipei, which are structured along north/south, rural/urban, and metropolitan/peripheral axes, which are a complex of ethnolinguistic identities, party loyalties, and, at root, economic viability. The wealthier school in Taipei could afford to open classes in three different languages, and Ms. Long said they would open more if they could find qualified teachers. The shortage for Mr. Tang appears to be budget related, at least in part; he emphasized that the county as a whole was poor compared to the rest of Taiwan, which put limits on available educational resources. It is difficult to find indigenous teachers in Taipei; it is difficult to find the money to pay them in Taitung.

Hakka speakers may be a minority in Taitung County, but constitute a majority in the central Taiwan county of Miaoli. Although they cannot be relied on to vote as a bloc along party lines, in terms of sociolinguistic and cultural politics they are highly organized; Hakka civil society groups have been active in locally-based language maintenance and revitalization, and pushing for national curriculum and language policy reform. For Mr. Chen, director of Miaoli County's bureau of education, the minimum standards set by national policy were insufficient for the goals of sustained language maintenance and revitalization. Concurring with Miaoli County principal Mr. Deng's approach to integrating both culture and language in MTLE, as mentioned above, Mr. Chen told me that:

> One session [hour] of Hakka language a week is not enough. From our experience, language is not a separate subject. Language has to be incorporated into daily life and culture to make itself living.

To address this perceived problem, Mr. Chen exercised Miaoli County's autonomy from central government by supplementing the minimum MTLE requirement with extra tuition. Miaoli County is wealthier than Taitung County, though the practicalities of additional language instruction were still restricted by the county's own budget as well as central government stipulations on other timetabled subjects:

> Therefore, besides one session of local language a week, the practice in our school is to have all the teachers and students get into some practical conversation lessons *taught by a language teacher on the internet from 7:45-8:30 on Monday morning*. (emphasis added)

Complaints about the limited time for MTLE were also made by Mr. Tang in Taitung and Ms. Long in Taipei, albeit for slightly different reasons; both thought that MTLE was a reasonable idea in theory, but rather pointless to put into practice since children could not effectively acquire these languages in such a short amount of time.

Languages in homes and schools

Taitung principal Mr. Tang's perspective aligned with that of Mr. Chen from Miaoli County, in that language maintenance and revitalization was important and desirable, and that it was not separate from daily life. However, Mr. Tang placed a different emphasis on the role of the school, suggesting that formal MTLE was secondary to revitalizing Hakka in the "low" diglossic domain of the home and family life, and that mandating language in schools at the national policy level – even at an hour per week – was unnecessary and overreaching. Parents, however, seemed to be enthusiastic or at least uncritical about MTLE national policy, which conflicts with the pedagogical concerns of principals and teachers:

> Mr. Tang:: Our experience is that the parents think the local language education is very good. They think that the local language is what belongs to them originally. We make kids learn the local language and the parents absolutely support this policy. But from our perspective, we think that this policy of the government has some problems. The local language should not belong to the formal education in schools; local language education should belong to education within the family. If we ask Amis kids to speak Amis language at home, Taiwanese kids to speak Taiwanese at home, and Hakka kids speak Hakka at home, this is the real promotion of the local language education among the next generation.
>
> Gareth: Do the teachers in schools also think so?
>
> Mr. Tang: Everyone thinks so.

Parental and family involvement in MTLE patterns in sociologically complex ways in Taiwan. As Ms. Long and Mr. Tang both explained separately to me, parents in rural areas often move to larger cities for socio-economic reasons, leaving children in the care of their grandparents (the dual-generation nuclear family rather than multi-generational extended family is a relatively recent sociological change in Taiwan, especially in these areas). However, they had different perspectives on what this meant for MTLE in schools and communities. For Ms. Long, national policy was unnecessary in rural areas where languages were, in her view, still vibrant:

> In the rural areas ... they often speak the local languages in the countryside, so they do not really have to learn. They speak the local languages with their grandparents. But the kids in Taipei don't speak the local languages. So, their parents want them to learn local languages from childhood. Those young parents might not speak the language themselves, even if they are Hoklo ... but they hope their kids do. In the rural areas, they use local languages all the time. Local languages are everywhere. So, they think that learning local languages is a waste of time.

Mr. Tang, however, pointed out that, with parents in the cities, children were learning languages from their grandparents, but language mixing and language shift among this generation created problems for language transmission:

> The grandparents are between 60 and 80 years old now. When they were young, they were ruled by the Japanese for 50 years. So, their Amis language is mixed with a lot of Japanese. They actually speak Japanese. It is difficult for the grandparents to teach their kids Amis because their language is not accurate.

Although language shift to and borrowing from Japanese is plausible, there may be an element of folk linguistics to this. Mr. Tang later told me that parents somehow spoke Amis "pretty well ... [they] just do not have the chance to live with the kids to teach them the Amis language at home", suggesting the parents managed to pick up this "mixed" and "not accurate" language from their own parents' generation. What might be a better linguistic explanation is that this is a classic case of intergenerational language shift, where the children are "receptive bilinguals" with their grandparents, capable of understanding the language but not proficient in producing it, though this also may well be the case if nominally Amis-speaking parents lived at home. The basic paradox for Mr. Tang, in either case, is the same: MTLE does not belong in formal school education but, for whatever reason, it is not being maintained or revitalized in the home. National policy, therefore, should be oriented towards increasing local language use in the family and civil society, not in the formal education system. It is unclear how this would work in practice: the logic that the state should intervene in family language practices is a dangerous one given the experience of language policies under the KMT during the martial law era. Yet in Taiwan, as in many other language revitalization contexts, incentives and encouragement are insufficient on their own to prevent language shift. Without community engagement on language and identity issues, the best-willed policies in the world cannot constrain social and political forces that flourish in a climate of indifference and apathy.

Mr. Tang's and Ms. Long's beliefs about parents' positive attitudes towards MTLE were somewhat contradicted by Director Wang from Taitung's county education bureau.

> Gareth: What do you think are parents' opinions about the local languages in Taitung county? Do they more agree or disagree [with the educational policies]?
>
> Director Wang: In fact, they neither agree nor disagree. What they think is just to ignore it. Parents ignoring the issues is the most difficult part in school education. It doesn't matter to the parents. [They think] as long as I send my kids to school, whatever you want to teach the kids doesn't matter to me.

However, he immediately qualified this construction of parents' lackadaisical attitudes, pointing to their instrumentalist framing of elementary education as the basis for navigating the minefield of Taiwan's rigorous and highly competitive national testing system, from middle school through to university.

> Director Wang: [But] the parents might think those things you teach are not helpful for the kids in the exams. The parents' main purpose is that their kids can get good grades to go to better schools in the big cities. They hope their kids can to go to national universities [better and more prestigious universities]. So, if you want to develop the courses with some special characteristics, like local language courses, the parents do not necessarily support that.

For parents in a poor county who have to migrate to urban centres for work, conflicting concerns are highly understandable. They may see the maintenance of languages and cultures as generally a good thing, or even essential to the maintenance of ethnic identities. However, educational achievement offers opportunities to avoid the trap of socio-economic marginalization, and thus the need for their children to migrate to urban centres as they have been forced to do. Local languages are not testable subjects, and thus they do not offer the cultural capital required for educational achievement. Yet again, the concept of "choice" is a relative one: parents are effectively being asked to choose between ethno-linguistic identity or socio-economic mobility.

Politicizing "mother-tongue"

Not everyone was uniformly positive about MTLE, particularly in the hard-line KMT context of Taipei City. Despite her enthusiasm for the general idea, Ms. Long frequently took issue with the "politicization" of MTLE, related to the perceived ethnic chauvinism of the DPP and, in her words, "the glorification of Hoklo". Retaining local languages for the purposes of maintaining cultural patrimony was one thing, but education could be a site for creeping officialization of multilingualism and the DPP's political independence ideology:

> I somewhat disagree with the policy because of the political factor. I think we should learn the local languages if we want to pass down and keep the cultures. But if you want to separate China from Taiwan and make the local language the official language in Taiwan, I don't think that's correct. If you take the point of view from the ROC, there is an official language [Mandarin] that everyone speaks and you can speak local languages freely, I think that is correct.

Mr. Lu, director of the bureau of education in Taipei City, was quite clear on his objectives:

> Here in Taipei City, our policy has two main axes. One, to teach Mandarin. Two, to teach English. And then, after that, local languages.

Indeed, he objected to the term "mother-tongue" itself, initially on semantic grounds but eventually implying that it was discriminatory against mainlanders:

Generally speaking, we don't use the term "mother-tongue" [*muyu*] too much. People born on the mainland, mainlanders ... suppose someone's mother speaks the Beijing dialect. But the Beijing dialect has now become *guoyu* [Taiwan Mandarin], so she doesn't use a "mother-tongue" as such, since that now refers to local languages. So, we use the term local or native [*bentu*] languages. Maybe my mother was from Jiangxi Province or Beijing, but I certainly cannot choose my "mother-tongue" as my elective class. Instead, I'll choose the local language, the strong language.

In this final quote, it is evident that decisions about language choice are not merely based on ethnic identification, but on pragmatic decisions about which language is "stronger" and offers the best potential for socio-economic advancement. As with many multilingual contexts, the notion of individual "choice" and autonomy favours the dominant languages. The shift in curriculum may have been from "Mandarin-only to Mandarin-plus" (Scott and Tiun 2007), but as Klöter (2006) puts it, "Mandarin remains more equal". In chapter six, we will see how another dominant language – English – is constraining local language choices even further.

5.6 KMT policies (2008–2016)

The KMT returned to power in 2008, with the election of Ma Ying-jeou as president and a legislative supermajority of 81 seats out of 116. Victory came as the DPP imploded under the weight of corruption allegations against Chen Shui-bian. He was convicted in 2009 and sentenced to life; the sentence was reduced to 19 years on appeal, and he was medically paroled in January 2015. For some opponents, he received a fair trial and due process, under a functioning judiciary and the rule of law; that is, within the very processes and structures of democratization that he spent his early career, as a member of the Tangwai movement, fighting so vociferously for. However, Chen's prosecution was branded by some supporters as politically motivated vengeance by the KMT for his actions during two terms in power. To be sure, the harshness of the sentence itself – and the undignified way Chen was made to serve it – concerned both domestic and foreign human rights observers. The very least that can be said is that it was a highly polarizing episode coming after Taiwan's otherwise largely untainted transition to democracy.

Born in Hong Kong in 1950 to a Nationalist family who had fled China after the Communist victory in 1949, Ma Ying-jeou took a law degree at National Taiwan University, graduating in 1972, before receiving his masters from New York University in 1976, and then a *juris doctor* from Harvard in 1981. One of his first roles in public service was as English-language interpreter for Chiang Ching-kuo. Ma served as deputy secretary-general of the

KMT through the lifting of martial law between 1984 and 1988, and as justice minister under the post-martial law KMT government between 1993 and 1996. He became deputy chairman of the KMT in in 2003, and then chairman in 2005, defeating Wang Jyn-pyng, fellow challenger for Lien Chan's former post. Like Chen Shui-bian, Ma Ying-jeou served as mayor of Taipei City (1998–2006). In the 2008 presidential elections, Ma beat former DPP premier Frank Hsieh by taking 58% of the vote; in 2012, he would be re-elected with a narrower margin against Tsai Ing-wen.

5.6.1 De-Taiwanization and re-Sinicization

As Dupré (2017: 125) argues, following Hughes (2014), "the KMT's cultural policy after 2008 was characterized by attempts to re-Sinicize Taiwan's cultural landscape and overturn some of the Taiwanization initiatives undertaken by the Lee [Teng-hui] and Chen [Shui-bian] administrations".[52] These attempts included reversing the gains of the DPP's Name Rectification Campaign (*Gaiming yundong*). As mentioned above, these became battles over the linguistic landscape. Changing the name of the National Taiwan Democracy Memorial Hall back to National Chiang Kai-shek Memorial Hall in 2009 was perhaps the most drastic and contentious change, taken by many to be an avowed refusal to engage in any meaningful transitional justice measures. But more subtle changes occurred; the name of the post office was changed back from "Taiwan Post" to "Chunghwa Post", *Chunghwa* being a reference to the ROC and "just short of the more explicit 'China Post'" (Dupré 2017: 125). In political discourse, references to Taiwan being part of the Chinese nation (*Zhonghua minguo*) became more common, as did casting Sino-Taiwan relations as being "one country, two areas" (*yiguo liangqu*) (Hughes 2014: 129, cited in Dupré 2017: 126). As Dupré (2017: 126) points out, this was not to overtly cement allegiance and identity with China, but to the legitimacy of "the idea of Taiwan as the Republic of China". As such, re-Sinicization was a form of cultural politics that fell back on a covert version of the older KMT ideology that the ROC was the only legitimate government of China.

These issues played out in the politics of orthographic reform. For many years, there was little standardization of *pinyin* in public life, often leading to the same road names being Romanized in different ways – usually in a mixture of simplified

---

52 Dupré's chapter (2017: 123–136) is, to my knowledge, the only published work on KMT language policies between 2008 and 2016, and so my analysis here draws heavily on his.

or modified Wade-Giles systems – on maps and even on different signs along the same street. In an attempt to make the system more navigable for foreigners, part of a broader internationalization of the island, in 2002 the DPP government introduced the standardized Tongyong system into official street signage, devised by Taiwanese linguist and language activist Boris Yu, though usage was voluntary for local governments. On returning to power, the KMT abandoned Tongyong in favour of the Hanyu system in 2009. The Hanyu system is the system used in the PRC, and thus contains ideological overtones. Many DPP-controlled counties and cities refused to comply, continuing to use Tongyong. At the time of writing, Tsai Ing-wen's administration had not reverted to Tongyong. Notably, national policy on *pinyin* usage did not extend to interfering in language use in the private sphere (nor, indeed, to the transliteration of names in passports, though according to Dupré the directive was allegedly intended to). However, the government did step into the private sphere in another controversy in 2011, concerning the use of simplified characters aimed at the burgeoning number of Chinese tourists visiting the island. The Taiwan Tourism Bureau was forced to delete simplified characters from its webpages, having taken this language policy decision unofficially, and the government "encouraged private businesses not to provide information, such as restaurant menus, in simplified characters" (Dupré 2017: 126). Again, the ideological justification here seems to be that traditional characters are associated with the legitimacy of the ROC, since the ROC retained this orthographic system while the PRC moved towards simplified characters in the 1950s and 1960s in an attempt to increase mass literacy. This is thus a complex process of de-Taiwanization and re-Sinicization, since it is not full de-Taiwanization in that it is making Taiwan – or the ROC – distinct from the PRC and, as such, it is re-Sinicization according to a particular interpretation of what "China" is.

5.6.2 The social consensus

While, as Dupré (2017) argues, de-Taiwanization and re-Sinicization was part of the KMT's policy, there were severe constraints on what could actually be done in terms of drastically altering the tolerance and promotion of multilingualism. A social consensus had been reached by 2008 that multilingualism was something to be protected, even if there were disagreements – such as over the NLDL – on the specifics of how it should proceed. A series of critical junctures and path dependencies had led to this situation. First, the KMT itself had initiated sociolinguistic and language policy reform under Lee Teng-hui, and the party "was not in a position to revert to its pre-Lee ideology of overt Chinese nationalism" (Dupré 2017: 125). Second, the DPP had capitalized on multilingual equality as a cornerstone of its *bentuhua* nationalist program, and the KMT had been forced into adopting some of those terms of reference simply by dint of broader processes of democratic reform. Third, a clue comes from considering not merely which government is in power, but the enduring bureaucracy of the state; the mandate and mission of the Council of Indigenous Peoples (CIP) and Hakka Affairs Council (HAC) remains to protect their respective constituencies' interests in sociolinguistic, cultural, and (to some extent) political development, regardless of the party in charge of the government. For example, Mayaw Dongi, Deputy Minister of the CIP between 2008 and 2013 and Minister between 2013 and 2016 under the KMT, initially worked under the DPP government between 2004 and 2008 as the CIP's chief secretary. Similarly, Liu Ching-chung, Minister of the HAC between 2014 and 2016, was a politically unaffiliated former Dean of the Graduate Institute at National Pingtung University of Education; his successor, Chung Wan-mei was appointed by Tsai Ing-wen for a brief stint in 2016, but had served in administrative roles under both the first DPP government from 2001, and the KMT government between 2008 and 2016. In other words, appointments within the bureaucracy were made less with consideration for partisan politics than bureaucratic competency.

Notwithstanding the continued refusal to grant the Hoklo their own bureau of cultural affairs, and the abolition of the National Languages Committee in 2013 – the only effective bureaucratic institution for Hoklo language promotion (Dupré 2017: 127) – no serious challenge to multilingual equality could have been undertaken without appearing to be tantamount to the re-imposition of the martial law era ban, with all the symbolic meanings that it entailed. It would have outraged civil society groups and many voters, alienating the KMT's constituents possibly to the point of mass disorder. In fact, in some respects, the KMT turned out to be *more* progressive on certain language issues than the DPP had. Their opposition to the NLDL seemed to spring more from sheer bloody-mindedness towards anything the DPP proposed while in power, rather than any true ideological commitment to some return to monolingualism. Specifically, the KMT drafted an Indigenous People's Languages Development Law (IPLDL) in 2015, which had earlier been drafted by the DPP as an alternative to the NLEL, and in 2010 passed the Hakka Basic Law (HBL), which was an amended version of an earlier DPP bill from 2005.[53]

---

[53] The IPLDL was drafted in 2015. We will see in the epilogue to this book that the DPP under Tsai Ing-wen eventually passed a version of the law as the Indigenous Peoples' Language Act in 2017.

5.6.3 The Hakka Basic Law

The Hakka Basic Law (HBL) was initially drafted as the Hakka Language Development Law (HLDL) by the DPP in 2005 as an alternative to the NLEL, before the DPP decided to pursue the NLDL (Dupré 2017: 127). The bill called for the creation of Hakka regions – counties and cities such as Miaoli and Hsinchu – where Hakka constituted over half of the population, in which "both Hakka and the official language(s) stipulated by the state would have official status" (HLDL sec. 1). Dupré (2017: 127–128, 135fn.2) summarizes the more specific provisions of the bill, including that: chiefs of local executives would be obliged to use Hakka in formal addresses; local governments were to create the conditions for Hakka language environments; certification of Hakka proficiency could be considered in hiring and promotion of bureaucratic personnel; Hakka could be used in courts and the legislature; the central government was to establish corpus planning Hakka research institutes; and national universities were to facilitate the training of Hakka teachers for acquisition purposes. Clearly based on the draft of the international UNDRM framework, adopted in 1992, and the UNDRIP framework, which was circulating but not promulgated until two years *after* the HLDL was proposed, the bill was concerned with promotion- and not merely tolerance-oriented rights, and had interlocking positive and negative rights that created specific affirmative obligations on the state.

In the end, the HBL that was passed in 2010 contained rather weak provisions for language development, and the co-officialization proposal was effectively dropped. Specifically, Dupré (2017: 130) points to Article 6 as the strongest guarantee of linguistic rights, which states that where Hakka form more than one-third of the population

> Hakka should be promoted as the language of public affairs; civil servants and teachers should enhance their Hakka proficiency; the acquisition of Hakka language proficiency certificates should be rewarded.

As such, Dupré (2017: 131) argues, "the term 'language of public affairs' is no more intuitive than the DPP's earlier proposal [in 2002] to make English a 'quasi-official' language". Language activists were scathing of the approach. Nevertheless, it represents a volte-face on the part of the KMT compared to the draconian approaches to banning minority languages under martial law.

When considering the development of the HBL by the KMT, Dupré (2017: 123) offers a more nuanced explanation than sheer opposition to DPP policies for the sake of it. Instead, he argues that "the Hakka minority has constituted a politically 'neutral' group whose recognition can fulfil ... the KMT's re-Sinicization agenda". At the same time, the DPP's support for a law that recognized the culture of a single minority group – in contrast to its earlier stated goals of ethnic equality under *bentuhua* – similarly comes down to the political neutrality of the Hakka minority; their recognition also fulfils the DPP's Taiwanization agenda, albeit in limited ways. Framed another way, the KMT and its allies can cast the Hakka group – who, as mentioned, are electorally significant and do not constitute a predictable voting bloc – as "ethnically Chinese" whose identity is not symbolic of Taiwanese independence, while the DPP and pan-greens can cast them as "native Taiwanese" (Dupré 2017: 131). At the heart of the matter – though Dupré does not use this term – are questions of transitional justice; the Hakka can be portrayed as victims of both Hoklo ethnic chauvinism and authoritarian KMT oppression. "No accusations of ethnic chauvinism are therefore readily possible [against the Hakka]," Dupré (2017: 131) writes, "except perhaps being part of the larger category of 'Chinese oppressors' of the Austronesian Aboriginals".

5.6.4 Language-in-education policies: The twelve-year national curriculum

A final note should be made about the KMT's approach to local language education in the proposed new comprehensive education curriculum, which was to expand the nine-year curriculum to twelve years. In late 2013, the MOE under Chiang Wei-ling had planned to build on earlier DPP policies that mandated compulsory mother-tongue language classes for elementary students in grades one through three. Instead, new policy would require that compulsory classes would be extended to junior high school students through grade six. Civil society groups quickly weighed in on the proposal. It faced opposition from the MOE's own Syllabus Research subcommittee (*Taipei Times* 2014), as well as from the Secondary and Elementary School Principals' Association who suggested that native languages should be learned in the setting of extra-curricular school social clubs (Lin 2014). The policy was supported by the Alliance for Taiwanese Mother-Tongues and the National Alliance of Parents, while the Union of Education in Taiwan believed that the policy would not go far enough, and compulsory local language education should be extended through grade twelve.

The KMT proposal, and Chiang Wei-ling's initially dogmatic stance on it in particular, is notable in that Chiang, former president of National Central University, was a strict ROC constitutionalist. Under other proposals, the curriculum was to be more China-focused: Zheng Zheng-gong, or Koxinga, and the

Zheng family regime were to be referred to as Ming dynasty rulers and not merely a family of warlords; the Dutch and Spanish merely "entered" Taiwan rather than colonized it; and the term "China" was to become "mainland China" in accordance with the Constitution and the Act Governing Relations between the People of the Taiwan Area and the Mainland Area (*China Post* 2014). Even the usually pro-KMT *China Post* lambasted the proposals as "juvenile attempts [by the DPP and KMT] to contradict each other". Ultimately, while the twelve-year compulsory education curriculum was adopted in 2014, the KMT backtracked on the language-in-education proposal, leaving DPP policy in place.

5.7 Conclusion

This chapter has traced the development of discourses about and policies towards multilingualism since the lifting of martial law. We have seen how language repression was intrinsically related to political repression, and thus that language liberalization accompanied – and perhaps was key to – political liberalization after martial law. By the late 1990s, campaigning monolingually in Mandarin was a political non-starter; the electorate, with the assertiveness that comes with a new democracy, demanded that candidates speak their own local languages. The DPP made multilingualism a cornerstone of their party platform of Taiwanese identity as a surrogate for claims to full political independence; in the absence of opportunities to enact legislation, this was achieved through the bureaucratic channel of national education policy. I have also assessed the transitional justice contexts of status planning scenarios, arguing that only true multilingual equality through language officialization meets transitional justice criteria. Language policy under the reformed KMT, who returned to power in 2008, was constrained by path dependencies and the social and political consensus developed not merely under the DPP, but by the nativist turn begun by KMT president Lee Teng-hui from the mid-1990s.

In itself, one hour a week of language instruction in elementary schools is not going to do very much to stem age-graded language shift and loss, particularly when education managers and school principals are ambivalent about policy implementation. But the subsidiary function has been to contribute to an overall revaluing of minority languages in public and political life. Positive discourses about languages and cultures are as important as laws and policies for maintenance and revitalization; whatever administrators, principals, and parents think of MTLE, there can be no denying that language revitalization has been put on the map, and local languages positioned as a cherished part of Taiwan's complex socio-political heritage. The battles over the NLEL and the NLDL are further examples of this discursive process. Like any other population, the Taiwanese do not vote solely on language and identity issues, but they are salient lodestars for party-political direction and deliberation in the public sphere. Just as the critical juncture of KMT reforms charted the course for sociolinguistic reform that the DPP continued (Dupré 2016), DPP policies created a path dependency that the KMT had to follow when they returned to power in 2008.

6 Globalization, neoliberalism, and immigration

6.1 Introduction

With the end of the Cold War, and contemporary globalization processes apparently deepening and intensifying inexorably, it became briefly fashionable to question whether the end of the nation-state was nigh (e.g. Guéhenno 1995). For Sassen (2007) and others, however, the nation-state is still the primary locus and final arbiter of the implementation of globalization. The resurgence of European and American nationalisms in response to globalization, particularly with the rise of the far-right since the 2010s, provide more empirical evidence that the nation-state has not withered away. But, with this said, nation-states, particularly weaker or emergent ones, cannot completely control the forces of globalization, and these issues are realized through sociolinguistic contexts in myriad ways. Taiwan is no exception. Its uncertain geopolitical status has given rise to a robust, if incipient, national identity framed by *bentuhua*, and yet state policies are shaped by global currents. Two main sociolinguistic outcomes can be identified. The first is Taiwan's management of its relationship with English, the global language that comes imbued with neo-imperialist and neoliberal doctrines and threatens the very egalitarianism that *bentuhua* nationalism is premised on. The second is the languages of the island's foreign spouses and migrant workers, which must be accommodated from the perspective of policy but do not fit into the categories delimited by the often-parochial tendencies of *bentuhua* nationalism.

This chapter is structured as follows. The first half addresses the mantra of "English for all?", arguing that, in practice, socio-economically and geographically stratified access to English language education (ELE) means English is only a useful linguistic capital for a few. I begin by contextualizing the DPP's framing of English as a means to "connect Taiwan with the world", essential for claims to political independence in the international community and for global economic competitiveness more broadly. From here, two sections examine the interrelationships between policies and discourses. Specifically, I analyze the construction of English as a valuable yet geographically stratified linguistic capital in the public education system, and the emergence of a shadow private education sector that causes further stratification along socio-economic lines. This data is based on interviews conducted with teachers, school principals, and education officials in 2007 and 2015. Cities and counties referred to are real, though schools and people are anonymized. The second half of the chapter addresses foreign spouses, new immigrants, and their "othered" languages. I begin with a brief ethnographic vignette of Taipei's metrolingualism, in order to demonstrate how these languages are invisible and unheard in civil society in general. The linguistic capital of foreign manufacturing and domestic workers is then addressed, before turning to the "language problems" of foreign spouses, whose linguistic and cultural assimilation is fundamental to how they are constructed as "good citizens" in the eyes of the state and "good Taiwanese" in the eyes of civil society.

6.2 English for all? Globalization, neoliberalism, and education

Although English is in theory a neutral lingua franca – one that potentially blunts Steiner's "razor edges of division" (Steiner 1998: 56–8) – English-spread has come under sustained criticism for contributing to economic, political, and social stratification between individual schools, districts, counties, and nation-states, particularly as it is framed within contemporary neoliberalism. In societies where it is not spoken as a primary language, it can only be acquired as a second language through education, whether implemented by the state or private providers in parallel sectors. English acquisition in these contexts is thus subject to many of the problems of stratification present in education systems more generally. For Park and Wee (2012: 1), "the spread of English is not only an apt demonstration of how our world has become increasingly interconnected; it is also a key example of the problems and dilemmas that globalization engenders or exacerbates". In this section, drawing on Price (2014), these issues are examined using Taiwan as a case study. Data from ethnographic work, including interviews with school principals and education managers, is contextualized using recent theoretical innovations in the sociolinguistics of globalization (Blommaert 2010) and language and neoliberalism (Block, Gray, and Holborow 2012). Neoliberalism venerates the ideals of "choice", "competition", and the "free market". For students and parents, however, English proficiency is less a "choice" than a necessity for success in education and employment, and "English for all" policies are thus imperatives rather than opportunities. The structural function of English as a valued capital is examined alongside language ideologies regarding the 'earlier-the-better' argument for L2 acquisition and the idealization of the native-speaking teacher.

6.2.1 Between localism and globalism: The context of DPP English language policy

During the 1990s and 2000s, a mania for learning English swept the island, which showed no signs of abating when I was last there in 2015. On practically every other block in Taipei, there is an English-language *buxiban* or private cram school for middle- and high-schoolers or an immersive *anjinban* or day care centre for kindergartners. Other large cities are the same; they can also be found in small towns, although they are not quite as densely packed, and more rarely in rural areas. All students must study English somehow, since it is a mandatory tested subject from high school through to tertiary education (in some universities, English competence is required not just for matriculation but also for graduation). After-work classes for adults are held in offices and factories or in the more voluntary sphere of civil society in private schools. One southern Taiwan municipality briefly required that its garbage trucks stop playing Beethoven to alert their presence – individual households deliver their household waste directly to the truck several evenings a week – and replaced it with recordings of "useful" English phrases. Although everyone seems to be learning English, few people speak the language to any degree of proficiency in wider society. But the structural effects on the political economy, the education system, and the valuation and circulation of linguistic and cultural capital, are profound. English, in short, is a means to achieve upward socio-economic mobility, whether in terms of actually acquiring it, or merely being seen to acquire it, in local, national, and global circuits. This translates into something of a national anxiety, felt by both citizens and the state.

There is some historical context to this obsession with English. In 1946, there was a belief in some parts of Taiwanese civil society and its resurgent public sphere that the US would soon assert political trusteeship of Taiwan and restrain the excesses of Governor Chen Yi. This led to the enthusiasm for learning Mandarin in 1945 to be put aside in favour of English: "English conversation classes flourished, radio programs offered English instruction, and a spate of new publications eagerly reprinted American stories and news commentary" (Kerr [1964] 2017: 167). The *Tai-oan Chheng Lian* magazine, suppressed during the later years of the Japanese *kominka* program but by now revived and presumably tolerated for its overall anti-Japanese stance, began printing an English edition, *Taiwan Youth Report*, which "encouraged English-language studies and stressed the need for strong international ties to advance Formosa's development" (Kerr 2017: 170). Other publications, such as *Liberty*, expressed similar opinions. The lead editorial in the first issue of *Formosan Magazine* in 1947, for example, opined that

> America does not hesitate to help [the Republic of] China, for the Chinese are a peace-loving people, and to understand American civilization and how Americans of late have made tremendous improvements, the first thing for the Taiwan people to learn is English, and then [read?] American books in every branch of learning. (Kerr 2017: 172)

Conversely, however, Chen Yi's government perceived this over-enthusiasm for the US to be harmful to the project of Sinification of Taiwan. In 1946, Chen's propagandist Stanway Cheng

> knew that Formosans ... were intensively pursuing the study of English, reading anything in English that came to hand. He therefore launched a new English-language journal, the *New Taiwan Monthly* with a dual purpose. It could be used as a vehicle for anti-American propaganda within Formosa, and it could be used abroad as a counterfoil to the popular *Formosan Youth* [sic] *Magazine* and *Liberty*. (Kerr 2017: 183)

Later, in 1952, the English-language *China Post* began life as a mouthpiece for the KMT, who were eager to portray a benign face to the outside world, again with American readerships uppermost in mind, and justify the ROC's designation by the USA as "free" China. The *China Post* is still in publication at the time of writing, though it became an online-only publication in May 2017.

Encapsulated in these historical discourses are some of the dilemmas that face policymakers and citizens in the contemporary context: the recognition that English, and by extension Westernization and Americanization, is essential to Taiwan's global survival, yet combined with a mistrust of foreign influences and foreigners who undermine the delimited categories of who belongs in *bentuhua*. The dilemma of English is, then, related to the paradox – not one entirely unique to Taiwan – in which the political economy of neoliberal globalization is juxtaposed against a localized and introspective ethnic and cultural nationalism.

It should be clear from preceding chapters that Taiwan's ambivalent geopolitical status exemplifies Putnam's (1988: 430) notion of a "domestic-international entanglement": a "two-level game" that must be played both at home and abroad. In other words, seemingly globally-oriented policies always have a domestic function, and vice-versa. The DPP played this game partly through language politics. Policies towards revitalizing local languages were not simply redressing past linguistic injustices; they signalled to the world important liberal-democratic credentials that were necessary for any claim to eventual political independence. English has a similar function; DPP nationalism had to engage with the outside world and structures of neoliberal globalization, and English is not only in the world, but the world is in English (Pennycook 1995). Enhancing English language competence among the population was considered key to enhancing Taiwan's political and economic visibility on the world stage; the metaphor of visibility invokes Pennycook's (1995: 14) observation that "English is the language of the global panopticon".

Chen Su-chiao (2006) perceptively argues that the emphasis on promoting both English and local languages created a tension between "indigenization and internationalization". In 2002 – the same year that Taiwan was accepted as a member of the World Trade Organization (WTO) – President Chen Shui-Bian suggested that Taiwan should adopt English as a second (or quasi-) official language in order to maintain the island's "competitive edge" and "to connect Taiwan with the world" (Ko & Yeh 2002), a proposal that was enshrined in the *Challenge 2008* six-year national economic development plan (CEPD 2002). For Dupré (2017: 105), co-officializing English, given that officializing Hoklo was barred as a legislative policy option, was the DPP's "next best option in displacing the status of Mandarin"; there is something appealing about this claim, although Dupré is probably overstating the case. Nevertheless, it was supported by the ultra-nationalist TSU, who quite probably did see this as an option, putting aside their emphasis on Hoklo ethnic nationalism to embrace a *foreign* language, in some impressive ideological gymnastics. This idea did not come to fruition in the face of bipartisan disapproval. According to media reports, then Mayor of Taipei Ma Ying-jeou acerbically noted that, given the present competence of the nation's bureaucrats and politicians (and citizenry), "making English as the second official language is not only unnecessary but, at the moment, also impossible". KMT stalwart James Soong thought it highly unlikely that "that in six years' time, even Chen or [then-Premiere] Yu Shyi-kun themselves will know how to speak English perfectly". Chen Shui-bian's own minister of education, Huang Jung-tsuen, demurred, calling the proposal "controversial" and suggesting that "before deciding which language should be the official language, we should consider [...] our own mother tongues". Wang Tuoh, chief executive of the DPP legislative caucus, refused to even comment on the proposal until it became policy.

Less controversially, *Challenge 2008* emphasized various mechanisms to "improve English proficiency among the whole population" (CEPD 2002: 18) through non-legislative bureaucratic channels and the state's influence in civil society. The "whole population" – or "English for all" – aspect was apparently intended literally; the plan went as far as specifying the need to enhance proficiencies among marginalized populations such as "senior citizens, farmers and fishermen, aborigines and people with learning disabilities" (CEPD 2002: 18). Improved English competence was explicitly rationalized within a neoliberal and globalized framework as central to "national adaptation to globalization and internationalization" (CEPD 2002: 18) and "improving [Taiwan's] international competitiveness" (2002: 19). An English-language summary of *Challenge 2008* (MOE, n.d.) further drew on this framework, emphasizing the need to "cultivate competitive citizens with international foresight" and "move forward into the new century" in a "world where national boundaries are disappearing", as well as "enhanc[ing] the international competitive advantage of higher education institutions". Here, competition is the neoliberal watchword; tellingly, there is little mention of choice.

Challenge 2008 included somewhat esoteric and ambitious proposals, including adopting bilingual street signage and insisting on the Anglicization of restaurant menus. The focus, however, was on the role of English in the compulsory education system, and spawned a raft of new policies. Elementary school English-language education (ELE) had been mandated to start from grade five in 2001, and from grade three beginning in 2003 though, as we will see, individual counties and schools were granted latitude to start earlier, depending on their own policies and resources. The General Scholastic Aptitude Test (GSAT) for university entrance replaced the older Joint Central College Examinations (JCCE) in 2002; while the JCCE had an English component, the broader push towards English meant it had an ever-more important gatekeeping function to higher education under the GSAT. This was complicated by the MOE's development of the parallel General English Proficiency Test (GEPT) which, from 2002, offered a means to demonstrate English proficiency from elementary to advanced levels outside of the GSAT. Many universities eagerly accepted GEPT scores for matriculation purposes; some even required high scores on the GEPT or other metrics of English proficiency in order for students to graduate. While it recognized that disparities in education provision between rural and urban areas were potential barriers to its "English for all" ethos, *Challenge 2008* offered little in terms of concrete policy proposals to reduce them. Crucially, it did not seem to anticipate the private sector seeking to profit by providing ELE in competition with the public sector, contributing further to stratification along socio-economic lines.

6.2.2 English as capital

English was framed as a valued capital in various policies, most obviously testing mechanisms in compulsory education, and discourses which both underpinned and emanated from such policies. However, access to English was stratified along rural/urban and socioeconomic lines by uneven resource allocation in public schools which disfavoured poorer, rural areas and the fact that *buxiban* (private schools) operated in wealthier, urban areas where it was economically viable to do so. Poorer, rural areas were thus disenfranchised by both the public and private sectors. As Director Chen, of Miaoli County's education bureau, put it in our interview:

> Starting times for kids to learn languages and the shortage of good English teachers are the most controversial issues in many areas. In 2001, we wanted to start ELE in the 3rd grade, since research shows this is a good time to start. But there were not enough English teachers in Taiwan, so we delayed implementation until the 5th grade. The MOE tried to recruit 3000 local Taiwanese English teachers. But most teachers were attracted to urban areas. [Director Chen, Miaoli County Education Bureau]

Assuming that Miaoli County's ELE policy was grounded in sound pedagogy, it was constrained by structural sociological factors. The MOE and the DPP were cognizant of iniquitous access to ELE along geographic and socio-economic lines. In 2002, *Challenge 2008* noted disparities between rural and urban areas due to differences in "economic capacity, teachers and resources" and the need to "improve English in rural areas". However, in 2007, five years later and towards the end of the program, it seemed little had changed: most of my interviewees mentioned continuing rural/urban gaps, and the issue surfaced regularly in media and political discourses. Director Chen made explicit reference to the difficulties of attracting teachers to already socio-economically disadvantaged rural areas. Even if salaries were comparable in rural areas, there are complex sociological reasons why teachers may prefer urban settings: rural areas have fewer amenities and "outsiders" often face challenges in integrating into local communities; paradoxically, teachers with children may be put off by the under-resourced local school systems that need teachers most.

Unequal resource distribution is by no means confined to Taiwan or to ELE, but the Taiwanese context had a political specificity in terms of competition between local areas. The DPP's nation-building *bentuhua* project had to contend with a historically delicate balance between the affluent north and poorer counties in central and southern Taiwan. This is not merely a rural/urban or even socioeconomic divide, but one which is political and cultural. Chinese immigrants who arrived with the KMT between 1945 and 1949 became political elites and settled in Taipei and surrounding areas in the north. The rest of the country, commonly referred to as "the South", continues to be inhabited by the historically marginalized Hoklo majority and minority Hakka and aboriginal ethnolinguistic groups. An editorial in the *Taipei Times* (Wang 2002: 8), concerning the DPP's new ELE policy proposals, warned:

> [As] the issue of language can influence the growth and decline of ethnic groups – not to mention that speaking English has usually been taken as a symbol of elitism in southern Taiwan – the issue may easily become a fight over ideologies that divides our ethnic groups. (Wang 2002: 8)

English was unlikely to literally ignite ethnic conflict in Taiwan, but its potential to precipitate even a "fight over ideologies" is important. The symbolic indexing of "elitism" – made concrete by the value of English as a cultural capital – positioned English as another site for the contestation of cultural politics. These were at least partly constituted by ethnolinguistic- and class-based structural inequalities which patterned along north/south lines. *Bentuhua* attempted to redress the injustices of the authoritarian KMT era and the disenfranchisement of autochthonous "southern" ethnolinguistic groups. English was not a language of any particular group, nor a lingua franca of anyone other than "an elite minority" (Mufwene 2002: 167). But while it might not itself hasten the demise of Hoklo, Hakka or aboriginal languages and identities, English devalues them as capitals within linguistic and educational markets. Principal Long, of Lan Hua elementary school in Taipei, further described the differences between Taipei and the rest of the island by invoking the notion of academic "pressure" and the expectations of parents who were positioned as consumers within neoliberalized discourses and policies:

> We are in Zhong Da district. There are many professors' kids studying at our school, so parents demand a lot from the school and the teachers. Let's put it this way (draws map of Taiwan on table with finger). Taipei City is here. Going south, the pressure becomes smaller. Taitung [an impoverished county in the South East] is here, the pressure is pretty small here. It is great in Taipei city. It is greater in Zhong Da district. And the pressure is greatest in Lan Hua School in Zhong Da district! [Principal Long, Lan Hua Elementary School, Taipei]

Principal Long links ELE with academic "pressure" and its importance in the compulsory education system. The reference to "professors'" is to some degree literal, given that Lan Hua School is near two prestigious universities. But "professors" might also be a heuristic for a broader middle-class dynamic. As Skeggs (1997: 9) argues, "social categories" such as class are not capitals themselves; instead "they provide the relations in which capitals come to be organized and valued". Education attainment – including attainment in English – is a highly important form of cultural capital valued by both "professors" and the imputed middle-class. Principal Long further configured pressure as a normative function of the national education system and presented it as concentric, radiating out from a single school in a single district in Taipei. Stratification within Taipei was indicated by the principal's distinction between Lan Hua School and others in the district, and between Zhong Da and other districts. She constructed the broader division, however, at the national level: between Taipei and "the south" and, implicitly, between rural/urban and poorer/wealthier areas. The concept of "pressure" – which might be a shorthand for "competition" – illustrates an important aspect of language-in-education policies (and education policies more broadly). In a compulsory education system, pressure would be theoretically equal; assuming access to educational resources was equal. However, a clearly iniquitous distribution of resources would mean that poorer, rural counties with less access to resources should be under more pressure to achieve; in short, they would have to do more with less in order to compete effectively in the educational market. So why did Principal Long see children in Taipei – and in her school specifically – as being under greater pressure? One explanation is that rather than, as Principal Long suggested, "going south, the pressure becomes smaller", it may be more accurate to say that going south, the opportunities become scarcer. Children in the south or rural areas lacked access to educational resources, and thus were ruled out of competing effectively in the education market. They were under less pressure to achieve, since their opportunities were already limited.

However, linguistic or educational markets are no longer solely bound by the nation-state (Park & Wee 2012); in contemporary globalization, these also have multiscalar dimensions in which regional dynamics have an additional global aspect. As Director Zhang put it:

> English is an important international language, and Taipei is an international metropolis. Taipei's children in future will have to compete globally, [and] participate in international exchanges. They will need to know English, and so we must teach them. [Director Zhang, Taipei City Bureau of Education]

Mr Zhang seems to concur with Principal Long that Taipei is the epicentre of the island's academic pressure, but also positions it as the capital city of a nation with aspirations towards achieving recognition of its sovereignty and one enmeshed in a constellation of other "global cities" (Sassen 2002). These cities form a network in which the centres of finance and capital in the global north, such as London, New York, and Hong Kong are increasingly linked with the global south through intermediaries such as Bangkok, São Paulo, and Mexico City. Sassen calls these linkages "the new geographies of centrality at the inter-urban level", that constitute a "transnational space for *the formation of new claims by global capital but also by other types of actors*" (2002: 17, emphasis added). "Claims by global capital" may correspond with the director's prediction that "Taipei's children [would] have to compete globally": here we see neoliberalism's catechism – competition and globalization – invoked. What the director phrased as "participat[ion] in international exchanges" perhaps reflects less the naked power of capitalism than the soft(er) power of what Sassen calls "claims ... by other types of actors", such as supranational political or cultural organizations. Taken together, English is a highly valued capital as the conduit through which these global economic, political, and cultural interactions were presumed to take place. These discourses reproduced the DPP's own rationale for "improving English competence among the whole population" in order to enhance "globalization and internationalization" (CEPD 2002: 18).

The paradigm of neoliberal competition which implicated counties and cities, schools and individuals, was put into even sharper relief by the parallel education system in the private sector. Neoliberalism approves of transferring traditional state functions to the private sector, but the existence of a private market for supplementary ELE in Taiwan provides a case-study in how even private markets are not "free" but constructed by state discourses and policies (and largely supports Piller & Cho's 2013 analysis of the South Korean context). The imperative to learn English under the DPP created opportunities for private schools, or *buxiban*, to profit from the perception that access to the valued cultural capital of English was lacking in parts of the public sector. There are two central paradoxes here. First, the demand met by the supposedly "free" market in the private education sector was created by state policies which emphasized ELE in the first place, despite neoliberalism being "philosophically opposed to any form of regulation, including language policy" (Piller & Cho 2013: 24). Second, parents were hardly exercising their "choice" within a free linguistic or educational market; rather, they were impelled to compete in it. Private *buxiban* offered an advantage within a compulsory system, but access to *buxiban* was dependent on socio-economic factors such as individual income level and whether aggregated wealth or income in a given community constituted a market which justified *buxiban* operating. Stratification occurred, therefore, along both class and geographic lines, which paralleled – and arguably exacerbated – that which occurred in the public education system. Neoliberal theory, however, does not take into account these structural barriers to the "free" market. For Director Wang, of rural Taitung County's education bureau, parents did not merely turn to the private education system because the public sector was perceived to be lacking; rather, the private education sector actively had a detrimental effect on the public sector. V.W. Chang (2007: 68) notes dryly that English learning in Taiwan is a "national sport", and Director Wang made a similar analogy:

> If the *buxiban* are run well, they help people get good grades in exams. It's a chicken-and-egg situation. If the *buxiban* did not help, then people wouldn't attend them. They are not positive for the education system. They are like the drugs people use in the Olympics. [Director Wang, Taitung County Bureau of Education]

Private supplementary education is not unique to Taiwan: Turkey has the *deshane* system; the US has "test preparation centres". Nor is it an entirely novel response to neoliberalism: Taiwanese *buxiban* share with South Korean *hagwon* (and contemporary Japanese *juku*) a common ancestor in the supplementary education systems developed by Japanese colonization of both countries in the early twentieth century (Zeng 1999: 66). Arguably, the Japanese, Korean and Taiwanese systems have even earlier antecedents in the private schools for the formidable Chinese civil service examinations, or *keju*, in operation from the seventh century to 1905 (Suen & Yu 2006: 48). However, "foreign language" *buxiban* in Taiwan mushroomed between the 1990s and 2008, paralleling the growth of neoliberalism globally and nationally, and the increasing commodification of English as essential to educational success and socio-economic advancement. In this regard should be noted the "symbolic added value" (Duchêne & Heller 2012: 10) of *buxiban* themselves. Private *buxiban* performed a surrogate child-care function in addition to their central raison d'être of increasing access to ELE, thus indexing a symbolic value linked to prestige and wealth. Mom-and-Pop operations at one end of the scale to Montessori-type schools at the other competed for the business of parents, and parents thus competed with each other on the socio-economic scale as to the perceived best or most prestigious *buxiban* to which to send their children. Though she did not keep records, Principal Long estimated that, of children in her elementary school in an affluent area of Taipei:

> [Probably] more than 80% go to the *buxiban*. They don't all necessarily take English classes, [but] most of them – maybe 85% – do. English is taught from the first grade. And then there are English tests in high school and the GEPT. So there ought to be many students. They need to take the tests, so they care about this. [Principal Long, Taipei]

There *ought* to have been many students studying at English *buxiban* because English is a gatekeeper in the form of tests in the public education sector from elementary school onward. Ironically, the principal acknowledges that the private *buxiban* offer the kinds of competitive advantages in ELE that are valuable capital in the public sector to which the principal belongs. State discourses and policies thus have a normative function in constructing a "free" market in the private sector. In a neoliberal system, both private and public functions overlap and compete, but in a competition in which the private sector inevitably prevails; in effect, the public sector is competing against itself, since it is always destined to lose either way. At root here, again, is the role of the state in setting the relative value of the capital of "educational attainment", a capital organized by social categories such as class. Students (or, more accurately, their parents) should be availing themselves of supplementary education, assuming that parents have the socio-economic means to do so. In Principal Long's affluent area of the capital city, this is less of an issue than for parents in more socio-economically disadvantaged areas, either elsewhere in Taipei or in the rest of the island. In contrast, Principal Tang, from Yang Shan elementary school in a remote and socio-economically underprivileged area in the mountains of Taitung County, said:

> People in Taitung are poor. They do not have money. It is expensive to go to the *buxiban*. Most people in Taitung are farmers and they can only make money to sustain their daily living. They can't afford to pay tuition fees for learning dancing, singing, and English. [Principal Tang, Taitung County]

Of course, not all people in Taitung are poor, since stratified wealth inequalities exist in micro-level contexts. But people in Taitung are poor relative to other areas; Taitung is impoverished compared to other counties, and particularly

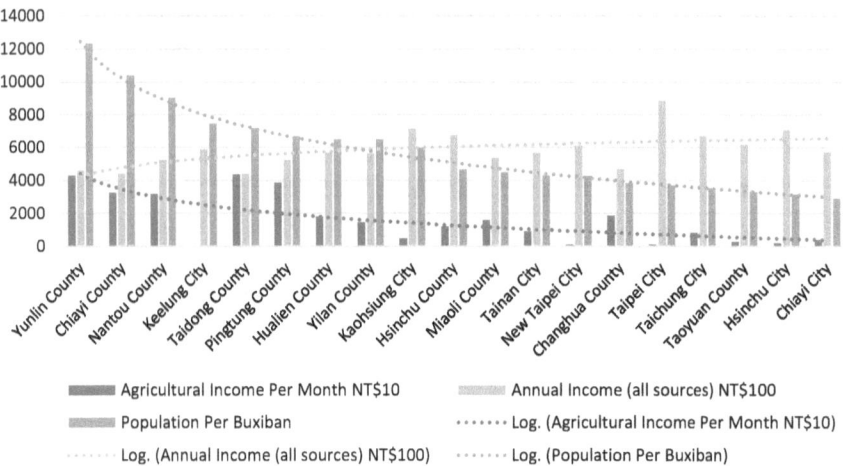

Figure 6.1: Population, income, and *buxiban* density by county and city.
Source: Taipei Board of Education (2013); DGBAS (2010); MOI (2010).

compared to urban areas, and especially compared to the capital, Taipei. The corollary of this is that private *buxiban* operate according to the iron logic of the market. *Buxiban* were not attracted to poorer areas where it is difficult, or impossible, to turn a profit. Figure 6.1 aggregates four datasets to demonstrate the distribution of *buxiban* geographically and socio-economically; these are official population data by county and city (MOI 2010); numbers of licenced *buxiban* (Taipei Board of Education, 2013); and average income and agricultural income (both DGBAS 2010).[54] Two broad correlations emerge. Below average income (<NT$586,534 per annum) correlates with a higher average population per *buxiban* (6,740 people per *buxiban*) and vice versa (>$586,534 per annum; 4,512 people per *buxiban*). Furthermore, counties with higher average agricultural income – indicating more rural areas – have fewer *buxiban* compared to population.[55] Rural and poorer areas (including, presumably, poorer areas within cities) thus tend to have less access to private ELE,

---

[54] Population per *buxiban* ranges from 12,332 (Yunlin County) to 2,926 (Chiayi City). Average annual income ranges from NT$438,229 (Taitung County) to NT$884,546 (Taipei City). Monthly agricultural income ranges from NT$0 (Keelung City) to NT$43,489 (Taitung County).

[55] TPBOE data is from 2013; since then, according to 2017 data, *buxiban* numbers have decreased. This is likely explained by the declining birth rate more than it is by a reduced fervour for learning English. With both datasets, the broad correlations hold between agricultural/overall income and population per buxiban.

compounding the structural problems of access to ELE in the public education sector. Furthermore, this disparity broadly falls along a north-to-south axis. Again, Principal Long's notion that "going south, the pressure becomes smaller" may be more accurately put as going south, the opportunities become scarcer. "Pressure" decreases as access to the cultural capital of English decreases: the stakes become lower, and disparities in public education between the north and south, between poorer and wealthier areas, and between rural and urban areas, are further entrenched by the private sector.

The correlation is not exact, however, and the rural/urban and north/south divides are not as rigid as they might seem. A more finely grained analysis of local socio-political and economic contexts reveals multi-layered and polycentric patterns of social stratification. Taipei City, for example, has the highest average employment salary but ranks fifth in *buxiban* density. This suggests quite considerable stratification, in terms of access to private ELE and thus socio-economically, within the city itself. The blue-collar, industrialized outskirts of Taipei – New Taipei City (formerly Taipei County) and Taoyuan County – have lower average incomes than the capital, but similar levels of *buxiban* density. Their proximity to the capital perhaps indicates aspirations towards upward social mobility. Hsinchu City, an hour or so by train from Taipei, meanwhile, has the second highest *buxiban* density on the island. Its size – around 416,000 people (MOI 2010) – and its status as a wealthy centre for the high-tech export industry (demonstrated by its high average employment income) suggests that socio-economic stratification is less stark, creating a favourable economic climate for the private education sector. In the south, Tainan City bucks the southern trend of low income and *buxiban* density; though this may be explained by local socio-economic development, such as the city's science and industrial park, as well as being the hometown of then president Chen Shui-Bian and thus a DPP heartland that benefited favourably from government economic policies between 2000 and 2008. The southern city of Chiayi has a low average income – Chiayi County, which adjoins it, is the poorest in the nation – but Chiayi City has the highest density of *buxiban* in the country. Changhua County, in south-central Taiwan is similarly incongruous: it has the fourth lowest income in the country, and its agricultural income ratio is reasonably high, but its *buxiban* density is only slightly lower than Taipei. However, both Changhua County and Chiayi City are home to important research universities. Professors, by definition, understand "the rules of the game" of the education system. They desire – and are able to afford – that their children gain a competitive edge, especially where the local education system lacks resources.

I asked Principal Tang what he thought was the best way to increase access to ELE in his rural area in Taitung. I expected him to suggest more resources or teachers for Yang Shan elementary school. Instead, he linked local socio-economic development with the creation of particular markets:

> If there were some tunnels to connect the west with the east, it may only take an hour to get here. And Taitung will have many chances to develop. Why? People will come to establish factories, businesses, or tourism. Once the population increases, the English *buxiban* and fast food restaurants [*maidanglao*/麥當勞] will come here. [Principal Tang, Taitung County]

The principal's comments echo, I suspect unintentionally, Spolsky's "only half-facetious" (2004: 15) dictum that the best way to increase ELE on the Navajo Reservation in the US was by "building more roads" (Spolsky 1974). For Principal Tang, broader socio-economic development of the local area – via the government investing in infrastructure – would grant greater access to *buxiban* and hence to a global language. Once again, we see the neoliberal paradox: state policy is fundamentally implicated in local socio-economic development and the creation of a supposedly "free" private *buxiban* market, which is held to be the only (or at least most efficient) way that children can compete in the public education system. Equating the arrival of *buxiban* with fast-food restaurants – the principal used *maidanglao*, the phonologically-assimilated name of the global and emblematically neoliberal McDonald's burger chain – rather aptly demonstrated the influence of neoliberal globalization in local contexts. English is not merely a tool for communication but, equated with globalization, indexes neoliberal values of competition, commodification, and the infallibility of the "free" market. Principal Tang finished our interview with this observation:

> English is a world language. People in Europe, America and Asia all speak English. I think learning English is more helpful in future than learning local languages. [Principal Tang, Taitung County]

There is a rather poignant irony in this quote. Due to physical and geographical constraints, local children had trouble getting outside their local areas and over the mountains without the national government building more roads and tunnels. In spite of these limitations, English was seen as the language to connect them to the rest of the world in the global context.

6.2.3 The-earlier-the-better argument

The emphasis on ELE, and its gate-keeping effect within the public education system, contributed to an anxiety among parents as to the most effective age to begin learning English and thus acquire a valued cultural capital. A persistent language ideology exists that foreign L2 acquisition is more effective the earlier it starts. Arguably, this is based on the "nativist" model of (L1 or actually bilingual) language acquisition whereby it is understood that babies learn language from birth and the dissemination in popular discourse that, as Lenneberg (1967) first proposed, there is a "critical period" between birth and puberty when language must be acquired. Lenneberg's hypothesis is in itself controversial and based on isolated cases of linguistic and social deprivation, and it was not originally intended to apply to L2 acquisition. Scholarly opinion differs on the optimum age for beginning L2 acquisition outside of a genuinely bilingual environment; this can be anywhere from around seven years old to adulthood, depending on how "optimum" is defined in various models of competence. This younger-the-better argument, which first gained credence in the late 1960s, pre-dates the emergence of neoliberalism in the late 1970s. But it is well suited to neoliberal discourses of competition for a language which is a valued capital. In January 2009, I received an email from an adult former student living in Taipei:

> I would like to buy some books and CDs from the UK for *my little baby who is five months old*. Could you give me some recommendations? I mean audio books. I want my baby to hear English at home. (Emphasis added)

Beginning ELE at five months old might seem extreme, but a whole industry is dedicated to early childhood (and even *in utero*) education, including language learning. It indexes the prevalence of the younger-the-better belief in Taiwan, which can be demonstrated beyond mere anecdote. Table 6.1 shows data from two separate surveys in 2002 (*United Daily News* poll data, cited in J. Chang 2004: 110) and 2008 (Y.F. Chang, 2008) as to the age Taiwanese parents believed ELE should start in public schools. Between the promulgation of the *Challenge 2008* national development plan in 2002 and its conclusion in 2008, the data shows a downward trend in the perceived optimum age for beginning ELE. Official policy arguably shaped public perception and vice-versa (Oladejo 2006); MOE policies which lowered the age that ELE must have begun in schools – to grade five (i.e. age 10–11) in 2001, and to grade three in 2003 – may have contributed to the perception that ELE should start earlier, and vice-versa. Desiring early access to ELE had as much to do with optimizing access to an institutionalized cultural capital (Bourdieu 1986) as it did with acquiring linguistic competence. Parents were forced into a competitive situation, whereby children with a head-start on ELE were perceived to gain an important competitive advantage later.

Teachers, school principals, and local education managers were similarly implicated in a competitive system. The younger-the-better issue in Taiwan was exacerbated by a quirk of DPP language policy: not all counties and cities started ELE in public schools at the same time. MOE policy specified the age at which

Table 6.1: Parental opinions on when ELE should start in public schools.

When should ELE start?	United Daily News Poll (2002)[1](%)	Y.F. Chang (2008: 429)(%)
7th grade (Junior High)	n/a	1.7
6th grade	26	5
5th grade		
4th grade	30	15.6
3rd grade		
2nd grade	30	36.3
1st grade		
Kindergarten	n/a	41.3

[1] United Daily News survey data does not total 100%: 14% did not know or thought ELE should start later than 6th grade; respondents were not asked about beginning ELE in kindergarten. Chang (2008) does not specify why her data totals 99.9%

English *must* have started – in grade five from 2001, in grade three from 2003 – but gave latitude to local education departments as to when it *could* start. V.W.C Chang (2007: 68) estimates that, as a result, 61% of children started ELE in grade three, 7% in grade two, and 32% in grade one. According to this data, almost a third of children started two years earlier before the rest of the country.

Y.F. Chang's survey data (2008: 429) also found that 83.6% of parents viewed inconsistent starting of ELE as "disrupt[ing] the curriculum continuity", and that 95.7% thought the MOE should ensure that all schools began ELE at the same grade level. For Ms. Long, principal of an elementary school in Taipei, this aspect was a pedagogical issue and one framed by neoliberal discourses of competition:

> We offer English lessons from the first grade at our school. This is a rule made by the Taipei city education department. There are two sessions of English courses each week. The schools [in the rest of the island] are different. English courses start from the third grade. English education *starts earlier and progresses faster in Taipei*. [Principal Long, Lan Hua Elementary School, Taipei;]

Principal Long's comments indicate the normative function of neoliberal competition. For her, an early – and thus competitive – start on ELE in Taipei compared to the rest of Taiwan was positive. She prefaced this, however, by stressing that her school's policy was dictated by a "rule made by the city education department". The city decided who began ELE when, not Principal Long. She was absolved of responsibility, as an educator, for directly contributing to stratified access to ELE. Her participation in an unequal system was justified, since she had little choice in a competitive system that entailed "a shift from pedagogical to market values" (Block, Gray, and Holborow 2012: 6). V.W.C Chang (2007: 68) found that at least two rural areas (Nantou and Taichung counties) started ELE at grade one even while they lacked teachers and resources, presumably as result of the pressure to compete. *Challenge 2008* recognized that "different starting points" for ELE constituted a disparity between urban and rural areas. Yet it refrained from adjusting policy to harmonize the age at which ELE began, ostensibly offering the neoliberal value of "choice" but (perhaps unintentionally) encouraging competition, illusory notions in the context of unequal distribution of resources. Furthermore, for various sociological reasons, parents are severely constrained in their ability to avail themselves of "choice" in a competition between different regions; it is very difficult to justify moving cities or counties simply to optimize early access to ELE.

The imperative to learn English under the DPP thus created opportunities for private schools, or *buxiban*, to profit from the perceptions that earlier ELE was more effective. Bilingual kindergartens proliferated in the decade up to 2008, as did after-school *buxiban* for elementary and middle school children. Kindergartens were formally forbidden from teaching English to children under six years old in 2004 (Ng 2004). Wu Tsai-Shun, director of the MOE's Department of Elementary Education, said at the time:

> The kindergarten curriculum should focus on health, games, music, general knowledge, [mother tongue] language, and identity. A second language is just not a priority in the education of kindergarten children.

The ban was presumably an attempt to stave off competition with the public sector from the *buxiban*s, although it was also framed by *bentuhua* nationalist discourses about exposing Taiwanese children to "Western" culture too early. But it was something of a paper tiger: lax enforcement of the ban, and the meagre threat of paltry fines – between NT$50,000 and NT$250,000 – could be construed as only symbolic state interference with the "free" market, and it meant kindergartens continued to operate with impunity.[56] Contrary to the minister's assertion, this suggests that second language education was very much an educational priority in the eyes of parents. *Buxiban* advertising eagerly reproduced the younger-the-better ideal:

---

56 The New Taiwan Dollar (NT$) is roughly pegged to the US dollar, with an exchange rate in 2017 of around 1 US$ = 33 NT$

> Learning English should be a very fun, enjoyable thing to do. The moment a baby opens his mouth and calls "Mom!" is the moment he starts his way through language. [Buxiban website]

At least in part, *buxiban* proliferated due to a perception that the public education system was lacking. Y.F. Chang (2008: 429) found that 56.7% of parents agreed or strongly agreed that if policy mandated ELE from the first grade in public schools island-wide, then the numbers attending *buxiban* would decline dramatically. Again, the notion of "choice" in the "free" market is chimerical. While parents were free to choose whether to send their children to bilingual kindergartens and *buxiban*, and were free to choose which *buxiban* to send them to, the exercise of "choice" is constrained by the notion of "competition" in the context of the younger-the-better belief in acquiring a valued cultural capital.

Closely related to the belief in the younger-the-better argument for L2 acquisition is the belief in the native-speaker as the ideal and most effective L2 teacher. As Director Chen, of Miaoli County's education bureau, described above, plans to introduce ELE in grade three were thwarted by the lack of local teachers. The MOE's attempts to recruit some 3,000 teachers to rural areas hit a wall when local teachers were not attracted to those areas for the kinds of sociological reasons alluded to earlier. It is not quite the case, then, that foreign native-speakers are necessarily the first choice for L2 teachers over their local counterparts in terms of national policy. But popular discourses play on the nativist argument, and policy follows. In 2004 the MOE proposed to address these local problems with a decidedly trans-national solution, by recruiting qualified foreign native-speaking teachers to rural areas. Parents and educators were generally enthusiastic about the idea. As Mr Tang, the principal of an elementary school in Taitung County, put it:

> It's very good if native-speakers teach our kids English. They are definitely able to teach English better than Taiwanese teachers because English is their mother-tongue. We do require the native-speakers to have some Chinese ability. Or we have to pay for an interpreter. [Mr Tang, Taitung County]

Mr Tang thought that native-speaking teachers were helpful in some areas of language acquisition, but not others. Sound pedagogy would suggest that at least some knowledge of the L1 background of L2 learners would be helpful. Unlike babies acquiring their L1, L2 acquisition does not proceed merely via linguistic osmosis. Nevertheless, he thought that native-speakers were better than Taiwanese teachers, and that, presumably, this was a way to ameliorate some of the rural/urban divides in access to ELE. However, the MOE recruited just five foreign teachers in 2004, vastly short of the original goal of 1,000 per year. The MOE seemed bemused by the lacklustre response. An MOE representative quoted by the *Taipei Times* in 2004 said: "Not many people are attracted to the project. We don't know why. Maybe it is in a remote area or we are not paying enough". While usually supportive of the DPP, the *Taipei Times* called the MOE's policy a "band-aid solution" (Freundl 2004). As with attracting local teachers, it appears that rural areas were simply unable to compete with urban areas for native-speaking teachers, for sociological reasons such as pay or amenities. The subsequent five years were similarly dismal: recruitment peaked at 104 teachers in 2006, and had a very low contract renewal rate (MOE 2010).

Arguably, MOE policy towards recruiting native-speaking teachers mirrored ideologies in the private *buxiban* sector. Two main types of *buxiban* characterize the industry. Larger operations feature "superstar" Taiwanese language teachers, who are sometimes accorded celebrity-like status. Often clustered around the *buxiban* mecca of Zhongxiao West Road and Nanyang Street, across from Taipei Railway Station, these schools exist to "sell English" (Chang 2013). Native-speakers are idealized as language teachers; in Taiwan and many other places, being a native speaker "involves the comprehensive grasp of a language", based on the misplaced notion that "a particular language is inherited, either through genetic endowment or through birth into the social group stereotypically associated with it" (Rampton 2003: 108). As *buxiban* increased under the DPP's tenure, so did foreign residents holding teaching visas: 3,812 as the DPP took office in 2000, to 5,967 in 2002; this number peaked at 6,831 in 2004 and remained steady at an average of 6,120 through 2008 (NIA 2017).[57] Foreign teachers were required to possess specific institutionalized cultural capital to be granted a teaching visa: a bachelor's degree (though not necessarily in English, linguistics, or education) and, at least as conventional wisdom would have it given that perception of policy is as important as policy itself, a passport from the MOE's somewhat mysterious designation of an "English-speaking country". In practice, this was a passport from Kachru's (1992) "inner-circle": the US, Canada, the UK and Ireland, Australia, New Zealand, or South Africa. Native-speakers from the Philippines or India need not apply, no matter how qualified. Native speaking teachers also possess embodied cultural capital, most obviously having English as a first language.

---

[57] In August 2017, the latest point for which National Immigration Agency figures were available, foreigners holding legal teaching visas – almost always from the US, Canada, UK, Ireland, Australia, New Zealand or South Africa, though approximately 10% are from Japan, presumably teaching Japanese – numbered 6,714 (NIA 2017). Almost half live in Taipei City (1,926) or New Taipei City (formerly Taipei County) (1,078); the rest are mainly in larger cities and wealthier counties. An unknown but likely small number live in Taiwan but work illegally, and thus do not appear in NIA statistics.

However, this trans-nationalized cultural capital was unevenly distributed among native-speaking teachers. Accents were (and remain) ranked in a preferred hierarchy, broadly from American to South African. This hierarchy was reflected in job advertisements requesting certain accents or nationalities (more than one advert seemingly confused concepts and stipulated "native American" teachers), or specifying that, for example, British accents were "acceptable". Differentiated salaries and tuition fees for different accents and nationalities are not unheard of. A further category of embodied cultural capital is racialized: white teachers were often preferred (Lan 2011; Chang 2004) and Asian-American teachers were often denied teaching jobs or offered lower salaries.[58] The higher the symbolic value of "superstar" local teachers or idealized (white, American-accented) native-speakers, the more that *buxiban* could charge in tuition fees, and the higher the symbolic capital associated with sending children to *buxiban*. While I was waiting to interview the director of education in Taitung County, an assistant was only half-joking when he stated to me very bluntly:

> If there is a foreign teacher [compared to a local Taiwanese teacher] the parents will definitely choose the foreigner. They think the foreigners are definitely better. If there are foreign teachers in the cram school, the parents think it's a good school and a good cram school. They think blonde hair is much better. [Assistant, Bureau of Education, Taitung County]

Again, as mentioned above, the *buxiban* themselves thus index different notions of class as much as English is a valued capital in the compulsory education system. It is moot whether a one- or two-year difference in starting times, or being taught by a native-speaking teacher, would have a significant impact on senior high school exam results where the institutionalized cultural capital really counts. But the *perception* of unequal access to a valued linguistic capital is problematic for a program, such as the DPP"s *bentuhua* nationalist movement, that is premised on notions of socio-economic and linguistic equality.

It is apparent that neoliberal notions of competition, choice and the free market shape national policies and discourses towards a global language, and how they percolate down into local contexts where policy is implemented. While "English for all" policies and discourses are framed as opportunities, there is little actual choice to acquire the cultural capital of English when it so fundamentally functions as a gatekeeper in and to education and employment

---

[58] This may be changing: in 2013, an Asian-American teacher successfully sued a *buxiban* for racially-based discrimination, in the first case of its kind.

markets. Regions, schools, and individuals are forced to compete with each other on anything but a level playing field given uneven resource allocation in the public education sector between rural and urban areas. The "free" market in the private sector is not really "free" when it exists to meet demand created by state discourses and policies, when it profits by ameliorating perceived or actual gaps in public education, or when it contributes to further stratification of access to ELE along socio-economic lines. The construction of English-as-capital further manifests itself in linguistic ideologies – the belief in the younger-the-better argument for L2 acquisition, and the idealization of the native-speaking teacher – which serve to further cement these neoliberal notions.

It is only comparatively recently that language study has begun to adequately theorize a sociolinguistics of globalization (Blommaert 2010; Park & Wee 2012) or the effects of neoliberalism on language and language policy (Block, Gray, and Holborow 2012), even if work on the commodification of language has a somewhat older provenance (see Heller 2010). The data presented here is thus analyzed in light of these theoretical innovations, particularly by heeding Piller and Cho's call to "look outside language and link language explicitly to the socio-economic order" (2013: 24). We might well ask: what is the real price of "English for all"?

6.2.4 The future of English

This study relies on data from fieldwork done in 2007, and therefore does not address the extent to which ELE policies changed, if at all, under the (substantially reformed) KMT government elected in 2008 and which held power until 2016. However, the world since then has arguably become more, not less, globalized and – either in spite or because of the global financial crisis of 2007–9 – neoliberalism has strengthened its ideological and structural grip. In interviews with KMT government officials in 2015, similar sentiments – the need for Taipei to become a global city, global economic competitiveness, and the problems of testing regimes – were raised. As with local language education, it seemed that little had changed in terms of discourses or policies towards English. Once again, these seem to be related to path dependencies laid down previously, but arguably English language education has its roots earlier than the DPP administration, instead being found in martial law-era education policies and discourses about connecting Taiwan – or at least the ROC – to a world that was increasingly switching diplomatic recognition to the PRC.

6.3 Foreign spouses, new immigrants, and "othered" languages

The migration to Taiwan of native-speaking English teachers from predominantly inner-circle nations contrasts with that of foreign labourers and foreign spouses from south-east Asia. The first contrast is in terms of sheer size: as of 2017, there are 7,000 or so migrants working as teachers, while there are some 665,000 foreign workers – in social care and industry combined – and 175,000 registered foreign spouses (MOL 2017a; NIA 2017).[59] The second contrast is in the push-pull factors: both groups are attracted by relatively high wages, but few English teachers are motivated by the prospect of propelling themselves and their families out of poverty; conversely, a significant motivation for many south-east Asian migrants is likely not the desire to travel the world out of a sense of adventure. The third contrast is in the relationship between these migrations, language policies, and linguistic capital. For foreign spouses, language policy is in the conventional position of reacting to migration; foreign spouses are constructed as having (or being) social "problems", and resolving them requires their linguistic and cultural integration into society in order to be "good" citizens. Foreign English teachers are in a rather different paradigm. For English teachers, rather unusually in the global scheme of things, their migration is *a consequence of* language policy: migration is reacting to language policy, not the other way around; the emphasis on English in the education system, and discourses about idealized native-speakers, creates a labour market. South-east Asian labourers are in more complex positions. For some – particularly from the Philippines – the ability to speak English is highly valued in high-tech manufacturing industries and domestic labour, though their situation is distinct from English teachers because the language capital they possess is only valued as a subsidiary outcome of the political economy of labour mobility. For others, their languages are not valued as capitals at all, and the lack of opportunity for permanent residency, means that there is little incentive to sociolinguistically incorporate them into citizenship regimes in the same way that foreign spouses are.

This section begins with an ethnographic vignette of Taipei written in 2015. From this, I focus on the issue of foreign labour – from manufacturing to domestic work – and the valuation of linguistic capital as a function of their labour roles (Lan 2003) and in the context of wider society. The final section

---

[59] This figure is for foreign spouses from south-east Asia excluding China, a distinction which will be explained below.

addresses the situation of foreign spouses, and how language policy reacts to intertwined perceptions of socio-political and sociolinguistic "problems".

6.3.1 Metrolingual Taipei: Visible and invisible languages

Most of my fieldwork in Taiwan was done in 2007, but in late spring 2015 I returned to spend a few brief weeks in Taipei. The small and very expensive apartment I rented was on the six-lane boulevard of Zhongxiao East Road in Xinyi district, almost directly above one of the entrances to Yongchun MRT station. The heart of the city is just a mile or so due west. My base at Academia Sinica, Taiwan's research campus, was due east. Walking south for ten minutes, I was at the head of the hiking trail up Elephant Mountain; foothills abut the city and funnel it into a basin, so that the only way for the urban to sprawl is upwards, from mid-rises with tin-roofed top-floor apartments to skyscrapers of glass and steel. Hulin Street, just around the corner from my apartment, runs north from Zhongxiao Road, and is the site of a traditional Taiwanese wet market. Hulin Street is long and narrow, with vendors' stalls down both sides and, in the evenings, carts along the middle. Between them, there is barely room for people to walk two abreast, although motorbikes periodically scatter them, sometimes with young children riding pillion and clutching their schoolbags from their English-language *buxiban*. Live fish are sold in tanks; these are for dinner, but the terrapins in a bucket, I am told, are being sold as pets. The pigs from which the pork belly comes are butchered elsewhere. When I arrived in mid-May, vendors occasionally had the expensive first crop of local lychees, bunches of their leathery red orbs poking out here and there. As the days and weeks went on, the lychees became more abundant and the prices dropped; I could rely on them being hawked at me with offers to try them to see their quality. Along with the lychees, fruit and vegetables abound; Japanese pears sit next to bunches of the leafy spinach-like *kongxincai*. The ubiquitous Taiwanese snacks – oyster omelettes, spring onion pancakes, chicken butts, and other assorted animal parts on sticks – are grilled or fried over gas burners or hot coals; I'm asked in Mandarin *"yaobuyao la?"* ("Do you want it spicy?") and when I say I do, I am looked at as if I cannot possibly have understood, since received wisdom is that *waiguoren* (or "foreigners") "aren't used to" Taiwanese food, and are not particularly great at speaking Mandarin either. I am never asked in Hoklo, which is otherwise the dominant language of the market. As with market traders anywhere in the world, their calls have distinctive prosodies that, amidst the cacophony, enable them to be heard over everyone else.

In the alleys off Zhongxiao Road, there are plenty of places to eat cheaply and well without having to buy it and cook it yourself. In the Taiwanese buffet canteens, my dish is weighed and I am charged accordingly; as in the market, the server switches from Hoklo with Taiwanese customers to Mandarin with me. The staff at the Hakka-style restaurant just across the alleyway may know Hakka but, despite several visits, I don't hear it spoken between themselves or to customers, and they certainly don't speak it to me; nevertheless, the link with Hakka culture is maintained through cuisine. I don't know everything on the menu, but it is in Mandarin and I can navigate my way through well enough to have a reliable guess at what I might be ordering. A shop nearby specializes in dumplings – pork dumplings, shrimp dumplings, dumplings in soup – making ordering from the menu rather easier. At the intersection of Zhongxiao and Songshan roads there is a Sushi Express – an English name for a Japanese chain that is the product of globalization, not colonization. Other English or foreign-language names can be seen: "Tartine" is a bakery with a French twist; I am not sure whether the Italian-style "Know Pasta" is an imperative or just one of the unusual translations that can be found all over the island, often derided as "Chinglish" but displaying their own logics and creativity. The use of foreign scripts is often indexical; they are not intended to communicate literal meaning, but point to what, for Taiwanese, is Western, modern, culturally "exotic", and higher class. At Starbucks, I am asked by the barista for my *xingming*, a word I cannot guess from context which bemuses me until it is translated literally as "star name", which is to be written on my coffee cup. Knowing that spelling out "Gareth" will be too complicated and cause embarrassment about English proficiency, I suggest "G", but a quizzical look and the miming of wings being flapped reminds me that this is a homophone for *ji* or chicken. Wondering why I didn't think of this before, I give them my Mandarin name, Fu Jing-ying (傅京英), but the barista only writes down the last character – *ying* (英) – which happens to be the first character in the word for "English". This apparently serves to sufficiently index my exoticness.

Mandarin, Hoklo, English, Hakka, French, Japanese: all these are part of the metrolingual landscape of Taipei, valued differently but all valued somehow. But less visible, and certainly less valued, are Taiwan's other – or "othered" – foreign languages from across South-East Asia: the languages of the cleaners, maids, nannies, and construction workers who work for a pittance and are at the mercy of both exploitative employers and unscrupulous labour "brokers"; the languages of "foreign spouses" who come to marry Taiwanese men, pushed by poverty at home and pulled by sociological and demographic changes here on the island. Their languages are not written on Starbucks cups or used as to index upmarket restaurants; they are not written on advertising billboards or emblazoned on children's schoolbags. Nor do I hear them spoken; literally and metaphorically, their languages are not shouted in the marketplace. They are, however, written in the window of the nearby Fubon Bank: instructions in Tagalog, Indonesian, and Vietnamese explain how to use Western Union to send remittances from meagre wages back home to dependent families. The following section examines these languages and their speakers in their political sociological contexts; in civil society (including within families), and in interactions with the state. These languages have largely been left out of Taiwan's embrace of multilingualism, and are arguably the most marginalized on the island.

6.3.2 Foreign workers and linguistic capital

Since the early 1990s, Taiwan's manufacturing industries have been attractive to skilled and semi-skilled labourers from south-east Asia who have sought to temporarily escape low wages and high unemployment in their home countries. At the time of writing in September 2017, 399,239 foreign workers out of 663,234 are employed in the manufacturing sector, mainly from Vietnam (42.53%), as well as the Philippines (28.3%), Thailand (14.42%) and Indonesia (14.71%) (MOL 2017a). Some of this migration was illegal, and a miniscule proportion still is (NIA 2016; though c.f. Lee 2010: 346), but much of it has been facilitated – albeit strictly controlled – through state immigration and work permit policies. In a nutshell, the state and industry have embraced these migrant labourers for familiar economic reasons; what foreign labourers consider a decent wage is cheaper than paying Taiwanese, since the latter have seen the overall standard of living rise through the "economic miracle" of industrialization; furthermore, as a result, Taiwanese do not want to do the most dirty, difficult, and dangerous jobs anyway (Lee 2010: 338). Keeping the manufacturing bases in Taiwan enables greater supervision of the production process and the quality of the product, particularly essential for Taiwan's high-tech manufacturing sub-sector, which employs over a fifth of all foreign manufacturing workers (MOL 2017a).

The non-manufacturing domestic work sector consists of jobs such as institutional and family nursing (14,717 and 229,772 people respectively), as well as housekeeping (1,968) (MOL 2017c). Of course, family nursing and housekeeping categories likely overlap in practice; the process for hiring foreign nurses is simpler and cheaper than hiring housekeepers. Of 246,485 workers – almost always women (99.3%; MOL 2017b), whom Lan (2006) calls "global Cinderellas" – most come from Indonesia (76.4%), followed by the Philippines (12.7%) and Vietnam (10.6%), with the numbers of Thai nationals a tiny fraction, in the region of five hundred individuals (MOL 2017c). Push factors are conventional economic ones: the desire for higher wages (or any wages whatsoever, in many cases) to support families back home. However, unlike manufacturing workers, the pull factors are as much sociological as macro-economic changes in Taiwan over the last two and a half decades. The increase in dual-generation nuclear families and the decline in the multi-generational extended family, particularly in urban areas, has driven the need for workers in these fields, as the elderly live longer and get sicker yet live apart from their children and grandchildren. Furthermore, the youngest generation also need looking after, as middle-class dual-career families work longer hours in highly skilled tertiary industries, and both need and can afford domestic assistance with childcare. In short, the phenomenon of foreign maids and caregivers is a function of intergenerational upward mobility. At least according to earlier Council of Labour Affairs data (CLA 1999, cited in Lan 2003: 137) most employers are established middle-class, dual income households in which one or two members have at least a university degree. Perhaps the key demographic difference now is that employing a foreign maid is a mark of the *aspirant* middle-class (Lan 2003: 156).

The sociolinguistic dimensions of foreign labour revolve around the sorts of linguistic capital that foreign labourers bring with them, and how they are valued in society and the economy. In the manufacturing sector, little premium is placed on native knowledge of Indonesian, Thai, or Vietnamese, but those who know Mandarin are likely valued as bilingual interfaces between Taiwanese managers and shop floor migrant workers. However, the high-tech manufacturing sub-sector is dominated by Filipino/a workers, at around 77% of the workforce (MOL 2017a); while Tagalog or other Philippine languages might not be particularly valued, most workers from the Philippines will know English given that it is a co-official language, which puts them at an advantage in terms of reading instructions for imported machinery and equipment, and other technical documents. Those who also speak Mandarin – the language is the medium of instruction in Philippine Chinese schools – or even Philippine Hokkien, which is mutually intelligible with Hoklo, have particularly valuable linguistic capital.

The English-speaking abilities of Filipina workers in the domestic labour sector are similarly valued. Lan's (2003, 2006) research investigates the nature of Filipina domestic workers' English linguistic capital, and how this intersects with class and status. For many Taiwanese, employing a maid indexes wealth. During one of Lan's (2003) interviews, a Taiwanese man indicated that the family chose their Filipina maid to match their middle-class status; in other words, her social skills, and cultural and linguistic capital, had to be middle class just to perform in a lower status occupation. In an overheard conversation in a coffee shop, an aspirant middle-class couple discussed getting a maid so their child could learn English, and so the wife had the time to attend a private English class on Saturday mornings; as we have already seen, learning English for both mother and child is a means, or at least perceived as a means, to upward socio-economic mobility. One interviewee related how her son's teacher had called and the maid answered the phone in English; "Is your family very rich?", the teacher asked the son the next day. Another suggested that "bad experiences" with maids were linked to Taiwanese employers who could not speak English and thus were unable to "set rules". Linguistic capital becomes a source of contention, as the quote in Lan's title from a maid aptly captures: "they have more money but I speak better English!". The linguistic capital of English is thus a substitute for class status, which many Filipino/a workers have exchanged for lower status but higher paid positions as domestic (and industrial) workers in Taiwan. For Lan (2003: 135), "[Filipinas] identify themselves as middle class based on their college education and previous occupations, but they are now employed in demeaning, deskilled jobs and treated as ethnic others in foreign countries".

Notable here is how the English varieties of maids and caregivers are evaluated differently compared to formal language instruction contexts, such as *buxiban*. As we have seen previously in this chapter, in the *buxiban* inner-circle varieties are valued as linguistic capital more highly than those of outer-circle varieties, such as Indian or Philippines English, which is partly a function of ethnicity, and this valuation is co-constructed by parents and school owners (and to some extent by the state, through de facto restrictions on teaching visas). The valuation of Philippines English in the context of domestic workers, however, changes rather significantly. The most compelling explanation for this is irreducibly socio-economic: particularly for aspirant middle-class families, when factoring in the cost of English-language *buxiban* or *anjinban*, it makes as much sense to have the "added value" of a maid for the not always substantial extra cost, with the trade-off being what is perceived to be a less than ideal accent.

6.3.2.1 *Othered languages in the public sphere*: Bao Bon Phuong

Manufacturing workers live and work under burdensome conditions. One day off a week is the legal minimum; employers will try to get away with less if they can, and employees often have little choice but to work overtime to pay off exorbitant labour brokerage fees of up to a year's salary. Even for those who do have free time, workers often live in dormitories in industrial zones, and have little opportunity for socializing or forming networks in civil society outside of these contexts (Huang and Douglass 2008). Particularly in urban areas, foreign domestic workers tend to have slightly more freedom. On Sundays, domestic workers' default day off, Indonesian and Vietnamese workers throng the concourse outside Taipei Main Station, having picnics and meeting friends. Filipinas develop more permanent and denser civil society networks which cluster around St. Christopher's Catholic church in the so-called Little Manila district in Zhongshan, where services are held in Tagalog and English. Developing social norms about the treatment of foreign domestic workers may be responsible for having allowed these freedoms, aided by the involvement of local NGOs and expatriate Christian groups sympathetic to migrant workers' plights. These have sought to depict positive representations of migrants in the public sphere and otherwise educate, persuade, or shame Taiwanese employers into adhering to minimum social (and legal) standards. These organizations replace the functions of the perennially indifferent or toothless Ministry of Labour.

By 2004, expatriate religious NGOs had set up a magazine, *Kaibigan*, aimed at Filipino/a workers and published in Tagalog. In December 2006, a secular alternative in the public sphere came with the publication of *Bao Bon Phuong* ("Four-Way Voice", in Vietnamese), a magazine issued monthly under the auspices of Shih Hsin University Press (*Lihpao*), and initially published in Vietnamese and Mandarin (Lin and Chen 2016: 91–98).[60] In 2008, a Thai language version was published; in 2011, Cambodian, Indonesian, and Tagalog versions followed. Per month, as of 2014, around 25,000 copies were printed in Vietnamese, 20,000 copies in Indonesian, 10,000 copies in Tagalog, 6,000 copies in Thai, and 3,000 copies in Cambodian, and free copies were distributed in places where foreign workers gather (Lin and Chen 2016: 92). The sizes of the print-runs in these different languages more closely follow the demographic spread of foreign spouses rather than foreign domestic workers. However, the magazine's ethos is to "welcome the newcomer and new immigrant to Taiwan", suggesting it is aimed at both permanent spouses and more temporary labourers.

As of July 2016, the print version of *Bao Bon Phuong* was still in circulation, and had also developed an online presence that reflects the increased use of smartphones and tablets for news consumption. NGOs were also instrumental in supporting the magazine, with awards and financial support (Lin and Chen 2016: 92), giving rise to a hybridized media model supported by purchases, advertising, and external donor funding. It seems that *Bao Bon Phuong* has had influence in other areas of the public sphere. As Lin and Chen (2016: 92–95) note, Radio Taiwan International began a Vietnamese language segment, while an unspecified TV channel carries a karaoke series called "Sing Four Ways", filmed by *Bao Bon Phuong* founding editor Cheng Chan. In addition, in 2014, the Taiwan Literature Award for Migrants was inaugurated, and continued the following year, with prizes of six months' salary awarded to winners of short story and article competitions.

---

60 http://taiwantoday.tw/news.php?unit=18,23,45,18&post=24,265

Whether these initiatives in civil society and the public sphere truly make headway in changing attitudes towards and perceptions of migrants and their languages is an unanswered question. There is a faint sense that, while well-intentioned, there is an element of spectacle about literature competitions and karaoke that, far from making migrant languages a part of public and political life, merely fetishizes them, creating a similarly othered image with the gloss of benevolence. The media economics of *Bao Bon Phuong* creates similar difficulties; with the best will in the world, a once-a-month freesheet, financially propped up by donor support, does not offer many opportunities for meaningful engagement – deliberation on issues and contestation against the state – within the public sphere. This is not to demean these efforts, but to point out the formidable structural obstacles to Taiwan's social and political integration of its temporary migrant worker populations, of which the language barrier is a particularly difficult one to traverse.

6.3.3 Foreign spouses, language "problems", and language policy

According to the last available National Immigration Agency statistics (NIA 2017), 526,769 foreign spouses were registered in Taiwan as of August 2017. Of these, 66.81% were from the PRC, Hong Kong, or Macau, while the majority of the rest – 28.56% – came from five south-east Asian countries, namely Vietnam, Indonesia, Thailand, Philippines, and Cambodia. At the peak of cross-border marriages in 2003, 31.86% of total Taiwanese marriages involved a Chinese or south-east Asian spouse (Tseng and Lin 2014: 14). This tapered off somewhat; in 2007, 18.3% marriages involved Chinese or south-east Asian spouses, but in 2011 the rate was still 13.1% (Tseng and Lin 2014: 14). Marriage migration is highly feminized, with 95% of marriages to spouses from the PRC, Hong Kong, or Macau, and 96.6% of south-east Asian marriages involving female foreign spouses (NIA 2017).[61] Aggregating various data (Hsieh and Wang 2006; Sheu 2007), 40.71% of foreign spouses graduated from junior high school, and 39.54% graduated from high school; the proportion of foreign spouses aged under 24 years old is 44.6%, aged 25–34 years old is 40.7%, and aged 35–44 years old is 10.8%. At its height, between 10 and 12% of all Taiwanese births were the result

---

61 The south-east Asian gender average includes the outlier of Thailand. There appears to be no literature, at least in English, on the phenomenon of Thai men making up nearly one-third of Taiwanese-Thai marriages. It seems related to the fact that Thailand is a cheap, easy-to-get-to, and popular holiday destination for Taiwanese, but this is far from an adequate sociological explanation and more research is needed.

of cross-border marriages (Tseng and Komiya 2011: 106), a figure high enough to influence educational and cultural policy.

The socio-economic, cultural, and political reasons for marriage migration are complex. In sending countries, women are often escaping rural poverty; it would be an over-simplification to reduce all motivations to economically-based "global hypergamy" (Tang, Bélanger, and Wang 2011: 137–138) in which women marry upwards for financial reasons, but the prospect of sending remittances home to families *also* stuck in rural poverty is surely a factor. In the host country of Taiwan, several interlocking structural changes in work and expected gender roles have made marriage to foreign female spouses desirable. Industrialization and then the transition to a high-tech and service based economy has required a larger, more skilled, and better educated labour force, which has in turn led to the increasing incorporation of women into paid work (King 2007: 145). As a result, Taiwanese women are postponing (or avoiding) entry into marriage or motherhood in favour of careers. In addition, sex-selective abortions have created a gender imbalance that favours males, with a 2011 Control Yuan report pointing to the fact that Taiwan's male-to-female birth ratio imbalance is internationally trailing only that of China (*Taipei Times* 2011). In sum, then, there are fewer women than men, and those women are less likely to marry and have children. For men, this creates a problem rooted in culture; marriage and reproduction – and ideally having a son – is considered a necessary mark of masculinity. Furthermore, the notion of "filial piety" requires a descendant to look after the parents in both old age and the afterlife; in addition, marriage is desirable because daughters-in-law are expected to look after the husband's parents. For men who cannot find a Taiwanese wife, and these tend to be somewhat older, lower- and lower-middle class men with lower educational levels, foreign wives offer ways out of these difficulties (Lan 2008).

We will turn to the linguistic barriers shortly, but cultural barriers can also be a problem, particularly for south-east Asian spouses. PRC spouses' understanding of the concept of "filial piety", both in terms of reproducing heirs and being a dutiful daughter to one's in-laws, as well as the expectations of rather rigidly defined patriarchal gender roles, is relatively similar to that of Taiwanese. For south-east Asian spouses, however, kinship systems and gender roles in their home cultures may differ from prescribed "Chinese" Confucian structures (Tang, Bélanger, and Wang 2011: 138). Furthermore, overt or latent racism from the community or in-laws may make the expected burdens on south-east Asian wives more onerous. Indeed, as Tang, Bélanger, and Wang (2011: 141–142) suggest, given the common countries of origin and economic logics of migration, the distinction between domestic worker and foreign spouse is often blurred; there are no separate categories for these roles in the program of *bentuhua*. Official institutional discourses further structure the roles of foreign wives as homemakers, bearers of children, and good citizens of Taiwan, which are often difficult to parse out from one another. As Su Jia-Chyuan, minister of the interior under Chen Shui-bian, put it in a preface handbook for foreign spouses in October 2005:

> With the tendency of globalisation and internationalisation, there are increasing number of marriages between our citizens and people from Mainland China [sic] and South East Asia ... These new migrant spouses have come from a long way and settle down in Taiwan as a result of their marriages. In addition to *living together with our citizens, they are also responsible to take care of family and nurture their children*. (My emphasis)

Despite the innocuous tone, this is nevertheless a paternalistic and patronizing "disciplining" of foreign spouses. The state has an incentive to facilitate cross-border marriages. Between the 1980s and 2000s, Taiwan's fertility rate plummeted; in 2010 it was just 0.9, well below the 2.1 needed for population stability, and a relatively large greying older generation combined with a shrinking tax base of younger workers creates difficulties for national social welfare budgets (and economic productivity in general). However, particularly under the DPP, policy has had to balance the long-term economic desirability of cross-border marriages with more immediate social and political concerns. In particular, the *bentuhua* nationalism that underpins DPP political legitimacy inevitably leads to some levels of xenophobia. Furthermore, given that foreign spouses (unlike foreign labourers) are meant to migrate permanently, the state must construct roles for foreign spouses that fashion them into "good" citizens and not social "problems". Crucial to this balancing act is the function of language in mediating interactions between foreign spouses, society, and the state.

6.3.3.1 Between multiculturalism and assimilation

Spouses from the PRC are more sought after – hence the larger proportion of marriages between them and Taiwanese – largely because language and cultural barriers are much more easily overcome than with south-east Asian spouses. Although they speak different varieties of Mandarin, or perhaps broadly mutually intelligible Hoklo and Fujianese *Minnanhua*, communication in Taiwanese-Chinese marriages can be achieved without an extraordinary amount of effort on both sides. South-east Asian spouses, however, may not speak or understand Mandarin well, and are even less likely to know Hoklo. They therefore do not have a common language to translate cultural or familial expectations, and therefore do not have a means through which to easily or quickly acculturate. For the rest of this section, which focuses on the construction of language "problems" and their resolution through policy, the term "foreign spouses" thus refers to south-east Asian spouses, except where specified; this follows the official statistical designation of "foreign" as not including Chinese spouses (Lan 2008: 832fn.2).

Yeh (2010: 210) examines language use within cross-border marriages and families. While Yeh's data is from 2002 and is confined to Tainan City, the sample is weighted and the demographic spread of cross-border nationalities has not changed substantially according to National Immigration Agency data from 2017 (NIA 2017b), thus making the study somewhat cross-comparable. According to Yeh, 52.8% of foreign spouses *expect* their children to speak both Mandarin and/ or Hoklo and the languages of foreign spouses at home, whereas 42.6% expect children to speak only Mandarin and/or Hoklo. In other words, slightly over half of all foreign spouses hope that their own languages will be used by children in the home. In terms of actual language practices, the situation seems rather different. The same respondents report that the language they mostly use at home with their children is Mandarin and/or Hoklo in 77.8% of cases, with only 21.3% reporting both the foreign spouse's language and Mandarin and/or Hoklo. In terms of foreign spouses' own language practices, 60.2% of Taiwanese partners expect the foreign spouses to only use Mandarin and/or Hoklo at home; 0% expect monolingualism in the spouse's native language; while 37% expect bilingualism in the native language and Mandarin and/or Hoklo. As such, most Taiwanese spouses expect their foreign partners to assimilate to the dominant language(s). A striking contrast is with reported language use in cross-border families where the spouse is American or European (in which case, the spouse is more likely to be male); just 36.4% reported using only Mandarin and/or Hoklo at home with children, while 54.5% reported using Mandarin and/or Hoklo and the spouse's native language. Several conclusions might be drawn from this. The first is that the intersection of gender and language may be significant, perhaps making the notion of a "mother" tongue problematic. Second, it points to the (often racialized) hierarchy of foreign linguistic capital in Taiwan, in which English (and to a lesser extent European languages) are valued over south-east Asian languages in families, reflecting and reproducing these valuations as they are constructed in wider society and by the state.

Although 77.8% of foreign spouses report mostly using Mandarin and/or Hoklo at home with their children, this does not necessarily indicate high levels of proficiency, especially since Yeh's data comes before the state began offering Mandarin classes precisely in response to low general proficiency and the related perceived "problems" of integration. In 2006, the *Taipei Times* (Hirsch 2006) reported an anecdote from a Vietnamese spouse named Ron Hsue-ming:

> Arguing with her Taiwanese husband once meant frantically flipping through a Vietnamese-Mandarin dictionary in search of the right word to yell at him.
>
> "Whenever we fought, I would grab my Vietnamese-Mandarin dictionary, and he would grab his Mandarin-Vietnamese dictionary, and we would go at it," Ron said.
>
> She added that their method of bickering was so absurd they couldn't keep a straight face, no matter how angry they were.

Not all arguments end quite as good-naturedly. While statistics are difficult to come by, domestic violence is considered a problem in cross-border marriages, with the language barrier a significant contributory factor (Williams and Yu 2006: 63). For example, the Good Shepherd organization, an anti-domestic violence NGO, prints a *Safety Guide for the Newly-Arrived* in several south-east Asian languages. However, the objective is to encourage foreign spouses to placate husbands and families, and extricate themselves calmly from situations. From a purely safety perspective this makes sense, but it echoes official discourses that more overtly link domestic violence problems to the foreign spouses' lack of cultural and linguistic integration, which is presumed to be their fault. As one Ministry of Interior leaflet from 2007 put it rather more explicitly:

> [The Ministry] has duly informed foreign and Mainland Chinese spouses about crisis and preventive ideas related to domestic violence and sexual assault through *the interactive instruction program, hoping to prevent social problems that arise due to cultural differences, language barriers and children's nurturing.* (My emphasis)

A perceived lack of linguistic and cultural integration, and the social problems this apparently engendered, became part of a broader narrative of crisis focused on foreign spouses. In part, it was related to state concerns that many marriages were a cover for economic migration, thus undermining the state's primary motivation of long-term population increase. More significantly, it was manifest as a function of the xenophobic impulses inherent in nationalist projects, and prevalent particularly in media representations. As Hsia (2007: 55) explains, foreign spouses were constructed as materialist gold-diggers, prostitutes, and prone to committing crimes and deserting their families; even somewhat more sympathetic depictions cast them as passive victims. Their husbands, meanwhile, were portrayed as "socially undesirable", physically or mentally disabled, and otherwise morally inferior. The pervasiveness of these depictions in the public sphere is pointed out by Hsia (2007: 56): government officials cited media stories to justify their own opinions when interviewed. These representations turn on the question of national anxiety over "good citizenship": whether foreign spouses can be "good mothers", which is their pre-determined social role, and whether they can be "good Taiwanese", which is something that nationalism constructs as something to be constantly strived for but always out of reach. As Sheu (2007: 180) notes, foreign spouses' Mandarin abilities – or lack of them – are linked to the perception of their ability to perform their pre-determined social role.

> Because many immigrant wives cannot speak Mandarin or read Chinese characters, their ability to teach their children to read and write, and to cooperate with school teachers, is questioned. In the end, their very capacity to be 'good mothers' has been questioned by both the families-in-law and Taiwanese society. (Sheu 2007: 180)

Language acquisition among children of cross-border marriages came in for questioning by the state during the 2000s. In 2005, the *Taipei Times* cited a MOE report (later contradicted by its own studies) to the effect that 8.2% of southeast Asian mothers were delayed in speech and language development. Once again, the foreign spouses' linguistic "problems" are blamed:

> The ministry report said sluggish language development among children born to Southeast Asian mothers may be related to their mothers' own linguistic problems. The survey also found that 24.13% of mixed-race children whose mothers can hardly speak Mandarin or Hoklo are slow language learners, while only 4.8% of mixed-race children with mothers able to fluently speak a local language have difficulties in language development.

Aside from the way that these "scientific" discourses can feed into and serve to legitimate xenophobic claims about genetic and thus ethnic inferiority compared to Taiwanese, they can have quite dramatic effects on language ideologies and practices. Mothers can feel shame about their own language, and pressured not to communicate with their children, as Yeh's (2010) data, above, suggests. However, it can also lead to the destabilizing of Taiwanese social structures that revere seniority and authority. Children, surrounded by Taiwanese relations, may acquire greater proficiency in Mandarin and/or Hoklo, and subsequently look down on their foreign mothers. Rather ominously, this in fact has a relatively recent historical context. As de Bernadi (1991: 7) describes, under the KMT children began to associate the ideology of Hoklo as a "bad" language with their Hoklo-speaking grandparents.

Some efforts were made by the state to provide Mandarin classes to better facilitate foreign spouses' integration. In 2003, the MOE considered requiring non-Mandarin speaking foreign spouses to take language classes as soon as they arrived in Taiwan. This was abandoned, in part because the MOI, and not the MOE would have jurisdiction in this area; instead, the following year, the MOE published a basic curriculum for foreign spouses. This was intended for 36-hours of classes provided by the government, usually in elementary school classrooms outside of school hours (Tseng and Komiya 2011: 108). 20,260 foreign spouses signed up for adult education classes between September 2005 and May 2006 (Lin 2006: 2).[62] Before this, a patchwork of immigrants' rights NGOs and sympathetic individual schools provided instruction, and so state-sponsored adult education is certainly a boon in important senses. However, Tseng and Komiya (2011) undertake a discourse analysis of the textbook used; compared to the textbooks of the island's relatively expensive Mandarin language institutes that specialize in teaching Mandarin to ("Western") foreigners, the *Happy Learning for a New Life* book conveys "messages to foreign spouses about what constitutes the most important aspects of their lives" (Tseng and Komiya 2011: 109). Unsurprisingly, these are grocery shopping, interactions associated with domestic chores, and communicating with family members. When mock dialogues are presented, "information is almost exclusively one-way traffic in the direction from those of higher authority to foreign spouses, with the latter hardly expressing their views or opinions" (Tseng and Komiya 2011: 109–110). The extended family is presented as the locus of immigrant life, rather than the nuclear family (Tseng and Komiya 2011: 111). The content of the textbook, in short, is as much about communicating the requirements of "good citizenship" as they are about language learning, and "citizenship" is not merely defined in terms of the expectations in civil society at large; instead, the state reinforces these expectations within the private sphere of the family.

A further issue that seems to have escaped policymakers is that the rural, lower-class men who mainly constitute Taiwanese partners are demographically likely to be speakers of Hoklo as much as Mandarin, particularly in informal or family domains. Learning Mandarin may well be an effective way to integrate foreign spouses into society, but only to the extent that Mandarin is in fact being spoken. It is perfectly feasible that, in many families, Mandarin is almost solely used to communicate with the foreign spouse. This means that Mandarin instruction is really only for the purposes of *following* instructions, and not for true integration into the affective sphere of family life or wider civil society. In fact, Mandarin instruction is likely most effective for integration with the order-giving and bureaucratic functions of the state.

In the absence of more holistic approaches to social integration through Mandarin instruction, NGOs have also been instrumental in pushing central and local government agencies to – albeit belatedly – implement bilingual provision of basic state services. In 2008, for example, the Pearl S. Buck Foundation partnered with the New Taipei City (formerly Taipei County) government to

---

[62] Lin Shu-min (2015) explores how these classes were also used to teach Mandarin to Japanese-speaking elders, which Lin casts as both othering and infantilizing.

provide translation, legal counselling, and social work referral services in six languages – Mandarin, English, Vietnamese, Burmese, Indonesian, and Thai – for both foreign spouses and foreign labourers. Significantly absent from this repertoire is Tagalog; presumably, Filipino/a immigrants are expected to use English.

Official discourses and policies appear to be changing. In 2010, the National Immigration Agency began Vietnamese classes for its employees, in order that bureaucrats could deal directly face-to-face with clients from the largest national grouping of south-east Asian spouses. In 2016, the DPP announced that its employees (though not, it seems, its politicians) would take classes in south-east Asian languages as part of its efforts to promote an "immigrant culture". Quoted in the *Taipei Times* (Gerber 2016), DPP Deputy Secretary-General Hsu Chia-ching stated that "because Taiwan is a diverse immigrant society, we hope to use the exchanges and stimulation of these courses to make Taiwan a richer nation". The *Taipei Times* further reported in 2016 that a high school in Kaohsiung set up a Vietnamese language club for children born to foreign spouses who were not conversant in their mother's language, and classes would be taught by an ethnically Vietnamese instructor (Huang and Chung 2016: 5). As the Taipei Times reported later the same year, a school in Taixi, in Yunlin County, along with immigrants' rights NGOs, set up a similar scheme, taught by a foreign spouse (Chen and Chin 2016: 4). But relegating new immigrant languages to extra-curricular clubs may not be the final word.

In December 2015, the KMT announced that new immigrant languages were to be included in the local language curriculum, taught alongside Hoklo, Hakka, and indigenous languages as a compulsory weekly subject between grades one and three, and as an elective between grades four and six. In the final analysis, it is not clear what motivated the KMT's policy. Outmanoeuvring the DPP on issues of social equality is one explanation, though it is clearly not about simple vote-buying: the families of foreign spouses constitute a very small and statistically insignificant voting bloc. Opposing the restrictive interpretation of *bentuhua* is another interpretation; undermining the DPP's nationalism by including "foreigners" dilutes the ostensible purity of ethno-nationalist claims. Of course, a more cynical view is that the policy was simply leaving the DPP with a poisoned chalice. After all, critical junctures and path dependencies have structured language politics since the KMT began its transition from martial law. The DPP are effectively powerless to reverse educational policies towards new immigrant languages. Whether that effectively changes discourses about and attitudes towards new immigrants remains to be seen.

6.4 Conclusion

As John Adams predicted in the eighteenth century, and W. Brackebusch declared had already happened by the nineteenth, English is the language of the world and, in Pennycook's (1995: 14) words, the language of the "global panopticon". Taiwan seeks visibility on the world stage in various ways; under Chen's DPP, it was a means to connect with the international community to appeal for recognition of its political independence; under the KMT between 2008 and 2016 it was primarily for the island's global economic competitiveness. One of these of course, cannot exist without the other: whether unfortunately or not, economic independence is a necessary prerequisite of political independence.

More research is needed on the actual language practices of foreign spouses, if for nothing else than to counter the unfortunate depiction of them as hapless and passive victims. Despite the language barrier, foreign spouses are, by virtue of taking the step to move to a different country and culture in the first place, resilient and resourceful enough to learn Mandarin on their own without the state's help, and strategically deploy languaging or translanguaging strategies to make themselves understood. Nevertheless, the state has an obligation to find solutions if it is going to actively construct foreign spouses as having problems with linguistic and cultural integration, or effectively challenge discourses in society that present them as such. Furthermore, it has a responsibility to embrace foreign spouses' languages and cultures alongside Taiwan's autochthonous languages if a truly multicultural, multi-ethnic, and multilingual society is to be fashioned out of new forms of diversity. The alternative is a parochial, xenophobic, and introverted nationalism that is hardly befitting of one of the world's youngest and most vibrant liberal democracies.

Epilogue: Taiwan as sociolinguistic laboratory

This book has demonstrated that the vicissitudes of Taiwan's history have made it a laboratory for studying the effects of macro-level geopolitics and historical-structural paradigms on language politics. This is not to say it is entirely unique; many countries have experienced various forms of colonization, nationalism, military occupation, authoritarianism, democratization, changing patterns of migration, and the effects of neoliberal globalization, and some have never achieved the status of a de jure independent state. But few places have run the gamut of these processes quite so exhaustively in such a way that they make visible and are made visible by their language politics. Perhaps the most remarkable aspect is that Taiwan has emerged from these scenarios not as a failed state, but one which is simply diplomatically unrecognized by a vast majority of the international community who are more concerned with placating the PRC than upholding their own ideals of self-determination and liberal democracy. The transitions from colonialism and authoritarianism have been relatively peaceful, and the country is a vibrant – if youthful – democracy, with respect for multilingualism as a core, though still evolving, value. This concluding epilogue serves three purposes. The first is to recapitulate the arguments made in the book as a whole. The second is to ascertain what the prognosis might be for multilingualism in Taiwan in view of its contemporary social and political contexts, which are still shaped by its particular historical circumstances. The third is to assess the contributions that a political sociology of language may make to understanding language politics beyond Taiwan.

1 The historical trajectory of language politics in Taiwan: A summary

The narrative of this book arguably began with the arrival of the ancestors of Taiwan's Austronesian-speaking indigenous peoples, who crossed what is now the Taiwan Strait some six millennia ago. It began in earnest, however, with the enmeshing of the diverse Austronesian languages of these groups into an alien socio-political system brought by the colonizing Dutch state in 1624. The Dutch missionary-colonial complex set the stage for socio-political interventions in Taiwan's Austronesian-speaking sociolinguistic situation. These were direct, in terms of codifying and learning local languages for the purposes of religious conversion and socio-political control, as well as somewhat half-hearted attempts to propagate the Dutch language among at least some indigenous groups. They were also indirect, but arguably more transformative: the "co-colonization" (Andrade 2008) of Taiwan by both the Dutch administrative system and the Sinitic-speaking – Hoklo and Hakka – migrant labour from China needed to operate the island as an agricultural colony, the latter settling the island in several waves that continued long after the Dutch had left. Notwithstanding the Kangxi emperor dismissing the island as a "ball of mud", initial wariness on the part of the Qing towards the restive province led to policies between 1683 and the mid-eighteenth century that partly sheltered indigenous languages and cultures from being overwhelmed by those of the Han migrant population (Shepherd 1993), effectively socio-spatially separating Han and indigenous communities, and limiting (or even reversing) immigration to the island. This gave way to indifference by the mid-eighteenth century, allowing Han populations to dominate in indigenous areas. The dynamics of this situation are more complex than the Han simply pushing the indigenous groups up into the mountains while they took over the fertile agricultural plains, but there is a certain logic to this as a theoretical explanation, since reports by anthropologists and travellers from the time indicate that linguistic and cultural assimilation proceeded much more quickly in the lowland areas.

Qing insouciance towards Taiwan meant that it ceded the island with relatively little protest at the conclusion of the first Sino-Japanese War in 1895; that is, it could give up a troublesome frontier territory without losing too much face, or at least that it was too preoccupied with internal tumult to care. Japan, which had dismantled feudalism in favour of a modern state based on the European and American models and adopted sociolinguistic reforms for the purposes of an efficient state and a national identity that legitimized the state's existence, took control rather more assertively. Initial policies, imbued with racist colonial ideologies regarding the supposed inferiority of both the indigenous and Han Taiwanese, deemed linguistic and cultural assimilation to be only necessary (or even possible) among Han elites, and even then, it was to proceed cautiously. The exigencies of colonial control and the dangers that the Taiwanese would begin to identify with China, with whom Japan was gearing up for another conflict, accelerated policies aimed towards Japanese-language spread, leaving an entire generation with at least some competence in the language. Upon taking control of the island at the end of the second Sino-Japanese War in 1945, the KMT adopted a similar logic: the danger now was that Japanese-speaking elites and many of the general Han population would identify as Japanese, a problem for the KMT's insistence that Taiwan was an ineffable part of China. As a function of martial law between 1949 and 1987, a highly effective – if ruthless – Mandarin-spread policy, particularly in compulsory education, transformed the island's sociolinguistic situation once again. Hakka and Hoklo were marginalized from public and political life, and a number of indigenous languages disappeared completely.

Political liberalization from the late 1970s culminated in the lifting of martial law in 1987, and with it the proclamation that punishing schoolchildren for speaking non-Mandarin languages was to be banned. It was a small, but highly symbolic, policy change, and paved the way for sociolinguistic democratization alongside political democratization. The first democratic elections were held in 1996 with, for various reasons (including many politicians campaigning in non-Mandarin languages), the reformist KMT retaining power. Forced to tolerate a certain amount of devolved political power as a condition for democratization, the KMT did not significantly oppose the decisions by some county governments to begin non-Mandarin instruction in schools during the 1990s. By the time of the election of the DPP in 2000, sociolinguistic reform was firmly on the political agenda, and under the remit of the nationalist *bentuhua* project the DPP expanded mother-tongue language education in schools and attempted the revaluation of non-Mandarin languages in public and political life. Returning to power in 2008, the KMT could hardly backtrack on the commitments to multilingualism that it had itself begun and, as Dupré (2017) argues, KMT language policy was forced (albeit with less enthusiasm) along the path dependencies that the DPP had forged during their tenure. Full sociolinguistic democratization, and a fully multilingual society, is still a long way off, however, and DPP legislative efforts to officialize Taiwan's non-Mandarin languages were consistently thwarted by KMT meddling and the difficulties of pleasing a variety of ethno-linguistically constituted political factions.

Further challenges to the management of Taiwan's sociolinguistic complexity come from the obsession with learning English, and the presence of languages of new immigrants, particularly those of (mainly female) "foreign spouses" from China and south-east Asia. The neoliberal construction – through both discourse and policy – of English as symbolic capital performing a gatekeeping function to higher education and upward socio-economic mobility may not (yet) directly threaten the vitality of Taiwan's indigenous and autochthonous languages, but it creates a political problem in that it challenges the notions of equality on which *bentuhua* nationalism and democratization are premised. Meanwhile, Taiwan's new immigrants do not easily fit into the sometimes parochial *bentuhua* categorizations of who is and who is not authentically "Taiwanese", and thus which languages deserve protection under democratized multilingualism. Although there is much work to be done, both policy and discourse appear to be shifting towards extending tolerance and inclusivity towards these groups.

2 The prognosis for Taiwan's languages

Temporally, the previous (and penultimate) chapter left us at the end of the KMT's two-term tenure between 2008 and 2016. In May 2016, Tsai Ing-wen, ethnically part-Hakka and part-Paiwan and educated at the London School of Economics (LSE), became the first woman, first part-indigenous, and only second DPP president of Taiwan. The DPP also comfortably won a parliamentary majority, ending eight years of KMT dominance of the executive and legislative branches. In her inauguration speech, Tsai emphasized the importance of implementing meaningful transitional justice measures in Taiwan; in August 2016, she issued a formal apology to indigenous peoples on behalf of the government (Coolidge 2016; Rowen and Rowen 2017). In a fitting denouement to our narrative, in January 2017, the Legislative Yuan proposed a bill to protect indigenous language rights in public and political life.[63] Swiftly clearing legislative hurdles – in stark comparison to the DPP's protracted and ill-fated attempts with the NLEL and NLDL during their first two terms in office – the bill passed into law, the thirty article Indigenous Languages Development Act, (ILDA; *yuanzhuminzu yuyan fazhan fa*) on May 26th, 2017.

The first article states that all indigenous languages have the status of national languages; meanwhile, their preservation and development is necessary in order to achieve "historical justice", which seems to be a way of couching the notion of transitional justice in slightly softer terms. The central ministerial authority for the law is the Council for Indigenous Peoples, though there is a strong decentralization to local government to implement its stipulations according to local sociolinguistic contexts. Both negative and positive rights are interlocked throughout the law – that is, the state is obliged to do more than simply refrain from interference – and there is emphasis on both linguistic human rights, or the rights to be able to use one's language to access other basic civil, social, and political rights, as well as language rights, or the rights to use, develop, and protect languages themselves. As well as simply regularizing the national status of indigenous languages, the law is highly specific in terms of ensuring corpus planning mechanisms – for online digital archives and dictionaries, for example – and shores up the language acquisition provisions in the forthcoming (KMT-drafted) twelve-year curriculum, slated to go into effect in 2019. Furthermore, it mandates indigenous language quotas in state-owned broadcast media. The law is clearly framed with the language rights provisions

---

63 As Dupré (2017: 135) notes, the ILDA has a longer provenance; first approved by the KMT executive in November 2015, it was in fact drafted by the DPP as an alternative to (and put aside in favour of) the NLDL.

enshrined in the UNDRM and UNDRIP in mind, usefully indexing Taiwan's credentials to the world as a robust, if young, liberal democracy.[64]

The drafting and consultation process similarly reflected the apparent desire to ensure a law that was as decentralized and sensitive to local sociolinguistic conditions as possible. The legislation was drafted under the purview of the Ministry of Cultural Affairs (and not, it seems, by the CIP), delegating much of the work to National Taichung University of Education (NTUE). Public forums were held to discuss the issues. One, held over the weekend of April 9th, 2017, had 270 individuals or groups signed up to speak, demonstrating the depth of feeling in civil society, but had to limit the number who could participate to around seventy and restrict others to commenting online. One report in the *Taipei Times* (Gerber 2017) curiously describes an official public hearing over terminology for the law that included discussions of including Hoklo and Hakka as national languages in the law. One language activist, and NTUE Hoklo professor, Ho Sin-han, said that the "the main objective of the law is to ensure that Hoklo has a definite budget and responsible government body". This is a familiar complaint: Hoklo activists have long described themselves as "the weakest majority" – the largest language group but with no Hoklo affairs ministry equivalent to that of the Hakka (HAC) or indigenous groups (CIP). Historically, they have had only a small sub-committee of the National Languages Committee (NLC) with a perennially uncertain (though certainly perennially diminished) budget, and in any case the NLC was dissolved under the KMT in January 2013.

More research is needed into whether the intention of the law somehow pivoted to focus on indigenous languages specifically, or whether Hakka and Hoklo activists were using public forums to advance their cause knowing full well that their languages were not included from the outset. In the end, Hakka and Hoklo were both excluded from the ILDA. But Hakka activists rode the wave of sympathy for multilingualism, and a proposal to co-officialize Hakka was approved by Tsai's cabinet in the Executive Yuan in mid-June 2017. This came in the form of a proposed amendment to the existing Hakka Basic Act, which the KMT had passed in 2010 and already contained certain (if somewhat vague) provisions for the protection and development of the language. It remains to be seen whether it actually becomes law, but the legislative path for officializing Hakka is easier than for Hoklo, given the latter ethnolinguistic group lacks any institutional clout at government level, and there is no equivalent "basic law" to

---

[64] Rowen and Rowen (2017) argue that this frames Tsai's transitional justice approaches in general, in that it is designed to signal a geopolitical strategy vis-à-vis China, and is not solely for domestic consumption or national reconciliation.

amend. The difficulty, of course, is that this leaves Hoklo, the numerically dominant language behind Mandarin, as the only language without official status. This creates a clear challenge to any notion of a transitional-justice focused language policy, since it misrecognizes the vast injustices visited upon Hoklo speakers by both the Japanese and martial law-era KMT regimes. Perhaps more perniciously, their alleged ethnic chauvinism renders them as the only group of speakers without enshrined language rights. For true sociolinguistic justice to be done, and to create both the sociolinguistic conditions for democratic pluralism and the democratic conditions for sociolinguistic pluralism, what Taiwan needs is a fully inclusive language regime.

The prognosis for Taiwan's languages is thus difficult to discern; or, framed another way, it is not clear whether any language maintenance and revitalization legislation will be too little, too late. Language shift is doubtless occurring towards Mandarin and, albeit to a lesser extent, Hoklo. The factors contributing to this are complex. Four centuries of pressure on non-dominant languages has created a path dependency, with critical junctures mainly being *which* languages have been repressed. Modern sociological factors continue to cause language shift and decline. Rural to urban migration for socioeconomic reasons is causing isolation in cities, and a breakdown in the traditional extended family structure and the ethnic bonds of local communities, making minority language communities vulnerable. Age-graded language shift is a particular problem, with younger generations increasingly only speaking local languages in schools (that is, within the confines of interacting with one aspect of the state) rather than in wider civil society. It remains unclear as to how to draft policies that actually have teeth beyond symbolic officialization to counteract this. State intervention in language practices in the family and civil society is constrained by liberal democratic norms that, post-1987, Taiwan has fought fiercely to construct and adhere to. In other words, the state can only facilitate and encourage language revitalization, not force citizens to maintain their languages. The continued dominance of Mandarin in the education system, the media, and popular culture, and mandating local language education only in elementary schools, does little to help. Neither does the spectre of English, which primarily rattles its chains in terms of exacerbating socio-economic inequality but may eventually directly threaten whether parents and students choose to acquire socio-economically less-valued local languages.

From a more optimistic perspective, however, in terms of indigenous languages globalization may – despite its association with English-spread – be the primary driver of language revitalization, as Taiwan continues to be influenced by liberal democratic norms and international minority rights regimes. To some extent, the same is true for Hakka, though perhaps the main factor is the symbolic raising of the status of Hakka through the efforts of the HAC and activists, and continued Hakka engagement in national politics. Despite the apparent age-graded language shift – which, as mentioned earlier in the book, may not be as steep as it might appear – Hoklo remains robust in private, public, and (to some extent) political life, and will remain (for better or worse) the primary language associated with Taiwanese national identity. Protection for south-east Asian spouses' languages may come from an unlikely confluence of political and economic factors in the context of globalization. President Tsai's "New Southbound Policy" intends to encourage favourable conditions for Taiwanese companies' investment into Vietnam and elsewhere, and this at minimum requires respecting the rights – including language rights – of new immigrants from these countries.

3 Beyond Taiwan: The contributions of a political sociology of language

The central theoretical framework advanced in this book is one of a political sociology of language, and there are two main reasons to think about how a political sociology of language may contribute to the understanding of language politics in other contexts beyond Taiwan. The first, however, is somewhat specific to Taiwan itself: the sad truth is that the reticence of the international community to adhere to its own ideals of respecting self-determination and liberal democracy means that Taiwan may well never exist as a de jure independent state, and China's increasing belligerence means that it is possible that it will cease to exist as a de facto one. Four centuries of a precarious geopolitical existence and internal political conflict that have nevertheless allowed multilingualism to survive may become moot, therefore, if China decides to pursue the ultimate military option of annexation. In such an event, it seems plausible that it would attempt ideological, cultural, and linguistic assimilation to quash any lingering political resistance on the island; the association of multilingualism with democratization and independence under *bentuhua* may mean that it is politically intolerable to an occupying PRC.

It is partly for this reason, in fact, that I have written this book: it serves as a historical record should Taiwan be absorbed and homogenized into the Sinosphere of the PRC. What Taiwan has achieved in the face of political adversity is a model for other movements – currently fifty or so (Middleton 2015) – that seek an independent homeland and that, in almost all cases, seek in tandem the right to speak their own languages. Political repression and resistance to repression, as we have seen, has in almost all scenarios throughout Taiwan's history implicated language politics, and democratization – and an embryonic approach to transitional justice – has been fundamentally premised on respecting sociolinguistic diversity. But the international community should be wary of complacency in terms of what conclusions other groups may draw. Decolonization and democratization are unfinished programmes in many parts of the world – indeed, even within supposedly established liberal democracies – and perhaps the real tragedy is that Taiwan is a salutary lesson that playing by the rules of international relations does not necessarily yield the desired outcome. It may well be that transitions to peace and stability within a liberal democratic framework that respects multilingualism and multiculturalism may prove, for more fervent separatists or irredentists, to be an example not to follow.

The second reason is more academic: put simply, a holistic and historicized understanding of politics and society is necessary to understand the complexities of multilingualism in any given context. As has been argued in chapter two, the central concerns of political sociology are the relations between society and the state. These include critical questions about the ethical and normative parameters of liberal democracy; who rules and who is ruled; how rule is conducted and how it is accepted or resisted; how symbolic and material resources are allocated; and what constitutes rights and how they can be distributed, claimed, and defended. These questions have sociolinguistic dimensions: which languages of the state are used to conduct the business of rule; the vitality and status of languages in civil society; how language is used to access rights; how democratic participation is structured based on language; how linguistic capital is valued within overlapping markets; and so on. The two constants in our narrative of Taiwan are, first, the presence of the modern state – which has manifested itself differently in different historical-structural paradigms – and its relations with multiple and overlapping dimensions of society, and, second, the tensions between repression and protection of languages, which have differed depending on perpetrators and victims of *political* repression.

At a general level, a political sociology of language is concerned with some of the problems posed by the fact that "we will never share a single language, nor be in complete agreement on what we view as the good life and/or the good state of society" (Peled, Ives, and Ricento 2014: 296). We can thus theoretically delimit a political sociology of language as an understanding of the relations between language and the state; that is, the state's manifestations through historical-structural paradigms of colonization, nationalism, and globalization, its role in the securing and disbursement of rights and (transitional) justice, and its obligation to facilitate a tolerant and democratic society. A political sociology of language thus aims to frame relations between society and the state as a sociolinguistic concern, and language as a concern for political sociology. We live, and will continue to live, in highly multilingual societies, and unless either (or both) the Marxists or libertarians are correct, we are quite likely to live under some form of the state for the foreseeable future. The protection of multilingualism requires the state to act ethically, and the role of society – in the broader sense – is to ensure that it does so. Perhaps respect for multilingualism is a fundamental guarantee of democracy, and vice-versa.

Appendix: Languages in Taiwan

All information in the following tables is adapted from Ethnologue (2017). EGIDS status refers to Lewis and Simons' (2010) Expanded Graded Intergenerational Disruption Scale. Austronesian sub-group status in Table A.3 is adapted from Blust (2014).

Table A.1: Sinitic (Chinese) languages.

Language	EGIDS Status
Mandarin	De facto national language (1)
Hoklo	Language of wider communication (3)
Hakka	Dispersed (5)

Table A.2: New immigrant languages.

Language	EGIDS status
Vietnamese	Unknown
Tagalog	" "
Thai	" "
Japanese	" "
Indonesian	" "
Mandarin and other Sinitic languages	" "

Table A.3: Austronesian (indigenous) languages.

Austronesian sub-group	Languages	Dialects	EGIDS status
Atayalic	Atayal	Ts'ole, Squliq	Developing (5)
	Seediq (Taroko)	Tgadaya, T[e]ruku, Toda	Educational (4)
East Formosan	Ketagalan	Basay, Trobiawan	Extinct (10); beginning 19th C.
	Kavalan	Kareovan	Nearly extinct (8b)
	Amis	Central Amis, Tavalong Vataan, Southern Amis, Northern Amis, Chengkung-Kwangshan	Developing (5)

(continued)

Table A.3 (continued)

Austronesian sub-group	Languages	Dialects	EGIDS status
	Amis (Nataoran)	Nataoran, Sakizaya, Kaliyawan, Natawran, Cikosowan, Pokpok, Ridaw	Nearly extinct (8b)
	Siraya	Siraya, Makatao, Taivoan	Extinct (10); end 19th C.
Puyuma	Puyuma (isolate)		Shifting (7)
Paiwan	Paiwan (isolate)		Developing (5)
Rukai	Rukai (isolate)	Budai, Labuan, Maga, Mantauran, Tanan, Tona	Developing (5)
Tsouic	Tsou	Duhtu, Luhtu, Tfuea, Iimutsu (extinct 1981)	Vigorous (6a)
	Saaroa		Nearly extinct (8b)
	Kankanabu		Nearly extinct (8b)
Bunun	Bunun	Central Bunun (Takbanuao, Takevatan, Takivatan), North Bunun (Takebakha, Taketodo, Takibakha, Takitudu), Randai, Shibukun (Sibucoon, Sibukaun, Sibukun, Sivukun), South Bunun (Ishbukun), Takopulan, Tondai.	Developing (5)
Western Plains	Taokas		Extinct (10)
	Favorlang/ Babuza		Extinct (10)
	Papora		Extinct (10)
	Hoanya		Extinct (10)
	Thao	Brawbraw, Shtafari	Nearly extinct (8b)
North-West Formosan	Saisiyat	Taai, Tingho	Threatened (6b)
	Kulon-Pazeh	Pazeh, Kaxabu	Pazeh dialect extinct (10), last speaker 2010; Kaxabu nearly extinct (8b)
Malayo-Polynesian	Yami		Threatened (6b)

Bibliography

Aarts, P. & F Cavatorta (eds.). 2013. *Civil society in Syria and Iran: activism in authoritarian contexts*. Boulder, CO: Lynne Rienner Publishers.

Adelaar, A. 2013. Reviving Siraya: a case for language engineering. *Language Documentation and Conservation* 7. 212–234.

Adornetti, I. 2015. The phylogenetic foundations of discourse coherence: A pragmatic account of the evolution of language. *Biosemiotics* 8(3). 421–441.

Adorno, T. W. 2000. *Introduction to sociology*. Stanford, CA: Stanford University Press.

Amenta, E., K. Nash & A. Scott (eds.). 2016. *The Wiley-Blackwell companion to political sociology*. Chichester: Wiley-Blackwell.

Anderson, B. 1991. *Imagined communities: reflections on the origin and spread of nationalism*. London: Verso.

Andrade, T. 1997. Political spectacle and colonial rule: The Landdag on Dutch Taiwan, 1629–1648. *Itinerario*, 21(3), 57–93.

Andrade, T. 2008. *How Taiwan became Chinese: Dutch, Spanish, and Han colonization in the seventeenth century*. New York: Columbia University Press.

Andresen, J. T. 2014. *Linguistics and evolution: a developmental approach*. Cambridge: Cambridge University Press.

Anter, A. 2014. *Max Weber's theory of the modern state: origins, structure, and significance*. Basingstoke: Palgrave Macmillan.

Anthonissen, C. & J. Blommaert (eds.). 2007. *Discourse and human rights violations* (vol. 5). Amsterdam: John Benjamins.

Arendt, H. 2006. *Eichmann in Jerusalem: a report on the banality of evil*. New York, NY: Penguin.

Arthur, P. 2011. *Identities in transition: challenges for transitional justice in divided societies*. Cambridge: Cambridge University Press.

ASA [American Sociological Association]. 2008. Symposium: Boundaries and relations between political science and political sociology. *States, Power, and Societies - Newsletter of the Political Sociology Section of the ASA*. from http://asapoliticalsoc.org/wp-content/uploads/2013/12/summer08.pdf (accessed October 2017).

Asen, R. 2000. Seeking the "counter" in counterpublics. *Communication Theory* 10(4). 424–446.

Ashcroft, B., G. Griffiths & H. Tiffin. 2002. *The empire writes back: theory and practice in post-colonial literatures* (2nd edn.). London: Routledge.

Atkinson, Q. D. 2011. Phonemic diversity supports a serial founder effect model of language expansion from Africa. *Science* 332(6027). 346–349.

Auer, P. 1998. From codeswitching via language mixing to fused lects: Toward a dynamic typology of bilingual speech. *International Journal of Bilingualism* 3(4). 309–322.

Bagehot, W. 1872. *Physics and politics: or thoughts on the application of the principles of "natural selection" and "inheritance" to political society*. London: John S. King & Co.

Baker, C. & S. P. Jones. 1998. *Encyclopaedia of bilingualism and bilingual education*. Clevedon: Multilingual Matters.

Baran, D. 2007. Linguistic practice, social identity, and ideology: Mandarin variation in a Taipei County high school. Cambridge, MA: Harvard University, unpublished PhD thesis.

Barclay, P. D. 2005. Cultural brokerage and interethnic marriage in colonial Taiwan: Japanese subalterns and their Aborigine wives, 1895–1930. *Journal of Asian Studies* 64(2). 323–360.

Beck, U. 2003. Toward a new critical theory with a cosmopolitan intent. *Constellations* 10(4). 453–468.
Beetham, D. 2012. Political legitimacy. In E. Amenta, K. Nash & A. Scott (eds.), *The Wiley-Blackwell companion to political sociology*. Chichester: Wiley-Blackwell.
Bellwood, P. & E. Dizon. 2008. Austronesian cultural origins: out of Taiwan, via the Batanes Islands, and onwards to Western Polynesia. In A. Sanchez-Mazas (ed.), *Past human migrations in East Asia: matching archaeology, linguistics, and genetics*. London: Routledge.
Bellwood, P. & A. Sanchez-Mazas. 2005. Human migrations in continental East Asia and Taiwan: Genetic, linguistic, and archaeological evidence. *Current Anthropology* 46(3). 480–484.
Bellwood, P., J. J. Fox & D. Tryon. 2006. The Austronesians in history: common origins and diverse transformations. In P. Bellwood, J. J. Fox & D. Tryon (eds.), *The Austronesians: historical and comparative perspectives*. Canberra: ANU E Press.
Benhabib, S. 1996. Introduction: the democratic moment and the problem of difference. In S. Benhabib (ed.), *Democracy and difference: contesting the boundaries of the political*. Princeton, NJ: Princeton University Press.
Benhabib, S. 1999. Civil society and politics of identity and difference in a global context. In N. J. Smelser, J. C. Alexander & S. Benhabib (eds.), *Diversity and its discontents: cultural conflict and common ground in contemporary American society*. Princeton, NJ: Princeton University Press.
Berlin, B. & P. Kay. 1991. *Basic color terms: their universality and evolution*. Berkeley, CA: University of California Press.
Bickerton, D. 1990. *Language and species*. Chicago: University of Chicago Press.
Black, M. 1959. Linguistic relativity: the views of Benjamin Lee Whorf. *The Philosophical Review* 68(2). 228–238.
Blake, M. 2003. Language death and liberal politics. In W. Kymlicka & A. Patten (eds.), *Language rights and political theory*. Oxford: Oxford University Press.
Block, D., J. Gray & M. Holborow. 2012. *Neoliberalism and applied linguistics*. London: Routledge.
Blommaert, J. 2010. *The sociolinguistics of globalization*. Cambridge: Cambridge University Press.
Blommaert, J. & B. Rampton. 2011. Language and superdiversities. *Diversities* 13(2). 1–22.
Blussé, L. 1995. Retribution and remorse: The interaction between the administration and the Protestant mission in early colonial Formosa. In G. Prakash (ed.), *After colonialism: imperial histories and postcolonial developments*. Princeton, NJ: Princeton University Press.
Blust, R. 1996. Beyond the Austronesian homeland: The Austric Hypothesis and its implications for archaeology. *Transactions of the American Philosophical Society* 86(5). 117–158.
Blust, R. 2014. Some recent proposals concerning the classification of the Austronesian languages. *Oceanic Linguistics* 53(2). 300–391.
Borao Mateo, J. E. 2009. *The Spanish experience in Taiwan 1626–1642: the baroque ending of a Renaissance endeavour*. Hong Kong: Hong Kong University Press.
Borao, J. E. 2001. The Dominican missionaries in Taiwan (1626–1642). In W. Ku (ed.), *Missionary approaches and linguistics in Mainland China and Taiwan*. Leuven: Leuven University Press.
Bourdieu, P. 1986. The forms of capital. In J. Richardson (ed.), *Handbook of theory and research for the sociology of education*. Berkeley, CA: University of California Press.
Bourdieu, P. 1991. *Language and symbolic power*. Cambridge: Polity.

Bourdieu, P. 1999. Rethinking the state: The genesis and structure of the bureaucratic field. In G. Steinmetz (ed.), *State/culture: state formation after the cultural turn*. Ithaca, NY: Cornell University Press.
Boxer, C. R. 1941. The rise and fall of Nicholas Iquan. *T'ien Hsia Monthly* 11(5). 401–439.
Brackebusch, W. 1868. *Is English destined to become the universal language of the world?* Gottingen: University of Gottingen Ph.D. thesis.
Breuilly, J. 1982. *Nationalism and the state*. Manchester: Manchester University Press.
Brown, C. 2002. *Sovereignty, rights, and justice: international political theory today*. Cambridge: Polity.
Brown, M. E. & S. Ganguly. 2003. *Fighting words: language policy and ethnic relations in Asia*. Cambridge, MA: MIT Press.
Brown, M. J. 2004. *Is Taiwan Chinese? The impact of culture, power, and migration on changing identities*. Berkeley, CA: University of California Press.
Bruce, S. & S. Yearley. 2006. *The SAGE dictionary of sociology*. London: Sage.
Bullock, T. L. 2008. Formosan dialects and their connection with the Malay. In H. Chang (ed.), *A chronology of 19th century writings on Formosa: from The Chinese Repository, The Chinese Recorder, and The China Review*. Taipei: Ts'ao Yung-ho Foundation for Culture and Education/SMC Publishing.
Butler, J. & G. C. Spivak. 2010. *Who sings the nation-state?* Chicago, IL: Seagull Books.
Cabestan, J.-P. 2005. Specificities and limits of Taiwanese nationalism. *China Perspectives* 62.
Calvet, L.-J. 1987. *La guerre des langues*. Paris: Payot.
Cameron, D. 1995. *Verbal hygiene*. London: Routledge.
Campbell, L., N. H. Lee, E. Okura, S. Simpson & K. Ueki. 2013. New knowledge: findings from the Catalogue of Endangered Languages. Presented at the 3rd International Conference on Language Documentation and Conservation (ICLDC), University of Hawai'i – Manoa http://scholarspace.manoa.hawaii.edu/handle/10125/26145 (accessed October 2017).
Campbell, W. 1903. *Formosa under the Dutch: described from contemporary records, with explanatory notes and a bibliography of the island*. London: Kegan Paul.
Campbell, W. 1915. *Sketches from Formosa*. Taipei: SMC Publishing.
Cardinal, L., & Sonntag, S. K. (eds.). 2015. *State traditions and language regimes*. Kingston, ON: McGill-Queen's University Press.
Cauquelin, J. 2004. *The aborigines of Taiwan: The Puyuma - from headhunting to the modern world*. London: Routledge.
CEPD [Council for Economic Planning and Development]. 2002. *Tiaozhan 2008: Guojia fazhan chongdian jihua [Challenge 2008: National development plan]* http://www.webcitation.org/6IJFw5X8J (accessed October 2017).
Chambers, J. K. 1995. *Sociolinguistic theory: linguistic variation and its social significance*. Oxford: Blackwell.
Chambers, S., & Kymlicka, W. 2002. Introduction. In S. Chambers & W. Kymlicka (eds.), *Alternative conceptions of civil society*. Princeton, NJ: Princeton University Press.
Chandhoke, N. 2004. The "civil" and the "political" in civil society: the case of India. In P. J. Burnell & P. Calvert (eds.), *Civil society in democratization*. London: Frank Cass & Co.
Chang, H., & Myers, R. H. 1963. Japanese colonial development policy in Taiwan 1895–1906: a case of bureaucratic entrepreneurship. *Journal of Asian Studies* 22(4). 433–449.
Chang, J. 2004. Ideologies of English teaching and learning in Taiwan. Sydney: University of Sydney unpublished Ph.D. thesis.

Chang, J. 2013. English teaching superstars http://www.languageonthemove.com/language-learning-gender-identity/english-teaching-superstars/ (accessed October 2017).
Chang, L. 2011. Telling histories of an island nation: the academics and politics of history textbooks in contemporary Taiwan. In G. Müller (ed.), *Designing history in East Asian textbooks: identity politics and transnational aspirations*. London: Routledge.
Chang, M. 2005. The movement to indigenize the social sciences in Taiwan: origin and predicaments. In J. Makeham & A. Hsiau (eds.), *Cultural, ethnic and political nationalism in contemporary Taiwan: Bentuhua*. Basingstoke: Palgrave Macmillan.
Chang, P. 2014. The political and diplomatic significance of interpreters/translators in seventeenth-century colonial Taiwan. In F. Federici & D. Tessicini (eds.), *Mediating and communicating power from the Middle Ages to the Modern Era*. Basingstoke: Palgrave Macmillan.
Chang, P. (ed.). 1974. *T'ai-wan ti-ch'ü kuo-yu yün-tung shih-liao [Historical materials on the national language movement in Taiwan]*. Taipei: T'ai-wan shang-wu yin-shu-kuan.
Chang, S. 1999. A Hakka view of language matters. *Taipei Times*, December 4, 1999, p.8.
Chang, S. Y. 1999. Taiwanese new literature and the colonial context: a historical survey. In M. Rubinstein (ed.), *Taiwan: a new history*. New York, NY: M. E. Sharpe.
Chang, V. W. 2007. A brief sketch of Taiwan's English education at primary level. In *Primary innovations regional seminar: a collection of papers*. London: British Council.
Chang, Y. 2008. Parents' attitudes toward the English education policy in Taiwan. *Asia-Pacific Education Review* 9(4). 423–435.
Chatterjee, P. 2004. *The politics of the governed: reflections on popular politics in most of the world*. New York: Columbia University Press.
Chen, K. 2010. *Asia as method*. Durham, NC: Duke University Press.
Chen, L. & W. M. Reisman. 1972. Who owns Taiwan: a search for international title. *Yale Law Journal* 81. 599–671.
Chen, P. 1999. *Modern Chinese*. Cambridge: Cambridge University Press.
Chen, P. 2001. Policy on the selection and implementation of a standard language as a source of conflict in Taiwan. In N. Gottlieb & P. Chen (eds.), *Language planning and language policy: East Asian perspectives*. Richmond: Curzon.
Chen, S.-C. 2006. Simultaneous promotion of indigenisation and internationalisation: New language-in-education policy in Taiwan. *Language and Education* 20(4). 332–337.
Chen, S.-C. 2010. Multilingualism in Taiwan. *International Journal of the Sociology of Language* 205. 79–104.
Chen, T., & Chin, J. 2016. Taixi school begins classes to teach pupils Vietnamese. *Taipei Times*, November 15, 2016, p. 4.
Cheng, R. 1985. A comparison of Taiwanese, Taiwan Mandarin, and Peking Mandarin. *Language* 61(2). 352–377.
Cheng, S. 2014. Police interpretation examinations in Taiwan during the period of Japanese rule. *Asian Education and Development Studies* 3(3). 253–266.
Cherubini, L. & J. Hodson. 2008. Ontario Ministry of Education policy and Aboriginal learners' epistemologies: a fundamental disconnect. *Canadian Journal of Educational Administration and Policy* 79. 1–33.
China Post. 2014. Is the MOE rewriting history or brainwashing the nation? *China Post*, January 24, 2014, p. n.p.
Ching, L. T. S. 2000. Savage construction and civility making: The Musha Incident and Aboriginal representations in colonial Taiwan. *Positions: East Asia Cultures Critique* 8(3). 795–818.

Ching, L. T. S. 2001. *Becoming "Japanese": Colonial Taiwan and the politics of identity formation*. Berkeley, CA: University of California Press.
Chiu, H.-H. 2008. *The colonial "civilizing process" in Dutch Formosa, 1624–1662*. Leiden: Brill.
Chiung, W. V. T. 2001. Romanization and language planning in Taiwan. *The Linguistics Association of Korea Journal* 9(1). 15–43.
Chomsky, N. 1965. *Aspects of the theory of syntax*. Cambridge, MA: MIT Press.
Chomsky, N. 1999. *Profit over people: neoliberalism and global order*. London: Seven Stories Press.
Chomsky, N. 2000. *New horizons in the study of language and mind*. Cambridge: Cambridge University Press.
Chou, C. P. & J. K. Yuan. 2011. Buxiban in Taiwan. *International Institute for Asian Studies Newsletter* 56(15).
Chou, W. 1991. The Kominka Movement: Taiwan under wartime Japan, 1937–1945. New Haven, CT: Yale University unpublished PhD thesis.
Chou, W. 1995. T'ai-wan-jen ti-i-tz'u te "kuo-yü" ching-yen – hsi-lunjih-chih mo.-chi te jig-yü hunting chi wen-T'ai [The National-language movement in Colonial Taiwan, 1937–45]. *Shin Shih-Hsueh [New History]* 6(2). 113–161.
Chrisomalis, S. 2009. The origin and co-evolution of literacy and numeracy. In D. R. Olsen & N. Torrance (eds.), *The Cambridge handbook of literacy*. Cambridge: Cambridge University Press.
CLA [Council of Labour Affairs]. 1999. *The 1998 investigation report on the management and employment of foreign workers in ROC*. Taipei: Executive Yuan.
Cohen, J. L. & A. Arato. 1992. *Civil society and political theory*. Cambridge, MA: MIT Press.
Colas, A. 2013. *International civil society: social movements in world politics*. Cambridge: Polity.
Colquhoun, A. R. & J. H. Stewart-Lockhart. 2008. A sketch of Formosa. In H. Chang (ed.), *A chronology of 19th century writings on Formosa: from The Chinese Repository, The Chinese Recorder, and The China Review*. Taipei: Ts'ao Yung-ho Foundation for Culture and Education/SMC Publishing.
Comaroff, J. & J. L. Comaroff. 1992. Home-made hegemony: Modernity, domesticity, and colonialism in South Africa. In K. Hansen (ed.), *African encounters with domesticity*. Newark, NJ: Rutgers University Press.
Constable, N. 2005. *Guest people: Hakka identity in China and abroad*. Seattle, WA: University of Washington Press.
Cook, S. D. N. 1995. The structure of technological revolutions and the Gutenberg myth. In J. C. Pitt (ed.), *New directions in the philosophy of technology*, 63–83. Dordrecht: Springer.
Coolidge, T. 2016. August 10. President of Taiwan offers historic apology to indigenous peoples for 400 years of abuse. *Cultural Survival*, August 10, 2016 https://www.culturalsurvival.org/news/president-taiwan-offers-historic-apology-indigenous-peoples-400-years-abuse (accessed October 2017).
Cooper, R. L. 1989. *Language planning and social change*. Cambridge: Cambridge University Press.
Copper, J. F. 1996. *Taiwan: nation-state or province?* Boulder, CO: Westview Press.
Corcuff, S. 2002. Taiwan's "Mainlanders": New Taiwanese? In S. Corcuff & R. Edmondson (eds.), *Memories of the future: national identity issues and the search for a new Taiwan*. New York: M. E. Sharpe.
Coulmas, F. 2002. Language policy in modern Japanese education. In J. W. Tollefson (ed.), *Language policies in education: critical issues*. Mahwah, NJ: Lawrence Erlbaum.

Coulmas, F. 2003. Sociolinguistics. In R. K. Aronoff & J. Ress-Miller (eds.), *The handbook of linguistics*. Oxford: Blackwell.
Crystal, D. 2000. *Language death*. Cambridge: Cambridge University Press.
Crystal, D. 2002. *The English language: a guided tour of the language*. London: Penguin UK.
Crystal, D. 2012. *English as a global language*. Cambridge: Cambridge University Press.
Curran, J. 1991. Rethinking the media as a public sphere. In P. Dahlgreen & C. Sparks (eds.), *Communication and citizenship: journalism and the public sphere in the new media age*. London: Routledge.
Dahaene, S., V. Izard, E. Spelke & P. Pica. 2008. Log or linear? Distinct intuitions of the number scale in Western and Amazonian indigene cultures. *Science* 320(5880). 1217–1220.
Dai, G. & Y. Ye. 1992. *Ai Zeng 228 [Love-Hate 228]*. Taipei: Yuanliu.
Davidson, J. W. 1903. *The island of Formosa, past and present. history, people, resources, and commercial prospects*. London/New York: Macmillan.
De Bakker, F. G., F. Den Hond, B. King & K. Weber. 2013. Social movements, civil society, and corporations: Taking stock and looking ahead. *Organization Studies* 34(5–6). 573–593.
De Bernadi, J. 1991. Linguistic nationalism: the case of Southern Min. *Sino-Platonic Papers* 25. 1–25.
de Greiff, P. 2012. Theorizing transitional justice. *Nomos 51*. 31–77.
de Lacouperie, T. 1887. Formosa notes on MSS., races, and languages. *Journal of the Royal Asiatic Society of Great Britain and Ireland* 19. 413–494.
de Varennes, F. 1995. *Language, minorities, and human rights*. The Hague: Martinus Nijhoff.
Deal, W. E. 2007. *Handbook to life in Medieval and Early Modern Japan*. Oxford: Oxford University Press.
Dean, M. & K. Villadsen. 2016. *State phobia and civil society: the political legacy of Michel Foucault*. Stanford, CA: Stanford University Press.
Delanty, G. 2001. Cosmopolitanism and violence - the limits of global civil society. *European Journal of Sociology/Archives Européennes de Sociologie/Europäisches Archiv Für Soziologie* 4(1). 41–52.
Della Porta, D. & M. Diani. 2006. *Social movements: an introduction*. Oxford: Blackwell.
DGBAS [Directorate General of Budget, Accounting, and Statistics]. (2010a). *Report on the survey of family income & expenditure*. Retrieved October 2017 from http://win.dgbas.gov.tw/fies/doc/result/99/a11/111.xls
DGBAS [Directorate General of Budget, Accounting, and Statistics]. 2010b. *Languages used at home for the resident nationals aged six years and over*. Taipei http://eng.stat.gov.tw/public/data/dgbas04/bc6/census022e(final).html (accessed October 2017).
Dos Santos, T. 1971. The structure of dependence. In K. T. Fann & D. C. Hodges (eds.), *Readings in U.S. imperialism*. Boston: P. Sargent.
Drake, M. 2010. *Political sociology for a globalizing world*. Cambridge: Polity.
Dryzek, J. 1990. *Discursive democracy*. Cambridge: Cambridge University Press.
Duchêne, A. & M. Heller (eds.). 2012. *Language in late capitalism: pride and profit*. London: Routledge.
Dupré, J.-F. 2016. Legislating language in Taiwan: From equality to development to status quo. *Language Policy* 15(4). 415–432.
Dupré, J.-F. 2017. *Culture politics and linguistic recognition in Taiwan: ethnicity, national identity, and the party system*. London: Routledge.
Easton, D. 1953. *The political system: an inquiry into the state of political science*. (2nd edn.). New York: Knopf.

Edwards, D. 1997. *Discourse and cognition*. London: Sage.
Edwards, J. 2011. *Challenges in the social life of language*. Basingstoke: Palgrave Macmillan.
Enjolras, B., K. Steen-Johnsen & D. Wollebaek. 2013. Social media and mobilization to offline demonstrations: Transcending participatory divides? *New Media & Society* 15(6). 890–908.
Errington, J. 2008. *Linguistics in a colonial world: a story of language, meaning, and power*. Oxford: Blackwell.
ESC (Election Study Center), N. C. C. U. 2017a. *Important political attitude trend distribution: Taiwanese/Chinese identification trend distribution in Taiwan (1992/06~2017/06)* http://esc.nccu.edu.tw/course/news.php?Sn=166 (accessed October 2017).
ESC (Election Study Center), N. C. C. U. (2017b). *Important political attitude trend distribution: Taiwan independence vs. unification with the mainland trend distribution in Taiwan (1992/06 ~ 2017/06)* http://esc.nccu.edu.tw/course/news.php?Sn=167 (accessed October 2017).
Ethnologue. 2009. 16th edn. http://archive.ethnologue.com/16/ (accessed October 2017).
Ethnologue. 2017. Ethnologue 2017: welcome to the 20th edition https://www.ethnologue.com/ethnoblog/gary-simons/welcome-20th-edition (accessed October 2017).
Evans, P. B., D. Rueschemeyer & T. Skocpol (eds.). 1985. *Bringing the state back in*. Cambridge: Cambridge University Press.
Fanon, F. 1967. *Black skin, white masks*. (C. L. Markmann, trans.). New York: Grove Press.
Faulks, K. 2000. *Political sociology: a critical introduction*. New York: New York University Press.
Feifel, K.-E. 1994. *Language attitudes in Taiwan: a social evaluation of language in social change*. Taipei: Crane.
Fell, D. 2007. Partisan issues in contemporary Taiwan: Is Taiwan's democracy dead? In J. Damm & G. Schubert (eds.), *Taiwanese identity from domestic, regional and global perspectives*. Munster: LitVerlag.
Fell, D. 2011. Taiwan's party system in transition: More or less space for identity politics? In *Taiwanese identity in the 21st century: domestic, regional and global perspectives*. London: Routledge.
Fell, D. & I. C. Chen. 2014. Lessons of defeat and success: Taiwan's 2012 elections in comparative perspective. *Journal of Current Chinese Affairs* 43(3). 13–43.
Feng, L. 2013. *Early China: a social and cultural history*. Cambridge: Cambridge University Press.
Ferguson, C. 1996. *Sociolinguistic perspectives: papers on language in society, 1959–1994*. Oxford: Oxford University Press.
Ferguson, C. A. 1968. Language development. In J. A. Fishman, C. A. Ferguson, & J. Das Gupta (eds.), *Language problems of developing nations*. New York: John Wiley & Sons.
Ferraro, V. 2008. Dependency theory: an introduction. In G. Secondi (ed.), *The development economics reader*. London: Routledge.
Ferrell, R. 1969. *Taiwan aboriginal groups: problems in cultural and linguistic classification*. Monograph No. 17. Nankang, Taipei: Academia Sinica, Institute of Ethnology.
Fishman, J. A. 1968. Some contrasts between linguistically homogenous and heterogeneous polities. In J. A. Fishman, C. A. Ferguson, & J. Das Gupta (eds.), *Language problems of developing nations*. New York: John Wiley & Sons.
Fishman, J. A. 1972. *The sociology of language: an interdisciplinary social science approach to language in society*. New York: Newbury House Publishers.
Fishman, J. A. 1991. *Reversing language shift: theoretical and empirical foundations of assistance to threatened languages*. Clevedon: Multilingual Matters.

Fishman, J. A. 2006. *Do not leave your language alone: the hidden status agendas within corpus planning in language policy*. Mahwah, NJ: Lawrence Erlbaum.
Foley, M. W. & B. Edwards. 1996. The paradox of civil society. *Journal of Democracy* 7(3). 38–52.
Fong, S. 1993. Achieving weak hegemony: Taiwanese cultural experience under Japanese rule, 1895–1945. Chicago, IL: University of Chicago unpublished PhD thesis.
Foucault, M. 1984. Truth and power. In P. Rabinow (ed.), *The Foucault reader*. New York: Pantheon Books.
Foucault, M. 1991. Governmentality. In G. Burchell, C. Gordon & P. Miller (eds.), *The Foucault effect: studies in governmentality*. Chicago, IL: University of Chicago Press.
Fraser, N. 1992. Rethinking the public sphere: a contribution to the critique of actually existing democracy. In C. J. Calhoun (ed.), *Habermas and the public sphere*. Cambridge, MA: MIT Press.
Fraser, N. 2014. *Transnationalizing the public sphere*. Cambridge: Polity.
Freundl, D. 2004. A band-aid solution for English-language learning? *Taipei Times*, September 5, 2004, p. 17.
Friedman, P. K. 2005. Learning "local" languages: passive revolution, language markets, and Aborigine education in Taiwan. Philadelphia, PA: Temple University unpublished PhD thesis.
Garcia, O. & L. Wei. 2014. *Translanguaging: language, bilingualism, and education*. Basingstoke: Palgrave Macmillan.
Gates, H. 1981. Ethnicity and social class. In E. M. Ahern & H. Gates (eds.), *The anthropology of Taiwanese society*. Stanford, CA: Stanford University Press.
Gee, J. P. 2011. *Social linguistics and literacies: ideology in discourses* (4th edn.). London: Routledge.
Geertz, C. 1973. *The interpretation of culture*. New York: Basic Books.
Gellner, E. 1964. *Thought and change*. London: Weidenfeld and Nicolson.
Gellner, E. 1983. *Nations and nationalism*. Ithaca, NY: Cornell University Press.
Gerber, A. 2016. DPP to study languages to promote understanding. *Taipei Times*, August 12, 2016, p. 3.
Gerber, A. 2017. Forum wrangles with questions on national language. *Taipei Times*, March 26, 2017, p. 3.
Giddens, A. 1985. *The nation-state and violence* (vol. 2). Berkeley, CA: University of California Press.
Gold, T. 1994. Civil society and Taiwan's quest for identity. In S. Harrell & C. Huang (eds.), *Cultural change in postwar Taiwan*. Boulder, CO: Westview Press.
Goswami, M. 2004. *Producing India: from colonial economy to national space*. Chicago, IL: University of Chicago Press.
Gottlieb, N. 2005. *Language and society in Japan*. Cambridge: Cambridge University Press.
Greene, D. 1978. Language and nationalism. *The Crane Bag* 2(1/2). 183–188.
Greenfeld, L. 1992. *Nationalism: five roads to modernity*. Cambridge, MA: Harvard University Press.
Greenfeld, L. & J. R. Eastwood. 2005. Nationalism in comparative perspective. In T. Janoski, R. R. Alford, A. M. Hicks & M. A. Schwartz (eds.), *The handbook of political sociology: states, civil societies, and globalization*. Cambridge: Cambridge University Press.
Greenhill, S. J., A. J. Drummond & R. D. Gray. 2010. How accurate and robust are the phylogenetic estimates of Austronesian language relationships? *PLOS ONE* 5(3). e9573.

Grin, F., C. Sfreddo & F. Vaillancourt. 2010. *The economics of the multilingual workplace*. London: Routledge.
Guéhenno, J.-M. 1995. *The end of the nation-state*. Minneapolis, MN: University of Minnesota Press.
Gully, J. M. 2011. Bilingual signs in Carinthia: international treaties, the Ortstafelstreit, and the spaces of German. *Transit* 7(1).
Gumperz, J. J. 1982. *Discourse strategies*. Cambridge: Cambridge University Press.
Gumperz, J. J. & S. C. Levinson. 1996. *Rethinking linguistic relativity*. Cambridge: Cambridge University Press.
Habermas, J. 1989. *The structural transformation of the public sphere: an inquiry into a category of bourgeois society*. Cambridge: Polity Press.
Hall, J. A. & G. J. Ikenberry. 1989. *The state*. Buckingham: Open University Press.
Hallett, D., M. J. Chandler & C. E. Lalonde. 2007. Aboriginal language knowledge and youth suicide. *Cognitive Development* 22(3). 392–399.
Halliday, M. A. K. & J. Webster. 2014. *Text linguistics: the how and why of meaning*. Sheffield/Bristol,CT: Equinox Publishing.
Happart, G. 1840. *Dictionary of the Favorlang dialect of the Formosan language*. (W. H. Medhurst, trans.). Batavia: np.
Harrell, S. 2011. *Cultural encounters on China's ethnic frontiers*. Seattle: University of Washington Press.
Harvey, D. 2007. *A brief history of neoliberalism*. Oxford: Oxford University Press.
Haugen, E. 1983. The implementation of corpus planning: theory and practice. In J. Cobarrubias & J. A. Fishman (eds.), *Progress in language planning: international perspectives*. Berlin: Mouton de Gruyter.
Heinrich, P. 2012. *The making of monolingual Japan: language ideology and Japanese modernity*. Clevedon: Multilingual Matters.
Held, D. 1992. The development of the modern state. In S. Hall & B. Gieben (eds.), *Formations of modernity*. Cambridge: Polity.
Heller, M. 2010. The commodification of language. *Annual Review of Anthropology* 39. 101–114.
Henrard, K. (2000). *Devising an Adequate System of Minority Protection: Individual Human Rights, Minority Rights, and the Right to Self-Determination*. The Hague: Martinus Nijhoff.
Heylen, A. 2001. Missionary linguistics on Taiwan: Dutch language policy and early Formosan literacy (1624–1662). In W. Ku (ed.), *Missionary approaches and linguistics in Mainland China and Taiwan*. Leuven: Ferdinand Verbiest Foundation/Leuven University Press.
Heylen, A. 2005. The legacy of literacy practices in colonial Taiwan. Japanese–Taiwanese–Chinese: Language interaction and identity formation. *Journal of Multilingual and Multicultural Development* 26(6). 496–511.
Heylen, A. 2007. An excursion into Cai Peihuo's colonial diary, 1929–36. *Journal of Chinese Overseas* 3(2). 239–262.
Hirsch, M. 2006. "Cross-border couples" discussed. *Taipei Times*, September 21, 2006, p. 2.
Hobsbawm, E. 1990. *Nations and nationalism since 1780: programme, myth, reality*. Cambridge: Cambridge University Press.
Hobsbawm, E. & T. Ranger (eds.). 1983. *The invention of tradition*. Cambridge: Cambridge University Press.
Hodge, F. S. & K. Nandy. 2011. Predictors of wellness and American Indians. *Journal of Health Care for the Poor and Underserved* 22(3). 791–803.

Hogan-Brun, G. 2017. *Linguanomics: what is the market potential of multilingualism?* London: Bloomsbury.
Horio, T. 1988. *Educational thought and ideology in modern Japan*. (S. Platzer, trans.). Tokyo: University of Tokyo Press.
Hornberger, N. 1994. Literacy and language planning. *Language and Education* 8. 75–86.
Hornberger, N. 2006. Frameworks and models in language policy and planning. In T. Ricento (ed.), *An introduction to language policy: theory and method*. Oxford: Blackwell.
Horowitz, D. L. 1985. *Ethnic groups in conflict*. Berkeley, CA: University of California Press.
Horowitz, D. L. 2001. *The deadly ethnic riot*. Berkeley, CA: University of California Press.
Hsia, H. 2007. Imaged and imagined threat to the nation: the media construction of the 'foreign brides' phenomenon as social problems in Taiwan. *Inter-Asia Cultural Studies* 8(1). 55–85.
Hsiao, H. M. 2011. Social movements in Taiwan: A typological analysis. In J. Broadbent & V. Brockman (eds.), *East Asian social movements*. New York: Springer.
Hsiau, A. 1997. Language ideology in Taiwan: The KMT's language policy, the Tai-yu language movement, and ethnic politics. *Journal of Multilingual and Multicultural Development* 18(4). 302–315.
Hsiau, A. 2000. *Contemporary Taiwanese cultural nationalism*. London: Routledge.
Hsieh, C. & C. Wang. 2006. Immigrant wives and their cultural influence in Taiwan. *Anthropology and Sociology* 53(2). 101–118.
Hsu, H. 1991. T'ai-wan kuang-fu ch'u-chi te yü-wen wen-t'i [Taiwan's language problem in the early years of the postwar period]. *Shu Yu Yen [Thoughts and Words]* 29(4). 155–184.
Huang, C. 2001. The Yamatodomashi of the Takasago volunteers of Taiwan: A reading of the postcolonial situation. In H. Befu & S. Guichard-Anguis (eds.), *Globalizing Japan: ethnography of the Japanese presence in Asia, Europe, and America*. London: Routledge.
Huang, C. & J. Chung. 2016. Kaohsiung school to run Vietnamese club. *Taipei Times*, May 13, 2016, p. 5.
Huang, J. 2003. Council says country to have no official language. *Taipei Times*, September 23, 2003, p. 1.
Huang, L. & M. Douglass. 2008. Foreign workers and spaces for community life Taipei's Little Philippines. In A. Daniere & M. Douglass (eds.), *The politics of civic space in Asia: building urban communities*. London: Routledge.
Huang, S. 1995. *Yuyan, shehui yu zuqun yishi: Taiwan yuyan shehui xue de yanjiu [Language, society, and ethnic consciousness: The study of Taiwan's languages and societies]*. Taipei: Crane.
Huang, S. 2000. Language, identity, and conflict: a Taiwanese study. *International Journal of the Sociology of Language* 143(1). 139–150.
Hughes, C. 1997. *Taiwan and Chinese nationalism*. London: Routledge.
Hughes, C. 2011. Negotiating national identity in Taiwan: between nativisation and de-sinicisation. In R. Ash, J. W. Garver & P. Prime (eds.), *Taiwan's democracy: economic and political challenges*. London: Routledge.
Hughes, C. R. 2014. Revisiting identity politics under Ma Ying-jeou. In J.-P. Cabestan & J. deLisle (eds.), *Political changes in Taiwan under Ma Ying-jeou: partisan conflict, policy choices, external constraints, and security challenges*, 120–136. London: Routledge.
Hwang, J. 2012. Democratic supervision of Taiwan-China agreements: On the ECFA and beyond. In P. Chow (ed.), *National identity and economic interest: Taiwan's competing options and their implications for regional stability*. Basingstoke: Palgrave Macmillan. //www.palgrave.com/us/book/9780230116481

Hymes, D. 1974. *Foundations in sociolinguistics: an ethnographic approach*. Philadelphia, PA: University of Pennsylvania Press.
ICTJ (International Centre for Transitional Justice). 2009. *What is transitional justice?* New York: International Center for Transitional Justice https://www.ictj.org/sites/default/files/ICTJ-Global-Transitional-Justice-2009-English.pdf (accessed October 2017).
Ignatieff, M. 2007. *The rights revolution*. Toronto: House of Anansi.
Jackson-Preece, J. 2014. *Beyond the (non) definition of minority* (brief no. 30). Flensburg: European Centre for Minority Issues.
Jacobs, J. B. 2005. "Taiwanization" in Taiwan's politics. In J. Makeham & A. Hsiau (eds.), *Cultural, ethnic and political nationalism in contemporary Taiwan: Bentuhua*. Basingstoke: Palgrave Macmillan.
Jacobs, J. B. 2016. Taiwan during and after the democratic transition (1988–2016). In G. Schubert (ed.), *Routledge handbook of contemporary Taiwan*. London: Routledge.
Jessop, B. 1990. *State theory: putting the capitalist state in its place*. University Park, PA: Penn State Press.
Jessop, B. 2007. *State power*. Cambridge: Polity.
Joseph, J. E. 2004. *Language and identity: national, ethnic, religious*. Basingstoke: Palgrave Macmillan.
Joseph, J. E. & F. J. Newmeyer. 2012. "All languages are equally complex": The rise and fall of a consensus. *Historiographia Linguistica* 39(2). 341–368.
Jung, C. 2011. Canada and the legacy of the Indian residential schools: Transitional justice for indigenous people in a nontransitional society. In P. Arthur (ed.), *Identities in transition: challenges for transitional justice in divided societies*. Cambridge: Cambridge University Press.
Kachru, B. 1992. *The other tongue: English across cultures*. Urbana, IL: University of Illinois Press.
Kaldor, M. 1993. Yugoslavia and the new nationalism. *New Left Review* 197. 96–112.
Kaldor, M. 2013. *Global civil society: an answer to war*. Chichester: John Wiley & Sons.
Kaske, E. 2008. *The politics of language in Chinese education, 1895–1919*. Leiden: Brill.
Katz, P. 2005. *When valleys turn blood red: the Ta-Pa-Ni incident in colonial Taiwan*. Honolulu, HI: University of Hawai'i Press.
Keane, J. 2003. *Global civil society?* Cambridge: Cambridge University Press.
Kedourie, E. 1960. *Nationalism*. London: Hutchinson.
Kerr, G. H. 1974. *Formosa: licensed revolution and the home rule movement*. Honolulu, HI: University of Hawai'i Press.
Kerr, G. H. 2017. *Formosa betrayed*. Manchester: Camphor Press.
Keyes, C. F. 1981. Towards a new formulation of the concept of ethnic group. *Ethnicity* 3(3). 202–213.
King, M., A. Smith & M. Gracey. 2009. Indigenous health part 2: the underlying causes of the health gap. *The Lancet* 374(9683). 76–85.
King, W. 2007. From exclusive to adaptive national identity: Taiwan's mainland spouses' immigration policy. In J. Damm & G. Schubert (eds.), *Taiwanese identity from domestic, regional and global perspectives*. Munster: LitVerlag.
Kitta, H. 1989. *Nippon no Romazi-undo 1789–1988 [The Romanization movement in Japan 1789–1988]*. Tokyo: Nippon Romazi-sha.
Kloss, H. 1968. *Research possibilities on group bilingualism: a report*. Quebec: International Center for Research on Bilingualism.
Klöter, H. 2004. Language policy in the KMT and DPP eras. *China Perspectives* 56.

Klöter, H. 2005. *Written Taiwanese*. Wiesbaden: Harrassowitz.
Klöter, H. 2006. Mandarin remains more equal: Changes and continuities in Taiwan's language policy. In D. Fell, H. Klöter & B. Chang (eds.), *What has changed? Taiwan before and After the change in the ruling parties*. Wiesbaden: Harrassowitz.
Klöter, H. 2008. Facts and fantasy about Favorlang: Early European encounters with Taiwan's languages. In A. Lubotsky, J. Schaeken & J. Wiedenhof (eds.), *Evidence and counter evidence: linguistic essays in honour of Frederik Kortlandt, vol. 2: general linguistics*. Amsterdam/New York, NY: Rodopi.
Knapp, R. 1999. The shaping of Taiwan's landscapes. In M. Rubinstein (ed.), *Taiwan: a new history*. New York: M. E. Sharpe.
Knight, C., M. Studdert-Kennedy & J. R. Hurford. 2000. Language: a Darwinian adaption? In C. Knight, M. Studdert-Kennedy & J. R. Hurford (eds.), *The evolutionary emergence of language: social function and the origin of linguistic form*. Cambridge: Cambridge University Press.
Ko, S. 2003. KMT says language policy stirring up ethnic strife. *Taipei Times*, September 25, 2003, p. 3.
Ko, S. & L. Yeh. 2002. English to be made official. *Taipei Times*, May 1, 2002, p. 2.
Kontra, M., R. Phillipson, T. Skutnabb-Kangas & T. Varady. 1999. *Language: a right and a resource. approaching linguistic human rights*. Budapest: Central European University Press.
Kopstein, J. & S. Chambers. 2008. Civil society and the state. In A. Phillips, B. Honig & J. Dryzek (eds.), *The Oxford handbook of political theory*. Oxford: Oxford University Press.
Kosonen, K. 2008. Literacy in local languages in Thailand: language maintenance in a globalised world. *International Journal of Bilingual Education and Bilingualism* 11(2). 170–188.
Krauss, M. 1992. The world's languages in crisis. *Language* 68(1). 4–10.
Kubler, C. 1985. *The development of Mandarin in Taiwan*. Taipei: Student Book Company.
Kubota, R. 2014. The multi/plural turn, postcolonial theory, and neoliberal multiculturalism: Complicities and implications for applied linguistics. *Applied Linguistics* 37(4). 474–494.
Kuo, Y. 2005. New dialect formation: the case of Taiwanese Mandarin. Colchester: University of Essex, unpublished PhD thesis.
Kymlicka, W. 1995. *Multicultural citizenship: a liberal theory of minority rights*. Oxford: Clarendon Press.
Kymlicka, W. & A. Patten (eds.). 2003. *Language rights and political theory*. Oxford: Oxford University Press.
Labov, W. 1972. *Sociolinguistic patterns*. Philadelphia, PA: University of Pennsylvania Press.
Lai, T., R. H. Myers & W. Wei. 1991. *A tragic beginning: TheTaiwan uprising of February 28, 1947*. Stanford, CA: Stanford University Press.
Laitin, D. & R. Reich. 2003. A liberal democratic approach to language justice. In W. Kymlicka & A. Patten (eds.), *Language rights and political theory*. Oxford: Oxford University Press.
Lamley, H. J. 1968. The 1895 Taiwan Republic: a significant episode in modern Chinese history. *The Journal of Asian Studies* 27(4). 739–762.
Lamley, H. J. 1970. Assimilation efforts in colonial Taiwan: the fate of the 1914 movement. *Monumenta Serica* 29(1). 496–520.
Lamley, H. J. 1981. Sub-ethnic rivalry in the Ch'ing period. In E. M. Ahern & H. Gates (eds.), *The anthropology of Taiwanese society*. Stanford, CA: Stanford University Press.
Lamley, H. J. 1999. Taiwan under Japanese rule, 18951945: the vicissitudes of colonialism. In M. Rubinstein (ed.), *Taiwan: a new history*. New York: M. E. Sharpe.

Lan, P. 2003. "They have more money but I speak better English!" Transnational encounters between Filipina domestics and Taiwanese employers. *Identities: Global Studies in Culture and Power* 10. 133–161.
Lan, P. 2006. *Global Cinderellas: migrant domestics and newly rich employers in Taiwan*. Durham, NC: Duke University Press.
Lan, P. 2008. Women's bodies as boundary markers: Reproductive crisis and sexual control in the ethnic frontiers of Taiwan. *Signs: Journal of Women in Culture and Society* 33(4). 833–861.
Lan, P. 2011. White privilege, language capital, and cultural ghettoization. *Journal of Ethnic and Migration Studies* 37(10). 1639–1693.
Lan, S. M. 2015. In pursuit of equality and liberty: Taiwan's indigenous political movement in the 1920s. In J. Kwak & K. Matsuda (eds.), *Patriotism in East Asia*. London: Routledge.
LaPolla, R. J. 2001. The role of migration and language contact in the development of the Sino-Tibetan language family. In R. M. W. Dixon & A. Y. Aikhenvald (eds.), *Areal diffusion and genetic inheritance: case studies in language change*. Oxford: Oxford University Press.
Laycock, D. 2001. Diversity in Melanesia: a tentative explanation. In A. Fill & P. Mühlhäusler, (eds.), *The ecolinguistics reader: language, ecology, and environment*. London: Continuum.
Lee, C. 2000. State, capital, and media: the case of Taiwan. In J. Curran & M. Park (eds.), *De-westernizing media studies*. London: Routledge.
Lee, I.-C., E. E. Chen, C.-H. Tsai, N.-S. Yen, A. L. P. Chen & W.-C. Lin. 2016. Voting intention and choices: Are voters always rational and deliberative? *PLOS ONE* 11 (2).n.p.
Lee, J. S. 2010. Taiwan: immigration to Taiwan. In U. A. Segal, D. Elliott & N. S. Mayadas (eds.), *Immigration worldwide: policies, practices, and trends*. Oxford: Oxford University Press.
Léglise, I. & B. Migge. 2007. Language and colonialism: applied linguistics in the context of creole communities. In M. Hellinger & A. Pauwels (eds.), *Language and communication: diversity and change*, 297–338). Berlin: Mouton de Gruyter.
Lenneberg, E. 1967. *Biological foundations of language*. New York, NY: Wiley.
Lévi-Strauss, C. 1961. *Tristes tropiques*. New York: Criterion Books.
Lewis, E. G. 1976. Bilingualism and bilingual education: the ancient world to the Renaissance. In J. A. Fishman (ed.), *Bilingual education*. Rowley, MA: Newbury House.
Lewis, M. P. & G. F. Simons. 2010. Assessing endangerment: expanding Fishman's GIDS. *Revue Roumaine de Linguistique* 55(2). 103–120.
Li, P. J. 2010. *Studies of Sinkang manuscripts*. Taipei: Academia Sinica, Institute of Linguistics.
Liao, P. 2006. Print culture and the emergent public sphere in colonial Taiwan, 1895–1945. In P. Liao & D. D. Wang (eds.), *Taiwan under Japanese colonial rule, 1895–1945: history, culture, memory*. New York: Columbia University Press.
Lin, C. Y. & J. Chen. 2016. *The impact of societal and social innovation: a case-based approach*. Singapore: Springer.
Lin, J. 2006. Foreign spouses flock to classes to learn Mandarin. *Taipei Times*, May 13, 2006, p. 2.
Lin, R. 2015. Most candidates ever take test on Hoklo proficiency. *Taipei Times*, August 24, 2015, p. 3.
Lin, S. 2014. Education groups call for changes to 12-year program. *Taipei Times*, July 24, 2014, p. 3.
Lin, S. 2015. Circulating discourses of minority education: The linguistic construction of modernity in globalizing Taiwan. *Anthropology & Education Quarterly* 46(1). 71–87.
Lippi-Green, R. 1997. *English with an accent: language, ideology, and discrimination in the United States*. London: Routledge.
Lipset, S. M. 1959. *Political man: the social bases of politics*. Baltimore, MD: Johns Hopkins University Press.

Ljubojevic, A. 2016. Speak up, write out: language and populism in Croatia. In L. Hancock (ed.), *Narratives of identity in social movements, conflicts, and change* (vol. 40), 29–55. Bingley: Emerald.

Lollini, A. 2011. *Constitutionalism and transitional justice in South Africa.* New York/Oxford: Berghahn.

Long, S. 1991. *Taiwan: China's last frontier.* Basingstoke: Palgrave Macmillan.

Luke, A., A. W. McHoul & J. L. Mey. 1990. On the limits of language planning: class, state, and power. In R. B. Baldauf & A. Luke (eds.), *Language planning and education in Australasia and the South Pacific.* Clevedon: Multilingual Matters.

Makeham, J. 2005. Introduction. In J. Makeham & A. Hsiau (eds.), *Cultural, ethnic and political nationalism in contemporary Taiwan: Bentuhua.* Basingstoke: Palgrave Macmillan.

Makoni, S. 2012. A critique of language, languaging, and supervernacular. *Muitas Vozes* 1(2). 189–199.

Makoni, S. & A. Pennycook. 2007. Disinventing and reconstituting languages. In S. Makoni & A. Pennycook (eds.), *Disinventing and reconstituting languages.* Clevedon: Multilingual Matters.

Mann, M. 1984. The autonomous power of the state: its origins, mechanisms, and results. *European Journal of Sociology/Archives Européennes de Sociologie /Europäisches Archiv Für Soziologie* 25(2). 185–213.

Mann, M. 1986. *The sources of social power vol. 1.* Cambridge: Cambridge University Press.

Mann, M. 1988. *States, war and capitalism: studies in political sociology.* Oxford: Blackwell.

Mansbridge, J. 1990. Feminism and democracy. *The American Prospect* 1. n.p.

Manson, P. 2008. A sketch of Formosa. In H. Chang (ed.), *A chronology of 19th century writings on Formosa: from The Chinese Repository, The Chinese Recorder, and The China Review.* Taipei: Ts'ao Yung-ho Foundation for Culture and Education/SMC Publishing.

March, J. G. & J. P. Olsen. 2006. Elaborating the "new institutionalism." In R. A. W. Rhodes, S. A. Binder & B. A. Rockman (eds.), *The Oxford handbook of political institutions.* Oxford: Oxford University Press.

Martin, H. J. 2005. The Hakka ethnic movement in Taiwan, 1986–1991. In N. Constable (ed.), *Guest people: Hakka identity in China and abroad.* Seattle, WA: University of Washington Press.

May, S. 2012. *Language and minority rights: ethnicity, nationalism, and the politics of language* (2nd edn.). London: Routledge.

McCarthy, T. 1989. Introduction. In J. Habermas, *The structural transformation of the public sphere: an inquiry into a category of bourgeois society.* Cambridge: Polity Press.

McWhorter, J. H. 2008. *Our magnificent bastard tongue: the untold history of English.* London: Penguin.

Meisner, M. 1964. The development of Formosan nationalism. In M. Mancall (ed.), *Formosa today.* New York: Frederick A. Praeger.

Mendel, D. H. 1970. *The politics of Formosan nationalism.* Berkeley, CA: University of California Press.

Middleton, N. 2015. *An atlas of countries that don't exist: a compendium of 50 unrecognised and largely unnoticed states.* London: Macmillan.

Migdal, J. S. 2001. *State in society: studying how states and societies transform and constitute one another.* Cambridge: Cambridge University Press.

Minns, J. 2006. *The politics of developmentalism: the Midas states of Mexico, South Korea, and Taiwan.* Basingstoke: Palgrave Macmillan.

MOE [Ministry of Education]. 2010. *Recruitment of teachers of foreign nationality* http://english. moe.gov.tw/ct.asp?xItem=7115&ctNode=502&mp=11 (accessed October 2017).
MOI [Ministry of the Interior]. 2010. *Population by sex and five-year age group for counties and cities (end of 2010)* http://www.ris.gov.tw/c/document_library/get_file?uuid=72bc52a7-292d-45f3-b8e1-e7205e28e2cc&groupId=11159 (accessed October 2017).
MOL [Ministry of Labour]. 2017a. *Foreign workers in productive industries and social welfare by industry and nationality* http://statdb.mol.gov.tw/html/mon/c12040.htm (accessed October 2017).
MOL [Ministry of Labour]. 2017b. *Foreign workers in productive industries and social welfare by industry* http://statdb.mol.gov.tw/html/mon/c12020.htm (accessed October 2017).
MOL [Ministry of Labour]. 2017c. *Foreign workers in productive industries and social welfare by various type and nationality* http://statdb.mol.gov.tw/html/mon/c12050.htm (accessed v October 2017).
Montgomery McGovern, J. B. 1922. *Among the head-hunters of Formosa*. T.F. Unwin, Limited.
Mouffe, C. 1992. *Dimensions of radical democracy: pluralism, citizenship, community*. London: Verso.
Mufwene, S. 2002. Colonisation, globalization, and the future of languages in the twenty-first century. *International Journal on Multicultural Studies* 4(2). 162–193.
Munsterhjelm, M. 2014. *Living dead in the Pacific: racism and sovereignty in genetics research on Taiwan aborigines*. Vancouver, BC: University of British Columbia Press.
Murakami, N. 1933. *Hsin-kang wen shu/Sinkan manuscripts*. Taihoku [Taipei]: Taihoku Teikoku Daigaku Bunseigakubu.
Nahir, M. 1984. Language planning goals: A classification. *Language Problems and Language Planning* 8. 294–327.
Nakajima, T. 1896. Seibanchi tantenki (jo) [Exploration of aborigine territory (Pt. 1)]. *Taiyu* 2(21). 241–248.
Nakamura, T. 1956. Shih ch'i shih chi Hsi-pan-ya jen tsai T'ai-wan ti pu chiao [Spanish missionaries in Taiwan in the seventeenth century]. *T'ai-Pei Hsien Wen Hsien Ts'ung Chi* 2. 21–36.
Nash, K. 2010. *Contemporary political sociology: globalization, politics, and power*. Oxford: Wiley-Blackwell.
Ndhlovu, F. 2016. A decolonial critique of diaspora identity theories and the notion of superdiversity. *Diaspora studies* 9(1). 28–40.
Neustupny, J. V. 1974. Basic types of treatments of language problems. In J. A. Fishman (ed.), *Advances in language planning*. The Hague: Mouton.
Ng, I. 2004. Taiwan to ban kindergarten English lessons. *South China Morning Post*, February 14, 2004. n.p.
Ngo, T. & H. Wang. 2011. Cultural difference, social recognition, and political representation in Taiwan. In T. Ngo & H. Wang (eds.), *Politics of difference in Taiwan*. London: Routledge.
NIA [National Immigration Agency]. 2016. *Ferreted illegal foreign residents* https://www.immi gration.gov.tw/public/Data/082514423871.xls (accessed October 2017).
NIA [National Immigration Agency]. 2017a. *Foreign residents* http://sowf.moi.gov.tw/stat/ month/m6-05.xls (accessed October 2017).
NIA [National Immigration Agency]. 2017b *Foreign spouses in various counties and cities according to nationality* https://www.immigration.gov.tw/public/Attachment/79181613865. xlsx (accessed October 2017).

Noble, J. 2000. Co-operation, competition, and the evolution of pre-linguistic communication. In C. Knight, M. Studdert-Kennedy & J. R. Hurford (eds.), *The evolutionary emergence of language: social function and the origin of linguistic form*. Cambridge: Cambridge University Press.
Norman, J. 1988. *Chinese*. Cambridge: Cambridge University Press.
Oladejo, J. 2006. Parents' attitudes towards bilingual education policy in Taiwan. *Bilingual Research Journal* 30(1). 147–170.
Ormrod, W. M. 2003. The use of English: language, law, and political culture in fourteenth-century England. *Speculum* 78(3). 750–787.
Orum, A. M. & J. G. Dale. 2009. *Introduction to political sociology: power and participation in the modern world*. Oxford: Oxford University Press.
Otsuji, E. & A. Pennycook. 2010. Metrolingualism: fixity, fluidity, and language in flux. *International Journal of Multilingualism* 7(3). 240–254.
Park, J. S.-Y. & L. Wee. 2012. *Markets of English: linguistic capital and language policy in a globalizing world*. London: Routledge.
Patrick, P. L. 2004. The speech community. In J. K. Chambers, P. Trudgill, & N. Schilling-Estes (eds.), *The handbook of language variation and change*, 573–597. Oxford: Blackwell.
Patten, A. & W. Kymlicka. 2003. Introduction: Language rights and political theory: context, issues, and approaches. In W. Kymlicka & A. Patten (eds.), *Language rights and political theory*. Oxford: Oxford University Press.
Pavlenko, A. 2017. Superdiversity and why it isn't. In S. Breidbach, L. Kusters, & B. Schmenk (eds.), *Sloganizations in language education discourse*. Clevedon: Multilingual Matters.
Peled, Y., P. Ives & T. Ricento. 2014. Introduction to the thematic issue: language policy and political theory. *Language Policy* 13(4). 295–300.
Pennycook, A. 1995. English in the world/the world in English. In J. W. Tollefson (ed.), *Power and inequality in language education*. Cambridge: Cambridge University Press.
Pennycook, A. 1998. *English and the discourses of colonialism*. London: Routledge.
Pennycook, A. 2001. *Critical applied linguistics: a critical introduction*. London: Routledge.
Pennycook, A. & E. Otsuji. 2015. *Metrolingualism: language in the city*. London: Routledge.
Phillips, S. E. 1999. Between assimilation and independence: Taiwanese political aspirations under Nationalist Chinese rule, 1945–1948. In M. Rubinstein (ed.), *Taiwan: a new history*. New York: M. E. Sharpe.
Phillips, S. E. 2003. *Between assimilation and independence: The Taiwanese encounter Nationalist China, 1945–1950*. Stanford, CA: Stanford University Press.
Phillipson, R. 1992. *Linguistic imperialism*. Oxford: Oxford University Press.
Phillipson, R. 2008. The linguistic imperialism of neoliberal empire. *Critical Inquiry in Language Studies* 5(1). 513–533.
Pierson, C. 2011. *The modern state* (3rd edn.). London: Routledge.
Piller, I. & J. Cho. 2013. Neoliberalism as language policy. *Language in Society* 42(1). 23–44.
Pinker, S. 2007. *The stuff of thought: language as a window into human nature*. London: Penguin.
Poggeschi, G. 2013. *Language rights and duties in the evolution of public law*. Baden-Baden: Nomos.
Poggi, G. 1978. *The development of the modern state: a sociological introduction*. Stanford, CA: Stanford University Press.
Poggi, G. 1990. *The state: its nature, development, and prospects*. Chichester: John Wiley & Sons.
Poulantzas, N. 1980. Research note on the state and society. *International Social Science Journal*, XXXII (4). 600–608.

Price, G. 2014. English for all? Neoliberalism, globalization, and language policy in Taiwan. *Language in Society* 43(5). 567–589.
Pullum, G. K. 1991. *The great Eskimo vocabulary hoax and other irreverent essays on the study of language.* Chicago, IL: University of Chicago Press.
Putnam, R. D. 1988. Diplomacy and domestic politics: The logic of two-level games. *International Organization* 42(3). 427–460.
Putnam, R. D. 1995. Bowling alone: America's declining social capital. *Journal of Democracy* 6(1). 65–78.
Qiu, P. 2015. *A preliminary investigation of Yilan Creole in Taiwan: discussing predicate position in Yilan Creole.* Alberta: University of Alberta unpublished M.A. thesis.
Rampal, K. R. 2011. The media's "public sphere" for civil society in Taiwan's democratic consolidation. *Taiwan Journal of Democracy* 7(2). 69–93.
Rampton, B. 2000. Speech community. In J. Verschueren, J.-O. Östman, J. Blommaert & C. Bulcaen (eds.), *Handbook of pragmatics*. Amsterdam: John Benjamins.
Rampton, B. 2003. Displacing the "native speaker"? Expertise, affiliation, and inheritance. In R. Harris & B. Rampton (eds.), *The language, ethnicity, and race reader*. London: Routledge.
Rawnsley, G. 2004. Treading a fine line: Democratisation and the media in Taiwan. *Parliamentary Affairs* 57(1). 209–222.
Rawnsley, G. & Q. Gong. 2012. The media and the vitality of democratic Taiwan. In S. Tsang (ed.), *The vitality of Taiwan: politics, economics, society, and culture*. Basingstoke: Palgrave Macmillan.
Ray, L. 2012. Civil society and the public sphere. In E. Amenta, K. Nash & A. Scott (eds.), *The Wiley-Blackwell companion to political sociology*. Chichester: Wiley-Blackwell.
Ren, S. 1923. *Taiwan doka saku ron [On Taiwan's assimilation policy].* Taihoku [Taipei]: Unknown.
Renan, E. 1992. *Qu'est-ce Qu'une Nation?* Paris: Presses-Pocket.
Rigger, S. 1999. *Politics in Taiwan: voting for reform.* London: Routledge.
Röhl, W. 2005. Generalities. In Willhelm Röhl (ed.), *History of law in Japan since 1868*. Leiden: Brill.
Roht-Arriaza, N. 2006. The new landscape of transitional justice. In N. Roht-Arriaza & J. Mariezcurrena (eds.), *Transitional justice in the twenty-first century: beyond truth versus justice*. Cambridge: Cambridge University Press.
Rosenblum, N. L. 2000. Primus inter pares: Political parties and civil society. *Chicago-Kent Law Review* 75(2). 493–529.
Ross, M. 2008. The integrity of the Austronesian language family: From Taiwan to Oceania. In A. Sanchez-Mazas (ed.), *Past human migrations in East Asia: matching archaeology, linguistics, and genetics*. London: Routledge.
Rowen, I. & J. Rowen. 2017. Taiwan's truth and reconciliation committee: The geopolitics of transitional justice in a contested state. *International Journal of Transitional Justice* 11. 92–112.
Roy, D. 2003. *Taiwan: a political history.* Ithaca, NY: Cornell University Press.
Rubio Marin, R. 2003. Language rights: Exploring the competing rationales. In W. Kymlicka & A. Patten (eds.), *Language rights and political theory*. Oxford: Oxford University Press.
Said, E. 1977. *Orientalism.* London: Penguin.
Sanada, S. & Y. Chien. 2010. Yilan creole in Taiwan. *Journal of Pidgin and Creole Languages* 25(2). 350–357.

Sandel, T. L. 2003. Linguistic capital in Taiwan: The KMT's Mandarin language policy and its perceived impact upon the language practices of bilingual Mandarin and Tai-gi speakers. *Language in Society* 32(4). 523–551.
Sanders, D. 1995. Behavioural analysis. In D. Marsh & G. Stoker (eds.), *Theory and methods in political science*. Basingstoke: Palgrave Macmillan.
Sapir, E. 1929. The status of linguistics as a science. *Language* 4. 207–214.
Sassen, S. 2002. *Global cities, linked networks*. London: Routledge.
Sassen, S. 2007. *Sociology of globalization*. New York: W.W. Norton.
Schiffman, H. F. 1996. *Linguistic culture and language policy*. London: Routledge.
Schmidt, R. 2000. *Language policy and identity politics in the United States*. Philadelphia, PA: Temple University Press.
Schmidt, R. 2014. Democratic theory and the challenge of linguistic diversity. *Language Policy*, 13(4). 395–411.
Schneider, E. W. 2007. *Postcolonial English: varieties around the world*. Cambridge: Cambridge University Press.
Schubert, G. & S. Braig. 2007. How to face a rising China? The DPP's identity politics and cross-strait relations at the end of the Chen Shui-bian era. In J. Damm & G. Schubert (eds.), *Taiwanese identity from domestic, regional and global perspectives*. Munster: LitVerlag.
Scott, M. & H. Tiun. 2007. Mandarin-only to Mandarin-plus: Taiwan. *Language Policy* 6(1). 53–72.
Shackleton, A. J. 1998. *Formosa calling: an eyewitness account of the February 28th, 1947 incident*. Manchester: Camphor Press.
Sharman, L. 1934. *Sun Yat-sen, his life and its meaning*. New York: John Day.
Sharp, G. 2008. *From dictatorship to democracy: a conceptual framework for liberation*. Boston: Albert Einstein Institution.
Shepherd, J. R. 1993. *Statecraft and political economy on the Taiwan frontier, 1600–1800*. Stanford, CA: Stanford University Press.
Shepherd, J. R. 1995. *Marriage and mandatory abortion among the 17th-century Siraya*. Arlington, VA: American Anthropological Association.
Sheu, Y. 2007. Full responsibility with partial citizenship: immigrant wives in Taiwan. *Social Policy and Administration* 47(2). 179–196.
Shih, C. & M. Chen. 2010. Taiwanese identity and the memories of 2–28: a case for political reconciliation. *Asian Perspective* 34(4). 85–113.
Simon, S. 2011. Multiculturalism and indigenism: contrasting the experiences of Canada and Taiwan. In T. Ngo & H. Wang (eds.), *Politics of difference in Taiwan*. London: Routledge.
Simon, S. 2012. *Sadyaq Balae! L'autochtonie formosane dans tous ses états*. Quebec: Presses de l'université de Laval.
Simon, S. 2015. Making natives: Japan and the creation of indigenous Formosa. In A. D. Morris (ed.), *Japanese Taiwan: colonial rule and its contested legacy*. London: Bloomsbury.
Sivan, E. 1989. The Islamic resurgence: civil society strikes back. *Journal of Contemporary History* 25(2/3). 353–362.
Skeggs, B. 1997. *Formations of class and gender*. London: Sage.
Skocpol, T. 1985. Bringing the state back in: strategies of analysis in current research. In P. B. Evans, D. Rueschemeyer & T. Skocpol (eds.), *Bringing the state back in*. Cambridge: Cambridge University Press.
Skutnabb-Kangas, T. 2006. Language policy and linguistic human rights. In T. Ricento (ed.), *An introduction to language policy: theory and practice*. Oxford: Blackwell.

Skutnabb-Kangas, T., R. Phillipson & M. Rannut (eds.). 1994. *Linguistic human rights: overcoming linguistic discrimination*. Berlin: Mouton de Gruyter.
Smit, H. 2014. *The social evolution of human nature: from biology to language*. Cambridge: Cambridge University Press.
Smith, A. D. 1986. State-making and nation-building. In J. A. Hall (ed.), *States in history*. Oxford: Blackwell.
Snow, D. A., S. A. Soule & H. Kriesi. 2004. Mapping the terrain. In D. A. Snow, S. A. Soule & H. Kriesi (eds.), *The Blackwell companion to social movements*. Oxford: Blackwell.
Soysal, Y. 2012. Post-national citizenship: rights and obligations of individuality. In E. Amenta, K. Nash & A. Scott (eds.), *The Wiley-Blackwell companion to political sociology*. Chichester: Wiley-Blackwell.
Soysal, Y. N. 1994. *Limits of citizenship: migrants and postnational membership in Europe*. Chicago, IL: University of Chicago Press.
Soysal, Y. N. & D. Strang. 1989. Construction of the first mass education systems in nineteenth-century Europe. *Sociology of Education* 62(4). 277–288.
Spaulding, R. M. 1967. *Imperial Japan's higher civil service examinations*. Princeton, NJ: Princeton University Press.
Spence, J. D. 1990. *The search for Modern China*. New York: W. W. Norton & Company.
Spolsky, B. 1974. Navajo language maintenance: Six-year-olds in 1969. In F. Pialosi (ed.), *Teaching the bilingual*. Tucson, AZ: University of Arizona Press.
Spolsky, B. 2004. *Language policy*. Cambridge: Cambridge University Press.
Stainton, M. 1999. The politics of Taiwan aboriginal origins. In M. Rubinstein (ed.), *Taiwan: a new history*. New York: M. E. Sharpe.
Steele, J. & N. Uomini. 2009. Can the archaeology of manual specialization tell us anything about language evolution? A survey of the state of play. *Cambridge Archaeological Journal* 19(01). 97–110.
Steere, J. B. 2008. The aborigines of Formosa. In H. Chang (ed.), *A chronology of 19th century writings on Formosa: from The Chinese Repository, The Chinese Recorder, and The China Review*. Taipei: Ts'ao Yung-ho Foundation for Culture and Education/SMC Publishing.
Steiner, G. 1998. *After Babel. Aspects of language and translation*. Oxford: Oxford University Press.
Stewart, W. 1968. A sociolinguistic typology for describing national multilingualism. In J. A. Fishman (ed.), *Readings in the sociology of language*. The Hague: Mouton.
Stiglitz, J. E. 2002. *Globalization and its discontents*. New York: W.W. Norton.
Stolojan, V. 2017. Transitional justice and collective memory in Taiwan: How Taiwanese society is coming to terms with its authoritarian past. *China Perspectives/Wanchai* 2. 27–35.
Stolz, T., & Warnke, I. H. 2015. From missionary linguistics to colonial linguistics. In K. Zimmerman & B. Kellermeier-Rehbein (eds.), *Colonialism and missionary linguistics*. Berlin: De Gruyter.
Storry, R. 1990. *A history of modern Japan*. London: Penguin.
Stout, D. 2010. Possible relations between language and technology in human evolution. In I. Davidson & A. Nowell (eds.), *Stone tools and the evolution of human cognition*. Boulder, CO: University Press of Colorado.
Strickland, C. J., E. Walsh & M. Cooper. 2006. Healing fractured families: parents' and elders' perspectives on the impact of colonization and youth suicide prevention in a Pacific Northwest American Indian tribe. *Journal of Transcultural Nursing* 17(1). 5–12.

Suen, H. K. & L. Yu. 2006. Chronic consequences of high-stakes testing? Lessons from the Chinese civil service exam. *Comparative Education Review* 50(1). 46–65.
Sugimoto, T. 1971. Japanese in Taiwan. *Current Trends in Linguistics* 8. 969–995.
Sunkel, O. 1969. National development policy and external dependence in Latin America. *The Journal of Development Studies* 6(1). 23–48.
Taintor, E. C. 1875. The aborigines of northern Formosa. *Journal of the North-China Branch of the Royal Asiatic Society* IX. 53–88.
Taipei Times. 2002. Education ministry dodges issue of language policy. *Taipei Times*, March 26, 2002, p. 4.
Taipei Times. 2009. Back to ground zero once again. *Taipei Times*, January 23, 2009, p. 8.
Taipei Times. 2011. Taiwan's gender balance worsening as more parents abort female fetuses. *Taipei Times*, December 8, 2011, p. 1.
Taipei Times. 2014. Education minister slammed by subcommittee over plans to make native languages compulsory. *Taipei Times*, January 1, 2014, p. 11.
Taipei Times. 2017. Tsai vows to investigate 228 incident. *Taipei Times*, February 24, 2017, p. 1.
Takekoshi, Y. 1907. *Japanese rule in Formosa*. London/New York/Bombay/Calcutta: Longmans, Green, and Co.
Takeshi, K. & J. A. Mangan. 1997. Japanese colonial education in Taiwan 1895–1922: precepts and practices of control. *History of Education* 26(3). 307–322.
Tang, W. A., D. Bélanger & H. Wang. 2011. Politics of negotiation between Vietnamese wives and Taiwanese husbands. In T. Ngo & H. Wang (eds.), *Politics of difference in Taiwan*. London: Routledge.
Tarrow, S. 1998. *Power in movement: social movements and contentious politics*. Cambridge: Cambridge University Press.
Taylor, C. 1995. Liberal politics and the public sphere. In *Philosophical arguments*. Cambridge, MA: Harvard University Press.
Taylor, C. 1997. Nationalism and modernity. In J. McMahan & R. McKim (eds.), *The morality of nationalism*. Oxford: Oxford University Press.
Taylor, P. J. 1994. The state as container: territoriality in the modern world-system. *Progress in Human Geography* 18(2). 151–162.
Teng, E. 2006. *Taiwan's imagined geography: Chinese colonial travel writing and pictures, 1683–1895*. Cambridge, MA: Harvard University Asia Center/Harvard University Press.
Teng, E. J. H. 1999. Taiwan as a living museum: tropes of anachronism in late-imperial Chinese travel writing. *Harvard Journal of Asiatic Studies* 59(2). 445–484.
Teufel Dreyer, J. 2003. The evolution of language policies and national identity in Taiwan. In *Fighting words: language and ethnic conflict in Asia*. Cambridge, MA: Harvard University Center for Science and Technology/MIT Press.
The Chinese Recorder. 2008. Missionary journal. In H. Chang (ed.), *A chronology of 19th century writings on Formosa: from The Chinese Repository, The Chinese Recorder, and The China Review*. Taipei: Ts'ao Yung-ho Foundation for Culture and Education/SMC Publishing.
The Economist. 1993. Grandpa would not approve. *The Economist*, August 7, 1993, p. 38.
The Economist. 2001. Kenneth Hale: Obituary. *The Economist*, November 2001 https://www.economist.com/sections/business-finance (accessed October 2017).
Thompson, L. G. 1964. The earliest Chinese eyewitness accounts of the Formosan aborigines. *Monumenta Serica* 23.163–204.
Tilly, C. 2004. *Social movements, 1768–2004*. Boulder, CO: Paradigm Press.
Tiu, H. 2007. Learning from India's policies on language. *Taipei Times*, January 7, 2007, p. 8.

TJWG. 2008. Transitional justice, reconciliation, and coexistence: Workshop report. Monrovia: TJWG (Transitional Justice Working Group of Liberia) http://heller.brandeis.edu/coexistence/pdfs/transitional-justice/transjustliberia08.pdf (accessed October 2017).

To, C.-Y. 1972. Education of the aborigines in Taiwan: an illustration of how certain traditional beliefs of a majority people determine the education of a disadvantaged minority. *Journal of Negro Education* 51(3). 183–194.

Tonkiss, F. 2000. Markets against states: neo-liberalism. In K. Nash & A. Scott (eds.), *The Blackwell companion to political sociology*. Oxford: Blackwell.

TPBOE [Taipei Board of Education]. 2013. *Licensed buxiban in Taiwan by area and subject*. http://bsb.kh.edu.tw/afterschool/english/?usercity=20. Archived at: http://www.webcitation.org/6IJIl5Xxn (accessed October 2017).

Troike, R. C. 1977. The future of English. *The Linguistic Reporter* 19(8). 2.

Trudgill, P. 1983. *On dialect: social and geographical perspectives*. Oxford: Blackwell.

Trudgill, P. 1996. Dual-source pidgins and reverse creoloids: Northern perspectives on language contact. In E. H. Jahr & I. Broch (eds.), *Language contact in the Arctic: Northern Pidgins and contact languages*. Berlin: Mouton de Gruyter.

Trudgill, P. 2000. *Sociolinguistics: an introduction to language and society*. London: Penguin.

Trudgill, P. 2010. *Investigations in sociohistorical linguistics: stories of colonisation and contact*. Cambridge: Cambridge University Press.

Ts'ao, Y. H. 1997. Taiwan as an entrepôt in East Asia in the seventeenth century. *Itinerario* 27(1). 94–114.

Tsai, H. C. 2009. *Taiwan in Japan's empire-building: an institutional approach to colonial engineering*. London: Routledge.

Tsai, S. H. 2005. *Lee Teng-hui and Taiwan's quest for identity*. Basingstoke: Palgrave Macmillan.

Tsao, F. 2008. The language planning situation in Taiwan. In R. B. Kaplan & R. B. Baldauf (eds.), *Language planning and policy in Asia, vol.1: Japan, Nepal, Taiwan, and Chinese characters*. Clevedon: Multilingual Matters.

Tse, J. K. 1986. Standardization of Chinese in Taiwan. *International Journal of the Sociology of Language* 59. 25–32.

Tse, J. K. 2000. Language and a rising new identity in Taiwan. *International Journal of the Sociology of Language* 143. 151–164.

Tseng, Y. & Y. Komiya. 2011. Classism in immigration control and migrant integration. In T. Ngo & H. Wang (eds.), *Politics of difference in Taiwan*. London: Routledge.

Tseng, Y. & P. Lin. 2014. Through the looking glass: migration into and out of Taiwan. In K. Chiu, D. Fell & P. Lin (eds.), *Migration to and from Taiwan*. London: Routledge.

Tsurumi, E. P. 1977. *Japanese colonial education in Taiwan, 1895–1945*. Cambridge, MA: Harvard University Press.

Tsurumi, E. P. 1979. Education and assimilation in Taiwan under Japanese rule, 1895–1945. *Modern Asian Studies* 13(4). 617–641.

Tsurumi, E. P. 1984. Colonial education in Korea and Taiwan. In R. H. Myers & M. R. Peattie (eds.), *The Japanese colonial empire, 1895–1945*. Princeton, NJ: Princeton University Press.

Tu, C. J., B.-K., Tsai & S. Chang. 2011. Are the Shau people in Taiwan of Dutch descent? *Social Behavior and Personality* 39. 55–64.

Turner, B. S. 1990. Outline of a theory of citizenship. *Sociology* 24(2). 189–217.

Turner, B. S. & H. Khondker. 2010. *Globalization: East and West*. London: Sage.

Twine, N. 1978. The Genbunitchi movement. Its origin, development, and conclusion. *Monumenta Nipponica* 33(3). 333–356.

Twine, N. 1991. *Language and the modern state: the reform of written Japanese*. London: Routledge.
UNPBF (United Nations Peacebuilding Fund). 2016. *Sri Lanka peacebuilding priority plan*. New York: UNPBF.
Urla, J. 1997. Outlaw language: Creating alternative public spheres in Basque Free Radio. In L. Lowe & D. Lloyd (eds.), *The politics of culture in the shadow of capital*, 245–261. Durham, NC: Duke University Press.
van Parijs, P. 2011. *Linguistic justice for Europe and for the world*. Oxford: Oxford University Press.
Vertovec, S. 2007. Super-diversity and its implications. *Ethnic and Racial Studies* 30(6). 1024–1054.
Vincent, D. 2000. *The rise of mass literacy: reading and writing in modern Europe*. Cambridge: Polity.
Walzer, M. 1984. *Spheres of justice: a defense of pluralism and equality*. New York: Basic Books.
Walzer, M. 1991. The civil society argument. *Statsvetenskaplig Tidskrift* 94(1). 1–11.
Wang, F. 2005. Why bother about school textbooks? An analysis of the origin of the disputes over Renshi Taiwan textbooks in 1997. In J. Makeham & A. Hsiau (eds.), *Cultural, ethnic and political nationalism in contemporary Taiwan: Bentuhua*. Basingstoke: Palgrave Macmillan.
Wang, F. 2009. Chiang Kai-shek plaque to return to memorial hall. *Taipei Times*, January 22, 2009, p. 3
Wang, H. 2005. National culture and its discontents: The politics of heritage and language in Taiwan, 1949–2003. *Comparative Studies in Society and History* 46(4). 786–815.
Wang, W. 2002. Choosing English over Hokkien. *Taipei Times*, March 30, 2002, p. 8.
Weber, M. 1946a. Bureaucracy. In H. H. Gerth & C. W. Mills (eds.), *From Max Weber: essays in sociology*. Oxford: Oxford University Press.
Weber, M. 1946b. Politics as a vocation. In H. H. Gerth & C. W. Mills (eds.), *From Max Weber: essays in sociology*. Oxford: Oxford University Press.
Weber, M. 1978. *Economy and society: an outline of interpretive sociology*. Berkeley, CA: University of California Press.
Wee, L. 2011. *Language without rights*. Oxford: Oxford University Press.
Wei, J. M. 2008. *Language choice and identity politics in Taiwan*. Lanham: Lexington Books.
Wert, M. 2013. *Meiji restoration losers: memory and Tokugawa supporters in Modern Japan*. Cambridge: Harvard University Asia Center/Harvard University Press.
Westney, D. E. 1982. The emulation of Western organizations in Meiji Japan. *Journal of Japanese Studies* 8. 307–342.
Whorf, B. L. 2012a. Science and linguistics. In J. B. Carroll, S. C. Levinson, & P. Lee (eds.), *Language, thought, and reality: selected writings of Benjamin Lee Whorf*. Cambridge, MA: MIT Press.
Whorf, B. L. 2012b. An American Indian model of the universe. In J. B. Carroll, S. C. Levinson, & P. Lee (eds.), *Language, thought, and reality: selected writings of Benjamin Lee Whorf*. Cambridge, MA: MIT Press.
Williams, G. 1992. *Sociolinguistics: a sociological critique*. London/New York: Routledge.
Williams, L. & M.-K. Yu. 2006. Domestic violence in cross-border marriage: a case study from Taiwan. *International Journal of Migration, Health and Social Care* 2(3/4). 58–69.
Wills, J. E. 1999. The seventeenth-century transformation: Taiwan under the Dutch and the Cheng regime. In M. Rubinstein (ed.), *Taiwan: a new history*. New York: M. E. Sharpe.

Winter, S. 2013. Towards a unified theory of transitional justice. *International Journal of Transitional Justice* 7(2). 224–244.

Wittgenstein, L. 1922. *Tractatus logico-philosophicus*. London: Harcourt, Brace.

Wolin, S. 2010. *Democracy incorporated: managed democracy and the spectre of inverted totalitarianism*. Princeton, NJ: Princeton University Press.

Wright, S. 2007. The right to speak one's own language: Reflections on theory and practice. *Language Policy* 6(2). 203–224.

Wright, S. 2016. *Language policy and language planning: from nationalism to globalisation* (2nd edn.). Basingstoke: Palgrave Macmillan.

Wu, M. 2009. Language planning and policy in Taiwan: past, present, and future. *University of Pennsylvania Working Papers in Educational Linguistics* 24(2). 99–118.

Wu, N. 2005. Transition without justice, or justice without history: transitional justice in Taiwan. *Taiwan Journal of Democracy* 1(1). 77–102.

Wu, W. 1992. *Jih-chü shih-chi t'ai-wan she-huei ling-tao chieh-ts'eng chih yen-chiu [A study of Taiwanese social leadership Under Japanese rule]*. Taipei: Cheng-chung.

Yeh, Y. 2010. Foreign spouses' acculturation in Taiwan: a comparison of their countries of origin, gender, and education degrees. In W. Yang & M. C. Lu (eds.), *Asian Cross-border Marriage Migration: Demographic Patterns and Social Issues*. Amsterdam: International Institute for Asian Studies/Amsterdam University Press.

Young, R. 1988. Language maintenance and language shift in Taiwan. *Journal of Multilingual and Multicultural Development* 9(4). 323–338.

Zeng, K. 1999. *Dragon gate*. London: Cassell.

Index

2-28 incident 135, 139, 141–142, 146, 150

Amis 176–181, 237, 238
Andrade, Tonio 76, 81, 82, 84, 93–96, 229
Assimilation 43, 70–73, 76, 96, 101–103, 106, 109, 110, 114–129, 148, 165, 171, 192, 221, 229, 234
Austronesian 75–76, 82, 95, 98, 107, 188, 228, 237, 238

Bellwood, Peter 75
Benhabib, Seyla 29, 69
Bentuhua 150, 158–161, 164, 174, 186, 188, 191, 194, 197, 207, 210, 220–221, 226, 230, 234
Birth ratio 220
Blommaert, Jan 53, 56, 63, 192, 211
Blust, Robert 75, 237
Bourdieu, Pierre 38–39, 55, 145, 173, 205
Brown, Melissa 20, 62, 80, 94–96, 102–103
Bukonsho 118
Buxiban 193, 196, 200–204, 207–210, 213, 217

Campbell, Rev. William 6, 7, 83, 85–92, 94, 96, 100, 105
Capital, forms of 118, 198
Chen Shui-bian 152, 156, 157, 160, 164, 167, 183, 184, 195, 203, 221
Chiang Ching-kuo 144, 150, 151, 153, 183
Chiang Kai-shek 130, 131, 140, 141, 146, 149, 150, 151, 156, 167, 184
Citizenship 1, 16, 21–22, 32, 44, 49, 116, 126, 127, 148, 173, 212, 223, 225
Civil society argument 1, 11, 26–28, 32, 71
Co-colonization 76, 82, 93–95
Colonization 7, 12, 20, 34, 42–47, 52, 54, 74–76, 82, 85, 93–95, 103–104, 107, 110, 115, 200, 214, 228, 229, 235
Common schools (Japanese) 115–121
Cooper, Robert 36, 38, 39, 73
Creole 128, 134, 157
Creoloid 134, 157
Curriculum reform 173–174, 175

Democratization 26, 65–66, 74, 109, 150–154, 158–159, 161–162, 166, 168, 170–178, 183, 228, 230, 234–235
Dependency theory 48
Doka 109, 110, 113, 120, 125, 126, 148
Dupre, Jean-Francois 162–165, 169, 173, 184–188, 190, 195, 230, 231

ELE (English-language education) 191, 196–208, 211
ESC (Election Study Center) 160
Ethnolinguistic chauvinism 157, 163–165

Favorlang 86, 88, 104, 238
Filial piety 220
Fishman, Joshua A. 2, 37, 46, 47
Foreign labour 212, 216
Foreign spouses 191–192, 212–227, 230
Fraser, Nancy 30–31, 67–71, 162, 171
Friedman, P. Kerim 122, 127

Globalization 7, 12, 16, 20, 23–24, 34, 52–53, 56, 74, 178, 191–227
Goto Shinpei 115

Habermas, Jurgen 29–31, 67–70
HBL (Hakka Basic Law) 186, 187
Heylen, Ann 85–86, 89, 91–92, 111, 119, 124–125
Hornberger, Nancy 36
Hsiao, Michael 147, 156
Hsiau, A-Chin 117, 120, 123, 126, 133, 135–137, 141–142, 144–146, 149, 153–154, 156, 165
Hymes, Dell 3

ILDA (Indigenous Languages Development Act) 231, 232
Implicit enclaving 70, 71
Interpreters 84, 88, 98–102, 108, 118–119
IPLDL (Indigenous People's Language Development Law) 186

Kerr, George 115–117, 119, 134, 137–140, 148, 193–194
Klöter, Henning 82–83, 86, 90, 114, 133, 135, 153, 155, 167, 183
Kokugo 116, 122
Kominka 109, 110, 113, 125, 126, 128, 148, 193

Lamley, Harry J. 95, 115–117, 121, 122, 126, 148
Lan, Pei-chia 124, 198, 206, 210, 212, 215–217, 220, 222
Landdag 84, 86, 88, 92
Language-based rights 57–62, 65, 162
Language maintenance 37, 72, 158, 179, 180, 233
Language movements 67, 72–73
Language revitalization 7, 24, 72–73, 181, 189, 233
Lee Teng-hui 151, 153, 154, 159, 161, 185, 189
Legitimacy (state) 1, 15, 17, 21, 32, 40, 45, 47, 52, 58, 62, 80, 84, 85, 97, 101, 110, 111, 115, 120, 129, 130, 142, 150, 151, 159, 184, 185, 221
Liberal democracy 16, 18, 26, 28, 32, 33, 51, 62, 72, 161, 166, 228, 232, 234–235
Linguistic capital 33, 89, 98, 100, 118, 191–192, 210, 212, 215–217, 222, 235
Literacy 19, 30, 40–41, 50, 70, 72, 75, 82, 89–91, 105–106, 111–116, 132, 146, 147, 185

Maejima Hisoka 111–112
Manchu 96, 131
Martial law 109, 124, 128–146, 150, 152–153, 160, 166, 174–176, 178, 181, 184, 186, 187, 189, 211, 226, 229–230, 233
Ma Ying-jeou 156, 160, 167, 183–184
Metrolingualism 53, 56–57, 191
Minority language 6, 51–52, 60, 67–73, 163–164, 168, 170, 178, 187, 189, 233
Missionary-colonial complex 43–44, 75, 82, 84–89, 107, 228
Modernization theory 47
MTLE (mother-tongue language education) 151, 173, 175–182, 189

Nationalism 1, 4, 7, 16, 20–23, 28, 32, 34, 37–38, 40, 46, 48–52, 72, 74, 91, 108, 112, 123–124, 130–131, 141–143, 154, 159, 161, 174, 185, 191, 194–195, 221, 223, 226–228, 230, 235
Native speaker 6, 208–209
Neoliberalism 28, 53–55, 177–178, 191–211
NGOs 27, 71, 218, 223, 225–226
NIA (National Immigration Agency) 209, 212, 215, 219, 222
Nihongo 116
NLDL (National Language Development Law) 150, 164–165, 170, 175, 185–187, 190, 231
NLEL (National Language Equality Law) 150, 162–165, 170, 175, 186–187, 190, 231

Paiwan 86, 104–106, 176, 231, 238
Pennycook, Alastair 2, 4, 31, 33–34, 49, 53, 56–57, 148, 194, 227
Pidgin 79, 94, 134
Pierson, Christopher 12, 13, 16–17, 20, 23, 26
Pinyin 184–185
Pirate radio 29, 147
Political economy 54, 74–76, 90, 93, 107, 159, 178, 193–194, 212
Political sociology of language 1–2, 33–74, 84, 90, 108, 129, 228, 234–236
PRC (People's Republic of China) 77, 129, 131, 150, 152, 154, 165, 185, 211, 219–221, 228, 234
Public sphere 2, 29–32, 66–70, 109, 120, 123–126, 136, 143, 145–147, 149, 162, 190, 193, 217–219, 223
Puyuma school 118

Radio and Television Law (1976) 146
Romanization 113, 124

Sapir-Whorf 8
Sassen, Saskia 12, 20, 53, 191, 199
Seediq 104, 128
Shuji, Izawa 115
Sinkan manuscripts 90
Siraya 86, 88, 90–94, 104–106

Social movements 25, 27, 28, 147
Soysal, Yasemin 22, 113
Spanish 54, 78, 81–82, 189
Status planning 36–38, 72, 112, 143, 161–162, 164, 170–172, 189
Sun Yat-sen 130–131
Superdiversity 56–57

Tai oan Chheng lian 124, 193
Taiwanese New Literature 124
Tangwai 147, 151–152, 183
Thao 104, 238
Transitional justice 34, 57–66, 74, 150, 154, 158, 161–169, 171–173, 184, 188–189, 231–233, 235
Translanguaging 53, 56–57, 227
Trudgill, Peter 2, 48, 134
Tsao, Feng-fu 133, 136, 142–145
Tse, John Kwok-ping 135, 155
Tsurumi, Patricia 114–117, 121–123
Twelve-year curriculum 231

UNDRIP (United Nations Declaration on the Rights of Indigenous Peoples) 51, 60, 61, 155, 162, 187, 232
UNDRM (United Nations Declaration on the Rights of Persons Belonging to National or Ethnic, Religious, and Linguistic Minorities) 51, 60–61, 155, 162, 187, 232

Weber, Max 1, 10–11, 13–19, 25, 39, 41, 80
Westphalia, Treaty of 20, 52
Whorf, Benjamin Lee 8
Whorfian 46, 47, 78
Wild Lily student movement 153
Wright, Sue 4–5, 7, 35, 40, 48–50, 58, 72
Writing 3, 5, 12, 15, 19, 28, 39–41, 61, 78–81, 89–91, 97, 99, 103, 105, 111, 113, 124, 128, 174, 185, 194, 215

Yilan Creole Japanese 128

www.ingramcontent.com/pod-product-compliance
Lightning Source LLC
Chambersburg PA
CBHW052214240426
43670CB00037B/445